NSTIGATORS

OF THE

APOCALYPSE

How Those With False Interpretations of the Book of
Revelation Influenced Wars and Revolution in the History of
Western Civilization

by

Award-Winning Author

KEVIN TIMOTHY O'KANE

I would like to thank Lore and Karen whose recommendations significantly improved this manuscript.

I would also like to thank Pamela, the former resource librarian from the Pacific Grove Public Library, who worked hard to locate and attain some difficult-to-find primary sources.

CONTENTS

Introduction   7

Chapter 1. Resurrection Now   13

Chapter 2. Crisis in Smyrna   21

Chapter 3. The New Prophecy and the Rise of the Alogia   31

Chapter 4. The Stone That Sharpens and the School of the Martyrs   39

Chapter 5. The Divine Institutes and Constantine   49

Chapter 6. Christ's Tomb and the Construction of the New Jerusalem   61

Chapter 7. The Millennium Now   73

Chapter 8. The First Crusade and the Last World Emperor   85

Chapter 9. Joachim and the Order of the Third Status   97

Chapter 10. The Florentine Jerusalem and the Protestant Reformation   105

Chapter 11. A Clash of Civilizations   127

Chapter 12. The Franciscan Millennium and the Mayan Inquisition   145

Chapter 13. Mary Tudor and the Revelation's Exiles   157

Chapter 14. Elizabeth Tudor and the Seven Vials   167

Chapter 15. Stuart, Cromwell, and the Puritan Revolution   179

Chapter 16. Men of Blood: The Fifth Monarchists   189

Chapter17. The Mark of the Beast and the American Revolution   197

Chapter18. The Whore of Babylon and the Rapture of the Church   211

Chapter 19. The Southern New Israel   227

Chapter 20. On the Threshold of the Nuclear Millennium   237

Chapter 21. Into the Last Days   253

Glossary   263

notes   265

About the Author   311

UNDER THE COVER of darkness, members of the Muslim militia crept into the Coptic Christian camp and slashed the throats of the leaders. An Islamic war cry woke up the rest of the Christians. Despite finding themselves surrounded, the Copts dashed into their enemy with flailing swords and daggers. When the battle ended, every Christian household in Egypt had lost at least one relative to death or prison.

The Coptic revolt in the year AD 750 was only one of many uprisings the Muslim Umayyad Caliphate had been dealing with. Just as the ruling army finished cutting down the Copts in Egypt, Abu Muslim gathered his Islamic insurgent forces in Khurasan and unfurled his black banners. Believing he was destined to fulfill prophecy, he then burned and pillaged his way down to the seat of the empire in Syria. As he planted his flags in Damascus, he brought an end to the Umayyad kingdom.

From at least the year AD 690 the Copts experienced maltreatment from the hands of their Muslim overlords. The Umayyad regime did not persecute Arab Christians or Arab Muslims. Rather, they focused on non-Arabs, including both Copts and Muslims, who suffered throughout the Dynasty. The rulers used the poll tax as the primary means of maltreatment. The Copt peasants groaned under the excessive penalty, for even those who could not afford bread had to pay the tax. Starting in the year AD 726, the Egyptian Christians responded to their afflictions with a series of violent rebellions. While the Copts failed, Abu Muslim's non-Arab Islamic insurgency ended the oppression for both the Christians and Muslims.

As it was with Abu Muslim, the contexts for the Coptic wars were not just political and racial, but also prophetic. Sometime around the year AD 691, a Syrian Christian monk put the final touches on a prediction known to us today as *The Apocalypse of Pseudo-Methodius*. Originally written in Syriac, copyists quickly translated the prophecy into Coptic and European languages. The document seemed to speak directly to the Umayyad government as it indicated that Islamic domination of Christians with its heavy taxation was one of the events that would precede the arrival of the Antichrist. According to the prediction, after numerous trials and tribulations, a last Christian emperor would emerge to lead an army to liberate Jerusalem, conquer Islam, and provide an age of peace prior to the return of Christ in the flesh.

Pseudo-Methodius blended Greek pagan notions of a last world king with certain interpretations of the Apostle John's book of Revelation that had permeated Europe and the Middle East starting from the fourth century AD. Such a perfect blend of religious and political predictions catapulted the idea of legitimate Christian holy war to the forefront of Christian theology and philosophy. History records the Coptic uprisings as among the earliest examples of Christians striking at their enemies, the direct results of the popularity of *Pseudo-Methodius*.

Besides inspiring Christians to violently strike back at their adversaries, *Pseudo-Methodius* would contribute to history other ominous incidents that are still being felt in our own day. The prediction of a last Christian world emperor started a counter reaction in Islam that resulted in Muslim prophecies which are currently being used to fuel world terrorism and the quest for weapons of mass destruction. In particular, the Islamic prophecy of the black flags that inspired Abu Muslim went through an evolution from predicting an attack on Damascus to one of prophesying the conquering of Jerusalem. The prophecy has resurged in modern times as Iran and terrorist organizations prepare their armies to retake Palestine in one of the final apocalyptic battles. In part, because of *Pseudo-Methodius*, the Middle East today is spiraling towards igniting a nuclear world war. One of the primary purposes of this book is to take you as the reader on a voyage through history to explore how these prophecies came about and their consequences that have yet to fully play themselves out. Our Journey will begin by investigating the primitive Christian church of Asian Minor.

During the first three centuries of the Christian era, by and large, the followers of Jesus acted passively in the face of persecution and martyrdom. Documents such as the letters from Ignatius of Antioch and the *Martyrdom of Polycarp* reflected the teachings of Jesus, the Apostle Paul, and the book of Revelation when they urged Christians to resist acting violently toward their persecutors. The fourth century, however, proved to be a pivotal turning point in the history of Christianity and western civilization.

Starting in the second half of the second century AD, the book of Revelation came under fire by certain mainstream church leaders who were paranoid about losing their positions of authority to a growing sect known as the Montanists. Also known as the New Prophecy, the faction based its theology on the Gospel of John and a literal understanding of the Revelation. Like other literalists, the New Prophecy preached patience and pacifism in relation to persecution and martyrdom. And like others holding a literal comprehension of John's Apocalypse, they maintained a hope in a soon returning Jesus who would establish a millennial kingdom of peace on earth. The ideological attack on the Montanists resulted in a slow transition away from literal to symbolic interpretations of Revelation. By the fourth century, the anticipation of Christ's return began to be replaced by spiritual understandings of certain chapters of John's book. The end result was that the Christian church came to believe it should and would usher in the thousand years of peace and prosperity, as opposed to waiting for Christ's return in the flesh to establish the millennium. Coupled with the pagan prophecy of the last world king, the stage was set for Christian holy wars.

In recent years this understanding of church history has come under attack in popular literature by two authors. The first, Jonathan Kirsch, in his *A History of the End of the World*, taught that the book of Revelation and its early literalist interpreters inspired hatred for Christianity's enemies. In this scenario, violent rebellion against the Roman Empire brewed under the surface of the Christian church for three centuries. During this state of affairs, the church fathers of the fourth and fifth centuries symbolized and spiritualized the book of Revelation in a failed attempt to keep the lid on the cauldron of violence that was slowly bubbling to the surface.

As you will see in this book, Kirsch's revisionist history fails on two fronts.

One, there is no evidence that the literalists of the first three centuries advocated committing acts of violence against their enemies and persecutors. In fact, it's just the opposite—they preached pacifism against their foes and left the judgment of enemies up to God. Concerning the second failure, the fourth and fifth century symbolizers and spiritualizers of Scripture and the Revelation are the ones who left a collection of writings advocating violence and the use of physical force against Christianity's adversaries. These include Eusebius of Caesarea and Ambrose of Milan, who supported the destruction of pagan and Jewish temples. This collection also contains the words of Augustine of Hippo. As part of his symbolic interpretation of the millennium, he encouraged government-enforced heresy laws against Christian schismatics. Augustine's theology helped lead to the first two crusades against the Muslims and the burning of heretics in the Middle Ages. As will be established in this manuscript, the reality of history and its facts are the exact opposite of what Kirsch tried to advocate.

The second and most recent author to attempt to rework history is Professor Candida Moss. In her depiction in *The Myth of Persecution*, the early centuries' eyewitness accounts of persecution and martyrdom, such as The *Martyrdom of Polycarp*, are forgeries created much later than most historians have believed. Somewhat similar to Kirsch's hypothesis, these fabrications inspired hatred for one's enemies by demonizing the Roman pagans and thus led the Christian church to eventually engage in holy war.

To buttress her theory, the University of Notre Dame lecturer cited the recent reaction to a terrorist bombing of a Coptic church in Alexandria and the deaths of twenty of its members. Upon the murderous act, Copts broke out into the streets vowing revenge and sacking a mosque. In her book, the primary culprit which inspired this violent response by the Christians was the document of the *Martyrdom of Polycarp*. But one is forced to ask the professor, no matter how or when this particular martyrology was written, how a manuscript that portrays a Christian pastor demonstrating acts of kindness to those who came to arrest him, and behaving passively in the face of his execution, could have caused the current and ancient Copt uprisings? Besides the modern event of the blowing up of the Coptic congregation acting as a contradiction to Moss's thesis that Christians were rarely persecuted in ancient Rome, her theory about the origin of *Polycarp* having been written in the later third century, rather than as an eyewitness account written in the middle of the second century, has several holes in it.

There are two linchpins to Moss's argument. One is that the document of *Polycarp* records that Christians prayed at Polycarp's tomb soon after he was executed. According to Moss, tombs weren't venerated until the late third century. Therefor, the document had to be a late third century forgery. The professor, however, ignored a debate that took place in Rome near the year AD 200, in which part of the argument revolved around the venerations of certain tombs that had already been taking place for some time in Rome and Asia Minor. The two debaters used the reverence of Christian tombs to argue whether Rome or Asia Minor should be the seat of authority for the Christian church. She also ignored the fact that *Polycarp*, in and of itself, can stand as evidence of early relic veneration. The evidences from the debate and *Polycarp* verify each other. The second linchpin is that Moss gives a late date for the origins of the Montanist sect, claiming it started many years after Polycarp's death. She bases this on a date given by the fourth century historian Eusebius of Caesarea and a slight revision of Eusebius by modern historian Christine Trevett. Once again, however, she failed to inform her readers of a contradictory date given by the fourth century chronicler Epiphanius, who dates the beginning of the Montanists to one year after Polycarp's execution in AD 156. The implication of the early date is that the Montanists emerged, in part, as a reaction to the pastor's execution as well as other persecutions that took place in Smyrna and Philadelphia at about the same time.

In one of her other arguments, the professor correctly cites evidence of a martyrology that advocated violence against Roman enemies entitled *The Martyrdom of Shenoufe*. But once again, she didn't bother to tell us that historians are unified that the document was written sometime between the late fourth and seventh centuries when the forces of symbolization were already well at work. Like Kirsch, Moss ignores ancient evidence that doesn't fit her thesis. More details in the weaknesses of Professor Moss's theory are given in the endnotes to chapter three of this manuscript.

This book provides a different answer from these authors' theories. At its heart, it is about the development of Christian eschatology (the theology of the end times) and the consequences of symbolic interpretations of John's Revelation. As a reader, you will travel through the centuries to gain an understanding of how the Christian church transitioned away from what has become known as the literal, futurist premillennialist interpretation when Christians waited patiently for Christ's return, to hyper-spiritualized viewpoints, such as historicism, preterism, postmillennialism, amillennialism, and variations and combinations of each, when the followers of Jesus no longer waited and took actions into their own hands to force the Kingdom of God upon the world. This book will begin with an exploration of the early passive Christian martyrs and church fathers from the west and Asia Minor, and it will end with a call to return to their eschatology.

While attending college, I read a book entitled *The Decline and Fall of the Roman Church* by Malachi Martin. The Catholic scholar's history of the papacy, starting from the third century, held me riveted from the opening pages to the final chapter. The beginning of Martin's manuscript focused on a bishop of Rome named Pontian, who waited for Jesus to return in the flesh. During the local persecutions perpetrated by the Emperor Maximinus against the clergy in the city of Rome, the pontiff remained patient in the midst of his incarceration and death in the salt mines of Sardinia. Martin then jumped to the fourth century when the Christian church transitioned to a new eschatology, a time when the pope grabbed at temporal, earthly power and wealth. I developed my own theory as a result of reading this book—many wars and revolutions throughout the history of western civilization emerged as products of postmillennial theology, or concepts similar to it. Postmillennialism claims that Jesus does not return until the end of the millennial era of peace and prosperity.

I spent time at seminary and subsequent years studying to learn if the hypothesis could be confirmed. I focused on primary sources as well as both established and more recent secondary research. During my inquiries, I was amazed at how much information exists which support my theory and equally amazed at how many mainstream histories and textbooks were either ignorant of, or have purposely ignored this evidence.

Five years ago, I decided to put the conclusions of my explorations in a book. The finished product is this volume, *The Instigators of the Apocalypse.* I hoped to make the text readable to the masses while maintaining academic integrity. With that in mind, I relegated some of the academic arguments to the endnotes while attempting to write as much of the main text as possible with a narrative and story-like style.

Along with the development of eschatology, I hope to inform you about some of the details of Christian church history and its relationship to the development of western civilization. As you read this book, you will experience the First Crusade against the Muslims with its massive bloodshed in Jerusalem. You will sail with Columbus in his discovery of the Americas and his dream of finding gold to finance a crusade to conquer Jerusalem from the Muslims. You will be drawn into Spain's conquest and subjugation of Mexico's natives and the portrayal of Hernan Cortes as the new Moses. You will climb into caves of the Yucatan to uncover the grisly remains of crucified children. You will witness a Franciscan inquisition of the Mayans. You will experience the divine healing of natives in Texas and New Mexico by the laying-on of hands from a Spanish conquistador. You will cross into Renaissance Florence and envision an uprising against the corrupt Medici family and parade down the streets of the city with ten thousand children singing a song to the New Jerusalem. You will observe the tortures of both Catholics and Protestants in England under the Tutors, as well as Oliver Cromwell's revolution against the English monarchy and the massacres Cromwell's Puritan army committed in Ireland. You will voyage across the Atlantic with the Puritans in their attempt to establish the New Jerusalem. You will witness the American Revolution with the colonials' cry of Britain as the Antichrist. You will read the sermons justifying American slavery and the South's hopes of establishing a millennial kingdom of human bondage.

You'll strut along with the Japanese invasion of Manchuria that was influenced by Japan's theology that mimicked certain aspects of postmillennial eschatology. And finally, you will gain a greater understanding of the present-day conflict between the West and Israel with apocalyptic Islam and the ancient Muslim prophecies that promote the terrorism of Al-Qaeda, the Taliban, the Islamic State, and Iran's current quest for weapons of mass destruction. You will travel back to the history of Abu Muslim's black flags and how they have now come to represent the apocalyptic war cry to establish the Islamic Kingdom of Allah on earth.

In the unfolding of each phase of history, this book will identify and explain each particular interpretation of John's Revelation that influenced the instigators of the apocalypse to initiate certain wars and violent revolutions. The first chapters, however, will recount the stories of those who waited for Jesus by refusing to strike back at their persecutors.

This book begins with a Christian named Ignatius who journeyed in chains across Asia Minor to endure ravenous lions in the Roman Coliseum. As he faced looming death, he begged the Christian church to remain meek in the midst of maltreatment and gentle in response to cruelty.

CHAPTER 1
RESURRECTION NOW

IGNATIUS STOOD in the center of the arena. Body parts of the bear-gorged mule lay strewn around him as the overpowering stench of animal blood rose from the saturated sand under his feet. His heart pounded as anguished roars of starved animals drew closer from somewhere below him.

Ignatius watched the ground across the Coliseum floor. He stepped back from two spots of shifting sand. Suddenly, trap doors slammed open and two lions sprang onto the arena floor, as if by magic. The mob in the levels above Ignatius howled and jumped to its feet. The lions spied their prey and crouched into attack position.

Trajan and Political Clubs

Some months earlier, in the year A.D. 107, the Emperor Trajan passed through the city of Antioch in Syria. As early as AD 101, political clubs emerged in various cities throughout the empire with some resulting in factious in-fighting and political disunity.[1] As a result, Trajan grew paranoid toward any new group that did not have long-standing traditions and well established ceremonies recognized by the political establishment.[2] Before his arrival in Antioch, the local authorities anticipated Trajan's attitude. They arrested Ignatius, the second leader of the Christian church in Antioch after the Apostle Peter.[3] As the Syrian pastor, Ignatius considered ceremony important to the unity of his congregation. In particular, he held a high regard for the Christian sacrament of Communion. Any edict keeping his congregation from worshiping and receiving Communion would have been difficult for him to accept.[4] With Trajan's attitude toward associations and unfamiliar ceremonies, the authorities took no chances and held Ignatius for trial before the emperor.[5] Trajan condemned Ignatius to die in the Coliseum at Rome.[6]

In Chains to Smyrna

A contingent of ten soldiers chained and hauled Ignatius overland and by sea through Western Asia Minor. The soldiers intended to stop in several cities to rest and replenish their supplies. One of Antioch's congregation members hurried ahead to spread the news. The report reverberated throughout the churches of what is today modern Turkey, and one church, in particular, looked forward to meeting with Ignatius.

Polycarp ruled over the church of Smyrna from the day the apostles appointed him to the office of pastor.[7] Polycarp may or may not have met Ignatius before his scheduled arrival, but he certainly knew of the man who succeeded the Apostle Peter. Polycarp now had his chance to meet Syria's pastor face to face.

Crossing overland from Antioch, the day finally arrived when the cohort marched into Smyrna. If the contingent had passed through the center of town, it would have yanked the shackled Ignatius past the Agora. This courtyard was the commercial, judicial and political heart of the city, its very center reserved for artistic activities and teaching. As the soldiers jerked Ignatius beyond the Northern Gate, he was exposed to the altar of Zeus, which included statues of the goddess Hestia, and the gods Hermes, Dionysus, Eros, and Heracles.[8]

Ignatius also would have noticed the trade guild buildings that lined the Agora's commercial area. As a port city, scores of commodities and goods flooded into this area from throughout the Roman Empire. Each product had its own dedicated guild: corn, wine, dyes, Chinese silk, silversmiths, goldsmiths and others. Each guild worshipped its own god. The guilds presented a particularly challenging problem for the churches of Asia Minor.

Trade guilds paved the path to financial prosperity. These financial associations forged connections and business partnerships. If you did not belong to one, you would find it difficult to rise out of poverty. For the Christians, the guilds' association with the Pantheon presented the primary stumbling block. Guild meetings included dedicating meat to the gods and to the emperor as a deity. The church at Smyrna apparently refused participation in the guilds, so Polycarp and his congregation lived in poverty.[9]

As Ignatius settled into the camp, he longed to meet with the Christians. They would revive his spirit. Throughout the journey, he tried to show kindness to the soldiers, but the more compassion he demonstrated the worse they treated him. Exasperated, he described the situation in his letter addressed to the church in Rome: "I fight with the beasts from Syria to Rome, by land and by sea, night and day, having been bound to ten leopards, that is, to the military attachment. By their mistreatment, I become more of a disciple."[10]

Polycarp, Tavia, Alce, Daphne, Uetecnus, and others came to greet Ignatius. But when the meetings ended, the Antiochian referred to Burrhus as the one church member who "revitalized me in every way."[11]

A party from Ephesus arrived to encourage the pastor. It brought news from the church at Rome. They planned on bribing the government officials.

Letters to the Churches

Ignatius's attitude toward the report was born out of years of struggling with leading his church at Antioch while yearning to be free from the vanity of human life. He had demonstrated no interest in or desire for wealth and power, whether political or personal. During his stay, Ignatius had time to write to several churches. He responded first to the Romans.[12]

After the opening greeting, Ignatius devoted a number of chapters to the heart of the issue. "I am somewhat afraid of your love for me, lest it do me wrong. . . . Do not prevent me from being poured out to God as a libation. . . . It is good that I should be like the setting sun from this world so that I may rise to God. . . . Let it all come upon me: fire and cross, fierceness of beasts, being cut up, torn apart, breaking of bones, beating of members, grinding of the whole body, torment from the devil. Only one thing remains: I desire to reach Jesus Christ."[13]

Although he recognized their good intentions, Ignatius believed the Romans' plan interfered with his destiny. Jesus Christ suffered, died, and physically rose from the dead. For Ignatius, the truest discipleship involved the same. "I seek him who died for us," he pleads. "I want him who rose for our sakes . . . permit me to be food for the beasts; through them I will reach God."[14]

After his plea to the Romans, Ignatius addressed a letter to the Ephesians. This letter and a later one written to the church at Philadelphia became two of the most important epistles in early church history. In them, he referenced concepts from what is one of the most controversial and debated books in the New Testament.

"Since in God I have received the much loved name that you purchased by a just nature in accord with the faith and love in Christ Jesus our savior; and since as imitators of God you rekindled yourselves in the blood of God. You perfectly completed the work of our family."[15] Ignatius applauded the Ephesians regaining a church unity that had been missing in earlier years. The book of Revelation told of an Ephesian church that had lost its first love.[16] And the First letter of John recounts an Ephesian congregation that had trouble defining love as it related to its own members.[17] Ignatius revealed that the Ephesians had "rekindled" their unity and love for one another. The word in the original Greek text implies a reigniting of what had smoldered out. Thus they found again their first love. This letter indicated that the Antioch pastor had in mind the notions from both the Revelation and the First Letter of John.[18]

Ignatius also stated that the Ephesians struggled with persecution. "Pray without ceasing in behalf of other men... Be meek in response to their wrath. And for their cruelty manifest your gentleness... Let us seek to be followers of the Lord (who was ever more unjustly treated?) so that no plant of the devil may be found in you."[19] For this pastor, the truest discipleship included not only suffering but doing so without striking back at the perpetrators. Showing kindness would help lead the persecutors to Christ. To strike back would allow the devil to enter the disciple.

Ignatius wrote two more letters while in Smyrna, one to the residents of Magnesia and one to the people of Trallia, both cities located in Asia Minor.[20] The epistles emphasized submission to the pastor, the elders, and the deacons and advice to steer clear of the heresies that plagued the churches at that time. These themes ran through most of his letters written in Smyrna and later in Troas. The emphasis on a hierarchical structure of church government is particularly interesting. In A.D. 107, the churches of Asia Minor were operating according to what has become known as the Episcopal form of church government—where the pastor, or "episcopos" in Greek, is the authority over the elders, or "presbyteroi," followed by the deacons.

In the New Testament, the congregational form of government ruled the churches. That is, a group of elders, elected or appointed, governed over the congregations. This is clear from the fact that the terms "episcopos" and "presbyteros" are interchangeable in the NT writings. The ultimate authorities, however, were the original twelve Apostles, and Paul held authority over the gentile churches that he had founded. As the Apostles began dying, one particular elder took over a given congregation as a replacement, and eventually, as seen in Ignatius' writings, "episcopos" came to specifically designate this lead elder or pastor. By the year 107, the Episcopal form ruled all the mainstream churches. In the centuries to come, a debate would rage in the Christian church over whether church should operate according to the Episcopal or congregational model. The dispute would erupt into warfare and Christians persecuting one another. But for now, in the early centuries, the churches remained unified under the Episcopal form.[21]

Ignatius and Revelation's Letter to Philadelphia

Eventually, Ignatius left Smyrna and traveled by ship to Troas.[22] He was another step closer to his confrontation in the Coliseum. But while in the city, the thought of gladiators and wild animals did not seem to enter his imagination. The problems in the church in Philadelphia engaged his attention and Ignatius wrote a letter to advise the people.

Judging from the epistle, the unity of the church was threatened by some who interpreted Christianity's relationship to the Old Testament in a different manner than what the Apostle Paul had taught. Perhaps they took a more legalistic stance on Christianity relating to the Law of Moses.

In describing these schismatics at Philadelphia, Ignatius made one of the most significant statements found in any of his letters: "They are pillars and tombs of the dead on which is written only names of men."[23] The Greek word for pillar is the same word the book of Revelation used to describe those Philadelphians who faithfully follow Christ: "He who overcomes, I will make him a pillar (stelai) in the temple of my God... And I will write on him the name of my God and the name of the city of my God, the New Jerusalem... And I will write on him my new name."[24] Here, Ignatius used the concepts in reverse —the heretics are pillars of mausoleums as opposed to the pillars of the temple of God, and they have written upon them only the names of men as opposed to the name and city of God. It is unmistakable that Ignatius had the book of Revelation's letter to the Philadelphians on his mind as he wrote his own letter to the same church.

Early church writers claimed the Apostle John wrote Revelation while exiled on the island of Patmos, off the Greek Coast, in about the year A.D.96.[25] Centuries later, scholars in the 1800s reported that Ignatius had no knowledge of the Revelation since he did not quote from it or reference it. Therefore, the Apostle could not have written the book. Ignatius's letters to the Ephesians and Philadelphians, however, seem to indicate that these scholars have either overlooked this connection, or have purposely ignored the obvious because it doesn't fit their agenda.[26]

Ignatius rarely quoted any New Testament writing.[27] In his letters, he made use of a number of concepts from Paul's epistles and from the Revelation's letters to Ephesus and Philadelphia. It's not hard to imagine why he doesn't quote verses directly. The soldiers were probably ordered not to allow Ignatius access to Christian writings, though he was permitted to write and speak with visitors. Therefore, he had to rely on memory. Before his arrest, Ignatius had possession of Paul's letters for decades, and had developed a cohesive theology centered on them. John's wrote the Revelation sometime in A.D. 96, and the document may have circulated to Antioch relatively late.[28] His pastoral concerns for the various churches ignited his use of Paul's teachings. Ignatius's view of persecution and suffering, however, mimics what is written in Revelation.

In Smyrna and Troas, Ignatius wrote seven letters in all, including a personal letter to Polycarp.[29] Besides a legalistic form of Christianity, another situation worried him. The problem first surfaced in Ephesus, some fifty years before, during the time of the Apostle Paul. It also became an unrelenting difficulty for the Apostle John as he oversaw many of the churches in Asia Minor. For John, as well as for Ignatius, some seven years after John's death, a counterfeit view of Jesus continued to gnaw at Christianity.

John addressed the issue with the Ephesian church: "Jesus is the Christ . . . And Jesus Christ shed his blood."[30] The philosopher Cerinthus had traveled from Alexandria, Egypt bringing with him a mix of pagan Greek thought and Christianity. For Cerinthus, Jesus and the Christ were two separate beings. The divine Christ descended upon and filled Jesus at his water baptism, giving the man from Nazareth extraordinary power and spiritual enlightenment. This divine being could not become flesh because all physicality was intrinsically evil. Only the soul was good and worthy of salvation. Furthermore, this divine being could not suffer. Therefore, the Christ left Jesus just before he was crucified. Only Jesus suffered, not the Christ.[31]

John wrote his letter to the Ephesian congregation outlining the correct theology concerning the nature of Jesus. There is no separation between Jesus and Christ, and Christ shed his blood. John also decided to write a gospel of Jesus. Three Gospels already existed, recounting aspects of Jesus' life, ministry, death, and resurrection. But John decided a fourth needed to be written, this one in response to a group with beliefs similar to Cerinthus. While Cerinthus bandied about in Ephesus, the Nicolaitans raged throughout Asia Minor.[32]

The Resurrection Now

After having been rejected by the church at Ephesus, the Nicolaitans turned their attention to other churches. While holding a similar view as Cerinthus about Jesus, the Nicolaitans had their own particular take on sexuality, martyrdom, and finances. The members were sexual libertines and believed that God never willed anyone to be martyred. At the same time, they believed God desired that everyone should be financially prosperous.[33] The Nicolaitans tied their view of suffering to their view of resurrection. There was to be no future resurrection of the body. Spiritual resurrection for the Christian church had already occurred at the moment of faith, or conversion. Therefore, Christians should live now free from all suffering.[34]

While John's epistle made the connection between Jesus and Christ, the Gospel of John demonstrated the life and theology of Jesus that hit on a number of themes in reaction to both Cerinthus and the Nicolaitans. The earlier chapters deal with the unjust persecution of Jesus; the latter chapters deal with the unjust persecution of his followers. In the late stages of Jesus' life, he promised to give his disciples the Holy Spirit, the Paracleat as John would refer to him in Greek, to give comfort and counsel in the time of persecution.[35] The Gospel ends with Jesus rising from the dead and appearing to his followers, promising them he would always be with them, even to the end of the age.[36]

While persecution is one of the main themes of the Gospel, it also stands out as a primary focus in John's Revelation. The book begins with John claiming he dwelled on the island of Patmos for the sake of his testimony for Christ. While he does not state that he is there because of persecution, the language is strikingly similar to the way he described those who will be martyred for their testimony for Christ.[37]

John's Revelation and the Gnostics

As John stood on the beach of Patmos, visions of the future illuminated his mind and soul. The themes he described play out like chronicles given in reaction to Nicolaitan theology. The saints in heaven sing a song in which the God of Jesus Christ physically creates the Universe: "You are worthy, our Lord and God, to receive honor and praise, for you created all things, and by your will they exist and were created." The Nicolaitans believed that an evil god created the physical universe, and such a song struck at the very heart of the Gnostic philosophy of good and evil.

John described martyrs who come from every tribe and tongue on earth and wash their robes white in the blood of martyrdom.[38] The white robe was meant by John as a symbol of martyrdom and acceptance of salvation by God. The Nicolaitans could not accept such an idea.

The Apostle goes on to explain that the martyred cried out and asked God how long it would be before He takes vengeance on those who are shedding their blood. God answers them that they must be patient until the full number of their brethren has been murdered. The extraordinary reply teaches the Christian church two things: the Nicolaitan view of martyrdom is in error, and Christians are to accept martyrdom passively and not take vengeance into their own hands.

John follows this with a vision of a beast rising out of the sea. The beast represents an empire and kings who slay with the sword. It is the antithesis of God's kingdom. The Apostle responded: "If any man shall kill with the sword, he must be killed. Here is the patience and the faith of the saints." [39] The prescription here is to resist picking up the sword in behalf of God's Kingdom, but patiently endure persecution. This passage in Revelation echoes Matthew, chapter 26:52, when Jesus said, "All those who have taken the sword, shall die by the sword." The context for this text in the Gospel is Jesus' example of accepting persecution because of who he was and what he taught as the guards from the Jewish leadership came to arrest him in the Garden of Gethsemane.

As the visions continued to unfold, another beast, who is the Antichrist, tries to force everyone to put a mark of devotion on their hand and forehead which allows them to buy and sell. Those who refused the mark cannot engage in legal economic activity. This part of the Revelation is particularly damning to the Nicolaitans, for it condemns their prosperity doctrine. At the time John had these visions, the Emperor Domitian encouraged a unification of economic activity with emperor worship by way of the trade guilds. In the Revelation, in spite of the Antichrist's control of the economy, this period would be a time of rapid inflation and price gouging similar to what took place during a famine that struck Galatia in A.D. 92.[40]

John marveled at a vision of the Whore of Babylon, a woman "drunk with the blood of the saints and with the blood of the martyrs of Jesus."[41] The woman represents the combination of religion, sexual impurity, and financial prosperity and is portrayed as responsible for shedding the blood of the saints. All aspects of Nicolaitan philosophy is condemned by the vision.[42]

In the final part of the Revelation, Jesus returned in the flesh, putting an end to the Antichrist and establishing an age of peace over the earth which lasts a thousand years.

In the early chapters of Revelation, letters to the seven churches of Asia Minor are particularly enlightening when it comes to understanding the prosperity doctrine of the Nicolaitans. John reveals that the churches of Pergamum and Thyatira were plagued by those who followed the Nicolaitans. To Pergamum: "I have this against you, because you have those who teach others to eat meat sacrificed to idols and commit sex outside of marriage. Thus you have those who follow the Nicolaitans." To Thyatira: "You allow your wife, Jezebel, who claims to be a prophetess, to teach my servants to eat meat sacrificed to idols and commit sex outside of marriage." During the trade guild meetings, meat was sacrificed to the emperor and to the city's patron god or goddess.

To Laodicea: "Because you say you are rich and need nothing, you do not know you are wretched." While the church at Laodicea probably did not accept the Nicolaitans' teaching on sexuality, it apparently accepted the prosperity doctrine and teetered on the brink of accepting the Nicolaitan view of martyrdom. The city of Laodicea was in the center of trade routes of the empire and its prosperity was tied to the trade guild in textiles. The city was also known for an eye medicine. It is likely the church became involved with the guilds to achieve its wealth.[43] Jesus warns the church to buy gold refined by fire and white garments. The statement reflects the New Testament's First Letter of Peter in its encouragement to Christians to endure suffering under persecution where their faith would be refined like gold.[44]

The letter to Smyrna would have been highly offensive to the Nicolaitans. "I know your poverty," John writes," but you are rich." According to John, Jesus predicts the Smyrneans will undergo a persecution that will last ten days and implies it will lead to martyrdom: "Stay faithful even to death." The letter reacts against the Nicolaitans' prosperity doctrine and their anti-martyrdom mentality. [45]

In spite of the warning by John's Revelation, the Nicolaitan heresy refused to die and a number of churches continued to flirt with some of its tenets well into the second century. By the time Ignatius entered Rome, Gnosticism broke down into increasing factions and sects. But most were based on the premise that Christ did not suffer and die. As Ignatius met with the various churches on his way to his appointment in the Coliseum, he knew it was his last opportunity to address the aberrant philosophy. It was his letter to the Trallians that best summed up his answer:

"And God the Word was truly born of the Virgin. . . . He who forms all men in the womb, was Himself really in the womb, and made for Himself a body of the seed of the Virgin, but without any intercourse of man . . . And when He had lived among men for thirty years, He was baptized by John, really and not in appearance . . . He who was Himself the Judge was judged by the Jews, falsely so called, and by Pilate the governor; was scourged, was smitten on the cheek, was spit upon; He wore a crown of thorns and a purple robe; He was condemned: He was crucified in reality, and not in appearance, not in imagination, not in deceit. He really died, and was buried, and rose from the dead."[46]

While this passage recalls John's Gospel, it was his attitude expressed in his letter to the Romans that mimicked John's attitude in the Revelation. As he mentally and spiritually prepared himself for his fate in the Coliseum, he wrote:

"May I enjoy the wild beasts that are prepared for me; and I pray they may be found eager to rush upon me, which also I will entice to devour me speedily . . . But if they be unwilling to assail me, I will compel them to do so. Pardon me. I know what is for my benefit. Now I begin to be a disciple . . . Permit me to be an imitator of the passion of my God."[47]

For Ignatius, God willingly died for mankind, and the truest discipleship rested in suffering as Jesus Christ suffered. He implored the Roman congregation to decline to fight to free him or to pay for his release.

The Final Resting Place

After Ignatius left Troas, many of the details in the final legs of the journey are not considered reliable tradition. But what might be authentic is the fact that he entered the city on the final day of the games and was condemned by the Magistrate. Then the city authorities hurried him into the Coliseum.

At the end of that day, church members slinked onto the arena floor and collected Ignatius's few remaining pieces. The body parts were taken back to Antioch where they remained buried in a cemetery outside the Daphne Gate. [48] In the seventh century, they were unearthed and returned to Rome and the Church of San Clemente, where they rest under the main altar.

While Ignatius left a legacy that helps us determine apostolic authority for the book of Revelation, and while the example of his death helped inspire the early church to follow the book's teachings to act passively in the face of persecution, the Nicolaitans also continued to exert their influence. In time, shades of their realized eschatology and their prosperity doctrine for the individual would be adopted by the church on a corporate level, resulting in corruption to the clergy.

In the meantime, however, Polycarp continued to battle Nicolaitan philosophy after Ignatius's martyrdom. And like Ignatius, Polycarp would face his own day of reckoning in the arena for the crime of being a Christian.

CHAPTER 2
CRISIS IN SMYRNA

NO MORE RUNNING. Pastor Polycarp felt too old and tired. After all, there is a time for every purpose under heaven: a time to live and a time to die. And didn't the dream confirm it? Three nights before, he had dreamt that his pillow caught fire. Now he reclined in his bed and waited for the soldiers.

Forty-eight years ago, two ravenous lions had torn apart and consumed most of Polycarp's friend, Ignatius, in the Roman Coliseum, and now persecution visited the church of Smyrna. Some days before, city authorities arrested a young congregant named Marcarius and threw him to the wild animals in the arena. The mob in the stands cheered and clapped at the carnage and then cried out for the authorities to find Polycarp.

When news of the persecution first broke, his flock convinced Polycarp to run and hide. At first, he resisted their overtures, but Jesus had made it clear that fleeing was an acceptable response to persecution and so they convinced him it might be God's will.[49] Now news reached him from church members that the authorities had tortured a young teenager and learned of his hiding place. Once again, the congregants tried to talk him into running. This time he waited.

From his bed, he heard the soldiers enter the house. He walked downstairs to meet them. They couldn't believe their eyes. Some of the guards grumbled. This is the guy who posed a danger to Rome? Why such an effort to capture an old man?

"Making haste is not our priority here," Polycarp assured the guards, speaking gently towards them. The pastor offered and gave to them as much food and drink as they wanted. He then asked them if they would allow him to pray for awhile. Incensed at the urgency their superiors had laid upon them, they granted his request.

Polycarp prayed out loud for two hours. In his supplication, he included all the people that he ever encountered, as best he could remember. After listening to him, many of the soldiers regretted becoming involved in the whole sorry business. But they were men of duty. At the end of the prayer, they loaded Polycarp onto a donkey and led him from the farmhouse back to the city.[50]

For years, the people of the church at Smyrna had enjoyed peace from government-sponsored oppression. Some fifty-nine years earlier, the Apostle John wrote in the *Revelation* that Smyrna would undergo a persecution that would last ten days: . . . *be faithful even unto death.* Year after year, the Smyrneans waited, but apparently, nothing happened. John probably appointed Polycarp to pastor the church after the Apostle returned from exile on Patmos in AD 96 or 97. Now, decades later, in 155, Polycarp's arrest signaled the fulfillment of the prophecy.[51]

Through the years, Polycarp followed the admonitions with which his friend, Ignatius, had left him: "Mitigate violent attacks by a gentle response. . . . Be long-suffering, therefore, with one another, in meekness, as God is towards you." But Ignatius also warned Polycarp not to tolerate the heresies of the Gnostics: "Do not let those who teach strange doctrine fill you with apprehension. Stand firm, as does an anvil, which is beaten."

In the decades of his episcopate, Polycarp had the letter copied and sent to other churches. His own letter to the Philadelphians reflected similar concerns:

"But He who raised Him up from the dead will raise up us also, if we do His will, and walk in His commandments, and love what He loved, keeping ourselves from all unrighteousness, covetousness, love of money, evil speaking, false witness; not rendering evil for evil, or railing for railing, or blow for blow, or cursing for cursing, but being mindful of what the Lord said in His teaching: 'Judge not, that ye be not judged; forgive, and it shall be forgiven unto you; be merciful, that ye may obtain mercy; with what measure you give out, it shall be measured to you again;' and once more, 'Blessed are the poor, and those that are persecuted for righteousness sake, for theirs is the kingdom of God.'"

"'For whosoever does not confess that Jesus Christ has come in the flesh, is antichrist;' . . . and whosoever does not confess the testimony of the cross, is of the devil; and whosoever perverts the oracles of the Lord to his own lusts, and says that there is neither a resurrection nor a judgment, he is the first-born of Satan."[52]

The Gnostics taught that there is no future resurrection of the body and that martyrdom for Christ's name was against the will of God. For Polycarp, as with Ignatius and the Revelation, keeping the church free from Gnostic heresy went hand in hand with passively accepting persecution and refusing to strike back at the persecutors.

The Revelation indicated that some of the Gnostics also intertwined their theology of resurrection and martyrdom with a prosperity doctrine. Apparently, at the time of his letter, Polycarp dealt with the same dogma infiltrating the church at Philippi. Valens and his wife fell into greed or avarice and had been expunged from the church. Polycarp addressed the issue: "I am deeply sorry for Valens, who was once made a presbyter among you, that he so little understands the place which was given to him. I advise, therefore, that you keep from avarice, and be pure and truthful. . . . Therefore, brethren, I am deeply sorry for him (Valens) and for his wife, and may the Lord grant them true repentance. Therefore be yourselves also moderate in this matter, and do not regard such men as enemies, but call them back as fallible and straying members, that you may make whole the body of you all. For in doing this you edify yourselves.[53] Thus Polycarp's letter implies he faced the heresy of the Nicolaitans or something similar.[54]

Having taught Philippi and his own church to stay strong against Gnosticism and act passively and meekly in the midst of persecution, Polycarp now faced the task of applying his instructions to his own situation. As the soldiers led the donkey into the city, as implied by the prophecy in Revelation, God was about to put him to the test.

Polycarp in the Arena

The soldiers stopped the donkey just outside of the arena, letting Polycarp off and marching him in. For hours, Smyrna had buzzed with rumors of the arrest and the stadium overflowed with the mob. As he walked in the crowd jeered. When the shrieks finally subsided, the proconsul addressed the old man. "Are you Polycarp?"

"I am."

"Then swear by the genius of Caesar and say away with the atheists."

"Away with the atheists," replied Polycarp, sarcastically.

"No, swear by the genius of Caesar! Take the oath and I will let you go. Curse your Christ!"

"I have served him for eighty-six years and he has done me no harm," Polycarp said, "How can I blaspheme my king who saved me?"[55]

"I have wild beasts and I will throw you to them. Swear by the genius of Caesar and repent."

"Then bring them in," answered the pastor. "We may go from evil to righteousness, not the other way."

"I will burn you alive if you don't repent."

"You threaten with the fire that lives but for a few minutes," rejoined Polycarp. "How I wish you knew the fire that burns the wicked forever. But do what you will."

The crowd erupted, crying such things: "This is the teacher of Asia, the father of the Christians, the destroyer of our gods, who teaches many neither to offer sacrifice nor to worship." And they called for Polycarp's death.

Wooden logs and twigs enveloped a large stake as swarms of men and women poured out from their arena seats and assisted in preparing the homicide. As some of them tied Polycarp to the post, he looked up to heaven. "I bless you Lord God Almighty that you have granted me this day and hour that I may share, among the number of the martyrs, in the cup of your Christ, for the Resurrection to everlasting life."

Torches thrown on the brushwood lit the fire. The flames funneled-up and surrounded the body but somehow refused to touch it. The sight stunned the mob. When it became apparent that the fire would not kill him, the authorities ordered a soldier to run him through with a sword. As the blade tore through his body, torrents of blood gushed over the fire, extinguishing the flames. The crowd, so vitriolic at first, sat astonished in silence as Polycarp gave up his final breath.

As the pastor of Smyrna died on February 23, 155, in Rome, thousands of miles away, one of his disciples felt pierced in his soul. At the second of Polycarp's demise, from somewhere around him, Irenaeus heard the words, "Polycarp is dead."[56]

The fire flared and mushroomed across the bottom of the bronze seat, roasting Blandina's flesh into a brown hue, the very color of the chair in which she was chained. The young woman did not shriek or cry out in pain.

After the authorities saw that her body was well scorched, they unchained Blandina, wrapped her in a net, and left her for the bull. Stoic in her expression till the end, Blandina accepted the impaling of the horns without a sound. The mob cheered as the bull ripped through her flesh.

Blandina's pastor, Pothinius, never witnessed her death, but he felt much of her pain in his own body. He lay motionless on the floor from both the inflicted wounds and from his arthritis. He probably knew he would never make it from the prison cell to the arena, for the torture was too much for his ninety-year-old body. Finally, the pastor of Lyons took his last breath. That moment robbed the mob of one more spectacle.

Before he died, perhaps Pothinius may have wondered who would take his place as pastor once he was gone. Perhaps he thought that Irenaeus, the pastor from Vienna, could handle two congregations, at least for awhile.

Irenaeus came to Rome to deliver a letter from the church of Lyons that described the persecutions, as well as to report on a sect known as the New Prophecy. At the time he pastored the church of Vienna, as well as acted as presbyter for Lyons.[57] After he returned from Rome, he succeeded Pothinius as pastor of Lyons.

Irenaeus grew up in the church at Smyrna. He and his boyhood friend, Florinus, sat under the tutelage of Pastor Polycarp. When they grew older, Florinus turned to Gnosticism. Irenaeus yearned to turn his early companion back to what they had learned as children. In a letter to Florinus, Irenaeus wrote: "I remember the events of that time more clearly than events of our own time. For what boys learn, growing with their mind, becomes joined with it; so that I am able to describe the very place in which the blessed Polycarp sat as he discoursed, and his goings out and his comings in, and the manner of his life, and his physical appearance, and his discourses to the people, and the accounts which he gave of his intercourse with John and with the others who had seen the Lord. And as he remembered their words, and what he heard from them concerning the Lord, and concerning his miracles and his teaching, having received them from eyewitnesses of the 'Word of life,' Polycarp related all things in harmony with the Scriptures."[58]

While in Rome, Pastor Eulithius asked Irenaeus to write an update of Justin Martyr's *Against Heresies*, written some fifty years before. Since Justin's document, Gnosticism had broken down into hundreds of factions. Various sects gleaned off some basic Gnostic ideas but then took them in new directions with different teachers giving them their own spin. It was a daunting assignment but Irenaeus accepted the challenge. When he returned to Lyons, after the persecutions subsided, he delved into his task. He titled the new manuscript, *Against Heresies: A Refutation and Subversion of Knowledge falsely so called.*

With Justin's manuscript at hand, certain writings from the Gnostics themselves, and the knowledge of Gnostic teachers he learned at the feet of

Polycarp, Irenaeus wrote the story of the origin of Gnosticism. Simon Magus stood at the heart of the heterodoxy's beginnings.[59]

The story of Simon begins in Samaria, where he proclaimed to be the Father of all and the power of God. Simon liked to preach in the shade of trees. One day, his followers gathered under an olive tree.[60]

He proclaimed to the crowd that all salvation existed within his own being. He explained that the Power of God is male but the Great Thought of God is female. The Father exists as both male and female although he appears as male before his pupils. "I have been separated from the great thought," he told them, "but I long to be reunited." For Simon, salvation would ultimately bring about all unification of males and females into one androgynous state.

The throng hung on every word as he taught them that the female Great Thought gave birth to the angels, who in turn rebelled against her and created the world and all that is in it. The physical creation, then, was the work of rebellious angels and their demon followers.[61]

Simon taught that God cannot be physical, and he proclaimed himself to be the one who came from Nazareth. Salvation is not found in suffering or the shedding of blood, for he himself came only in the appearance of a man, and only appeared to suffer in Judea. Simon lectured that salvation is in the knowledge he, himself, offered.

As he stood teaching in the shade of that tree, Simon noticed someone watching him from a rooftop of a brothel. Her pleasing figure gleamed in the sunlight. Finally, he thought, he had found her.

Helen of Troy

As he gazed at her magnificence, a revelation struck his mind. This must be the one he had been waiting for. She was the Great Thought that destiny would reunite him with. Beautiful as she was, how could she be anything else?

Helen probably blushed from the prolonged stare. Could this great teacher really be noticing her? Pride must have welled up within her.

In Simon's belief system, the rebellious angels captured the Great Thought and shut her up in a human body where she spent the centuries traveling and reincarnating into various bodies. How fitting, he must have reflected, as he found out her name. Here was the face of Troy that launched a thousand ships.[62]

From that moment, the two became inseparable. Simon found the love of his life. And in Helen, he would reunite with the Great Thought.

Simon's followers became known as the Simions and would eventually separate into two groups. One group advocated celibacy, trying to put an end to the endless regeneration of human bodies, thus freeing the soul once and for all. The other took the opposite view, advocating sexual libertinism, teaching that what was done in the body is of no consequence to the soul. Both would reject the suffering of Christ and the physical resurrection of the body.[63]

With the origin of Gnosticism explained, Irenaeus described the teacher Menander. Menander added a couple of new wrinkles to the Simion tradition. Those who were baptized in the name of Menander could never suffer or grow old and die.[64] Perfect health was now available to those who followed the true knowledge and put their faith in him and the resurrection that has already occurred.[65]

After Menander, Saturninas and Basilides followed, one from Syria and the other from Alexandria. Judging from his writing, the Egyptian Basilides particularly astonished Irenaeus. Through supernatural hocus-pocus, Christ in Jesus took the appearance of Simon of Cyrene, who the Gospels record helped Jesus carry the cross up Calvary. Simon took on the appearance of Jesus, so when the Romans thought they were crucifying Jesus, they were actually crucifying Simon. Jesus then stood watching and laughing at the Romans and at the angels who created the world, having pulled a fast one on them all.

After having witnessed some of the persecutions in Lyons, Irenaeus must have felt insulted by the theology and logical conclusions of Basilides. The Syrian believed that one must not confess the Crucified, for Christ's death was an illusion. If one is faced with denying Christ or suffering martyrdom, then deny Christ. If one eats meat in sacrifice to idols, think nothing of it. It is no sin. In fact, all suffering is a result of sin. Christians who have faith, therefore, should never suffer.[66]

Basilides put the blame of martyrdom squarely on the suffering Christians. The end result is that the orthodox, mainstream Christians risked everything for the sake of their beliefs, while many of the Gnostics risked nothing.[67]

The Origin of John's Gospel

Irenaeus represented Cerinthus as a man educated by Egyptians who taught that God did not create the world, but it was made by an ignorant being far beneath Him. Irenaeus then goes on to write: "He (Cerinthus) represented Jesus as having not been born of a virgin, but as being the son of Joseph and Mary according to the ordinary course of human generation. . . . Moreover, after Jesus' baptism, Christ descended upon him in the form of a dove from the Supreme Ruler, and that then he proclaimed the unknown Father, and performed miracles. But at last Christ departed from Jesus, and that then Jesus suffered and rose again, while Christ remained impassible, inasmuch as he was a spiritual being."

"The Nicolaitans . . . lead lives of unrestrained indulgence. The character of these men is very plainly pointed out in the Apocalypse of John, [when they are represented] as teaching that it is a matter of indifference to practice adultery, and to eat things sacrificed to idols."[68]

In chapter three of his book, the apologist from Lyons explained why John wrote his Gospel: "John, the disciple of the Lord, preaches this faith, and seeks, by the proclamation of the Gospel, to remove that error which by Cerinthus had been disseminated among men, and a long time previously by those termed Nicolaitans, who are an offset of that "knowledge" falsely so called."[69]

Here, Irenaeus set the context for the Nicolaitans in the sixth chapter of 1Timothy where they descended from Gnostics who taught a prosperity doctrine. For Irenaeus, however, the 'knowledge falsely so called' referred to all Gnostic teachings. As he worked through his manuscript detailing the various teachers and doctrines of this false knowledge, Irenaeus set the stage for his final two chapters where he explained Satan's end game. Ultimately, Gnosticism is destined to lead to the emergence of the Antichrist.

In no uncertain terms, this author of *Against Heresies* informed his readers that Polycarp's mentor, the Apostle John, wrote the book of Revelation: "John also, the Lord's disciple, when beholding the sacerdotal and glorious advent of His kingdom, says in the Apocalypse: . . ."[70] In the overall context of his manuscript, Irenaeus referred to "John, the Lord's disciple," as the Apostle John. In his last chapter, he explained the time in which the Revelation was written as he expounds why the Antichrist's identity should remain hidden: "We will not, however, incur the risk of pronouncing positively as to the name of Antichrist; for if it were necessary that his name should be distinctly revealed in this present time, it would have been announced by him who beheld the apocalyptic vision. For that was seen no very long time since, but almost in our day, towards the end of Domitian's reign."[71]

The Roman Emperors and the Beast

The historical background to Domitian, and a fresh reading of the Revelation, helps verify the correctness of Irenaeus's statements. The Emperor Domitian came to power in A.D. 86 and, over the years, became paranoid about losing his hold on the throne. He waged a pogrom which infiltrated all aspects of Roman society. Political street preachers, members of the Senate, and Jews spilled their blood in the emperor's execution halls. The slaughter grew so bad that the Senate designated Domitian with a term that meant "Nero back again" referring to the idea that the spirit of Nero had returned. During this time, the emperor exiled John to Patmos. The nightmare finally ended when Domitian's wife conspired with his best friend and assassinated him, cutting the emperor to pieces as he slept.

Some modern scholars advocate that the number 666 in Greek numerology spells out the name Nero and, therefore, they conclude that John wrote Revelation in Nero's time and with Nero in mind as the Antichrist. However, a careful analysis of how John portrays the Antichrist reveals that the Beast encompasses aspects of the reigns of Nero plus the three Flavian Family Emperors: he persecutes the church as Nero did, he wages war effectively as Vespasian and Titus did, including a rampage against Jerusalem which they carried out in AD 70, and he encourages all religious, political and economic aspects of life to be merged under emperor worship as Domitian attempted to do. John paints a composite portrait of an antichrist which encompasses the facets of four emperors.

As the above quote indicates, Irenaeus did not accept either Nero or Domitian as John's Beast, but the identity of the Antichrist remained hidden. John's explanation of the Antichrist helps verify Irenaeus's timing of authorship.

After Domitian's assassination, Nerva became ruler of Rome. The new emperor brought fresh hope to Rome as he reversed Domitian's destructive policies. Even the Christians could let out a sigh of relief as Domitian's exiles were allowed to return, including the Apostle John.

Irenaeus and the Suffering Church

During his instruction on the various Gnostic sects, Irenaeus wrote of the time when the Antichrist shall persecute the true church and the reason for suffering of Christians. He stated that the afflictions under the Antichrist are in preparation for the Marriage Supper of the Lamb, which the Revelation claims will take place at the end of the Great Tribulation period. "Why is tribulation dropped upon the church? Why must we suffer martyrdom and other sufferings? The reason is to separate the wheat from the chaff. Tribulation is for the saved to be mingled with the word of God and fire so we may be suited for the Kingdom of God and the Marriage Supper of the Lamb."[72] For Irenaeus, the reason Christians will suffer in the time of the Great Tribulation will be the same reason many Christians have suffered persecution for the name of Christ. That is, they suffer as a test of their faith in Christ.

Irenaeus took a literal reading of John's Revelation. In opposition to modern scholars who claim the literal interpretation incited wars and revolutions, the pastor of Lyon's commentaries on John's book are evidence that the early church's literal interpretation helped lead to passivity towards persecution and martyrdom. In the same book where Irenaeus discussed the reason for persecution and tribulation, he repeated the warning from Revelation 13:10, which had referenced Matthew 26:58, concerning those who take up the sword. "If any one shall lead into captivity, he shall go into captivity. If any shall slay with the sword, he must be slain with the sword. Here is the endurance and the faith of the saints." [73]

Irenaeus had two copies of the Revelation before him, one of which had a different number for the Beast—616. The pastor from Lyons claimed the text with 666 was the correct one because it was the manuscript that was approved by those "men who saw John face to face bearing their testimony [to it]. . . . I do not know how it is that some have erred. . . I am inclined to think that this occurred through the fault of the copyists."[74] This appears to have been the only difference in the Revelation copies at this time, but at some point, a significant variation surfaced, altering the text of 13:10 from referencing Mathew 26:58 to referencing a passage in Isaiah which predestined some to die by the sword: "If anyone is to be killed with the sword, with the sword he will be killed." For Irenaeus, however, the particular text he used was the one accepted by those he knew had encountered the Apostle John and experienced him personally. At the time of Irenaeus' comments in the second century, the evidence suggests that the text of 13:10 quoting Matthew 26 was the version known and accepted throughout the west, Asia Minor and North Africa.[75]

In an earlier section, Irenaeus gave a description of Stephen's martyrdom from the New Testament's book of Acts. The pastor of Lyons emphasized Stephen's passivity in persecution and forgiveness toward his murderers: "Stephen . . . was stoned . . . and praying for those who were slaying him, in these words: "Lord, lay not this sin to their charge."[76] Irenaeus correctly viewed the Revelation as consistent with the rest of the New Testament, as well as with the

the *Martyrdom of Polycarp*, in teaching that Christians should not strike back at their enemies.

Irenaeus turned his attention to the day of resurrection for believers and writes of the period just preceding it: "For all these and other words were unquestionably spoken in reference to the resurrection of the just, which takes place after the coming of Antichrist, and the destruction of all nations under his rule." The day of resurrection occurs at the end of the Antichrist's rule, at which time the Christians will set their sights on Christ in the flesh.[77]

This view of the resurrection of believers echoes other early church writers on the subject. In a patristic document known as *The Didache*, the author proclaims that the day of resurrection occurs after the arrival of the Antichrist: "Then shall appear the world-deceiver as Son of God, and shall do signs and wonders, and the earth shall be delivered into his hands, and he shall do iniquitous things which have never yet come to pass since the beginning. Then shall the creation of men come into the fire of trial, and many shall be made to stumble and shall perish; but those who endure in their faith shall be saved from under the curse itself. And then shall appear the signs of the truth: first, the sign of an outspreading in heaven, and then the sign of the sound of the trumpet, and third, the resurrection of the dead." [78]

Irenaeus also confirms Justin Martyr who believed the church would suffer under the Antichrist: "He (Christ) shall come from heaven with glory, when the man of apostasy, who speaks strange things against the Most High, shall venture to do unlawful deeds on the earth against us the Christians, who, having learned the true worship of God from the law."[79]

Irenaeus never used the term millennium in his manuscript, *Against Heresies*. However, he wrote of how God created the earth in six days and how each day can be equated with six thousand years of earth's existence. He then continues to teach that the seventh day of rest for God can be equated with the time of rest that will occur for God's people after the demise of the Antichrist and the return of Christ. Thus Irenaeus believed that Christ in the flesh will inaugurate the Kingdom of God on earth that will last a literal thousand years.[80]

In chapter thirty-five of book five, Irenaeus explained the purpose for the millennium. The thousand-year-kingdom will be designed for the conversion of Israel and the resurrected will aid in this task: ". . . and those whom the Lord shall find in the flesh, awaiting Him from heaven, and who have suffered tribulation, as well as escaped the hands of the Wicked one. For it is in reference to them that the prophet says: 'And those that are left shall multiply upon the earth.' . . . as many believers as God has prepared for this purpose, to multiply those left upon earth, should both be under the rule of the saints to minister to this Jerusalem." In his theological scheme, the heavenly Jerusalem which has literally descended will be the home of those Jews who had rejected Christ: "For the footmen have gone forth from thee, while they were drawn away by the enemy. God shall bring them in to thee, being borne with glory as the throne of a kingdom. . . . that Israel, the glory of God, may walk in safety."

Irenaeus's account of John's Revelation and its theology was based on Justin Martyr and the traditions handed down to him through Polycarp. It was a theology born out of contention with the realized eschatology of the Gnostic sects and their rejection of suffering and martyrdom, their denial of a material resurrection, and their dismissal of a material but spiritual earthly kingdom. The pastor from Lyons believed that Gnosticism was destined to play an important part in leading society to accept the Antichrist when he eventually arrives. In time, the Christian church would lose sight of Irenaeus's theology and put forth competing interpretations of the Revelation that would be the exact opposite of John's intention.[81]

Heartbreak in Carthage

About the time Irenaeus finished his manuscript, in AD 180, a trial was in process in the North African city of Carthage. Twelve Christians stood before Saturninus, the proconsul, as he spoke to the group. 'You can win forgiveness from the emperor, if you return to a sound mind."

Speratus, the one who appeared to be the leader of the Christians answered. "Proconsul, we have never harmed anyone or spoken badly about anyone, and when we are ill-treated we give thanks. When we are put down for our beliefs, we pay reverence to our King."

Saturninus had no desire to execute these people and sought a way out of the proceedings. "I will delay the sentence for thirty days. I implore you to think about what I have said and consider relenting."

"There is no point for the delay, we are Christians," replied Speratus.

"Very well, then." The Proconsul then read the decree from the tablet: "Speratus, Nartzalus, Cittinus, Donata, Vestia, Secunda, and the rest have confessed that they live according to the Christian ceremony. They have refused the opportunity to return to the Roman rite. Therefore, it is decreed that they be put to death by the sword."

Saturninus replied, "We give thanks to God."

Then one of the other Christians said, "Today we are all martyrs in heaven, thanks be to God." And then they all said, "Thanks be to God."[82]

After the persecutions in Carthage, things remained peaceful for Christians until the turn of the century when Emperor Septimius Severus outlawed conversions to Christianity and Judaism. However, the persecutions in Carthage created an environment in North Africa that became ripe for the acceptance of a new movement that was based on the book of Revelation and had been taking the Christian church by storm. In the early third century, a young woman named Perpetua would embody the new movement as it finally reached Carthage. In reaction, an extreme countermovement would develop that would attack Irenaeus's claim of the Revelation's apostolic authorship.

CHAPTER 3
THE NEW PROPHECY AND THE RISE OF THE ALOGIA

IN A TOWN some ten miles outside the North African City of Carthage, shouts roared from a small house. Those outside listened closely.

"Perpetua, I will tear your eyes out!"

"Father, a flower vase can only be a vase, she replied, "and I can only be what I am." Her father stormed out of the house.

For the next several days, she studied and prepared for her baptism. And government spies watched and took note of everything she did.

As she studied her lessons, she sensed a revelation: pray for endurance, Perpetua. The impression proved genuine, for in time, government officials terminated her house arrest and hauled her to a dungeon in Carthage.

The soldiers pitched her into the darkest reaches of the military prison. Their rough handling made the moment all the more bitter as her fear mingled with the gloom of the cell.

"Who will care for my baby and breast feed him?" Perpetua moaned out loud as she stared into the black.

The next day, the guards took her to a better part of the prison where the light-streamed cell illuminated her visitors—her mother, brother, and son. She learned that two church deacons bribed the guards, leading to the improved situation.

"Please do your best to take care of my son while I am gone," she pleaded as she grasped the child to her breast.

After the three left, the twenty-two-year-old mother spent the next three days haunted by grief and worry for the child.

On the fourth morning, her brother rushed into the cell. "Perpetua, your payers are answered. The soldiers have changed their minds! The baby can stay with you."

"I am in a palace! The prison is now my palace," she said, beaming as she took the child and looked into his eyes. "Now I would rather be here than any other place in the world."

He dropped his voice. "Sister, it's time you ask for a vision so that you may know whether you are to die or be set free."

The comment didn't surprise her. As members of the New Prophecy, the brother and sister believed in prophetic gifts with dreams and visions.

"I know Jesus will tell me," she responded, "for I have suffered all this for His name. Come back tomorrow and I will tell you."

After her brother left, she prayed and immediately the image of a high, bronze ladder illuminated her mind. From both sides of the ladder protruded weapons of iron spears, swords, hooks, and knives. She knew that if she climbed without looking straight up her flesh would be torn to shreds. Slithering around the foot of the ladder wrapped a serpent. The snake had one mission—to terrorize anyone who tried to ascend the ladder.

Her friend, Saturus, stood at the top of the ladder. "Come, Perpetua, I am waiting for you. But be careful that the serpent doesn't bite you."

"He shall not hurt me, in the name of Jesus Christ," she shouted. She stepped on the serpent's head, and she began to climb.[83]

The Birth of the New Prophecy

In the year AD 203, Carthage city authorities arrested Perpetua and four other members of the New Prophecy. They were transported to a military prison in the city to await their trial. Saturus voluntarily gave himself up to the authorities when he learned of the arrests.[84]

The New Prophecy began as a movement of self-proclaimed prophets that emerged from the Asia Minor Provence of Phrygia starting in AD 157. Immediately controversial, many in the mainstream ecclesiastical hierarchy moved swiftly against the new group. The controversy began when its founder, Montanus, and his two prophetess partners, Priscilla and Maximilla, prophesied the return of Christ.[85]

Montanus became a convert to Christianity in the city of Hierapolis in Asia Minor. He soon traveled to Philadelphia and the rural areas of Phrygia, prophesying, reveling in ecstatic visions, and uttering proclamations in tongues.

While reading the letter to the church of Philadelphia in John's Revelation, Montanus believed that he experienced a vision about the heavenly New Jerusalem. The letter foretold the city's name would be written on those who endured persecution. For Montanus, his prophecy gleaned from the letter included the imminent descent of the heavenly city. But it would not drop down in Palestine, as many assumed. Montanus interpreted the letter in such a way as to claim that the New Jerusalem would descend near Philadelphia.[86]

As Montanus traveled through the rural areas of Asia Minor, he found that the perfect spot for the New Jerusalem appeared to be the plains between the villages of Pepuza and Tymion that rested some fifty miles east of Philadelphia. The message spread rapidly and Christians throughout Asia Minor flocked to Pepuza, yearning to witness the descent. Other Christians stayed in their churches but embraced the message of the new prophet.[87]

As the days wore on, Montanus brought forward more prophecies: "The righteous will shine a hundred times brighter than the sun, and the small ones among you who are saved will shine a hundred times more than the moon."[88] The meaning of the prophecy was clear to those listening: his followers were destined to be the martyrs John spoke about in his Revelation, the ones who would be murdered by the Antichrist.

The historical situation explains the attraction of Montanus to the churches of Asia Minor. Just two years earlier, government-sponsored persecution and executions struck the Christian communities in the cities of Smyrna and Philadelphia. John's Revelation predicted the onslaught in Smyrna when he wrote, "Do not fear those things which you are about to suffer. . . . Be faithful until death and I will give you the crown of life". [89] For the followers of the New Prophecy, the torments in Smyrna signaled the beginning of a worldwide persecution prophesied in John's Revelation.[90]

Among the first to embrace his message were Priscilla and Maxima, and they joined him as the initial leaders of the movement.

"This place is holy and in this place Jerusalem will come down from heaven."[91] Priscilla echoed Montanus as she helped him spread the word that the inhabitants of Pepuza would soon witness the return of Christ.[92]

Maximilla also did her part in proselytizing Christians to the New Prophecy and helped garner an expectation of the end times. In explaining her mission she prophesied wars and revolutions. She considered herself the mouthpiece of God to interpret the coming holocaust upon their followers. "The Lord has commissioned me as an illuminator and interpreter of this suffering and covenant and promise."

The word she chose for "suffering" is rare in the New Testament; John used it, however, to describe the pain that's destined to be abolished at the descent of the New Jerusalem.[93] For Maximilla, the temporary suffering of persecution did not compare to the glory to be experienced when the heavenly city finally arrived.

The New Prophecy endeavored to prepare Christians to endure the massive persecution foretold in John's Revelation. "Do not hope to die in bed nor in an abortion nor in languishing fevers, but in martyrdom, so that He who died for you may be glorified." In Montanus's prophecy, Christians needed to forget the idea of living long lives in this temporal world. Instead, it set their minds on professing the name of Christ in front of the authorities.[94]

For the mainstream church hierarchy, the New Prophecy presented a number of problems. First, Montanus and the two female prophets did not request permission from any church authority before prophesying.[95] Second, their ecstatic behavior, while prophesying, caused some church authorities to question their prophecies. Third, their claim to be the martyrs of John's Revelation implied an authority of their own that put themselves on an equal footing with the church hierarchy. Fourth, they supported the idea that one could voluntarily give oneself up to the Roman authorities, as Saturus eventually did.[96] And finally, the movement supported a doctrine forbidding remarriage after widowhood.[97]

Priscilla and Maximilla dissolved their marriages when they became filled with the Spirit. By doing so, they followed the orders of Montanus, who taught that the leading prophets should be celibate. Priscilla came to believe that the Holy Spirit had remade her into a virgin. This worried the church authorities even more, as it implied the members of the New Prophecy were not only the martyrs of Revelation, but were among the 144,000 special prophets singled out by John.[98] For a handful of church leaders, this gave the new prophets a self-importance that put them above the church hierarchy. These leaders became known as the Alogia. [99]

Members of the hierarchy took a proactive approach in responding to the new prophets. Synods or councils of bishops met across the empire to deal with the issue. Some churches sent exorcists to cast out demons from Priscilla and Maximilla. Despite the invectives against them, the movement continued to grow. Christians hungered for a move of the Spirit, and with looming threats of persecutions by the Roman authorities, they flocked to Pepuza to hear the prophecies and await the New Jerusalem. From there, New Prophecy evangelists carried their message across the Roman Empire.

By the summer of A.D.177, the controversy reached a fever pitch as the movement began to knock on the doors of Rome. Eleutherus, the pastor of the Roman Church, could not make up his mind about its validity even though his two predecessors condemned it. In desperation, he welcomed the advice from Irenaeus, the pastor from the church in Vienne.

Irenaeus brought *The Letter of the Churches of Lyons and Vienne* to Rome to describe the persecution that had broken out against the church in Lyons. Along with the descriptions of the martyrdoms, the envoy included a letter advocating toleration and negotiation with the New Prophecy. After all, from the standpoint of Irenaeus, most of the new prophets were orthodox in their view of the nature of God and Christ, and their prophecies had yet to be proven false.[100]

But when it came to reconciliation, many of the mainstream leaders refused to consider it. Eventually, while writing his *Against Heresies*, Irenaeus described the situation: "To be sure, others, in order to suppress the gift of the Spirit, which, in the last days by the Father's good pleasure has been poured out on the human race, do not allow that concept . . . in which the Lord promised to send the Paraclete (Holy Spirit). . . . They reject both the Gospel and the prophetic spirit."[101]

As an overreaction to the New Prophecy, a number of church leaders argued against allowing the prophetic gifts of the Spirit to be practiced in their churches. These "others," as Irenaeus indicated, would eventually become known as the Alogia, which means "those who oppose the Word." They introduced novel ideas. In their desperation to dispute the New Prophecy and maintain their own authority, they claimed the gifts of the Spirit came to an end with the death of the Apostles, and that the Apostle John did not write the Gospel of John.

Supernatural phenomena, however, reigned in the churches of Gaul, as well as Asia Minor. "Some have foreknowledge of things to come," wrote Irenaeus referring to the gifts of the Spirit. "They see visions and utter prophetic expression. Others heal the sick, laying their hands on them and making them whole. The dead have even been raised up and remained with us for many years. ... It is not possible to name the number of the gifts which the church scattered throughout the whole world has received from God."[102]

From what Irenaeus penned, one may come to the conclusion that the new prophets gained widespread popularity because the churches operated in prophetic gifts and, therefore, were willing to give the new movement an ear. [103]

Despite the existence of the supernatural gifts in many churches throughout the empire, Irenaeus sought negotiations with the New Prophecy rather than complete acceptance. He understood that there were problems with the group that needed to be addressed and he pressed the Roman Church to engage the new prophets in dialogue. For Irenaeus, judging from his manuscript, the bigger problem came from the Alogia.

"The Gnostic Cerinthus wrote the Gospel of John and The Revelation," bellowed the Alogia.[104] When Irenaeus wrote his *Against Heresies,* he claimed the Apostle John specifically wrote his Gospel against the Gnosticism of Cerinthus and the Nicolaitans. The Nicolaitans, whom Irenaeus claimed were forerunners to Cerinthus, figured heavily in Revelation.[105] The First Letter of John was also written in reaction against the theology of Cerinthus.[106] For Irenaeus, the overreactions of the Alogia posed a serious threat to the apostolic authority of John's Gospel.[107]

Clearly, both the Gospel of John and Revelation are anti-Gnostic polemics, advocating passive martyrdom and the physical resurrection of Christ and his followers. It is highly unlikely that a Gnostic would have written either.

The Alogia also claimed that Cerinthus taught a material millennium on earth. While this is hypothetically possible, the idea is unlikely since Gnostic theology ran counter to such a belief.[108]

In the light of the dangers that the Alogia posed for Scriptural authority and the practice of the spiritual gifts, Irenaeus did his best to convince the Roman pastor to negotiate with the New Prophecy. It worked. Pastor Elueutherus sent a letter of peace to the churches of Phrygia and Asia, advocating tolerance for the New Prophecy.[109]

The letter did nothing, however, to extinguish the opponents' passion. A man named Praxeas made false allegations against the New Prophets and fell in line with the Alogia, denying the gifts of the Spirit. In his dogged quest to discredit the New Prophecy, Praxeas convinced Eleutherus to change his mind and rescind the letter.[110]

Despite continued resistance, the New Prophets persisted in Rome and eagerly sought opportunities to defend the movement. When a presbyter named Victor ascended to the Roman pastorate in A.D. 189, he gave his consent to a debate between Proclus, a New Prophet, and Gaius, a Roman presbyter.

The Debate that Changed History

Gauis prepared well for the debate as he stood at the podium. In the midst of his bellowing, he reflected the attitude of the Alogia. "But Cerinthus, too, through his written revelations that he would have us believe were given by a great apostle, brings before us marvelous things, which he pretends were shown him by angels; alleging that after the resurrection the kingdom of Christ is to be on earth, and that the flesh dwelling in Jerusalem is again to be subject to desires and pleasures. And being an enemy to the Scriptures of God, wishing to deceive men, he says that there is to be a space of a thousand years for marriage festivals."

John's Revelation made no such claim about marriage festivals or carnal desires, but it mattered little as Gaius put forth the Alogia's rumors that the heretic Cerinthus wrote the Revelation. Besides making such false allegations, the presbyter fought an uphill battle to convince the Roman Church to reject a book that it had already accepted as authoritative for over thirty years. The Roman document known as the *Shepherd of Hermas,* which had been written sometime between AD 90 and 140, had used a number of concepts from John's Revelation in its own text. An example of Hermas' use of Revelation is found in his likening of the Great Tribulation as a rising sea beast with fiery locusts coming from its mouth. This echoed Rev. Chapters 6, 12, and 13.[111]

Not withstanding any acceptance by Rome of the Revelation or Hermas, Gaius attacked the ninth chapter of John's Apocalypse with Psalm 72. "How can the lawless be tormented by locusts when the Scripture says that sinners prosper and the righteous are persecuted in the world. This is just ridiculous."[112]

Gaius then turned to using the Gospel of Matthew. "Matthew does not say that angels shall war nor that a quarter of mankind shall be destroyed, but that nation shall rise against nation. And how can Satan be bound here, as it says in Revelation, when Matthew says that Christ entered into the house of the strong man and bound him and took away his goods?"[113]

When Proclus rose in his turn to speak, he focused on the second chapter of Acts in order to make the case that his movement rested on the scriptural tradition of the prophet Philip. "There were four daughters of Philip at Hierapolis in Asia Minor. The tomb of the prophetesses is there, along with the tomb of their father."[114] These are the only words attributed to Proculus from the debate. Obviously he must have made a point of using the book of Revelation and John's Gospel to make his arguments, but because of the purging of schismatic writings that were to take place in the future by the mainstream church, nothing more remains.

Proclus's use of the tradition of Hierapolis was probably a fatal error in his argument. Gaius almost certainly waited for just this moment in the contest. In his shrewdness, the presbyter appealed to Rome's desire for supremacy. "I can point to the bones of the Apostles," answered Gaius. "If you go to the Vatican, or to the Ostian Way, you will find the remains of those who founded the church."[115] The Roman presbyter referred to the tombs of the Apostles Peter and Paul. In one sentence, he turned the debate into one about the authority of Rome versus Asia Minor and which one should be considered the center of Christianity. Not surprisingly, at the end, the bishop of Rome sided with Gaius and condemned the New Prophecy.[116]

In spite of its failure to win back Roman support, the New Prophecy remained entrenched in Asia Minor and had made inroads into North Africa. At the turn of the third century, the persecutions inspired by Emperor Severus and carried out against Christians in Carthage helped plow even more fertile ground for the growth of the new sect. The young convert, Perpetua, was just one example of the suffering Christians endured in this region. Tertullian, a mainstream Christian teacher who eventually converted to the New Prophecy, became an eyewitness to the final stage in Perpetua's story.

The Passion of Perpetua

On that early March day of A.D 203, Perpetua's dream concluded. As she reached the top of the ladder, she found herself in a garden-like paradise. A white-haired shepherd met her and gave her a piece of cheese to eat.[117] Then she woke.

The next day she recounted the dream to her brother. They both knew what it meant. They embraced for the last time.

Three days later, the authorities announced that she and the others would stand trial. Upon hearing the news, her father dashed to the prison. As he pushed through the cell door, he plunged to his knees and groveled at her feet. "Lady, between you and your brothers, you were always my favorite."

Her heart stirred as he had never before addressed her in such an honorable fashion. Tears streamed down his face as he grabbed her hands to kiss them. "Think of your family," he pleaded. "Think of your son who will not survive if you die! Give up this oath to your God or none of us will survive."

"Father," she replied, "what occurs in this life is not done according to our own power, but according to God. His desire will be done at the trial." His hopes ruined, her father skulked out of the prison.

Finally the day came. As news of the trial spread, a mob anticipated the verdict and filled the amphitheatre. In the court room the authorities demanded each Christian to sacrifice to the deities and to the emperor. Each one, in turn, refused and confessed their Christianity until they came to Perpetua.

Her father broke in before she had a chance to answer. "Offer the sacrifice," he screamed. "Have mercy upon your son!"

"I am a Christian," she responded. The procurator pronounced sentence on all the accused to face the wild beasts in the amphitheatre.

On March 7, Perpetua stood in the center of the arena. The crowd in the stands hissed as the maddened bull charged, trampling the young Christian and trying to gash her with its horns. When the animal lost interest, Perpetua struggled upright, pulling her torn robe to conceal her breasts and midsection, which became exposed in the rampage.

With the animal no longer an instrument of torture, the authorities determined that she would be executed after the show. But as she left through the Gate of the Living, the mob refused to leave and shouted for her to be brought back.

Perpetua limped back into the arena. The authorities sent a gladiator to finish the job. He walked up to her with his hands shaking. He was a novice and new at murdering women. He stabbed her once but the cut was superficial, missing vital organs and causing more pain than a swift kill should. She reached out to steady his trembling hand and guided it up until the base of the sword rested against her neck. As he slashed the blade across her throat, her body crumpled to the ground. By the end of that March day, Perpetua and the other five members of the New Prophecy reached the top of the ladder.

Despite the mainstream church's condemnation of the New Prophecy, the followers of Montanus continued to congregate at Pepuza well into the sixth century. Rome's early rejection, however, proved fatal to the movement. The Christian Emperor Justinian sent soldiers to Pepuza to deal with the sect. They found and incinerated the enshrined tomb that contained the bodies of Montanus and the two prophetesses. Justinian also ordered the abundant Montanist writings to be destroyed. Today, the only pro-Montanist texts to survive are by Tertullian. The rest of what we know comes from the ancient criticisms of the movement and the few quotes of prophecies those critics recorded.

The New Prophecy's effect on history, however, traveled well past the sixth century. The gifts of the Spirit remained in some mainstream churches after the second century, but the reference to them steadily diminished. At the same time, while support for the authority of the Book of Revelation remained strong, the Alogia's criticisms helped move the church away from the literal interpretations. The eastern churches, in particular, chose hyper-symbolic explanations. And modern critics have taken up the Alogias' false rumors and now spread the ancient gossip that Cerinthus wrote the Apostle John's vision.

As we have seen, Irenaeus hoped for dialogue and negotiation with the New Prophecy. He knew there were problems with the movement, but he believed the greater danger lay in the overreaction against it. As it turned out, Irenaeus was right.

While Irenaues and Montanus preached passivity in the face of martyrdom, the Christian church's move toward symbolic interpretations of Revelation eventually resulted in wars and violent revolutions. The church lost its patience, and no longer waited for Christ to return in the flesh before inaugurating the millennium.[118]

At the start of the third century, the symbolic interpretation of Revelation began permeating the church's intelligentsia. As we will see in the next chapter, at the head of the movement came a brilliant teenager from Alexandria. The seventeen-year-old son of a martyr was destined to help change the course of western civilization.

CHAPTER 4
THE STONE THAT SHARPENS AND THE SCHOOL OF THE MARTYRS

NAKED, ORIGEN STORMED into his room. He demanded that his mother tell him where she hid his clothes. She refused. How could he go naked into the street? The young Origen longed to join Leonides in martyrdom, for why should his father die alone? Knowing her son's brash, impulsive temperament, his mother concealed his garments hoping he would not leave the house unclothed.

The plan worked. After Origen collected his emotions, he sat down to write his father a letter of encouragement. Above all, he penned, his father should not be concerned about the family. "Be careful not to change your mind because of us." After he finished, he sent one of his brothers to deliver the message.

The next day, Origen's brothers watched as the soldiers led his father to the place of execution. The officials placed the prisoner's head on the block and sliced through his neck with the sword. Along with Leonides' execution, the authorities took possession of all the family's belongings and property. Origen and his family were on their own and penniless.[119]

In the year AD 202 Alexander Severus usurped the Roman throne. He opened his reign spewing inflammatory words against the Christians, and he aimed to persecute Roman citizens converting to the new faith. He cared little that slaves, plebes and peasants converted in high numbers. But he wondered how the nobles of Rome could convert. For him, the very idea was unthinkable!

The imprisonments and executions ordered by the emperor touched the nobles and intellectuals, not their families. But the confiscation of all property left their families in abject poverty. Being the oldest, Origen had to find a way to provide for his loved ones.

All of Leonides' biblical manuscripts were confiscated, but fortunately, the authorities left the Greek philosophies and grammars. At seventeen years of age, Origen used the library to his advantage, finding work teaching secular literature and grammar. Even though the job paid little, it allowed Origen to make a living using his keen mind. What's more, the work honed his teaching abilities. Before long, he gained a reputation as a brilliant teacher of philosophy. He attracted pagans by his shrewd integration of Christian theology with the writings of Plato and Aristotle. Among those who noticed Origen's brilliance was the pastor of the Alexandrian church.

One day Pastor Demetrius took Origen aside. Persecutions had depleted the theological school of all the teachers and scholars. Even the renowned Clement fled lest he be counted among the tortured.[120] The pastor implored Origen to become head of the school. Origen gave the obligatory humble response: "I'm only eighteen." He knew his young age made little difference to Demetrius, as it made even less to himself. He had proved himself in the short time he had lectured, and he knew God was opening the door for him.

The pastor had one concern, however, for he feared the authorities might target Origin. But the young man's youthful exuberance and determination won Demetrius's confidence. So in the year AD 203, the prelate of Alexandria appointed Origen as head of the catechumen school of the church.[121] The official position would mark a watershed moment for Origen. From this point, he would emerge as one of the great philosophers and theologians of all time.

As head of the school, and following his earlier success, it did not take long before Origen gained a reputation as a dynamic teacher who could attract both Christians and pagans. Over the years, Origen increased his uncanny ability to demonstrate to pagans how Christianity could inform and enlighten certain aspects of Greek philosophy, but at the same time show the superiority of the Christian faith. At the heart of his instruction lay the basic premise that both the Greek philosopher Plato and Christianity had one thing in common: God endowed the individual with free will. While most Gnostics heavily followed the idea of predestination and rejected Plato on that point, Origen also integrated an aspect of Plato followed by the Gnostics: the body is the tomb of the soul. The end result is that many pagans and Gnostics converted to his theology.

The School of the Martyrs

Two such Gnostic students were Plutarch and Heraclas. The pagan brothers applied to the school after hearing of Origen's instructional exploits. Overwhelmed by the man's genius and abilities, it did not take long before they converted to the new faith. Plutarch's conversion was particularly ardent and soon his devout faith caused his pagan friends to seek the help of authorities to try to reconvert him. Plutarch refused to deny Christ. Prison and condemnation followed.

Origin accompanied Plutarch to the place of execution, encouraging him the best he could. The mob gathered to watch and jeer. Cries could be heard throughout the audience, including, "This Origen stole our friend's soul from us and now he comes to watch him die!"

The executioner pushed Plutarch to his knees and forced his head into the proper position. The sword swiftly decapitated the victim. As the body slumped and the blood surged over the ground, a cheer roared from the mob. Men and women hurled insults at Origen as he prayed over Plutarch's departing soul.

Plutarch was only the first of Origen's martyred students.[122] As the school grew and gained its notoriety among Alexandrian society, the list of the murdered included Serenus, who would be burnt alive. And it didn't stop there as a newly baptized student named Hero met his end with decapitation. Six martyrs also included Herais, a female student burned to death before her baptism. But, as Origen wrote concerning her, "she was baptized by fire."[123]

For Origen, the blood of the martyrs cemented spiritually, the foundation that bolstered the Alexandrian school. The institution not only prepared students for Christian conversion and baptism, but it endured as a training ground for those students who would soon be persecuted. Origen taught by his own example. He visited the Christians in prison and accompanied them to their execution, whether they were among his student body or not. So enamored with Origin's teaching and model of behavior, one of his students, Gregory of Nazianus, remarked, "Origen is the stone that sharpens us all."[124]

While Origen avoided prison from the authorities, at times he came dangerously close to joining his beloved martyrs. One day while walking down the street leading into Alexandria's Greek quarter, he soon passed near the great temple of the god, Serapis. Inside stood the huge statue of Serapis, an image resembling the Greek god, Zeus. Serapis began as an Egyptian animal god, but in the religious syncretism of the Gecko-Roman world, many of the gods began to look alike.

As Origen grew nearer the temple, the mob that came to worship the god spied him and immediately erupted, yelling and screaming. In a frenzy, they clutched and dragged Origen up the steps of the temple. They forced him into the robe of a priest and put the sacred pagan crown on his head.

Having forced him into the garb of the pagan high priest, the mob ordered him to take palm branches and distribute among the worshippers. Origen calmly did as he was ordered, placing the branches in the hands of each person. Blessing the palms, he cried out to the crowd to come and receive them, not from idols but from Jesus Christ. Origen's preaching stunned the crowd into silence. As he left unharmed, the crowd murmured and dispersed. [125]

Satan's Salvation and Origen's Banishment

By the year 230, Origen's reputation knew no bounds and church leaders throughout Palestine sought his counsel and teaching. In their exuberance, pastors in the Palestinian towns of Caesarea and Jerusalem ordained Origen an elder. Back in Alexandria, pastor Demetrius did not appreciate the gesture.

Incensed over the fact that Origen was ordained outside his proper jurisdiction, Demetrius brought back an old allegation. A Gnostic had once accused Origen of teaching that Satan would one day repent and be saved. In fact, Origen only taught this as a hypothetical possibility, since Satan still has free will. The crux of the debate had centered on free will versus predestination and Origen hypothesized on behalf of free will.[126]

At the time, Demetrius dismissed the Gnostic's allegation as much ado about nothing, but now it served his purpose to bring it back. After all, the Palestinian pastors and Origen bucked his authority. And besides, Origen was just getting too popular. It was time for excommunication.

Demetrius banished Origen from Alexandria and the teacher made his new home in Caesarea, where he knew they appreciated him. But inside he seethed. "Like the Israelite slaves, I have been freed from bondage in Egypt," Origen wrote in disgust.

Origen had always tried to hold no grudges against anyone, no matter how they may have treated him. But it's also clear he struggled with forgiveness. However, after awhile, he was able to calm his temperament. In writing to a friend he stated: "such men deserve pity rather than hate, and we must pray for them rather than curse them. We have not been created to curse but to bless."

In the early days of Caesarea, Origin spent time working on the preamble to his commentary on John's Gospel. This document shows his view of scriptural interpretation. For Origen, there was a literal, simple meaning to all scripture, but also a deeper, more allegorical and spiritual meaning. In his thinking, many of the Christian church leaders could not get beyond the simple meaning. In other words, they were simpletons.

Eventually, Origen would write about those who followed premillennial thinking: "Certain persons, then, refusing to work their minds, and adopting a superficial view of the letter of the law, and yielding rather in some measure to the indulgence of their own desires and lusts, being disciples of the letter alone, are of opinion that the fulfillment of the promises of the future are to be looked for in bodily pleasure and luxury; and therefore they especially desire to have again, after the resurrection . . . as may never be without the power of eating, and drinking, and performing all the functions of flesh and blood, not following the opinion of the Apostle Paul regarding the resurrection of a spiritual body. And consequently they say, that after the resurrection there will be marriages, and the begetting of children, imagining to themselves that the earthly city of Jerusalem is to be rebuilt . . . Such are the views of those who, while believing in Christ, understand the divine Scriptures in a sort of Jewish sense, drawing from them nothing worthy of the divine promises."[127]

For Origen, Irenaeus also followed that tradition, for the pastor of Lyons put forward a literal view of John's Revelation. The crassness of the simple meaning probably caused Origen to cringe as he read the portions of Irenaeus describing a literal, physical recreation of the world as Christ returns in the flesh.

What bothered Origen the most was Irenaeus's acceptance of the writings of Papius, who described earth during the millennium as producing fruit in greater abundance than has ever been known to mankind. For Origen, the resurrection body would be spiritually physical and would have no need for such carnal pleasures and desires such as eating. Origen's point was a valid one, but what he failed to consider was the possibility that the resurrected will not need to eat but may do so anyway, and of the non-resurrected existing beside the resurrected. In the pre-millennial theology of Irenaeus, there are two purposes of the millennium. One is to bring about the final restoration of Israel and the Jewish people. The other is to lead the resurrected into becoming one with the divine nature.[128]

What is perhaps the most interesting aspect of Origen's theology of the restoration of all things is that it is not so different from Irenaeus's viewpoint. Origen simply had no need for such a carnal, intermediate period as the millennium to bring about a merging with the divine nature. Christians should progress into this nature while traveling along a completely spiritual path. The Holy Spirit would lead Christians down this path, not the return of a physical Christ and a physically recreated earth. However, as slight as this distinction may appear to be, it would have grave significance since much of the Christian church would embrace Origin's eschatology and renounce that of Irenaeus.[129]

While the followers of platonic free-will rushed to hear Origen, his reputation became so great that even many hard core advocates of predestination piled into his classes. One such Gnostic was the Valentinian, Ambrose. While attending Origin's class, Ambrose revealed why he chose to follow the Gnostic teacher Valentinus. He explained that he could not stand the shallow teachings of the psychic church with its emphasis on the body and the literal interpretations of Scripture.[130] Most followers of Gnosticism accepted only symbolic interpretations of Scripture, giving no place to the literal.

In Ambrose, Origen saw himself when he was young: always wanting to know more. He looked upon his student as a man who was never satisfied, just like himself. Ambrose convinced himself that Scripture held deeper things, and in the quest to find the spiritual meaning that lay behind what appeared to be a simple, even carnal meaning, Ambrose turned to the theology of Valentinus. The Gnostic taught his followers to spiritualize and symbolize all Scripture. Origen knew how to appeal to such students. The professor responded that there truly is a deeper meaning to scripture, but it's not found among the Gnostics. He explained that his theology would lead Ambrose in the proper path to God.

Origen began by teaching Ambrose that true Christianity was not alien to seeking deeper meanings in Scripture. Valentinus taught that there is no value to the literal interpretation. The difference was that the literal interpretation was not to be abandoned, altogether. For Origen, Scripture had layers of meaning. The first was the literal, and there may be truth in the simple, literal interpretation. But the truer, deeper truth was found beyond the literal, into the symbolic. Thus Origen merged Gnostic principles of exegesis with the more orthodox principles.

The allegorical and symbolic interpretation became predominate in early Greek culture during the fifth century BC. Hellenistic philosophy held that divine inspiration influenced allegorical explanations of Greek myths. And this was particularly true of the analysis of Homer's writings.[131]

The Alexandrian Jew, Philo, borrowed from Hellenistic culture in supporting the allegorical approach as he applied it to the Old Testament. Later, Clement of Alexandria applied the method to the New Testament, but with one innovation: One could use the literal approach as a starting point to finding the deeper meaning in the symbolic. Thus the literal method was not wholly ignored. In Clement, the literal was meant to stimulate the curiosity of the spiritually advanced to find the deeper and most proper meaning.[132]

Origen added further wrinkles to the method. The literal interpretation held and exposed historical facts, such as the resurrection of Jesus. Thus literal understanding had an important place in teaching theological truths. But corruption existed within the literal comprehension. Scripture could only be thought of as inerrant in its symbolic understanding.

In his apologies combating Gnosticism, Irenaeus took great pains to warn the church against relying too heavily on symbolism, but Origen ignored him. As we have seen in earlier chapters, certain factions of Gnosticism followed a prosperity doctrine. Valentinism was based on the basic idea that the resurrection occurs when one has faith, for there is only a spiritual resurrection, not a physical one. But the followers of Valentinus could swing in either direction: to extreme asceticism or financial prosperity. Ambrose was no ascetic when it came to money.

After the initial session, Ambrose committed to Christianity and put himself in Origen's hands. For Origen, Ambrose was a godsend. One of the wealthiest men in Alexandria, Ambrose offered to help the struggling school and more than that, funded a publishing house for Origen, complete with stenographers, copyists, and calligraphers.

But the money came with strings attached. Ambrose expected something in return—hard work. Origen wanted to devote more time to writing, but found it difficult to set aside the necessary hours. Most of his effort focused on finding ways to keep the doors of the school open.

Ambrose is going to be my taskmaster, he thought, as he picked up his pen to write. "As the Hebrews had the Egyptian taskmaster to make them work, I will have Ambrose. I will answer to God through Ambrose."[133]

Funny, thought Origen, God would send a Valentinian to be the scourge of the Valentinians. Now Origen could finally deal with all the writings the heretics had been spewing. And he could reach those Gnostics that the teachers of the great Church had not been able to reach with their own defenses, explanations, and shallow interpretations. Origen remembered saying this very thing to Ambrose during his lesson on the Gospel of John: "Ambrose, the Gnostics are rising up and bringing their compositions in many books, announcing interpretations of the texts both of the Gospels and of the apostles. If we are silent they will prevail. You yourself became a follower of the Gnostics because you refused to follow irrational and unlearned interpretations and instead turned to these writings of the knowledge falsely so-called. But now you have turned to the best understanding and the proper knowledge."[134]

Origen presided over the school of theology at Caesarea for almost twenty years, producing most of his writings, including two works he dedicated to Ambrose. During this period, one of his converts, Gregory Thaumaturgus, became known as the Wonder Worker. Gregory practiced healing by laying hands on the sick, curing them in the name of Jesus and converting many to the new faith. This period was relatively peaceful for Origen, and the Christian church at large experienced rapid growth in the numbers of new converts. But in the midst of the peace, storm clouds of persecution formed. By the year 249, a new emperor took the throne and the time of tranquility was about to end.

Decius and the Advent of Persecution

In history, the Emperor Decius is known for two things: as a builder in the infrastructure of Rome with roads and bridges, baths and walls and as a reformer of Roman society that led to the persecution of Christians. For Decius, good Roman citizenry meant conforming to the state-backed mode of religious worship. In fact, no man could be a true citizen who did not adhere to Roman polytheism. A proper Roman citizen gave public allegiance to the Caesar-cult. On the other hand, privately, one could worship Christ all he wanted as long as he outwardly showed allegiance to the emperor. Most Christians, however, would not tolerate such a compromise.

Prior to Decius, for forty years the Roman government regarded the growth of Christianity with apathy. In the midst of this indifference, Christianity spread and flourished throughout the eastern and western empire. Christians everywhere built cathedrals and houses of prayer.[135]

During these years persecution emanated from the people whose fanaticism fired them to take the law into their own hands or whose outcries forced provincial governors to enforce old laws that were otherwise allowed to lie dormant. But such persecutions were localized and slight in numbers. Under Origen's tutelage, his school witnessed an inordinate amount of persecution of its students compared to the Alexandrian church and many churches in the empire. Origen believed such lack of opposition for Christianity was the calm before the storm.

His sharp eye to what the future held was born out of the condition of the overall Christian church during these years. A number of leaders alleged the thriving church spread hand in hand with unsavory elements that had infiltrated local congregations. The problem seemed particularly endemic to the churches in the larger cities. Origen complained that factions ripped apart the church at Athens. Bishop Cyprian complained that many of the celibate clergy and supposed virgins engaged in continuous sexual relations, and mixed marriages with pagans had worked to break down the apostolic tradition in many large city congregations. The quest for wealth by both clergy and laity had particularly troubled him. He would write of the problem: "In old days people laid up treasure in heaven, and sold their property and laid it before the apostles for them to divide among the poor. But now we never pay tithes on our patrimony, we disobey our Lord's command to sell our goods, and instead, we buy and get gain. Hence our spiritual vigor is weakened, and the strength of believers is crippled."[136] For both Origen and Cyprian, the Christian church's condition ripened the time for God's discipline.

When Decius came to power, he championed the old laws against illicit religion that had been allowed to lay dormant during Christianity's growth. His edict appeared toward the end of the year 249, or early 250, and commanded every inhabitant to sacrifice to the gods and swear to the genius of the emperor. The edict would be the first to try to enforce a systematic sacrifice throughout the entire empire. The Roman authorities summoned men and women by name suggesting they had lists of residents of every city.[137] All were expected to show up and sacrifice by a particular date or face persecution. The authorities assumed those who did not come were Christians.

To try to get Christians to comply with the order, local magistrates had the right to inflict every kind of torture short of death. The proconsul alone could require capital punishment. If any Christian withstood the torments, the proconsul was called.

The fierceness and thoroughness of the persecutions caused many Christians to sacrifice to the gods and the emperor. Some clergymen gave in quickly. One named Eopostus not only renounced his faith but persuaded many in his congregation to follow him in apostasy. Others tried their best to withstand the torment but ultimately broke and gave in to the authorities. Cyprian records the words of one example: "I was anxious to struggle bravely, and remembering my oath, I put on the armor of faith and devotion, but endless series of tortures overcame my resolution. My mind stood firm, my faith was strong, and for a long while the pains of torture made no impression on my soul. But when the fury of the judge had broken forth again, and my weary body was being torn with lashes, bruised with clubs, stretched on the rack, pierced with hooks, and burned with fire, my flesh failed, my weakness overcame me, and pain subdued my body, though not my heart."

After the persecutions subsided, a number of clergy who gave in to the authorities wanted to return to the priesthood and the pastorate. Again, these actions particularly troubled Cyprian. He wrote of one such bishop named Fortunatrianus: "He dared to claim the priesthood which he had deserted, as though it were allowable to pass from the altars of the devil to the altar of God." Cyprian's attitude would eventually help give rise to a reform movement called Donatism. The Donatists insisted clergy undergo a period of probation and rebaptism before returning to ecclesiastical office after renouncing their faith during a future persecution under the Emperor Diocletian.[138]

By the time of the edict, Origen was well acquainted with government-sponsored persecution as local authorities had targeted his students in the past. He knew the potential for atrocity and he warned his congregation: "The kings of the earth have assembled together, the senate and the people and the leaders of Rome to blot out the name of Jesus and Israel at the same time. For they have decreed in their laws that there be no Christians. Every city, every class, attacks the name of Christians."[139]

The authorities prized Origen. When the soldiers arrested him they were forbidden to kill him. They intended to make him a supreme example by forcing him to recant his faith and showing the world that even the mighty Origen is susceptible to their torture. They laid him in the deepest and darkest recesses of the prison. A heavy iron collar weighed him down as the torturers inflicted torments upon his body. For four days stocks stretched his feet apart by four spaces. The authorities continually threatened him but they made sure they did not create another martyr. Encouraging the Christian community was the last thing they wanted.

Origen refused to recant. While suffering under the torture, no doubt he reflected on his own teachings to his student Ambrose. When faced with martyrdom, Origen taught Ambrose to prepare himself by first embracing a martyrdom of the soul—an inner reflection which allowed the victim to suffer passively and not strike back at one's torturers. Repeatedly, Origen instructed Ambrose that "during the whole time of testing and temptation," he should not corrupt his soul "by any word foreign to our confession, and … bear from opponents every reproach, mockery, laughter, slander, and pity." Neither should he be diverted by affection "for children or for their mother or for any of those we hold dearest in life to hold onto them and to stay alive," but instead "suppose, that we turn away from all of them and belong totally to God and to life with him and near him."[140]

Eventually, the authorities released Origen after they failed to make him give up his faith. But the tortures had a lasting effect, and at the age of sixty-nine, Origen died of his wounds. His followers buried him in the city of Tyre, where for centuries his tomb formed the main decoration in the Cathedral of the Holy Sepulcher.

While there is much to admire about the man Origen, his overall theology is problematic. For the study in this chapter, the most troubling aspect has to do with the eschatology he developed in line with his interpretation on the symbolic view of Scripture.

Origen promoted a spiritual view of God's Kingdom and a symbolic view of the future millennium on earth. At the heart of the issue was the question of how to interpret Revelation, chapter twenty. The literal reading of the passage indicates that Christ will return in the flesh and establish a material kingdom that lasts a thousand years. But was there a deeper, truer meaning behind the literal words of the chapter? Origen believed so and dismissed any notion of a literal, material millennium put forward by the likes of Papius, Justin Martyr, Irenaeus, and Tertullian.

While some of the differences between Origen and Irenaeus might seem mundane and inconsequential to some, they would, in fact, have a disturbing impact on both the Christian church and the development of western civilization. The rejection of the literal interpretation of Revelation's chapter twenty set in motion a plethora of allegorical interpretations. These interpretations led Christians to no longer act passively in the face of persecution, but to react with violence against their persecutors. Martyrdom continued, but the definition of the term would change to include those who die while violently defending Christianity. With the aid of allegorical interpretations, coupled with influences by those denouncing Montanism, as seen in the last chapter, Christians eventually turned to become the persecutors.

As the church moved into the fourth century, some of Origen's followers took the allegorical approach to the kingdom of God on earth and believed the millennium should be ushered in by the church, rather than through Christ's return in the flesh. Ambrose of Milan would justify the burning of Jewish synagogues by renegade Christians, and Eusebius of Caesarea would defend and advocate the violent suppression of pagan religion. Most assuredly, Origen would never have supported such applications of his own theology, but nonetheless, his theology did indeed help lead the Christian church to embrace violence against its enemies. The logical conclusions of his eschatology would prove to be a turning point in the history of western civilization.

But before Ambrose and Eusebius made their marks on history, two other important figures would emerge and influence those holding the symbolic view. A premillennial Christian apologist would put forward the idea that an age of peace could be attained before Christ returned, and he would inspire a young pagan military and political leader. The apologist Lactantius would help convert Constantine to Christianity. After that, the Roman Empire and the Christian church would never be the same.

CHAPTER 5
THE DIVINE INSTITUTES AND CONSTANTINE

BEFORE THE FOURTH CENTURY, the Christian church experienced sporadic, localized persecutions. As the new century unfolded, however, a greater persecution reverberated across the entire eastern empire. At the same time, a countermovement rose to challenge the violence and forever change the face of Rome. As the story of the countermovement unfurled, a Christian scholar and a sun-worshipper converged with each other to become unlikely allies in turning the Roman Empire upside down. Just as important, the two also helped change the church and its theology of Christ's second coming. The first significant event in this story occurred some years before the two met. In the city of Nicomedia, a ceremony commenced.

The Emperor Diocletian looked on as attendants brought the goat to the altar and laid it flat. With the servants holding the legs, the priest plunged the knife deep into the animal's midsection and carved out the liver. As he searched for signs in the organ, two other of Diocletian's servants made the sign of the cross. The priest caught sight of the two in the corner of his eye as he searched the liver. He leered at the Christians. "There are profane persons here who interrupt the sacred rites," shouted the priest. "I cannot read the future!" Diocletian screamed at the two Christians to sacrifice to the gods or be scourged.[141]

For several decades the Christians enjoyed a respite from persecution, even intermixing with pagan society. The churches brimmed with new converts, overflowing with those interested in the ways of the young religion. The imperial palace, the schools, businesses, and the army witnessed Christian converts occupying places within these institutions. But with interference in the practice divination, it became clear to the emperor that something had to be done. He needed the ceremonies in order to make proper decisions regarding the direction of the empire. As far as he was concerned, Christians acted unpatriotically.

After the incident, in the year A.D. 299, Diocletian gave his first order of persecution. Everyone in his household must sacrifice to the gods or risk scourging, and those in the army must sacrifice or face dismissal. Many of the Christian soldiers refused to bow the knee to any other but Christ and found themselves stripped of their rank and discharged. While this order stopped short of putting anyone to death, Diocletian's edict shot the first round in a campaign that spiraled into atrocities.

The Great Persecution

The next important incident on the road to what became known as the Great Persecution occurred in the year 302, in the mountain region of Transdanubia. The priestess, Romula, gathered the townspeople to the feast of the Great Mother and her son, the god of vegetation. But some did not show. The scorn in Romula's voice betrayed her bias as she demanded to know where the Christians were. "They fast and pray against me," the priestess bellowed against the followers of Jesus. She took comfort, however, in that her son Galerius hated the Christians as much as she did. And he had the power to do something about it.

Romula's hatred blew in with the winter of 303 as Galerius met in closed-door meetings with Diocletian.[142] The priestess's son stood as second in command of the empire. The Christians' refusal to honor his mother was bad enough, but that was far from the worst of it. He believed that Christians threatened the very constitutional law of Rome and undermined Diocletian's hope for a golden age.

The hope of returning Rome to a period reminiscent of the era of Augustus possessed Diocletian since the beginning of his rule. In the early years, despite progress, revolts and invasions threatened unity, and the army's drive for power always stood as a looming threat to stability. In his quest, the emperor knew he needed to consolidate the empire's defenses and instill the Roman people with a sense of security, while at the same time keeping the army at bay. Diocletian came up with a plan that would become known as the rule of four.

Earlier in the year 285, Diocletian conceived a plan to share his power.[143] He divided the empire into east and west, each having its own primary leader, or Augustus. Each Augustus would have an understudy referred to as Caesar who would eventually take over as Augustus. Diocletian ruled the east and Maximian ruled the west. Constantius was appointed Caesar of Gaul and Britain, while Galerius was appointed the Caesar of Italy. It was a rule of four, or a tetrarchy as it would be named by Diocletian. The plan gave an imperial presence to every corner of the empire, and by 297, peace finally ruled Rome.

As the secret meetings progressed, Galerius became adamant in declaring that the peace and future of Rome was at stake. As far as he was concerned, the past edicts and punishments were not comprehensive and intense enough. His solution: force the Christians to sacrifice; kill them all, if necessary.

Diocletian raised his eyebrows as he listened to the words. The thought of so much bloodshed disturbed him. And unlike his colleague, he did not hate Christians. He just wanted them to become good patriotic Romans, supporting his government and taking part in a unified Roman religion. He ended the session without a decision.

At the next session, Diocletian brought in a number of advisors. But he emphasized two, in particular: one, a governor, and the other a philosopher who had once been sympathetic to Christianity. The Emperor decided to go slowly with edicts and give the Christians time. An intellectual appeal to them to give up their faith stood at the heart of his agenda: demonstrate the superiority of true religion, and give them every opportunity to repent.

Diocletian continued to address the meeting with his explanation. He would give the Christians a two-pronged treatment. First, a series of public lectures would be held by Governor Hierocles and the philosopher named Pophyry. Their job would be to convince the Christian hearers to give up aberrant religion and embrace the gods of Rome. Second, after the lectures begin, an edict would be passed to burn their writings and destroy their churches.

In some ways, the lectures employed an ancient equivalent of the good cop, bad cop concept. The Christians would be caught between two lecturers: one who lambasted Jesus as a charlatan and practitioner of witchcraft—a man who deserved to be put to death. For Governor Hierocles, Jesus should be completely rejected. Pophyry, on the other hand, believed Jesus to be a good man and a wise philosopher.

A Philosopher's Attack

In his earlier days, Christianity fascinated Pophyry. In his desire to learn about the religion, he moved to Alexandria to study under Professor Origen at the Christian School of Theology. Later, in the city of Tyre, he fell into depression and came to reject the basic tenets of the Deity of Christ and monotheism. Pophyry returned to his pagan roots, but adopted a belief that Jesus wasn't bad, just misunderstood.

On the day of the first lecture, the crowd gathered in anticipation. Pophyry took his place at the podium. "Jesus did not require worship," Pophyry boomed. "His wisdom is similar to the oracles of Apollo and Hecate, and a true understanding of his teachings should lead us to the proper worship of these gods."[144]

The audience sat spellbound, hanging on every word. The pagans were not used to hearing one of their own say positive things about Jesus. But to at least one member of the audience, nothing positive came forward. Lactantius taught rhetoric at the court of Diocletian, and in spite of his Christian beliefs, the professor gained a reputation as a brilliant instructor and lecturer. But as he listened to the speech, Lactantius sensed danger with every uttered word.

I want to shut my ears to this, Lactantius thought, but I need to keep listening. I need to know how to respond. [145]

Pophyry continued his speech: "The true Roman gods are proclaimed everywhere, in every city, in every kind of temple, by every emperor, lawgiver, and philosopher. If Christians don't react properly to the true teachings of Jesus and take part in the Roman religion, to what sort of penalties might we not justly subject such people? Any and all!"[146]

There it was, thought Lactantius. His fears proved right. The reference to lawgivers particularly troubled him, for it implied that all Christians struck at the very heart of the Roman Constitution. And all penalties implied death.

Lactantius hurried out of the lecture hall, determined to give an answer to the claim that Christians deserved persecution. He probably knew it would not be long before he had to give up his chair in the royal court. But at least that would afford him time to write his response.[147]

The first edict of persecution was publicly posted in Nicomedia on February 24, 303. But by the night before, city authorities already knew the edict was on its way and started dismantling the newly built Cathedral Church of Nicomedia. The celebration of Terminus, the god of boundaries, must have seemed a fitting night for church burning. Thus the edict started the suspension of Christian worship, the destruction of church buildings and the burning of Scriptures.[148]

The second edict followed within hours. The law removed all Christians from posts of authority and declared them liable to torture if they would not sacrifice to the emperor and the gods. The law stopped short of bloodshed and the burning of all Christians for which Galerius had pushed for. At the same time, it gave local officials discretionary power to torture. Many took the opportunity to torture unto death.

The first to die was Eutius. As the cathedral in Nicomedia smoldered, he ripped the edict from the wall. "Here is what I think of your victories over the Goths and Sarmatians!" He held up the paper and shredded it in front of the crowd that had gathered to read it. The two guards standing by wasted no time in responding. After a series of tortures in the dungeon, the authorities completed the job by setting the Christian on fire.[149]

After this, Nicomedia began persecuting the Christians in earnest. A man named Peter was one of the next. They brought him up before the magistrates and commanded him to worship. When he refused, the guards chained his wrists and hoisted him off the ground. They bashed his entire body with rods until their own hands tired from the strain.

They commanded him to sacrifice, but he refused. They couldn't believe his response as they looked upon the bones protruding through his flesh. They mixed salt with vinegar, pouring the mixture over the most mangled parts of his body. Still he refused. Next they brought a gridiron and fire and slowly placed parts of his body over the flame, being careful not to burn his entire body all at once and kill him too quickly. Still he refused. Finally his mortal life succumbed to the flames as the fire engulfed his entire person.

Peter stood as a typical example. Many others followed in Nicomedia, and the pattern persisted in other cities with both individuals and whole families dying by fire, the sword, or by drowning.[150]

As persecution spread throughout the eastern provinces, some Christians in Syria and Melitine rebelled.[151] And in Nicomedia, the imperial palace mysteriously caught fire twice. After the second fire, Galerius decided to get out of the city. Although lightening probably caused the combustions, the rebellions stroked his paranoia, convincing him the Christians were out to kill him. Perhaps now Diocletian will listen to me, he thought as he fled, and burn them all.[152]

Diocletian started to listen. Believing that things were spinning out of control, he passed another edict—this one ordering the arrest of all church leaders. Prisons filled-up with pastors, elders, deacons, teachers and exorcists. The dungeons couldn't hold them all, so the authorities released common criminals in order to make room for the other prisoners. For the government, it was better to set free the murderers, rapists, and thieves than set free the usurpers of an entire empire and the offenders of the gods.

In January of the year 304, Diocletian passed the last edict. It was his final solution to the Christian problem. All Christians—men, women, and children, had to gather in a public place and sacrifice to the gods. If they refused, they would be burned alive. Galerius finally realized his hopes.

Many of the eastern provinces enforced the edict, but in the west, Caesar Constantius refused. From the beginning, Britain enforced only the first law. Constantius sympathized with Christians and may have been a closet Christian. He had named his daughter Resurrection.

His son, Constantine was a pagan, and although he had an affinity for

Apollo, he seemed to concentrate his worship on the Sun god as the supreme deity.[153] Thus even in early years Constantine leaned towards monotheism. He may have been influenced by his father since he took no part in the persecutions while working under Diocletian in Rome. As one historian put it: "In the grand scheme of what was playing out in front of him, the suffering of those who refused to sacrifice, the abdication and apostasy of those who could not stand the torture, and the delight of the torturers, Constantine witnessed the best and worst of human nature. He watched and learned."[154]

Despite his best efforts to do what he thought necessary for the sake of the empire, the end of Diocletian's reign was near. Not long after the final edict, Diocletian suffered mental exhaustion and decided to abdicate.[155] Maximian determined to join him. Galerius was set to become Augustus in the east and Constantius Augustus in the west. Rumors swirled that Constantine would be named Caesar under his father. A new era for the empire was about to begin.

On May first, 305, three miles outside the city of Nicomedia, in front of the statue of Jupiter, Diocletian gathered the army. The soldiers anticipated the announcement: Constantine and Severus would be made Caesars.

"The new Caesars are Severus and Maximin Daia!" The shout stunned the crowd. Maximin? Who's Maximin? The murmuring reverberated from bystander to bystander. No one could believe it, but no one objected as they were all too dumbfounded to make a move. "Perhaps Constantine changed his name," some exclaimed. Better to wait before making an outcry.

Diocletian took off his purple robe and placed it on Maximin. In his royal robe, he entered the chariot and drove toward the streets of Nicomedia. The shocked crowd looked on and wondered what it meant for the future of the empire.

Humiliated, Constantine returned to his father in Britain. When the elder died shortly after, the troops in Britain proclaimed Constantine Caesar. Constantine's acceptance planted the seeds for civil war.[156]

The Divine Institutes

In the year 306, with the persecution in full swing, Lactantius worked feverishly on his *Divine Institutes*. The dissertation rebutted Pophyry, pitting the superiority of Christianity against Paganism. But anyone reading between the lines knew the criticism struck much deeper.[157]

Lactantius despised the Tetrarchy. Diocletian never sought senatorial validation for his rule. Like a number of emperors before him, he owed his power to the army, and like the others, he kept the army happy with bribes. Ultimately, he knew that he couldn't trust the soldiers and so he divided power among four rulers. But for Lactantius, many rulers mimicked many gods. Underlying the *Divine Institutes* was an attack on Diocletian's form of government. Because the Roman Empire was divided under four emperors and because each one was claimed to be divine, the system failed to reflect the true natural order. Lactantius reasoned that there is one monarch ruling in heaven, so only one emperor should rule Rome.[158]

Lactantius forged the *Divine Institutes* at the same time Constantine observed the onslaught of Diocletian's policies against the Christians. Initially, Constantine was committed to the Tetrarchy, but he began to see the fallacy of religious intolerance. After watching and learning from the persecutions, and after he attained power as Caesar of the West, he came under the influence of Lactantius.

Sometime after the year 310, the *Divine Institutes* played its part in convincing Constantine he was destined by God to return the empire to Lanctantius's proper pattern of divine rule. But early in 306, the rule of four still held sway, and Constantine's journey to consolidate the empire had just begun.

Initially, Galerius seethed over Constantine's usurpation of power, but after he collected himself, he elected to avoid war. Maxentius, however, the son of the retired Augustus Maximian, remained in a rage. Like Constantine, he had been passed over when Diocletian and Maximian abdicated. Now Constantine had power while he remained stagnant. Maxentius determined to do something about it. After all, years ago, a seer had predicted it.

"When the right moment comes, Rome will submit to your son's right hand." The words still burned in his mind as Maxentius recalled his father's meeting with the fortuneteller. From sixteen years of age, he believed his rule was inevitable.[159] Maxentius started his road to rule by making friends with those who gained a reputation as emperor-makers.

Civil War Begins

Three months after the army in Britain made Constantine Caesar, the Praetorian Guard proclaimed Maxentius emperor. As the emperor's special guards, the Praetorians hoped to remain relevant. Diocletian had siphoned their power and put them on the path to obsolescence. The Praetorians had a history of determining the next emperor, but their days of glory were coming to an end. Still, they believed they had one more hand to play. The Praetorians marched out of Rome and conquered Southern Italy for Maxentius.

All out rebellion gripped the west and south as Africa and Spain declared in favor of Maxentius. In the winter of 307, Severus marched against Maxentius. When he reached Rome, most of his army turned against him and joined Maxentius, thus bringing his defeat. He died in captivity, possibly committing suicide.

With Maxentius entrenched in Rome, in the summer of 308, Galerius replaced the dead Severus with an old drinking companion and comrade-in-arms, Licinius. The man rose out of peasantry to gain power by his military genius. At his appointment, he was expected to wage war against Maxentius, but Licinius knew the weaknesses of his army and elected to bask in his new authority rather than risk losing it in a new campaign.

Meanwhile, while resting securely in Rome, Maxentius perpetrated a reign of terror in the city. He murdered senators for their money, kidnapped young women from their homes for nights of sexual debauchery, and ripped open children's bowels in order to try to read omens. The news of his depravity caused Spain to break its alliance with him and return to Constantine. Maxentius responded by forging a fateful alliance with the notorious persecutor of the Christians, Maximin Daia, strengthening his grip on the rest of his jurisdiction.

In the year 310, another event took place that would help lead to civil war. Toward the end of that year, Galerius fell sick. A tumor struck his testicles and spread into his intestines. The authorities ushered in the most famous physicians to treat the disease. Throughout the year, however, the condition worsened until the situation turned critical. His intestines began to emerge from his body and his gluteus putrefied.

The sight horrified the physicians. Worms formed throughout Galerius's body and started devouring his bowels. The stench spread throughout the palace.[160] Try as they did to eradicate the worms, the insects laid swarms of fresh eggs, defying the physicians' actions. The stench became so horrible that many of the doctors couldn't stand it. Guards surrounded the palace to keep them from fleeing and threatened to kill any refusing to go back in. Some doctors refused. The guards butchered them on the spot.

Those who went back could do nothing to eradicate the disease. As it became apparent that the emperor was going to die, the guards slaughtered all of the doctors for their incompetence.

In his hour of desperation, Galerius considered that his misfortune might have been the vengeance of God and thought of the suffering he perpetrated upon the Christians. With his dying breaths, he put forth his last royal edict. "Leave the Christians alone to build their churches and worship as they desire. But also, they must pray for my wellbeing."[161] He ordered that the edict be put forth in the name of all the emperors, except Maximus Daia. With that, he died in the year 311.[162]

Perhaps Galerius knew Maximin Daia would never assent to have his name on the edict. When he read the document, Maximin refused to circulate it in his jurisdiction, but he reluctantly gave the order to ease persecution. In his quest to gain as much power as possible, the risk of denying a royal edict could cause unrest. But soon, however, he couldn't stand to leave the Christians alone. "Okay, we won't kill them," Maximin proclaimed. "But if they refuse to sacrifice, mutilate their ears and nostrils, and slice off their hands and feet."

The death of Galerius left a vacuum of power. Maximin took the opportunity in such an unstable moment to march into Asia Minor. In response, Licinius marched his troops into Bithynia. The two came close to war, but they were able to ease tensions with a temporary peace treaty.

Despite the treaty, Licinius distrusted Maximin Daia, and when Constantine proposed an alliance, Licinius jumped at the chance. In the year 311, the stage was now fully set for war, Maximin Daia and Maxentius pitted against Constantine and Licinius. Constantine was ready. For over a year he had spent hours learning theology from Lactantius and about the proper form of government he believed God desired for the empire. The time had come for Diocletian's tetrarchy to disintegrate.

A Golden Age before Christ's Return

Earlier, in the year A.D. 310, Constantine offered Lactantius a job tutoring his son in Latin grammar. The *Divine Institutes* was finished and now Lactantius had direct access to the emperor.[163] The *Divine Institutes* gave a theological reason to return the empire to a lone monarchy. God desired one emperor, not four.

In part of the *Institutes,* Lactantius veiled this theology by criticizing an empire based on the rule of the gods Hercules and Jupiter. Galerius had likened himself to the son of Hercules, and Diocletian to the son of Jupiter. By criticizing the reign of these two gods, Lactantius, in effect, criticized the Tetrarchy. At the same time, he wrote supportively of the rule of Saturn, which was equated with the golden age of Augustus. Augustus impressed him for two reasons: one, Augustus refused to proclaim himself a god, and two, he did not persecute monotheists. Lactantius believed the ruler had set a precedent that enabled Christianity to flourish under the following emperor, Tiberius. Thus, one ruler patterned after Augustus's reign of Saturn could return the empire to a golden age in which Christianity could flourish.

By using the Roman Pantheon in such a way, Lactantius put forth a disguised political tract advocating a return to one monarch. He was adept at using pagan imagery to make his point to the pagans.

The overall agenda of the *Institutes* claimed the superiority of Christianity over paganism, while also arguing that government should practice tolerance for all religions.[164] Lactantius used one more pagan prop to make this point. The Greek and Roman societies had long held the Sibylline Prophetesses in high esteem. Their oracles were studied to help understand the future of the world. By the first century, the writings had so permeated everyday life that certain Anti-Roman Jews made up and added a Jewish prophetess and oracle to the list of prophetesses and oracles. The Jewish oracle prophesied the coming destruction of Rome. Lactantius ignored the Jewish oracle and focused on a list of ten well-known pagan prophetesses.

Christianity is so superior, he argued, that even the pagan Sibyls received divine revelation concerning the second coming of Jesus Christ and an ensuing golden age: "Then God will send a king from the sun who will free the whole earth from evil war. And another of the Sibylls says: Behold, He will come in gentleness to release the unbearable yoke of slavery that lies upon our necks, and he will undo Godless laws and the bonds of violence."[165]

When he started writing the *Institutes* he was a classic premillennialist and the Great Persecution was the tribulation period just before the final millennium. For Lactantius, "The king from the sun" was a clear reference to Christ, who will inaugurate a golden age. By 310, however, things were changing. It was not so clear that this was the final persecution of the Antichrist. In his thinking, Christ would not return for perhaps another two-hundred years. Thus it became hypothetically possible for a temporary golden age to take hold of the empire if the right ruler came along.[166] By 311, it just so happened that a "king from the sun" was coming into his own.

The March toward One Monarch

Constantine's army camped at Saxa Ruba, a suburb of Rome some nine miles outside of the city. In the middle of October, in the year 312, ninety-thousand soldiers joined him in crossing the Italian Alps. Although Maxentius had done nothing to personally provoke Constantine, he determined to end the tyranny of Italy.

Maxentius's troops and Praetorians camped along the banks of the Tiber River, alongside the ruined Milvian Bridge. He had the bridge destroyed to slow down any advance from Constantine. Maxentius and a large contingency remained barricaded in Rome. It was a smart move. Altogether, his army outnumbered Constantine's by almost two to one, and if the enemy were to somehow defeat the first legions, it would still have to assault a barricaded Rome. Maxentius had defeated Severus with this strategy. On this night, the two adversaries waited for daylight to engage in the final clash.

For over a year, Constantine had the opportunity to learn from Lactantius through discussions, lectures, and readings from the *Divine Institutes*, giving Constantine insight into the thought processes of his teacher. Constantine would have learned of Lactantius's vision of a government that shunned persecuting religion and a monarchy based on a lone monarch in heaven. He also would have found he had some things in common with this Christian scholar besides disliking the persecution of religion. They both believed the pagan Sibylline Prophetesses could be rightly interpreted, and just as importantly, they both hated Maxentius's debauchery. Consequently, when he set out on his campaign in October, he believed right was on his side.

On this night, however, as Constantine faced two-to-one odds, he had his doubts. Was it right to attack without provocation? Did he really have a divine mandate to unify the western empire under one ruler, thus striking at the heart of the Tetrarchy? With only a few hours left before sunrise, he fell into a troubled sleep.

As he slept, he dreamt: "Paint this symbol on your shields," commanded the voice in the dream.[167] The symbol of the Chi-rho hung in the haze of his mind.

Christianity adopted the symbol of the Chi-rho in the beginning of the fourth century. For some time in Christian circles, the letters X AND I in Greek had stood for the word, Christ. The Chi-rho was an X with a perpendicular line drawn through the middle with the top turned to suggest the letter I. But the Chi-rho had another meaning associated with it. For some pagans it represented the solar god.[168]

Constantine awoke with a renewed sense of purpose. For him, the divine mandate came with the perfect symbol. The sign of the Christians and the sign of the solar god would go into battle and God would give the victory. Perhaps in his mind, he considered the solar god and the Christian God as one and the same.[169] In any case, he lost all doubt as he marched his troops against Maxentius.

With the Chi-rho painted on their shields, Constantine's troops clashed with the enemy. The outnumbered army of the Chi-rho divided the enemy troops. Before long, confusion reigned in many of Maxentius's undisciplined soldiers and they fled, leaving the Praetorians to hold the line. As the battle raged, Maxentius grew impatient. He sought an omen from the sibylline books and interpreted it to mean that he should meet the enemy outside Rome. Going against his earlier strategy, he ordered his troops to make a makeshift bridge to replace the Milvian, and he and the rest of his troops joined the battle. It was his downfall.

The Praetorians fought ferociously, but they could not stop the advancing shields of the Chi-rho. By the thousands, the Praetorians and the rest of Maxentius's troops sought to escape and plunged headlong into the River. Their attempt to flee failed, however, and Constantine's army descended upon them, cutting them to ribbons.

At the end of the battle, the bodies of Maxentius and his butchered troops floated down the bloody water of the Tiber River. Maxentius's body washed up on the one of the banks. Victorious soldiers decapitated his head, presenting it to Constantine for a trophy. With the head on a stick, Constantine marched into the city of Rome. The senate wasted no time in proclaiming him Supreme Augustus. He then ruled almost half the empire.

After the battle, Lactantius provided a post-script to the *Divine Institutes*. He placed his "Oration to Constantine" just before his final exposition on the Second Coming of Christ.

"All fictions, oh holy Roman emperor, have been laid to rest ever since God the most high has raised you up to protect the abodes of Justus and to protect the human race.... The providence of the one true God has promoted you to supreme power so that you in the trueness of your piety may rescind the wicked laws of others."[170]

Prior to Constantine's ascent, Lactantius believed that it was hypothetically possible for a golden age to occur before Christ returned. But with the Tetrarchy in place, he also believed such a utopian era was highly unlikely unless an emperor sympathetic to Christianity, like Constantius, could come to power with sole rule. With Constantine's victory, the unlikely occurred. After the battle of the Milvian Bridge, three emperors still divided the empire. But now, Lactantius could see the goal in sight. With his thinking that Christ might not return for two hundred years, a golden age was definitely possible.

After the battle at the Milvian Bridge and his coronation in Italy in 313, Constantine urged Licinius to wage war against Maximin Daia. He cited Daia's continued persecutions as a legitimate reason to put him out. Likely, once again, the *Divine Institutes* played its part in influencing Constantine's decision to eliminate Daia. The end result of the war saw Daia's army wiped out and the persecutor roaming the mountains until he died of Cholera.

Constantine and the Sibylline Prophecy

By 324, a final civil war erupted between Licinius and Constantine, with Constantine the victor. Now he alone ruled the empire. Lactantius finally realized his dream of one monarch patterned after the one monarch in heaven.

In his *Oration to the Saints* in the year 324, after he unified the empire, Constantine mimicked the *Divine Institutes* in using the sibylline prophecies and referencing the age of Augustus. In one section, Constantine writes: "The Erythraean Sibyl, then, who herself assures us that she lived in the sixth generation after the flood, was a priestess of Apollo, who wore the sacred fillet in imitation of the God she served, who guarded also the tripod encompassed with the serpent's folds, and returned prophetic answers to those who approached her shrine; having been devoted by the folly of her parents to this service, a service productive of nothing good or noble, but only of indecent fury, such as we find recorded in the case of Daphne. On one occasion, however, having rushed into the sanctuary of her vain superstition, she became really filled with inspiration from above, and declared in prophetic verses the future purposes of God:

> "On judgment's seat earth's kings their God shall own.
> Uplifted then, in majesty divine,
> Radiant with light, behold Salvation's Sign!
> Cross of that Lord, who, once for sinners given,
> Reviled by man, now owned by earth and heaven,
> O'er every land extends his iron sway.
> Such is the name these mystic lines display;
> Saviour, eternal king, who bears our sins away."

In 324, pagans objected to certain aspects of the sibylline prophecies because they believed both Jews and Christians had interjected fraudulent prophecies into the sibyllines. Constantine rejected this claim. Like Lactantius, he proclaimed the Erythraean Sibyl as correctly prophesying the first coming of Christ, while he implied the Augustan golden age helped allow the proliferation of the Gospel. In effect, both Lactantius and Constantine helped de-paganize the sibylline prophecies.

In centuries to come, the effect of the sibylline prophecies, and the desire for a golden age inaugurated by a mortal ruler, would help spin events into some of the bloodiest wars ever known in the western world. But before these things came, another piece of the historical puzzle needed to be added.

A follower of Professor Origen's symbolic view of Scripture would take prominence in the Christian church and profoundly change the way people viewed the Second Coming of Christ. Eusebius of Caesarea would question the authority of the book of Revelation, and at the same time, symbolize its twentieth chapter, proclaiming that the New Jerusalem would descend by way of one of Constantine's building projects. It would be a structure Christians would eventually kill and die for.

THE GUARDS GRIPPED Fausta's arms as she struggled to keep them from dragging her toward the steaming room. She kicked and flailed at the doorway, but finally gave in as the guards overpowered her. They threw her in and barricaded the opening. Other guards tossed more wood on the fire under the baths that lay beneath the room. The boiling water forced increasingly more gas up into the pipes and out through the gaps that lined the walls. The normal ceiling exit had been boarded up. With sweat drenching her clothes, steam filled her burning lungs. Sinking to her knees, she clawed at the door.

Fausta's death did not pacify Helena. How many times had she warned Constantine not to trust that woman? Now her favorite grandson, Crispus, was dead, and the queen's demise would not bring him back. Just as troubling, Fausta's three sons stood as sole heirs to the throne, and not one of these remaining grandsons had Crispus's integrity, courage, and common sense.

A Plot is Hatched

Twenty-six years earlier, in the year 300, Constantine's concubine gave birth to Crispus. [171] The father delighted in him and kept the boy close by his side. He employed Lactantius to tutor the boy at an early age.[172] The lad grew to become a leader revered by the Roman people. His cunning strategies defeated Licinius in the final civil war and brought the entire empire under his father's rule.[173] Both Constantine and the Roman people anticipated him as heir to the throne.

In the year 308, Constantine married Fausta as part of a political alliance with Maximian, her father. By 326, however, Constantine's paranoia reached fever pitch, leaving the emperor ripe for Fausta's intrigues. They had three sons together, but Crispus remained the first heir in succession. However, Fausta was not about to let a bastard push her sons aside. She hatched her plot when she summoned Crispus to her bed side.

She fawned over Crispus and professed her love. Her words shocked him. He tried to back away as she clutched him and pulled him closer. But finally he freed himself.

As he slammed the door behind him, Fausta continued to plot. She had intended to call the guards in the middle of his groping her. Even with her plan's failure, she knew her word would be good enough. She left her bedchamber and sobbed forced tears as she told Constantine his son tried to rape her. [174]

Fausta correctly discerned Constantine's state of mind. For months, conspiracy rumors swirled through the palace. He suspected anyone and everyone of coveting the throne. Her accusation may have surprised him, but at this point, even his beloved Crispus might be guilty of desires for the queen and plots to seize the empire. In defiance of his mother, Helena, the emperor condemned Crispus to death.[175]

Fausta's plan worked perfectly until the night Constantine caught her in adultery with one of the servants. The emperor realized he had been played for a fool. Outraged by his wife and seized with grief for his son, Constantine ordered her into the scalding sauna.

Fausta's death consoled Constantine, but not Helena. In the emperor's mind, the more she railed about it the more embarrassing it became. And on top of it, the whole sordid affair would eventually become known to the Christian community and jeopardize his standing in the church. Constantine needed to act quickly to deflect Helena's attention while giving the Christians something to reflect on besides his shortcomings.

He decided to send her on a pilgrimage to Palestine. The news thrilled Helena. She dreamed of the Holy Land and had expressed her desire to find the relics of Christ and the places where He walked.[176] The emperor gave her full use of the treasury with no expense too great.[177]

Born a pagan, Helena converted to Christianity by way of Constantine's influence.[178] Ever since the battle of the Milvian Bridge, Constantine considered Christ to be his military and political ally. The emperor returned confiscated property to its rightful Christian owners, building churches, and elevating the clergy to prime positions as advisors in the government. Helena took delight in helping to direct the building of the churches. And she dedicated herself in service to the poor and the sick.[179]

With the death of Crispus temporarily in the back of her mind, Helena made her way to Palestine. When she arrived, Bishop Eusebius of Caesarea and Bishop Macarius of Jerusalem met and accompanied her.[180] In Jerusalem she made inquiries as to where Jesus had been crucified and buried. Local townspeople pointed her to the site of the pagan temple of Venus.[181]

Back in the year AD 120, the Emperor Hadrian sought to bury the Christian holy places by building pagan temples on top of them. He reasoned that if Christians continued to worship Christ at these spots, they would, by proxy, be worshipping the pagan gods. The most important sites deserved the most attention. The Temple of Venus betrayed its importance as an acute work of engineering. Laborers had brought dirt from far distances and built a mound covering all that lay underneath. They over-laid the mound with stone before constructing the temple. Statues of Venus stared down at Helena as she surveyed the site.[182]

Some of the townspeople informed the queen that they believed the cross Jesus died on may have been buried under the temple. She responded by ordering the temple destroyed. With the aid of the bishop of Jerusalem and the consent of Constantine, the excavations began. First, the laborers demolished the statues. Then both the stone and timber by which the temple had been built were torn apart and transported far away from the site. Likewise, they shoveled the mound and dug to a considerable depth, hauling the dirt to remote vicinities. As the workers dug, the uncovered treasures astonished Helena.

As layer after layer of dirt was pushed away, a rock-cut tomb emerged. Further excavation at the bottom of where the mound had been, revealed three wooden crosses. Most surprising, one of the crosses had a headboard attached with three lines of writing: Aramaic, Hebrew and Greek. Translated, each line read, "Jesus, King of the Jews."[183] Helena had found the cross on which Christ had died and the tomb of his burial and resurrection.[184]

The discovery convinced many, including Constantine, that a new age was about to dawn over the empire. The timing seemed perfect, for it came on the heels of Constantine's defeat of Licinius. The discovery also came just in time to help quell a doctrinal controversy that had ripped the Christian church apart. The controversy had been officially dealt with at the first ecumenical council but the decision did not pacify everyone in the church. Now, one year later, the cross and tomb would help solidify Constantine's part in the council and the final choice that was wrought.

The Council of Nicaea

One year prior to the discovery of the tomb in Jerusalem, in the year 325, Constantine called for the first empire-wide ecumenical council. The assembly was to decide several issues, but the main problem concerned the doctrine of Christ's relationship to the Father and the overall issue of the nature of God.

As early as the second century, one of the primary controversies within the mainstream churches centered on whether God exists as three persons in a trinity, or Modulism, which taught that God exists as one person, who manifested Himself in three modes of being.[185] Debates raged between individuals, but no council was called to decide the issue, even though evidence suggests the majority fell on the side of the Trinity. As time wore on, many holding to Modulism emphasized Christ's deity over his humanity, some even going so far as to claim that Christ was never human.[186] This inspired a counter reaction, particularly in the eastern churches and among the followers of Professor Origen's theology, where points of discussion continually centered on Christ's humanity and deity. The Alexandrian presbyter, Arius was one of these. He went beyond Origen, however, grabbing-hold of some of Origen's concepts and taking them to an extreme.

Origen taught that a "community of substance" existed between the Father and the Son, and the Son was an "outflow of one substance" from the Father. The word used by Origen that is translated as "one substance" is "homoousios" in the Greek.[187] At the same time, he taught that Christ was a kind of second God, lower than the first. In this, the teacher was trying to relate Christ to Gnostics schooled in the theology of the neo-Platonist philosopher Numenius, who claimed that there existed three Gods whose essence was interrelated. Origen used other similar methods to try to convert Gnostics to Christianity.[188] However, such blending of Christian orthodox and unorthodox concepts opened the door for Arius.

Arius taught that Christ was a created being who had a different essence and substance from the Father. His theology implied Christ was something less than God and emphasized the human aspect. The popularity of Arius, particularly in the eastern churches, threatened to increase the discord in the church. For Constantine, the unity of the empire depended on a harmonious Christianity. He called for a church-wide council to convene in the city of Nicaea. The council convened over two months, arguing and debating the issue. On August 25, the last session met to make a definitive decision.

The assembly met in the central building of the palace. On each side of the interior, the clergy bustled into their seats, which were set up according to each occupant's rank. As they were fully seated, a hush fell over the meeting, everyone anticipating the arrival of the emperor.

Friends and family members entered first. Then all rose to their feet as the attendant gave the signal. Constantine arrived, clothed in a purple robe highlighted with gold and precious stones. He advanced to the front which elevated above the seats and where he remained standing. Then a chair of radiant gold was placed before him. After he sat down, the rest of the assembly took their seats.

To Bishop Eusebius of Caesarea, Constantine looked like some heavenly messenger. He would later write of Constantine's presence: "He (Constantine) surpassed all present in height of stature and beauty of form, as well as in majestic dignity, strength and vigor of men. . . . His mental abilities were above all praise."

After everyone sat, Eusebius stood from his place at the right of the Assembly and gave a speech thanking God in behalf of the emperor. When he finished the prayer, Constantine rose to speak. "Dearest friends, the impious, violent tyrants have been removed by the power of God our Savior. I believe, however, internal strife and division within the Church of God is far more evil and dangerous than any of the acts of the persecuting emperors. I pray, therefore, that you will be united in one judgment and that the spirit of peace will prevail among you."[189]

Following the speech, Constantine allowed one more session for debate. Almost immediately, the assembly broke out with shouts and bickering, members of each side accusing the other and vice versa. The emperor ordered calm, but then allowed each side to have its say. When all were finished, he gave his own opinion.

Before the Council, Constantine seemed to favor the idea that Christ and the Father were of two different substances. But now, probably as a result of the debates, he sided with the term "homoousious." Jesus and the Father were one substance.

The assembly voted. "Homoousious" prevailed. Prior to the Council, Eusebius favored Arius. But at least for now, he did not question the council's decision. After all, Constantine was proving himself to be Christianity's champion, and the emperor's quest for unity was not only for the empire, but was essential in establishing the Kingdom of God on earth. In his thinking at this moment, Eusebius's eschatology hindered on such unity in the church, for it was the church that would establish the Kingdom, not Christ's return in the flesh. It's easy to understand how he came to this view if one becomes aware of his background and how he was nurtured under the methods of Scriptural interpretation emerging from eastern churches.

The Ridicule of John's Revelation

Eusebius was born sometime between the years 260 and 265 and probably in Palestine.[190] When he grew of age, he received an education in philosophy and theology. He eventually became a devoted follower of Pamphilus, who had devoted himself to the theology of Professor Origen.

Eusebius first caught a glimpse of Constantine in Caesarea while the future emperor worked for, and traveled with Diocletian through that area in 296. During the years leading up to the Great Persecution, Eusebius enjoyed studying at the house of Pamphilus, which stood as a gathering place for Christian scholars. Here, he became influenced by Origen's allegorical approach to Scriptural interpretation. With Pamphilus, Eusebius also studied the scholar Dionysius, best known for his analysis of John's book of Revelation.

As a student under Origen at the School of Theology at Alexandria, Dionysius became head of that school in the year 231. Fifteen years later, he served as bishop of the city. While bishop, he dealt with a certain controversy concerning the Revelation. Another Egyptian bishop named Nepos wrote a book entitled *A Refutation of the Allegorists*, and the book spread throughout the churches of Egypt, unsettling them as many had come under the sway of Origen's allegorical interpretations. In reaction to Nepos, Dionysius wrote his own book called *On Promises*.

The second part of *On Promises* specifically dealt with the book of Revelation. Dionysius relates how he had come into contact with people who rejected the book as Scripture and who claimed it wasn't written by the Apostle John. Rather, it was written by the heretic Cerinthus.[191] "But I could not venture to reject the book," wrote Dionysius, "as many brethren hold it in high esteem."[192] The Alexandrian bishop could not discard the book because of the strong support in the churches, but the idea that the Apostle did not write the book intrigued him. Perhaps, he theorized, another John wrote it: "*But I am of the opinion* that there were many with the same name as the apostle John. . . . I think that he (the author) was some other one of those in Asia." Then the bishop added that he had heard that there were two memorials to John in Ephesus and he attributed them to two different Johns. [193]

Dionysius began an in-depth grammatical study and comparison between the Revelation with the Gospel of John and the First Epistle of John to see if the same person authored all three documents. As he engaged in his analysis, he noticed that the Gospel and Letter were written with proper Greek grammar and an excellent linguistic style, while the Revelation had improper grammar and an atrocious style. Dionysius would write: "The first two are written not only without any blunders in the use of Greek, but with remarkable skill as regards diction, logical thought, and orderly expression. It is impossible to find in them one barbarous word, or solecism, or any kind of Vulgarism."[194]

But of the Revelation and its author, he wrote: "The language and style are not really Greek: he uses barbarous idioms, and is sometimes guilty of solecism. There is no reason to pick these things out now; for I have not said these things in order to pour scorn on him-do not imagine it-but simply to prove the dissimilarity between the books."

Dionysius may have left us examples of these problems in Revelation but, unfortunately, *On Promises* is lost to us, and we have only excerpts recorded by Eusebius.[195] However, the many grammatical errors convinced him that Revelation was written by a John other than the Apostle.

In spite of rejecting the Alogia's claim that Revelation was not Scripture, one might surmise that Dionysius helped undermine the book's authority by attributing it to someone other than the Apostle John. His chief influence on the book, however, emerged with his agreement with Professor Origen in accepting a symbolic interpretation as superior over the literal: "There is a concealed and more wonderful meaning in every part . . . I suspect that a deeper sense lies beneath the words." [196] Thus Dionysius paved the way for those who would come after him seeking hidden meanings with various mystical interpretations.

As far as the grammar was concerned, Dionysius never considered that the Apostle John had little formal learning and did not have access to a scribe to help him write the Revelation while exiled on Patmos, as John probably had in Ephesus when he wrote the Gospel and letter.[197] But if Dionysius did not consider this, neither did Eusebius. And Eusebius went a step further in criticizing Revelation. He stopped short of claiming that the Gnostic, Cerinthus authored the book, but just barely: "Gaius, whose words we quoted above in the Disputation (with Proculus) which is ascribed to him, writes as follows concerning this man: 'But Cerinthus also, by means of revelations which he pretends were written by a great apostle, brings before us marvelous things which he falsely claims were shown him by angels; and he says that after the resurrection the kingdom of Christ will be set up on earth, and that the flesh dwelling in Jerusalem will again be subject to desires and pleasures. And being an enemy of the Scriptures of God, he asserts, with the purpose of deceiving men, that there is to be a period of a thousand years for marriage festivals.'"[198]

While Dionysius is careful not to mention Gaius or any other members of the Alogia, Eusebius clearly references the man who claimed Cerinthus authored the Revelation, and used the published transcript of the debate with Proclus to put forward details about Cerinthus that Irenaeus never claimed. At the same time, both Dionysius and Eusebius failed to mention Gaius's and the Alogia's attack on the Gospel of John.[199]

Eusebius, however, did not throw out the Revelation altogether. In his own theology, the Revelation's New Jerusalem figures prominently. He would keep the tradition of Origen's and Dionysius's symbolic interpretations and their search for hidden meanings. In his theology, the hidden meaning of the New Jerusalem would be found in the discovery of Christ's cross and tomb.[200]

Eusebius and the Age of Peace

After the years spent with Pamphilus, Eusebius would go on to be imprisoned during the Great Persecution. He survived without being tortured or killed probably because of prior connections he had made with government officials.[201]

In the coming years, as he studied Origen, Eusebius's own intellect became well known and he attracted the attention of Constantine. He eventually became one of the emperor's favorite scholars. As the bishop of Caesarea, his presence loomed large at Nicaea.

At Nicaea's conclusion, Eusebius determined to stay in fellowship with

Constantine and the council's decision concerning Arius. In time, he waffled back and forth on the Arian issue, but at this point in his life, unity was all-important.

Shortly after Nicaea, he returned to Caesarea and penned his *Commentary on Isaiah*.[202] He wrote of the role the bishops play in establishing the Kingdom of God on earth. In the document, Constantine's importance is similar to Augustus, in that he helped pave the way for the Gospel to go forward into the world. But the bishops were the real players in the fulfillment of prophecy. Constantine's role is minor by comparison. Shortly thereafter, however, the discoveries in Jerusalem changed his thinking. The unearthing of the tomb coupled with the study of Lactantius's *Divine Institutes*, convinced Eusebius that Constantine played a greater role in the fulfillment of prophecy. As will be demonstrated in this chapter, by the year 335, he was ready to announce to the world that the emperor had already established Lactantius's age of peace.

The Oration to Constantine and Divine Prophecy

In the year 336, Constantine called for the bishops to assemble to celebrate his Tricennial. It had been thirty years since he was proclaimed Caesar and the bishops came to Constantinople to rejoice in all that had transpired for the emperor and the Christian church. Eusebius, in particular, looked forward to the assembly. A year earlier he had given the oration at the dedication of the Church of the Holy Sepulcher, and now Constantine selected him to provide the opening address at the Tricennial.[203]

As the bishops gathered in the palace, Eusebius stood overlooking the audience. He prepared his lesson well. Judging by his lecture, he knew exactly where he wanted the speech to take his audience. He believed this very day was in the midst of fulfilled prophecy.

"I do not come forward with a fictional account, or with eloquent language to tickle the ear, as with the song of the siren." His introduction captured the crowd's attention. "No. I do not wish to follow the vulgar crowd. I come to celebrate our emperor's praises in a new way, giving an account of his deeds to those who have attained divine knowledge and have been persuaded by a proper theology."

As Eusebius moved through the first few paragraphs of his notes, he came to the part that could be said to be the topic sentence explaining the purpose of the entire speech. "Let the sacred prophecies, not given by occult madness, but by divine inspiration lead us to understand the mysteries of the emperor's deeds."

Diving into the main portion of the speech, the bishop hammered at the topic of prophecy. "Our emperor, acting as interpreter of the Word of God aims at calling the whole human race to the knowledge of God. And now that the fourth decade of his reign has extending his imperial power by appointing other rulers, thus fulfilling the predictions of the holy prophets, according to what they uttered in past ages: 'and the saints of the Most High shall take the Kingdom.'"[204]

Eusebius referenced the Prophet Daniel, but the saints "taking" the Kingdom, was a personal embellishment. The correct translation of the passage is the "Saints of the Most High shall 'receive' the Kingdom." What seems a small matter of translation had huge political and theological implications. In this new eschatology, the saints should no longer wait for their day of resurrection and Christ to return in the flesh to give them the Kingdom, but under Constantine, with political help, they should take the kingdom by force over the world.

Eusebius goes on in his Oration to reflect the political theology and eschatology of Lactantius: "He (Constantine) directs his gaze above, and frames his earthly government according to the pattern of that Divine original, feeling strength in its conformity to the monarchy of God. . . . He frames his earthly government according to the pattern of the Divine original, gaining strength in its conformity to the monarchy of God . . . who decrees that all should be subject to the rule of one. . . . And surely monarchy is superior to every other constitution and form of government: for democracy, which is its opposite, may rather be described as anarchy and disorder, for there is one God, and not two, or three, or more."[205]

The concepts of Lactantius were not lost on the bishops as most, if not all by this time, had to be familiar with the Divine Institutes. Lactantius criticized Diocletian's rule of four emperors and taught that an age of peace could be attained prior to Christ's return if one monarch ruled the empire and sympathized with monotheism.

Politics and the Age of Peace

This age of peace was a work in progress. In Eusebius's eschatology, the age that Lactantius hoped for began with the resurrection of Jesus: "But when that instrument of our redemption, the holy body of Christ . . . was raised, at once the abolition of evil spirits was accomplished. The manifold forms of government, the tyrannies and republics, the siege of cities and devastation of countries caused by those forms of governments were now no more, and one god was proclaimed to all mankind."[206]

The bishop explained how the power of the Resurrection was now guiding the Roman Empire to complete peace over the world: "Meantime, the Roman Empire . . . its object being to unite all nations in one harmonious whole, much of which has already occurred, and destined to be more perfectly attained . . . through the aid of that Divine power which facilitates and smoothes its way."[207]

Eusebius believed the era of harmony was settling over the known world. Constantine brought the world out of warfare and anarchy and was instilling it with the knowledge of God.

Now that Eusebius had established Constantine as the emperor that had been dreamed of in the Divine Institutes, he continued in his oration to demonstrate another proof in the emperor's fulfillment of prophecy. Progression toward the ultimate fulfillment of the Kingdom of God on earth came with the building of the Church of the Holy Sepulcher.

"On the very site of the Lord's sepulcher, he (Constantine) has raised a church of noble dimensions, and adorned a temple sacred to the salutary Cross with rich and lavish magnificence, honoring that everlasting monument, and the trophies of the Savior's victory over the power of death." According to his lecture, no less instrumental to the age of peace was the discovery of the cross and tomb and the construction of the edifice housing them.

In this part of the *Oration*, however, Eusebius made what seems to be startling omission. He does not claim that Helena found the Cross and the Tomb. The speaker credits Constantine with the findings. Helena established three sites in Palestine marked by caves: the sites of the Transfiguration, the Ascension, and the Resurrection. In his speech, Eusebius recounts the discovery of the sites: "In the same country he (Constantine) discovered three places venerable as the localities of three sacred caves: and these also he adorned with costly structures . . . and the victory (the Resurrection) which crowns it, at the third."

Conspicuously missing from the talk was any mention of Helena. In Eusebius's mind, God used Constantine's mother as an instrument in the fulfillment of prophecy, but the real credit belonged to the emperor.[208]

Not only did he obscure Helena, but the Cross is given second place in importance to the Tomb. In many churches and for many bishops, the Cross became the most important part of Helena's discoveries. The Tomb took a backseat. As pieces of the Cross were disseminated to churches throughout the empire, it did not take long before special rituals were implemented around the pieces.[209] For Eusebius, however the Tomb represented the most important find, for the fulfillment of the kingdom of God on earth was found in the Resurrection of Christ and the impartation of Christ's Spirit in Constantine.[210]

In the middle of the Oration, Eusebius switched from the grammatical voice of the third person to the second and no longer glanced from bishop to bishop. Eusebius focused his eye contact on Constantine. "And now, mighty and victorious Constantine, let me lay before you some of the mysteries of Christ's sacred truths."

After he re-capsulated much of what he had already said, Eusebius ended his speech with a direct discourse to the emperor on the importance in human history of building the Church of The Holy Sepulcher: "Such doubtless are the reasons, and such convincing proofs of your Savior's power, which caused you to raise that sacred edifice . . . ascribing victory and triumph to the heavenly Word of God."

That day, the Bishops left the Tricennial celebration with a clear understanding of the role Constantine and the discovery of the Tomb played in the fulfillment of prophecy. A new dawn had descended over the world and the emperor and tomb were the catalysts by which the Kingdom was arriving.

Eventually Eusebius included the Tricennial Oration in the document, The Life of Constantine. In that biography, he gave a detailed account of the discovery of the Tomb and the erection of the Church of the Sepulcher. In chapter twenty-three, Eusebius wrote a statement that struck an emotional spark that would one day set the Middle East on fire: "…on the very spot which witnessed the Savior's sufferings, a New Jerusalem was constructed . . . It was opposite this city (the old Jerusalem in its spiritual decline) that the emperor now began to rear a monument to the Savior's victory over death, with rich and lavish magnificence. And it may be that this was that second and new Jerusalem spoken of in the predictions of the prophets."

After he became a disciple of Origen, it would be the only time Eusebius claimed validity to any concept from the book of Revelation. He symbolized the twentieth chapter in keeping with Origen's allegorist tradition. There was to be no descent of a literal, physical metropolis out of Heaven, but a spiritual city already descended in the construction of the Church of the Holy Sepulcher.

Eusebius and the Violence of Constantine

As indicated in prior chapters of this book, some modern historians have claimed that the fourth century fathers advocated the allegorical and spiritual interpretation of John's Revelation as a way to try to stop the looming violence inspired by a literal interpretation. However, Eusebius, one of the greatest allegorists and spiritualizers of Scripture and Revelation, strongly advocated and supported war and suppression of pagan religion in the name of Christ.[211]

In his biography of Constantine, he described how the emperor used the symbol of the cross to bring about the defeat of Licinius. "Indeed, wherever this appeared, (the cross) the enemy soon fled before his victorious troops. And the emperor perceiving this, whenever he saw any part of his forces hard pressed, gave orders that the salutary trophy (the cross) should be moved in that direction, like some triumphant charm against disasters: at which the combatants were divinely inspired, as it were, with fresh strength and courage, and immediate victory was the result."[212]

In support of laws passed by the emperor to forbid pagan practices, Eusebius wrote: "Soon after this, two laws were promulgated about the same time; one of which was intended to restrain the idolatrous abominations which in time past had been practiced in every city and country; and it provided that no one should erect images, or practice divination and other false and foolish arts, or offer sacrifice in any way."[213]

Eusebius expressed in the biography how Constantine destroyed pagan temples: "He razed to their foundations those of them which had been the chief objects of superstitious reverence."[214] In the context of his document, Eusebius seemed to suggest that the emperor demolished many pagan temples. In reality, he tore down only four, and these four were involved with extreme occult practices which some pagan emperors before him had not favored, such as cult prostitution. At the same time, Eusebius ignored the fact that Constantine actually built two pagan temples for the sake of his pagan subjects.[215]

As shown to you in the early chapters, the church fathers with the greatest claim for apostolic connection and succession rested with those leaders who emerged out of Asia Minor and the West.[216] And their theology was clearly futurist pre-millennial. And as readers have seen, a number of disparate elements emerged to attack that eschatology. These elements ranged from the prosperity doctrine taught by the Nicolaitans, to the overreaction by the Alogia against the New Prophecy, to the symbolic interpretation and exegesis of Scripture advocated by Professor Origen, to the church's establishment of an age of peace before Christ's return as put forward by Lactantius.

In the fourth century, all of these elements merged in Eusebius's theology and eschatology. He supported Constantine's bestowing financial and political power upon the church. He transformed Lactantius's concept of an age of harmony into the millennial era of peace that occurs without the return of Christ in the flesh. As one of the great disparagers and allegorists of the book of Revelation, he led the charge for waging war and suppressing religion in the name of Christ. And finally, he did one more thing of significance. He allegorized the Church of the Holy Sepulcher with the descent of the New Jerusalem.

In the centuries ahead, a new religion called Islam would rise and take control of Jerusalem. In what would become known as the Great Crusades, the Church of the Holy Sepulcher would become a battle ground as Christians fought, killed, and died in trying to regain control of the New Jerusalem to fulfill the prophecies concerning Eusebius's age of peace.

In the meantime, leading into the fifth century, the writings of a member of a reform sect known as the Donatists will have a profound effect on the theology and eschatology of a North African bishop named Augustine. The bishop would be destined to become one of the most influential thinkers in the history of western civilization. In time, his theology of love would inspire Christians to burn those they considered apostates and aid the coming onslaught in the march to holy wars and revolutions.

CHAPTER 7
THE MILLENNIUM NOW

WINGS OF FLAME burst up the inner walls of the synagogue, sweeping across the ceiling and crawling back down to the floor of the altar. Columns of smoke billowed from the windows as the Christian monks continued to fling torches. Within minutes the blaze gained mass and strength, swallowing the building in a torrent of scorching gases. As the fire reached its pinnacle of intensity, the bishop of Callinicum called off the rabble. The arsonists had completed the task he had assigned them.

The synagogue still smoldered when the news reached the Christian emperor, Theodosius. Outraged, he ordered the perpetrators arrested and then sent an edict commanding the bishop to rebuild the synagogue out of church funds. As far as he was concerned, the bishop violated Roman law and acted contrary to proper civil order. More important, the uncouth and violent act on the part of the Christians arsonists contradicted the teachings of Jesus.

When the reports of the arson and the emperor's reaction reached Ambrose, the bishop of Milan, the clergyman fired off a letter to Theodosius, chastising him for his response. This dispatch alarmed the emperor. The incident became another highlight in a fourth century roused with the fusion of church and state and another turning point leading to violence perpetrated by the church.

Originally the governor of Milan, Ambrose became bishop after the death of the pro-Arius bishop, Auxentius, who left a power vacuum in the struggle between Arian and pro-Nicene Christians in the city. In spite of Ambrose's own Nicene leanings, both parties favored him to fill the vacant church office. Ambrose was seen as a compromiser and someone who could work with all sides. Ecclesiastical authorities sped him through priestly ordination and consecrated him bishop on December 7, 374.

At first, having little theological training, Ambrose tread lightly on the city's pro-Arian majority and spent a great deal of time studying the likes of Philo and Origen to increase his knowledge and hone his preaching skills. Eventually, he came out strongly against the Arians, but his most important legacy for history lay in his particular view of church and state and his support for Origen's system of Scriptural exegesis.

Ambrose followed Origen and his symbolic interpretation of Scripture. Somewhat Similar to Origen, Ambrose taught a threefold meaning: the literal, the mystical, and the moral. Of the three, the mystical was the most important, for it can "help us out of the contradictions the literal meaning may lead us into."[217] And for Ambrose, there could be a plurality of meanings for the same passage.[218] At the time of the burning of the synagogue, Ambrose had popularized Origen's theology and the symbolic interpretation of Scripture in the west, while Eusebius's symbolizing of the millennium slowly permeated the empire.

While Origen's theology impacted Ambrose and Eusebius, the two bishops applied that teaching to the relationship of church to state in both similar and divergent ways. Eusebius had championed the idea of the Christian emperor as the fulfillment of prophecy and the instigator of the millennium. In this dictum, the church should be subordinate to the king while aiding him in his task.

Ambrose believed that the emperor had the duty to ensure a proper order for the church so that it could go forward and convert the world to Christianity. Unlike Eusebius, however, the bishop should be the emperor's authority. But like Eusebius, Ambrose believed that Rome should merge with the church and the church merge with Rome. Good Romans are Christians. For both Ambrose and Eusebius, it was the duty of the emperor to promote Christianity.[219]

Ambrose wrote the emperor, complaining of his decision concerning those responsible for burning the synagogue. The monarch knew that it was not politically astute to completely defy such a well-respected bishop. The theology of the letter also made Theodosius uneasy about the state of his own soul should he dismiss the bishop altogether. After he finished reading the letter, Theodosius sought to compromise. He rescinded his order that the church pay to rebuild the synagogue, but the monks would still be incarcerated. Ambrose, however, was not pacified.

The bishop wrote a second letter chastising the emperor and insisting the whole affair be dropped. "There is no adequate reason for the commotion," Ambrose wrote in defense of the perpetrators, "that the people should be severely punished for the burning of any building; much less seeing that it is a synagogue that has been burnt, a place of unbelief, a house of impiety, a receptacle of madness, which God Himself hath condemned."

As he continued his letter, Ambrose insisted that the burning of the Synagogue paid back Jews and pagans that had burned a church sometime in the past. "At Alexandria too, the most beautiful church of all was burnt down by the Gentiles and Jews. The church has not been avenged, then shall the Synagogue be?"

Ambrose finished the memo with an appeal to the emperor that the subject should now be finished and that he would not have to chastise him any further. "Assuredly I have done what is most respectful to you: I have sought that you should listen to me in the palace that you might not have to listen to me in the church."

Theodosius remained silent. The emperor was scheduled to attend mass soon in the Cathedral of Milan. Ambrose had chastised him in the palace. Now he would have to do the same to him in the church.

A Subservient Government

Theodosius swaggered into the cathedral, strutting up to the front to sit with the clergy. Ambrose motioned him to go to the back of the congregation. "Sit with the laity." The emperor did as commanded.[220]

As the service commenced, Ambrose began to preach. Midway into the sermon, he referenced Deuteronomy 33:24: "A blessed son is Asher, and he shall be acceptable to his brothers, and shall dip his feet in oil. With this oil, the Church anoints the necks of its children."

After explaining that the oil of which he spoke was spiritual in nature, Ambrose began the climax of the sermon. "The synagogue has not this oil." He then made eye contact directly with the emperor. "Wherefore, oh emperor, I direct my words not only about you, but to you . . . guard the whole body of Christ, that He may protect your kingdom." Theodosius understood the rebuke—pardon those who burned the synagogue at Collincum, or God will act in revenge against the empire.

All eyes in the congregation focused on both Ambrose and the emperor as bishop ended the sermon and came down from the pulpit to meet Theodosius in his seat. "You spoke about me," the emperor said.

"I spoke that which is to your benefit."

"I admit I dealt too harshly with the bishop, but I amended that," pleaded the emperor. "The monks, on the other hand, commit too many crimes."

For some time, the two men faced each other in silence, Ambrose refusing to back down. Finally, Ambrose demanded. "I will not offer you the Eucharist with a bad conscience." Theodosius nodded in agreement but failed to speak out loud that he would pardon the monks. Ambrose instructed him that he should end the investigation, once and for all. At last, Theodosius agreed.

Now that he had the promise, Ambrose walked up to the altar and made ready the Eucharist. With the emperor properly humbled, disciplined, and repentant, the clergyman gave Theodosius the wafer. Ambrose quivered under what he believed was the grace of God as he put the Eucharist in Theodosius's mouth. And afterwards, the monks went free, and the state demanded no retribution for the synagogue's burning.

While Eusebius and Ambrose were important voices that eventually helped lead the Christian church to wars and revolutions, another controversy emerged, fueling the brewing storm. In the middle of the fourth century, prior to Ambrose's time, a group known as the Donatists and a violent groupie-type sub-faction, inspired an overreaction that would result in the implementation of government-sponsored heresy laws.

The Donatists

Approximately fifty years before the persecution under Diocletian in 305, a council was held in Carthage under Bishop Cyprian to decide what should be done with clergyman who had apostatized during the persecution under the Emperor Decius. The council determined that bishops and other clergymen who had succumbed to the persecution were to be forever excluded from their ecclesiastical offices. While they were allowed back into the church if they were willing to undergo penance, they were not permitted to return to their previous positions.

Under Diocletian, many Christians in North Africa followed the prescriptions of the earlier council. However, when the emperor ordered that the Holy Scriptures should be handed over, there were some bishops that believed they could follow the order in good conscience, arguing that turning over objects was not the same as denying Christ.

At the end of the Diocletian persecution, the church of Carthage had broken down into factions: those who supported the complete forgiveness of those clergymen who had handed over the Scriptures or denied Christ and those who refused to allow them back in to their ecclesiastical offices. Bishop Donatus led a faction that refused to allow reentry of the lapsed without rebaptism and re-ordination. Donatus re-baptized and ordained lapsed clergy without appealing to the Roman Church who had advocated that the clergy did not need to go through the rituals again. Donatus, however, re-baptized only those who completely denied Christ. For those who cooperated with the authorities but had not denied Christ, he advocated only a period of penance and restoration by the laying on of hands.[221] By 313, the controversy split the church in Carthage in half with two congregations following two bishops—the rigorists following Donatus and those who followed Ceacilianus, who adopted the more lenient position.

From there, the controversy spread through the entire province of North Africa with most following Donatus. Initially, outside of Africa, most of Christianity recognized Ceacilianus as the rightful bishop. However, through the decades leading to the year 345, Donatism spread throughout the empire by making inroads with the lower classes and economically impoverished.

As the mainstream church aligned itself with the government, it achieved accolades, prestige, and wealth. A growing throng resented this direction. They identified with members of the Donatists who associated with the slaves and lower classes. In the year 345, a crisis erupted within the Donatist churches when a number of congregants joined a band of brigands hell-bent on changing society by literal class warfare.

The Violence of the Circumcellions

Members of the Circumcellions forced the deed into the creditor's hand and ordered him to tear it up. The certificate represented a large sum to be sure, but what good would the money be to him if he were bludgeoned to death? In spite of how much the creditor was owed, he tore up the document. Then the thugs forced him to his knees and commanded him to beg forgiveness and pray for repentance.

While the creditor groveled at the feet of the Circumcellions, a scene unfolded outside the creditor's house that would play itself out in provinces throughout North Africa. A chariot passed by with slaves running in front. When other members of the Circumcelloin mob saw the chariot, they rushed the horses and stopped the carriage. They yanked down the driver and put the two slaves into the chariot. The mob ordered the slaves to drive while they forced the owner to run in front. The Circumcellions sought to turn the class structure of the empire upside down.[222]

As the roving bands of brigands gained popularity, Donatist bishops became concerned at what was happening within the ranks of their churches. A number of Donatist congregants enlisted in the Circumcellions and joined in the violence. Nothing the bishops said to the contrary made a difference. At their wits' end, the bishops wrote a letter appealing to Taurinas, a military general, for help. The content of the correspondence claimed, "Men of this kind cannot be corrected within the church. They can only be brought back by force."[223]

Taurinas acted immediately ordering the death of the rebels by sword and decapitation throughout the provinces of North Africa. Many within the Donatist fold considered the slaughtered Circumcellions martyrs and tried to bury them in Donatist church cemeteries. But the Donatist bishops ordered the dead bodies dug up and cast out. The hero worship heaped upon the slain Cicumcellions by the poor would eventually inspire some of them to engage in suicide so that they might be counted with the martyrs.[224]

In spite of the opposition of the bishops and the military action, some congregants continued to join the ranks of the Circumcellions. Then, in 348, an event occurred that would cause the critics of the Donatists to forever associate the schismatics with the violence of the Circumcellions. A Donatus priest enlisted the brigands to stop what he considered a ploy by the mainstream church to render the Donatist faction as irrelevant.

The Macarian delegation approached the outskirts of the North African city of Bagai carrying large amounts of food and clothing. The sizable number of government troops accompanying the group prepared for a fight. When they reached the border of Bagai, the Circumcellions were waiting for them. If the delegation continued to enter the town, it would be over their dead bodies. As the mission came closer, the blockading mob hurled insults. Finally, the Circumcellions grabbed several of the delegation's emissaries and beat them. The troops that trailed the delegation charged forward, plunging into the throng, mercilessly slicing off heads and arms. When the battle ended, all the Circumcellions lay massacred.

What led up to this slaughter was that the leaders of the mainstream church realized they had lost touch with lower classes and economically impoverished. The hierarchy decided to send delegates to the North African provinces to distribute food and material to the poor. Perhaps, they thought, the act could help win back the schismatics to the true church. The Donatist leaders, however, considered it a ploy to turn the masses against them and eliminate what they considered to be the true church.

One of the Donatist priests in Bagai called for the Circumcellions to gather at the city to stop the delegation. It was the first time a Donatist clergyman associated himself with the thugs. Eventually, the mainstream church used the affair at Bagai as an opportunity to paint all the Donatists as violent and turn the government against the entire movement. The majority of Donatist bishops, however, continued to reject the Circumcellions and any association with violence. By the year 377, a Donatist layman named Tychonius made it clear that the Circumcellions stood outside of the Donatist communion when he wrote, "These men do not live in the same manner as other brothers do but kill themselves as if in the love of martyrdom. . . . In Latin we call them Circumcellions, since they live in the country. They roam around the provinces because they do not allow themselves to be in one place with the brothers in single-mindedness or partake in communal life, so that they might live with a single heart and soul according to the apostolic custom."[225]

So at least up to the year 377, the evidence from Tychonius demonstrates that the majority of Donatists rejected the violence of the Circumcellions and wanted nothing to do with this group. The critics of the Donatists, however, would go on to smear the Christian schismatics with a broad brush, making no distinction between them and the aggression of the brigands.

In the meantime, Tychonius put forward an interpretation of the book of Revelation that impressed even the most ardent critics of the Donatists. The premillennial interpretation was in retreat in the east as a result of Eusebius, and Ambrose helped to put it in withdrawal in the west with his hermeneutic of symbolization. The result was the growing acceptance of the violent suppression of non-Christian religion. In spite of his own rejection of violence, Tychonius would continue the trend. His seven rules of Scriptural interpretation would spell the end of the premillennial interpretation in the church for centuries to come.

Tychonius and the Seven Rules

Tychonius lived at a time when paganism seemed to be in retreat in the empire and Christianity appeared to be on the verge of triumph. The idea that Christ should soon return in the flesh to end persecution seemed increasingly archaic. Throughout the empire, as stated above, symbolic interpretations of the book of Revelation came into vogue and the eschatology of Irenaeus was rejected. The situation was no different in North Africa. By the year 388, Tychonius began writing his book of rules to help interpret the "mysteries" of prophecy. In the same year, the Council of Constantinople met to emphasize the deity of the Holy Spirit. For Tychonius, reliance on the Holy Spirit factored heavily in the rules as both the Spirit and the rules would illuminate and guide the reader while "walking through the immense forest of prophecy."[226] The end result of Tychonius's exegesis of this immense forest was a highly symbolized view of Revelations' description of the millennium.

Tychonius proposed seven rules to help interpret prophecy: The Lord and His Body, The Lord's Bipartite body, The Promise of the Law, The Particular and the General, On the Measurement of Times, Recapitulation, and The Devil and his Body.

In rule five from the "On the Measurements of Time," Tychonius speculated that some measurements of time in the Old Testament were meant to be half times or only part of the time that was stated. For example, when a day was proposed, sometimes only part of the day was meant. Rule six, or Recapitulation, stated that a narrative that seems to progress chronologically in fact "covertly switches backward to earlier matters which had been passed over."[227] Both of these rules influenced Tychonius's view of the millennium.

In a straightforward, literal reading of Revelation, chapter twenty, John recorded that Jesus returns in the flesh and personally establishes the millennium or a thousand years of peace. In accordance with rule six, Tychonius proposed that the thousand years of Christ's reign had already begun. In harmony with rule five, Tychonius interpreted the millennium to mean a period of 350 years, rather than a literal thousand, and it began at Christ's crucifixion. Thus the end of the millennium would come by about the year 383. For Tychonius then, the church was already in the midst of the millennium and Christ would return within a decade.[228]

As a result of rule five, the Donatist teacher gave a symbolic meaning to John's description of the first resurrection. In Revelation chapter twenty, John claims that those beheaded by the Antichrist come to life in the first resurrection. In a literal reading, those who were beheaded are resurrected and reign with Christ on earth. This description suggests that this is the day of the physical resurrection of the righteous which is then followed by the millennium. John goes on to explain that there is another physical resurrection at the end of the millennium, this time for the unrighteous.[229] For Tychonius, however, the millennium, or 350 years, encompassed the first resurrection which was symbolized as the spiritual resurrection that occurs through the sacrament of baptism.[230] The second resurrection would be a literal rising of the body from the grave of both the righteous and unrighteous and would occur at the end of the millennium.

For Tychonius, his rules helped him to understand that the Christian curch is made up of both good and evil together and only God can determine the tares (those who are evil) at the end of time.[231] This flew in the face of traditional Donatist theology which claimed that God helps the church determine the good and evil through persecution, as it separates the tares from the wheat. This difference caused Parmenian, Tychonius's bishop, to excommunicate him. In spite of his expulsion, Tychonius always considered himself a Donatist.

Tychonius's eschatology represented another change in how the church viewed the millennium. But it was not unlike Eusebius in that for both men, the millennium had already begun. Tychonius, and one might argue Eusebius, gave birth to what has become known as the historical interpretation of the book of Revelation. The historical view claims that many of the portions of what the Revelation describes will occur in the future have, in fact, already occurred. For example, Irenaeus believed that the Antichrist would arrive sometime in the future, but Tychonius claimed that the Antichrist was now in the process of charming the church by means of the great deception. But the Antichrist was not a literal lone figure as Irenaeus professed. All the tares collectively made up the Antichrist. The Antichrist, or tares, would continue to plague the church until Christ literally returned in the flesh and separated the good from the bad. By symbolizing the term Antichrist to mean the tares, Tychonius could claim that the presence of the Antichrist was a fact of history from the time of Christ's resurrection and not someone or something to wait for in the future. In the centuries to come, this highly symbolic and historical interpretation would be one of the hallmarks by theologians and political thinkers as they would justify the Christian church's waging war and striking back at its enemies.[232]

The role of the bishops in Donatist theology shaped the Donatist view of the return of Christ. A clergy free from the sin of denying Christ's name or giving up the Scriptures during the time of persecution would mold a pure church and prepare for Christ's return. In one sense, the eschatology is not unlike Eusebius's view of the bishops prior to Constantine's discovery of Christ's tomb, where the bishops played an instrumental role in bringing about the Kingdom of God.[233] One difference, however, lay in the view of persecution. For Eusebius, persecution was becoming a thing of the past as the kingdom of God swept across the world. For the Donatists, God used persecution to purify the church and separate the wheat from the chaff or tares, with the chaff comprising those who rejected Christ under the pressure of torture.

Beyond this similarity and difference with Eusebius, it is difficult to ascertain Donatus eschatology. Outside of the fragments of Tychonius, little is known of the movement's view of Christ's return because the mainstream church eventually obliterated Donatist writings.

Today, most scholars assume that Donatism taught a traditional, premillennial theology. But as stated above, with the influences of Lactantius's age of peace, Origen's eschatology, and Eusebius's view of the millennium, the fourth century witnessed a sea change in how the church viewed the millennium. Tychonius, a Donatist, embodied this change. When Parminian excommunicated Tychonius, it was specifically because of Tychonius's view of the church and the fact that the church could not determine the tares, not because of his eschatology as a whole, or his view of the millennium.[234] One can say, then, that at the time when Tychonius wrote, the church, both mainstream and Donatist, swung toward a highly symbolic view of Revelation. It's possible then, and likely, that throughout the latter part of the fourth century, Donatism reflected the mainstream church in its eschatology and was made up of some who held to premillennial theology and many who held to more symbolic notions.[235]

By the end of fourth century, the symbolic view of John's Revelation, chapter twenty, pervaded much of the Christian church's thinking. Eusebius and Ambrose's ideas on the relationship of church and state and Tychonius's view of the millennium would profoundly influence a bishop of North Africa. Augustine would become one of the church's greatest theologians. He would also strike the theological match that would one day instigate the church to burn heretics at the stake.

Augustine of Hippo

Augustine was born to a Christian mother and a pagan father in Algeria in the year 354. At the age of nineteen, he joined a group called the Manichees, who taught, among other things, that the God of the Old Testament was an evil demon. Although a member, he found certain aspects of the religion unsatisfactory and he had many questions. He continually sought answers from those who were supposed to be experts in Manichaean theology, but they disappointed him because they could not give him the information he sought.

Augustine applied for and won a teaching position in rhetoric in the city of Milan. There he came under the influence of Bishop Ambrose, about whom he later wrote, "At Milan I came to Bishop Ambrose, who had a world-wide reputation, was a devout servant of yours [referring to God] and a man whose eloquence in those days gave abundantly of the spiritual riches of God to the people of Milan."[236]

As often as he could, Augustine attended Ambrose's services, listened to his sermons, and sought his counsel. By using the allegorical interpretation of Scripture derived from his studies of Origen, Ambrose broke down Augustine's resistance to the Old Testament and taught him to believe in a deeper truth that existed beneath the literal interpretation. With Ambrose's explanations, Augustine lost his objections to Scripture, and one night in his garden, he heard the voice of a child in the yard next door singing, "Take it and read it, take it and read it." He picked up and opened a copy of the Scriptures and read the first passage he saw, "Not in rioting and drunkenness, not in chambering and wantonness, not in strife and envying: but put on the Lord Jesus Christ, and make not provision for the flesh in concupiscence." [237] On the night before Easter, in AD 387, Ambrose baptized Augustine.[238]

Shortly after his baptism, Augustine left Milan for Hippo in North Africa and became bishop of that city in the year 394. While in North Africa, Augustine became one of the chief critics of the Donatists. At the same time, Tychonius's theology of symbolism fascinated him. He would later write two books that would have a great impact on Christianity and western civilization in the coming centuries: *Confessions* and *City of God*. Tychonius underpinned the theology of *City* and it was this book that outlined Augustine's view of the book of Revelation.

Augustine and the Millennium

Many citizens of Rome laid dead or dying in the streets. As famine and severe distempers ravaged the city, men, women, and children fell like weakened sheep in the midst of ravenous wolves. Proba, a Roman noblewoman living in the city, had seen enough. Born of great wealth and prestige, her societal rank meant nothing now and she could see no reason to hold out any longer against the siege of the Visigoths. The enemy leader, Alaric, had promised he would not kill any Roman citizen who took refuge in the Cathedrals of Peter and Paul. Sick of seeing the dying around her, on August 24, 410, Proba led a contingent of Visigoth slaves and opened the gate known as the Porta Vinaria. The barbarians rushed in and proceeded to ransack the city for three days. But Alaric kept his word, leaving the Cathedrals untouched.[239]

"How could this happen?" asked Augustine. Rome was the eternal city that was supposed to protect the church and kingdom of God on earth. He would later write of the event in his *City of God* and claim he found the answer. It came as he poured over the theology of Tychonius.

Borrowing on a spiritual and carnal two-city concept that Tychonius first put forward, Augustine claimed that Rome and all political entities make up the city of man, but the Christian church makes up the city of God, and it is God that will protect and keep the spiritual city until the end of time. As he developed his theology, Augustine would write that the church as the city of God had already begun the thousand-year reign of God on earth, for the church itself represents the millennium. At the end of the millennium, or church age, the dead would rise physically and Christ would carry the church into heaven.[240]

Continuing to glean off Tychonius, Augustine symbolized the Antichrist as an entity of evil, or the tares that already existed in the church. There would be no literal beast or man of sin that would come in the future. Thus Augustine continued the trend of symbolizing the millennium and book of Revelation begun by Origen, Eusebius, and Tychonius. At the same time, the millennium was spreading over the world as the church branched out and Christianized the world. Augustine's theology coalesced with Eusebius's idea that the world was progressing into the Kingdom of God. And like Ambrose and Eusebius, God would use civil government to play a violent role in protecting the church to insure its survival and growth.

Augustine and the Suppression of Heresy

The unrepentant Donatist knelt at the block with his hands tied as the guard prepared the flogging. The soldier reeled back the whip and then launched the lead-tipped throngs deep into the man's back, the metal gouging his flesh. Pulling the tips out, the sentinel whirled the whip back and repeated the action again and again. By the time the guard finished the punishment, the prisoner's lifeless body lay sprawled across the block.

The Edict of Unity that passed in AD 405 left scores of Donatists dead from the floggings. Other members of the religion had their property confiscated and many Donatist bishops were exiled. Augustine approved of most of the measures, as he had of the earlier edicts.[241]

Even before the sack of Rome, Augustine developed his theology of the state as it related to the Donatists. Before and after the year 410, the unity of the church always remained of utmost importance. Donatists threatened that harmony and therefore had to be suppressed.

In the year 402, Augustine exchanged letters with a Donatist bishop named Petilian. Augustine replied to a number of charges by the man that the Catholic Church advocated violence against the Donatists. Petilian tried to make the case that this proved that the Donatists were the true Christians because they followed the teachings of Jesus against the use of violence. Petilian wrote, "Here you have the fullest possible proof that a Christian may take no part in the destruction of another. But the first establishing of this principle was in the case of Peter, as it is written, 'Simon Peter having a sword, drew it, and smote the high priest's servant, and cut off his right ear. Then, said Jesus unto Peter, put up thy sword into the sheath. For all they that take the sword shall perish with the sword.'"[242]

Augustine answered by painting the Donatist movement with the brush of Circumcellions. "Why then do you not restrain the weapons of the Circumcelliones with such words as these?"[243]

Each time Petilian tried to portray the Donatists as non-violent, Augustine responded by associating the entire schismatic movement with the violence of the Circumcellions. Throughout the letters, as recorded by Augustine, Petilian appeared to remain silent to the fact that some Donatis congregants had latched onto the violent sub-faction and reacted to Augustine's charges by saying in effect, "What does the violence of the Circumcellions have to do with us?" Augustine, however, through the course of the letters, refused to acknowledge that most Donatist bishops rejected the Circumcellions, and he insisted the entire movement advocated violence. Thus the Circumcellions became a convenient argument for Augustine to justify the suppression of all Donatists by civil law.

Augustine justified the use of force against heretics on his supposition that suppression can be an act of love. In the midst of his argument against Petilian he wrote, "For what did we order beyond this, that you should be arrested, brought before the authorities, and guarded, in order to prevent you from perishing." As long as the government did not put the heretics to death, it could rightly use force for the schismatics' own good to keep them from eternal damnation.[244]

Augustine also believed that coercion by the church kept the heretics from influencing others to their own destruction. Thus, again, love was the motivating factor. "Why, therefore, should not the church use force in compelling her lost sons to return, if the lost sons compelled others to destruction."[245] While Augustine stopped short of advocating death, it took only a small philosophical step for the church to eventually execute heretics for the sake of the church's unity and to keep others from following the heretics into damnation.

As Augustine developed his eschatology of the millennium after the sack of Rome, the suppression of the Donatists continued to play an important role. In his letter to Boniface written in the year 417, he applauded and justified the measures against the Donatists, for the millennium is the age of Christian kings who maintain the unity of the church in the face of heresy. "But as to the argument of those men who are unwilling that their impious deeds should be checked by the enactment of righteous laws, when they say that the apostles never sought such measures from the kings of the earth, *they do not consider the different character of that age, and that everything comes in its own season.* For what emperor had as yet believed in Christ, so as to serve Him in the cause of piety by enacting laws against impiety." [246]

After explaining that the church under the apostles was of a prior age when violence should not have been preached, Augustine finished his thought with the idea that people of his time now lived in a different age. *"Wherefore, if the power which the Church has received by divine appointment in its due season, through the religious character and the faith of kings*, be the instrument by which those who are found in the highways and hedges—that is, in heresies and schisms—are forced to come in, then let them not find fault with being forced."[247] In the age of the "millennium now," Augustine justified the use of force to try to bring back the schismatics to the unity of the church.[248]

Some modern historians have argued that Augustine attempted to put a lid on the violence that the literal interpretation of the book of Revelation inspired. For them, Augustine was one of the great heroes of history. Nothing could be further from the truth. These commentators focus on certain portions of the *City* while ignoring the eschatology Augustine put forth in his letters.[249] By investigating the primary sources of his own writings, Augustine, in fact, stood in the long line of spiritualizers and symbolizers of the Revelation that advocated violence and physical force to help bring about the kingdom of God on earth. Conversely, other historians have correctly painted his preaching as the idea of the Church Triumphant which helped usher in wars and revolutions and the burning of heretics during the Middle Ages.

A number of scholars have tried to support the idea that Augustine's theology led to a period of what they call "the taming of the apocalyptic tradition" with the result being peace and harmony for a number of centuries in the empire where religion was concerned. A truer explanation for the seeming harmony is found in the effectiveness of the heresy laws. The mainstream church, in conjunction with civil government, successfully squashed the schismatics and their dissent by way of violence and censorship. This is testified in history by the fact that Montanist and Donatist writings all but disappeared by the sixth to seventh centuries.[250]

In the centuries to come, Lactantius's and Eusebius's age of peace ushered in by civil force and the theology of Ambrose and Augustine concerning church and state would be merged with pseudo-prophecies concerning a last world emperor who many believed would rescue the New Jerusalem of the Holy Sepulcher from the hands of infidels. While Christian schismatics, Jews, and pagans suffered at the hands of the spiritualizers and symbolizers of Revelation, the cauldron of violence was just beginning to heat up. In the seventh century, a new monotheistic religion of violent conquest would emerge to challenge Christianity's dominance over the known world. And the full weight of the force instigated by the spiritualizers would be brought against it.

Chapter 8
The First Crusade and the Last World Emperor

"BUT I SAY TO YOU, love your enemies and bless the ones who curse you, and do what is beautiful to the one who hates you, and pray over those who take you by force and persecute you." These words by Jesus recorded in the fifth chapter of Matthew's Gospel never made it into the sermon given at the Council of Clermont as Pope Urban II described persecutions of Christians by Muslim insurgents in Turkey. Instead, the pontiff focused on inciting the crowd to outrage while advocating his own desire to unite the western churches with the eastern congregations.

Urban stood in front of the cathedral, addressing the three hundred clerics assembled in the open air. After reading the list of atrocities, the pope encouraged the throng to think beyond Asia Minor. He reached the climax of his speech when he described Christ's burial tomb in Jerusalem: "Let the Holy Sepulcher of the Lord our Savior, which is possessed by unclean nations, especially inflame you, as well as the holy places which are now treated with shame and irreverently polluted with their filthiness." After referencing a passage of Isaiah the prophet, he continued to rouse the crowd. "Most beloved brethren, if you reverence the source of that holiness and you cherish these shrines which are the marks of His footprints on earth, if you seek God to fight in your behalf, you should strive with your utmost efforts to cleanse the Holy City and the glory of the Sepulcher." He finished the sermon with the cry for the knights of Western Europe to liberate all the eastern churches and lay siege to the Holy Land, "before the approaching time of the Antichrist."

The mob stirred into an uproar. Many of the priests and abbots screamed, "It is the will of God! It is the will of God!"

Moved by the clerics' response, Urban rejoined, "Let this then be your war-cry in combat, because this word is given to you by God. When an armed attack is made upon the enemy, let this one cry be raised by all the soldiers of God: It is the will of God! It is the will of God!"

After the close of the council on November 28 of the year A.D. 1095, Urban and the clerics spent three months preaching the crusade throughout France and Western Europe. His own motivation centered on finding a cause by which he could unite the western church with the eastern congregations that had begun to split in the year 451. However, the desire for church unification alone, or putting down some Muslims in the regions around Constantinople for persecuting Turkish Christians would never galvanize enough support to wage war against the entire Islamic world. In his shrewdness, the pontiff focused on a popular prophecy that concentrated on the Church of the Holy Sepulcher.[251]

For centuries, churches had been preaching a prophecy foretelling of a last world emperor that would rise and liberate Jerusalem from the infidels just before the return of Christ in the flesh. The prophecy merged symbolic interpretations of the book of Revelation and the millennium, which Eusebius, Tychonius, and Augustine taught in the fourth and fifth centuries, with the pagan sibylline prophecies that Lactantius Christianized and Constantine supported. Lactantius and Eusebius had been particularly instrumental with advocating postmillennial concepts. To postmillennialism, Eusebius added the notion that the Church of the Holy Sepulcher represented the symbolic descent of the New Jerusalem. Thus he helped make the church and the tomb of primary importance in later European ideas on Christ's return.

The destruction of the Church of the Holy Sepulcher by the Muslims in the year 1009 laid further groundwork for popular support for Urban II's crusade. Even though the church was rebuilt soon after, the pope's backing of its liberation from Muslim control caught the imagination of the Christian populace.[252]

The response overwhelmed Urban's own expectations. The pontiff had hoped to gather only knights and military men to venture to the east, and during his preaching tour throughout France, he attempted to forbid scores of women, monks, the lame, and the sick from answering the call. He failed. By the time the march to the Middle East began, the army included more peasants than knights, with many of the civilians leaving before the knights. They all vowed to make their pilgrimage to the Church of the Holy Sepulcher.[253]

On June 7, 1099, after a number of battles and skirmishes along the way, the crusaders finally reached Jerusalem. Out of the one hundred thousand that had originally gathered for the crusade at Constantinople, only fifteen thousand set eyes on the metropolis.

After several failed attempts to take the city, Bishop Adhemar, who had joined the crusade with other clergy, appeared before Father Peter Desiderius, "Speak to the princes and all the people, and say to them: 'You who have come from distant lands to worship God and the Lord of hosts, purge yourselves of your sins, and let each one turn from his evil ways. Then with bare feet march around Jerusalem invoking God, and you must also fast. If you do this and then make a great attack on the city, it will be captured. If you do not, all the evils that you have suffered will be multiplied by the Lord.'"

The clergy and certain military men assembled the people and addressed them. One of them shouted, "If we make this procession around the walls, for the honor and glory of His name, He will open the city to us and give us judgment upon His enemies and ours, who now with unjust possession contaminate the place of His suffering and burial."

The clergy led the march while holding up crosses and relics of the saints, while the knights and all able-bodied men followed in bare feet carrying trumpets, flags, and weapons. While they strutted around the city, Muslim warriors on top of the city's walls jeered and ridiculed them by putting up crosses and beating upon them.

The final assault took place on July 13. As one eyewitness chronicler put it, "Then our leaders planned to attack the city with siege machines, in order to enter it and adore the sepulcher of our Savior"[254] The two towers had been built with wood carried in from great distances. When finished, the crusaders placed one at the north side of the city and the other at the south.

The European militants fought and struggled for two days as the Muslim warriors attempted to destroy the towers by hurling stones, flaming arrows and pottery full of Greek fire, a mixture of sulfur and pitch. Time and time again, the Muslims set the towers ablaze, but each time the crusaders extinguished the flames with water, vinegar, and by beating out the fire.

On July 15, the crusaders made their final push. At about noon, they finally broke through the fortifications. Muslim soldiers fled back from the walls. Many Islamic women and children hunkered down in their houses, while some sought sanctuary in the mosque on the Temple Mount. Most of the city's Jews took refuge in their synagogue. As the crusaders poured over the barricades, all Muslims and Jews trembled. [255]

The events that led up to this fateful day in July of 1099, can be said to have begun some four hundred years earlier when a pagan claimed to have a new revelation about God and Christ. A man named Muhammad took his message and initiated a religious and political revolution that spread across the Middle East.

The Rise and Conquests of Islam

Muhammad ibn Abdallah burst into the house. "Cover me, cover me," he implored his wife, Khadija. She covered him until he stopped trembling.

"What has happened to you?" she asked. Muhammad professed that he had an experience in the cave on nearby Mount Hira. It was a place he often went in order to meditate and pray to Allah, the moon god of the Meccans. On this night, he claimed that the Angel Gabriel visited him.

"Recite," the angel commanded.

"What shall I recite?"

Muhammad told Khadija that Gabriel grabbed him in a vice-like grip and squeezed him until words poured out of his mouth. Thus began a sequence of words that would form the basis for a new religion that would become known as Islam.[256]

Muhammad was born in about the year 570 in the town of Mecca, in Arabia. In his youth, it is believed that he made expeditions to Syria and discussed religion with a Syrian Christian monk who questioned the doctrine of the Trinity. In about the year 610, he claimed to have had his first visions from the Angel Gabriel and began preaching a message of strict monotheism. His initial announcement was simple. Only one God exists, Allah, and He sent Muhammad as his messenger. The prophet also taught that the souls of the virtuous in this life would be rewarded in death with a paradise of a green and delightful garden. The wicked, however, would burn in hell.

The first converts to Muhammad's faith were those of his closest family and friends. As the Meccans worshipped many gods, he feared a backlash from the townsfolk, and so he kept his revelations a secret for three years. In another vision, however, he believed Allah told him to make the religion public. Thus he gained a small local following.

Although Polytheists, the Meccans did not find the emphasis on one God unique. They already considered the moon god, Allah, to be the highest in the Pantheon and had attributes not shared by any other god. Also, the influence of the Jewish and Christian religion made its mark on the townspeople in that they did not make statues of Allah or depict him in paintings, while all other gods had their graven images. Muhammad's emphasis on making himself Allah's exclusive prophet, however, found few adherents. The political overtones of such a message worried the Meccans.[257]

Escaping persecution at Mecca, Muhammad and his followers migrated in the year 622 to join up with recent converts at the town of Yathrib or Medina, as it eventually became known, 275 miles north of Mecca. During the first eighteen months of his stay, he established his credentials as a warrior.

Muhammad's followers lost their livelihood when they moved to Medina. The prophet tried to rectify the situation by carrying out a number of raids against unguarded merchant caravans. One of the raids infuriated the pagans, as it took place during the holy month of Rajab when bloodshed was forbidden, and several caravan members were killed. In each case Muhammad initiated the raids. The Meccans had had enough and so they galvanized their pagan forces against Muhammad and his Muslims, as his adherents became known. Muhammad personally led a contingent and defeated a numerically superior army near the oasis of Badr, southwest of Medina, carrying home a substantial amount of booty and prisoners.

The Slaughter of Jews

In Medina, tensions had been brewing for several years between Muhammad and three tribes of Jews. During the years 624 and 625, the Muslims expelled two of the tribes with only the Quraysh tribe remaining. The final conflict revolved around the control of the Kabah shrine which the Jews and Muslims believed had been built and purified by Abraham. According to Muhammad, the Jews barred other people from visiting the holy place.[258]

Certain leaders of the Jewish tribes invited the Quraysh to join them in a confederacy with the pagan Meccans to attack the Muslims.

The Muslims dug trenches to the North of Medina to try to mitigate any hand-to-hand battles. The Meccans tried to assault the trenches but the Muslims repelled them easily. The winds also aided the Muslims as a sand storm helped turn back the attack. The Meccans and their allies withdrew, ending the battle of the trenches.

Negotiations began for the surrender of the Medina Jews. The Quraysh agreed to arbitration, allowing a Muslim named Sad, whom they believed to be moderate in his views toward them, decide their fate.

Sad came to Muhammad riding on a donkey and sat down next to the Muslim leader. "These people are ready to accept your judgment," said Muhammed.

Sad responded, "He who is subjected to razors (i.e. the male) should be killed, women and children should be enslaved, and property should be distributed."

The Prophet remarked, "You have decided in confirmation to the judgment of Allah, above the seven heavens."[259]

To avoid mass rebellion, the Muslims marched small batches of Jews to the edge of the trenches. They forced the prisoners to kneel, then raised their swords and lopped off their heads. That day, The Muslims butchered over 600

Jewish prisoners.[260]

The slaughter of the surrendered Jews is an example of Muhammad embracing a policy of brutality in accordance with his religious beliefs. Various Muslim historians have gone out of their way to justify the executions, usually with the claim that the Jews engaged in political treason. Others simply ignore the event.[261]

The attacks on the caravans and the executions, however, demonstrate an affinity with Christianity that emerged after the third century. Holy war and slaughter in the name of God came to permeate religion during the middle ages. Islam today accepts Jesus as a prophet who preached peace, but Muhammad embodied all the characteristics of all the prophets and was the culmination of them all. Islam, according to this view, is a religion that needs to be protected by force. Muhammad, like the Christianity of his day, shunned the teaching of Jesus that His followers should not strike back at their enemies.[262]

As early as 626, Muhammad sent small forces to fight hostile tribes in the area of Dumat al-Jandal, some five hundred miles northeast of Medina. He also sent emissaries into to a number of prominent Arab and non-Arab rulers, including Byzantine, Iranian, and Ethiopian emperors, demanding they convert to Islam. In 630, he led an army of thirty-thousand to the frontier of Byzantium, some five-hundred miles north of Medina, forcing a treaty on the Christian ruler of Aylah, at the northern tip of Aqaba. The Christian leader agreed to an oath of Allegiance and the payment of annual tribute. When he returned, Muhammad prepared a campaign into Transjordan and southern Palestine. His death by illness in 632 cut short his plans.[263]

Muhammad's attacks on unarmed caravans, his victories over the consequential forces that rose against him, his slaughter of unarmed, surrendered Jews, and his forages into Syria left a legacy for his followers to emulate in the future.

The Islamic Empire

After Muhammad died, his father-in-law, Abu Bakr took command of the Muslims. He consolidated his control over Arabia and Iraq and set his sights on the Byzantine-held region of the Levant in Syria. He battled his way to Damascus, laying siege to the city beginning in August of 634. With the capture of the city, the Muslims could establish a base of operation by which to conquer the entire region. During the blockade, the elderly Abu Bakr died.

Umar succeeded Abu Bakr that same month. Upon the fall of Damascus in September, Umar laid the foundation for the conquests to follow by commanding his warriors: "Do not settle on the conquered territories but leave them for the whole Muslim Community. Keep riding and continue to conquer new territories." Umar established a form of payment as an incentive for the warriors to keep moving and take possession of the land.

After ravaging many of the Christian regions of Syria and Palestine, the Muslim warriors believed the "Sword of Allah" commanded them to march to Jerusalem. In of July of 636, they reached the outskirts of the city. In plotting their siege, the tradition of Muhammad's night journey must have inspired as they looked upon the city.

Thirteen years before, Muhammad had stood in front of his disciples to relate his experience. "One night the angel Gabriel came to me, bringing with him a white horse." Muhammad described how he mounted the horse and flew in the air with Gabriel to the city of Jerusalem. From there, they ascended through the seven heavens. At various levels, they stopped for the angel to introduce Muhammad to the prophets who had come before him including, Adam, Jesus, Joseph, and Moses. When Moses met Muhammad, he began to cry.

"Why the tears?" asked Gabriel.

"I led many of my followers to paradise, but this young prophet, who has come after me, will lead many more than me."

Muhammad then described reaching the seventh heaven where a voice told him his followers must pray fifty times a day. Muhammad returned to Moses to recount the voice's command. "I tried to make my followers pray fifty times a day," Moses said, "but they failed. Go back to Allah and ask for the number to be reduced."

After returning, Allah reduced the number to forty." Still too many," Moses said upon his meeting Muhammad again. "Revisit Allah and plead for the number of prayers to be reduced." This exchange occurred several times until Allah agreed to reduce the number to five.

The number still did not satisfy Moses, so he commanded Muhammad to go back again. Muhammad refused. "My Lord has shown me so much mercy that I shall not return."[264]

Now, toward the end of the year 636, as they believed they looked upon the city of Muhammad's night journey, Muslim forces plotted how they might conquer such a well-fortified metropolis. They concluded that success would come by starving the inhabitants. The warriors surrounded Jerusalem, cutting off all supplies and reinforcements.

After four months, the Christian Bishop of Jerusalem, Sophronius, decided to capitulate and negotiated terms of surrender. Not trusting the Muslim warlords, Sophronius agreed to give up only if Umar traveled from Medina and personally took control of the city.

Umar arrived dressed in shabby clothes as a sign of humility, unlike the Muslim warlords who dressed in splendid robes. The grungy appearance offended the Bishop. As the two of them toured the Church of the Holy Sepulcher, Sophronius whispered in Greek to one of his attendants, "Surely this is the abomination of desolation standing in the holy place spoken of by Daniel the Prophet."[265]

Christians had come to believe that a certain foundation site with retaining walls rising up in the northern part of Jerusalem was the original site of Solomon's Temple. In the fourth century, a Christian tourist from Bordeaux, France claimed a tradition of Jews giving reverence to a stone somewhere on top of the retaining walls. The tradition concluded that it must be the original foundation for the Temple. He wrote back to Rome with his assumption. The letter circulated and the site became known as the Temple Mount. By that time, however, the Church of the Holy Sepulcher took prominence as the temple of prophecy in many people's thinking, replacing Solomon's Temple. By the seventh century, The Jewish Temple mentioned in Daniel and the book of Revelation was now seen as symbolic for the Church of the Holy Sepulcher.[266]

Umar confiscated the site of the Temple Mount, erecting an edifice over the area that became known as the place where Muhammad took his night journey. He called it the Dome of the Rock. He then built a mosque a short distance from the Dome. Sophronius recorded the construction. "They took with them men, some by force, others by their own will, in order to clean that place and to build that cursed thing, intended for their prayer and which they call a mosque." The bishop also recorded the reason why he thought the Christians lost the city. "The godless Saracens (Muslims) entered the holy city of Christ our Lord, Jerusalem, with the permission of God and in punishment for our negligence."[267]

The loss of Jerusalem and the Holy Sepulcher shocked many Christians. As a result, certain monks from Syria studied the Judaized and Christianized Sibylline prophecies advocated by apologist, Lactantius. Originally the work of Greek pagan prophetesses, one of the divinations had come to reflect Lactantius's hope for an age of peace that he believed could arrive in the fourth century if the right emperor could take the Roman throne. From the latter part of the fourth century, after the Christian emperors had failed to deliver the new age, the prophecy needed updating. By the seventh century, the prophecy needed revising again. By 691, the Syrian monks understood the prophecy to mirror the rise of Islam, its conquest of Jerusalem, and the treatment of Christians under Muslim rule.[268]

The Last World Emperor

Starting in the year 660, in the Muslim controlled city of Singara, Orthodox Christian abbots put their pens to paper, calling for war against the Islamic infidels. The abbots wrote using a pseudonym—Methodius, a Christian martyr from the early fourth century, giving the work an air of authority. An anonymous monk put the prophecy in its final form in 691.[269]

Pseudo-Methodius began by echoing Bishop Sophonius's reason why the followers of Muhammad conquered Syria. "And so the Lord God will give them (i.e., the sons of Ishmael) the power to conquer the land of the Christians, not because he loves them, but because of the sin and iniquity committed by the Christians." As the prophecy continued, it appeared to reflect the heavy taxation levied on Christians by their Muslim overlords in 691. "The inhabitants of Egypt and Syria will be in trouble and affliction, seven times the greater for those in captivity. The Land of Promise will be filled with men from the four winds under heaven."

The author, however, brought hope to his Christian readers as a last world emperor rises to exact revenge upon Islam with the end resulting in the millennial age of peace. "The whole indignation and fury of the king of the Romans will blaze forth against those who deny the Lord Jesus Christ. Then the earth will sit in peace and there will be great peace and tranquility upon the earth such as has never been nor ever will be any more, since it is the final peace at the End of time."

The book of Revelation is then brought into play and chapter twenty's description of a final battle at the end of the millennium. "Then the 'Gates of the North' will be opened and the strength of those nations which Alexander (i.e. the last emperor) shut up there will go forth. The whole earth will be terrified at the sight of them; men will be afraid and flee in terror to hide themselves in mountains and caves and graves."

The Syrian monk then described the rise of the Antichrist and the last emperor's rule in Jerusalem "After this the king of the Romans will go down and live in Jerusalem for seven and half-seven times. When the ten and a half years are completed the Son of Perdition will appear. . . . When the Son of Perdition has arisen, the king of the Romans will ascend Golgotha upon which the wood of the Holy Cross is fixed, in the place where the Lord underwent death for us. The king will take the crown from his head and place it on the cross and stretching out his hands to heaven will hand over the kingdom of the Christians to God the Father."

The Syrian monk finished his prophecy with the return of Christ in the flesh and the destruction of the Antichrist. Thus *Pseudo-Methodius* is a hodgepodge of a sibylline prophecy mixed with John's Revelation and a postmillennial return of Christ in the flesh.[270]

By the eighth century, the Syriac original of the prophecy was soon translated into Coptic, Greek and then into Latin.[271] A number of similar prophecies emerged out of Syria and Egypt, having been written between the years 690 and 720 and generally reflect the politics of the moment. While these do not mention the idea of a last world emperor, they speak of the idea of the rise of Islam as the great apostasy at the end of time. By the year 900, however, both ideas permeated Europe. Depending on the particular advocates of the prophecy, the final world emperor would come from France or Germany.[272]

Germany and France in Prophecy

Adso, the monk of Montier-en-Der responded to a request by his queen of France, Gerberga, wife of King Louis the Fourth. With Louis's authority questioned by western Frankish dukes, Adso sought to comfort and convince the queen that prophecy, not the whims of politicians, ruled the fate of France. The monk reassured Gerberga that her empire will not fully disintegrate when he wrote, "As long as the kings of the Franks, who possess the Roman Empire by right, survive, the dignity of the Roman Empire will not perish altogether, because it will endure in the French kings."

In Adso's mind, however, the kingdom would do more than survive. The abbot went on to predict that one day, a French King will rule the world with an age of peace. "Certain of our learned men tell us that one of the kings of the Franks, who will come very soon, will possess the Roman Empire in its entirety. And he will be the greatest and last of all kings. He, after governing his kingdom prosperously, will ultimately come to Jerusalem and lay down his scepter and crown on Mount Olivet. Immediately afterwards, Antichrist will come."

Adso encouraged Louis to take up the mantle of the last world emperor.

The death of Louis in 954, however, put an end to the abbot's hopes. But others were not disillusioned, as the prophecies of the last world emperor continued to permeate the minds of Europeans.

While Adso conditioned France for the last world emperor, Benzo of Alba laid the groundwork for Germany and Italy. He ardently supported King Henry IV of Germany, and in the year 856, wrote seven books in support of the German claim over Italy as part of the Holy Roman Empire. Benzo sought to convince Henry to assume the mantle of the last emperor. "For a long road remains to him (Henry IV) as the prophecy of the Sybil testified. . . . He will lead an expedition to Jerusalem and having rescued the Sepulcher and other sanctuaries of the Lord. . . . Then will be the fulfillment of what is written: 'And His Sepulcher will be glorious.'" By 1091, the various prophecies of a last world emperor and the defeat of Islam had ripened Europe for the idea of conducting a pogrom into the Middle East to deal with the Muslim problem.

Emperor Alexius and the Muslim Threat

"They circumcise young boys over the baptismal fonts, pouring their blood into the basin and force the boys to piss into the blood." The Byzantine Emperor's letter shocked Duke Robert of Flanders. "Then they drag them around the church, forcing them to blaspheme the Holy Trinity. Those who refuse are punished in various ways and eventually killed."

In the Year 1091, Alexius I, king of the crumbling Byzantine Empire of the east, wrote a desperate letter to Robert in the Latin West, hoping for a contingent of mercenaries to come and help save his reign. Along with the above descriptions of persecutions, Alexius described the relics owned by the Eastern Church that are under threat by the Muslim insurgency. "For it is better that you should have Constantinople than the pagans because in that city rest the precious relics of the Lord: the pillar to which he was bound, the lash with which he was scourged, the scarlet robe in which he was arrayed, the crown of thorns with which he was crowned . . . the linen clothe found in the sepulcher after his resurrection."

In his shrewdness, Alexius knew the mentality of the knights of the west and he sweetened the pot by not only promising the relics, but all the riches of Byzantium to those who would help. "However, if they should be unwilling to fight for the sake of these relics, and if their love of gold is greater, they will find more of it in Constantinople than in all the world." Alexius's feared that if the treasure fell into the hands of the enemy, the Muslims would seduce his remaining forces to switch sides. So it would be better to give the treasure to the Latins and possibly save his reign.

The emperor finished the letter by referencing the prophecies that circulated in the Christian churches, as well as a warning of an invasion of France by the Muslims: "If Byzantium falls, I fear that by means of this treasure the Muslims will gradually seduce our covetous soldiers, as did formerly Julius Caesar who by reason of avarice invaded the kingdom of the Franks and as antichrist will do at the end of the world after he has captured the whole earth. Therefore, lest you should lose the kingdom of the Christians and, what is greater but the Lord's Sepulcher, act while you still have time." Despite the passionate pleas and the promise of riches, initially no mercenaries answered his call, perhaps because they did not trust him, knowing his tendency to manipulate his alliances.[273] They also may have wanted to await the pope's response.

The letter caught the attention of Pope Urban II. The perfect scenario had just dropped into the pontiff's lap—Alexius's willingness to put the church of Constantinople under the authority of Rome. However, he needed more than the situation in Constantinople. As the evidence from the prophecy of the last world emperor testifies, Western Europe desired the liberation of Jerusalem. Urban was in a position to create the perfect storm—persecutions of Christians in Turkey, and the hope of liberating the Holy Sepulcher to bring about Christ's return, could amass a crusade to reunify all of Christianity under his reign. The pope may have persuaded Robert to wait for the proper time for a crusade that he hoped would reach much further than Constantinople.

Over the next few years the situation became dire for Alexius. It was clear he needed to give a greater incentive for the mercenaries to come and help him. By the year 1095, he sent envoys to Pope Urban's Council of Piacenza, urging the liberation of Jerusalem. If mercenaries wouldn't come for the riches of Constantinople, he may have thought they would be enticed by both the riches of the entire Middle East and the liberation of the Holy Sepulcher.[274] At the Council, Pope Urban urged many to take an oath to help Alexius against the Muslims.[275]

In July of 1095, the pontiff laid the groundwork for the Council of Clermont by beginning his tour of France. When he reached Burgundy, believed to be in late October, members of a regional council in Autun witnessed the first vows for the Jerusalem journey.[276]

Urban underestimated the appeal of his preaching as throngs answered his call for Holy War. The end result, however, pleased him as the fifteen thousand remaining crusader knights made it to Jerusalem and breached its defenses in July of 1099. When they climbed over the walls of that city, they had one thing on their mind—cleanse Jerusalem and the Holy Sepulcher of the infidels.

The Crusaders' Final Onslaught

As the siege towers helped open the walls and crusaders poured into Jerusalem, the Muslim warriors in the south retreated to the area of the Dome of the Rock and the mosque while news of the breach caused those in the northern part of the city to flee to the Citadel. The Jews barricaded themselves in their great synagogue. In the south, the Christian soldiers overtook the defenders before they could fully secure the Temple Mount, slaughtering most of the Muslim warriors. The survivors sought refuge in the mosque, along with many of the Muslim civilians who gathered at the holy site for Friday prayers. The crusader commander, Tancred called a halt to the killing, promising safety to those inside.

Tancred's promise came to nothing as his men ignored the pledge and tore through the mosque, slaughtering ten thousand people. Raymond of Aguilers recounted the carnage. "But these were small matters compared with what happened in the Temple of Solomon, a place where religious services are normally chanted. What happened there? If I tell the truth, you would not believe it. Suffice to say that, in the Temple and Porch of Solomon, men rode in blood up to their knees and bridle reins. Indeed, it was a just and splendid judgment of God that this place should be filled with the blood of the unbelievers, since it had suffered so long from their blasphemies. The city was filled with corpses and blood."[277]

Robert may have been exaggerating in order to relate the slaughter to the book of Revelation, chapter 14:20. There is no doubt, however, that the carnage was significant. Another witness expresses what might be considered a more accurate account of the overall killing in Jerusalem when he wrote, "Indeed, if you had been there you would have seen our feet colored to our ankles with the blood of the slain. But what more shall I relate? None of them were left alive; neither women nor children were spared."[278] And Albert of Aachen, a critic of the crusade who interviewed a number of returning crusaders, wrote this: "The Christians gave over their whole hearts to slaughter, so that not a suckling little male child or female, not even an infant of one year would escape alive the hand of the murderer."

The crusaders showed no more mercy to the Jews than they did to the Muslims. Perhaps they had the theology of Ambrose of Milan in their minds as they set fire to the Synagogue, burning men, women, and children in the blazing ordeal. Some of the Jews had been captured outside the Synagogue and later put to work piling bodies of the slain outside the city for cremation.[279]

When the killing ended, a mass of dead bodies littered Jerusalem. The priests, monks, and knights sloshed their way through the blood–drenched streets. As they reached the Church of the Holy Sepulcher, they funneled into the building. And they worshiped God.[280]

While Urban II called for the first crusade, it can be said that the crusaders actually took their marching orders from the symbolizers of the book of Revelation. Unlike the early premillennialists, the knights of Europe refused to wait for Christ to return in the flesh before attempting to implement the millennium. Following the theology of the fourth century church fathers, the crusaders tried to realize the age of peace by massacring their enemies and liberating the Sepulcher.

In the years to come, Islam struck back, and the age of peace remained elusive. As you will see later in chapter twenty, Muslims reacted to the loss of Jerusalem with its own version of a prophecy that mimicked aspects of the last world emperor. They transitioned an Islamic prophecy from the early eighth century concerning a march to capture Damascus and reconfigured it to predict a re-conquering of Jerusalem. The prophecy would continue to attain followers long after the middle ages. Some nine-hundred years later, this prediction concerning black flags from the ancient region of Khurasan would be used to incite terrorist activities across the globe and inspire the current quest for weapons of mass destruction.[281]

For Christians, despite of the failure of the First Crusade to realize the millennium, they would continue to hold to symbolic interpretations and put faith in Christianized pagan prophecies. And the Church of the Holy Sepulcher would remain at the forefront of prophecy. In the midst of future Islamic wars, a new voice would arise, claiming a new vision of John's revelation. While Joachim of Fiore would put forth the idea of a peaceful transition to the millennium, his historicist interpretation would eventually be used in later centuries to help usher in more violent conflicts and revolutions as the Christian church would continue its pursuit of the millennium.

RICHARD THE LIONHEARTED dispatched a message to Joachim, the head of the monastery at Fiore. Many believed this monk possessed the gift of prophecy and had been given supernatural insights into the book of Revelation. Richard craved knowledge of the future, for he planned to launch a third crusade to retake Jerusalem after the city had fallen to the cunning Muslim warrior, Saladin. Richard hoped Joachim would offer him good news about things yet to come.

On a winter's day in the city of Messina, Sicily, in the year 1190, Joachim met with Richard and his entourage of English clerics. The monk opened Revelation, chapter 16 and began to expound. "Of the dragon with seven heads, the first five have fallen." Joachim interpreted the five as Herod, Nero, Constantine, Muhammad, and the Muslim leader, Melsemutus. "Saladin is the one that is," he continued, "but he will fall." The abbot turned to Richard. "The one who has not yet come, this is the Antichrist. He is fifteen years old, but not yet in power."

"Where was the Antichrist born," asked Richard, "and where is he to reign?"

"He was born in Rome, and he will attain the office of the papacy."

"If born in Rome and to occupy the Apostolic See, then I believe the Antichrist is Clement who is now pope," responded Richard, for the count despised Clement. Richard then put forward the standard belief that the Antichrist is supposed to rule in Babylon. Upon his statement, the priests erupted into a heated debate, calling Joachim's views into question. The count, however, took solace in that Joachim had prophesied the defeat of Saladin. Richard continued to prepare for war.[282]

In time, Joachim would alter his view of the Christian crusades, prophesying a peaceful transition to the millennium. For now, however, he still followed the current prophetic tradition that foresaw the Muslims' downfall as one step in the march to the age of peace. After the victories of the First Crusade, Muslim counterattacks had retaken much of the Syrian territories, including Jerusalem. With the losses, some doubts began to seep into Europe concerning the prophetic idealism of the First Crusade. It would take one more crusader defeat to shake Joachim into a new theology of the book of Revelation. The first defeat began forty-four years before Richard's meeting with Joachim and ended with the emergence of a new Muslim hero.

The Second Crusade and Rise of Saladin

With no trained army, Edessa's Christian population had no knowledge in anti-mining tactics to counteract the siege. After the tunnels undermined the wall's foundation, a portion collapsed, allowing the Muslim warriors free access into the city. The Muslim forces rushed in, slaughtering all they encountered—

men, women, and children. As one chronicler put it, "They butchered the widow, the stranger, the orphan, the youth, the virgin, and the old man."[283]

As the enemy hoard moved to the inner parts of Edessa, hundreds of Christians dashed to barricade themselves in the citadel, hoping to find respite from the massacre. Scores of people suffocated in the throngs that squeezed through the doors, groping and trampling over one another. Archbishop Hugh died in the chaos. The chronicler wrote that the cleric had accumulated vast sums of money for his personal benefit. If he had spent some of the money on an army, he might have averted the disaster.[284]

The county of Edessa was one of three crusader states established after the First Crusade. Its collapse in 1144 alarmed the west and fear spread that all crusader gains would soon be lost. In the year 1145, Pope Eugenius III penned his encyclical *Quantum Praedecessores* calling for a second crusade. He appealed for a new war based on the idea that if one truly loved God, he would slay Christianity's enemies, for those who answered the call for the First Crusade had been "fired by the passion of love."[285] With his Bull, he brought a new take on Augustine's proclamation that state-sponsored heresy laws were acts of love to maintain the unity of the church. The assault by the Muslims put the unity of Christendom at stake, and the pontiff's thought was a natural progression in Augustinian theology.

Despite of the alarm that they may lose Jerusalem, Western Europeans gave a lukewarm response to Eugenius. The pope recruited Abbott Bernard of Clairvaux to incite the masses. Both the peasants and the monarchs responded to the monk's fiery preaching. The Second Crusade was launched in 1146.

The crusade proved disastrous. It failed to recapture Edessa, and more important, it energized the Muslim world. The mystique of crusader invincibility drained away with the spilled blood of the fallen Christian knights. Now the Muslim's hope of re-conquering Jerusalem and the other crusader territories became more than wishful thinking. The optimism gave rise to one of the greatest of Muslim warriors. Saladin would lead his forces to Jerusalem's door steps.

In the year 1137 a man of Kurdish background named his new-born son Yusuf. Soon after his birth, the boy's father was banished in shame from the city of Takreet on the Tigris River. The Muslim world would normally view such an event so close to Yusuf's birth as a bad omen for the son. Later, however, it would be said, "Good may come out of adversity. And such was the case with Yusuf."[286]

Yusuf grew up as a Muslim in Damascus. In his adolescence, he chased after wine and women, but at some point, he converted to a strong Islamic faith, renouncing his former ways. Under his mentor, Nur ad-Din, it was said that he learned to walk in the path of righteousness, to act virtuously, and to be zealous in waging war against the infidels.[287] Eventually Yusuf became known as Saladin, meaning "righteousness of faith."

In 1163, Nur ad-Din sought to strike back at the crusader occupation of Syria and ordered Saladin to accompany his uncle in invading enemy territory. After a number of failures, Saladin took control of the army and led warriors to a series of victories. By 1175 he took power over Egypt and Syria. After being heralded Sultan of Egypt he proclaimed, "When God gave me the land of Egypt, I was sure He meant Palestine for me as well."[288]

By 1187, Saldin had captured almost every crusader city in Palestine. Jerusalem remained. By September 20 of that year, Saladin's forces arrived outside the city.

The Muslim Siege of Jerusalem

Some sixty thousand Christians flocked to Jerusalem hoping the city's sacredness would protect them from the Muslim onslaughts. The Christian military prepared for siege by deepening the moat and fortifying the walls. The population prayed that the strengthening of the defenses and God's blessing would be enough to stop Saladin. They knew well the stories of the slaughtering of Muslim women and children that took place at the hands of the first crusaders. And Saladin knew them as well.

As the Muslims laid siege to the city, Saladin addressed his commanders: "I want to take Jerusalem the way the Christians took it from the Muslims ninety-one years ago. They inundated the city in blood, leaving it not a moment's peace. I will slaughter the men, and the women I will make slaves." [289]

The Muslims' intense bombardment and mining tactics created a breach in the northern wall. The Christian Franks knew no reinforcements were coming. In desperation, the City's commander, Balian, threatened to kill all Muslim hostages and obliterate the Mosque and Dome of the Rock if Saladin refused to negotiate. Saladin agreed to make terms and took possession of Jerusalem with no bloodshed. The Muslim leader, however, looted the churches, enslaved sixteen thousand people, collected ransoms from others, but set the elderly free.

Saladin's entourage met to discuss the future of the Church of the Holy Sepulcher. Perhaps a decision to destroy the edifice might have mitigated prophetic speculation by the Christians. The Muslim leader, instead, chose to allow the building to stand and bring revenue into Muslim coffers with a heavy charge to all pilgrims visiting it.[290]

With the fall of Jerusalem, Saladin had now conquered most of the crusader territory. It was Jerusalem's capitulation, however, that most captured and enraged the imaginations of Europe. Pope Eugenius put forward the call for the Third Crusade. Richard the lionhearted answered the plea.

The Third Crusade

Richard met with Joachim in the winter of 1190, receiving the prophecy he had hoped to hear. By the summer of that year, he set out for the crusade, joined by the Germans and the French. After fighting for over a year and following a series of victories, the prize of Jerusalem lay within their reach.

The coastal city of Darum had fallen to the crusaders in May of 1191, eliminating a strategic stronghold for Saladin and laying open a march to Jerusalem. Richard, however, fell into depression. Domestic problems at home called for his attention, and he contemplated abandoning the crusade and returning to England.

As the armies moved north, Richard continued to receive bad news from home. In June 5, while camped at Ascalon, Richard wandered aimlessly in an orchard outside the city. A monk confronted him. "May God forbid that uncertain reports from overseas turn you away from recovering this land. Remember when you came here from the Western world, you were everywhere victorious and your enemies lay in chains at your feet."

The following day, Richard addressed the troops. He proclaimed to the army that he would not depart for home but stay until the following Easter. He ordered his soldiers to prepare for the siege of Jerusalem. When they heard his words, the crusaders dropped to their knees and prayed in thanksgiving. With Richard leading the way, they were fully confident that the nave of the Holy Sepulcher would, once again, run red with the blood of Muslims and Jews.[291]

On June 24, the crusaders camped at Beit Nuba on the outskirts of Jerusalem. Saladin evacuated civilians from the city. The European knights brimmed with confidence. Two days prior, however, a monk with the gift of prophecy had strutted into the crusader camp and prophesied to Richard that his quest would fail. Richard lost his nerve.

With depression appearing to rule his emotions and the ability to make sound decisions, Richard met with members of his council and told them the situation remained hopeless. The council erupted, but no protest could assuage or change his mind. On July 6, the crusader force retreated from Bet Nuba. The Third Crusade ended in defeat. [292]

The failure of the Third Crusade began to raise doubts that military crusades could take back the Holy Sepulcher and lead to the emergence of the last world emperor. Even before the latest campaign, however, one seer questioned that the crusaders could pave the way for the age of peace. A prophet named Matthew would help influence some to shy away from military might and turn to hope for a peaceful transition to the millennium.

Matthew of Edessa

Abbot Mathew lived and wrote in Edessa during the years leading up to the Muslim conquest of 1144. Some historians believed he died in the city's collapse.

As a member of the Armenian Orthodox Church, he marked a contrast against the Latin belief that the crusaders would help usher in the last world emperor and the age of peace. Part of Matthew's agenda was to explain why the crusader capture of Jerusalem in 1099 failed to lead to the millennial golden era. For Matthew, the crusaders encompassed both virtue and villainy. At times, they acted with compassion toward the Muslims and Greek Christians. Other times, however, they were capable of gross atrocities and lewd conduct. Matthew wrote that Islam had to resurge as a result of crusader inconsistencies with Christianity.

Matthew used prophecy as the foundation for a chronicle of the Armenian people. The Abbot proclaimed that God would punish the Armenians for their sins, but they could look forward to the eventual redemption through God's mercy. In this scenario, God was not finished using the Muslims as an instrument of his judgment.

Gleaning from an earlier prediction by a man Matthew names as Mark the hermit, the monk explained how Mark predicted a period of thirty years of Muslim re-conquests. Matthew wrote: "He (Mark) prophesied about the Franks that when they took the holy city of Jerusalem, the Persian nation (Islam) would again strengthen itself and would come with the sword up to the coast of the great sea, which indeed we have seen."

As Muslim warriors began to retake large portions of crusader territory, Matthew took a pessimistic view of the immediate state of affairs and the crusaders' ability to quell the onslaught. In spite of his cynical view toward the crusaders, however, he believed that the last world emperor would soon arise as the Abbot pointed to a "great and marvelous comet" that had appeared in the year 1106. This portent marked the birth of the emperor: "The wise men and the experienced ones said, 'This is a royal star; a king will be born in this year who will rule over all creation, and his kingdom will stretch from sea to sea, like the great Alexander of Macedon.'"[293] So Matthew abandoned the hope that the crusaders would lead to the millennium but maintained the idea of the last world emperor.

With the fall of Edessa and the failure of both the Second and Third Crusades, Matthew's pessimism spilled into the west. As his writings took an evolutionary turn, Joachim of Fiore would not only de-emphasize the crusades but also the last world emperor and the very concept of violence leading to the millennium. He would not, however, return to the theology of Irenaeus and the early church's futurist premillennial understanding of the book of Revelation. For Joachim, a group of spiritually endowed monks would help guide the world into the age of peace.

Historical Interpretation and the Third Status

Joachim wrote his exposition on the book of Revelation in 1180 and spent the next two decades revising it until his death in 1202. While he initially appeared to support the Lionheart's expedition, one of his greatest revisions came with Richard's defeat at Jerusalem. In Joachim's new thinking, neither the crusades nor a last world emperor would bring about the age of peace. The monk came to criticize the church's reliance on materialism and its use of force to protect itself.[294]

As his eschatology evolved, the book of Revelation represented the entire span of church history. Joachim's overarching theology divided history into three ages or 'status,' as he called each of the ages. He borrowed from the fourth century teacher Tychonius in symbolically interpreting literal days into years. He differed from Tychonius, however, in that he applied 1260 days mentioned in Daniel and Revelation into 1260 years for each status. The second status began with the advent of Christ and would run 1, 260 years, ending in A.D. 1260. Thus he believed he stood on the threshold of the third status. While Tyconius put forth concepts that would lead to the historical understanding of Revelation, Joachim systematized and developed the interpretation.[295]

"The likeness of the third status must be sought in the birds that fly up to heaven; in the clarity of the sun. Its marks are liberty and spiritual understanding." Joachim wrote in poetic metaphors in his description of the millennium. Its spiritual intelligence, according to the Abbot, would proceed from the authority of the Old and New Testaments and it would be established by a new, contemplative monastic order. All the current orders of monks and priests were meant to pass away. Thus a revolutionary concept emerged out of Joachim's pen—the whole current established church hierarchy was destined to become extinct and replaced by a new social order.[296]

This new order, however, would still have its ruling pontiffs, for the contemplative order will include seven divisions—five devoted to the monastic life, one division to the clergy, and one to married men. In the third status, all mankind would merge into the new order with a select contemplative group of monks at the head of the hierarchy. The third status would be marked with a transition stage preceded by conflict with the Antichrist. The transition stage would be heralded by the sounding of the seventh trumpet recorded in Revelation, chapter fourteen. Upon the trumpet blast, one of the divisions of monks would descend from the contemplative life of prayer to the preaching life, and effectively evangelize the world.

Joachim saw the church as corrupt and decadent. Helping to pave the way for these monks in the transition from the second status would be the angelic pope. Joachim believed this pope would be angelic in his divine message and would reform the corrupt nature of the church from within.[297]

Within his framework of history, Muslims played their part as God's instrument of chastising the church, helping to lead to its reform. The crusades, however, could not bring about the third status. At the appointed time God would convert the Muslims, the Jews, and the Greek Christians to the fold of the Latin Church by way of the preaching by the angelic pope and the spiritual monks.

Joachim de-emphasized any need for the church to rely on the civil government to help bring about the millennial age. This era of peace, however, would manifest itself prior to the second coming of Christ. Thus the Abbot maintained the postmillennial ideas that began in the fourth century with Lactantius and Eusebius. As the centuries progressed, his writings and theological concepts would be joined with other writings that purported to be written by the monk. In spite of Joachim's hope for a peaceful transition to the millennium, pseudo-Joachimist documents would maintain the idea of a last world emperor and postmillennialism would continue to inspire future conflicts and wars.[298]

Pseudo-Joachim and the Last World Emperor

Although Joachim's writings ignored politics and political solutions, followers of the seer sought to apply the concept of the third status to the realm of political prophecy. In about the middle of the thirteenth century, a document purported to be written by Joachim to the Emperor Henry VI, described the

German Fredrick II as the seventh head of the dragon, or in other words, the Antichrist. The work emanated from an Italian group.

Germans countered the Italians, recasting Fredrick as the last world emperor who Joachim supposedly prophesied would chastise the church and bring about its renewal. Another German document proposed a third Fredrick. And still another, this time with a French bias, proposed a political champion who destroys Fredrick and helps the angelic pope in ushering in the third status. The thirteenth and fourteenth centuries witnessed a barrage of such writings, merging Joachim's third status with the political.[299]

Perhaps the most influential of the pseudo documents were those that found their way into Spanish culture. As Spain began to embark on an age of discovery, A young Genoese dreamed of finding a new path to the Indies. Christopher Columbus would cite Joachim as his inspiration as he came to believe God had destined him to find fame and fortune in his journeys across the Atlantic. Convinced God had called him to finance a crusader army, Columbus would seek an age of gold that he hoped would lead the king of Spain to the doorsteps of Jerusalem and the Holy Sepulcher. Instead, the prophecies of pseudo-Joachim and the discovery of a new world would help lead a young Spanish conquistador to wage war in the mountains of Mexico.[300]

Just prior to Columbus's first voyage, however, pseudo-Joachim would also influence a fiery Italian monk to take on the corruption and decadence of church and government. You will now experience how Savonarola sought to create a New Jerusalem in Renaissance Florence with the hope of shedding its light to the entire world.

IN THE MONASTERY OF SAN MARCOS, Cardinal Giovanni de Medici donned the robe of a monk, pulling the hood over his forehead to keep his face from being seen. On this day of November 9, 1494, the city of Florence blazed with rebellion as mobs rushed the streets and back allies. In the turmoil, the rabble cried-out for the deaths of the ruling Medici family. Several hours earlier, Giovanni had collected gold, jewels, and coins from the family palace, bringing them to the abbey. With the help of monks still loyal to him, he slipped into the attire of a Franciscan. Now, taking his treasure with him, he used the disguise to flee the city to safety. When the mob realized he eluded them, they put a price on his head. The cardinal, however, would one day return in an attempt to capture and re-control the city as a stepping stone to becoming one of the most powerful men in Europe.

The uprising had been brewing for some time, sparked by a Dominican monk named Savonarola. The monk had locked horns against Lorenzo, Giovanni's father. The Medici had created a city that helped to perpetuate the humanist movement of what became known as the Renaissance. In contrast, Savonarola sought to remake Florence as a New Jerusalem that would become a spiritual light to what he viewed as a corrupt society and church. As Giovanni took flight from the city, it appeared that Savonarola won the day.

As he made his way from Florence to seek refuge in Rome, the cardinal must have wondered how an ugly little monk had risen to such a state as to successfully challenge the power of the Medici family. Now the rebellion threw everything into doubt, including his father's dream for Giovanni to ascend to the rank of the papacy. The cardinal knew he would have his work cut out for him to reestablish his control of Florence.

The battle between Savonarola and the Medici would demonstrate how a city could erupt into revolution. One day Giovanni would inspire an even greater rebellion against him. This revolt would not only cause the upheaval of a city, but turn much of the known world upside down. The story of Savonarola and the Medici, however, began twenty-six years earlier in AD 1482 when the monk first entered Florence.

Lorenzo's Florence

As Savonarola walked into Florence through one of its immense gates, he strode down streets of multistoried houses and passed people of every class: noblemen, laborers, beggars, slaves, and gangs of rowdy adolescents casting stones at each other in dangerous street games. Above all the groups, however, these unruly youths caught the monk's attention. One day they would become the focus of his compassion, and in turn the young people would follow Savonarola with an intense devotion.

The city Savonarola found stood at the forefront of a cultural transformation in Italy that began in the fourteenth century. By the fifteenth century, spurred by an industry in producing textiles, the city boasted a population of 40, 000 individuals and seventy banking houses—more than in any other country in Europe. A wide variety of artists and poets sought prosperity in Florence. The city's uniqueness could also be seen in its form of government. While princely aristocracies ruled many municipalities, a republic ruled the Florentines by way of a pyramid of councils ascending to the top with the eight-person Signori and the Gonfalonier of Justice who were selected by lot every two months.[301]

The time for the people to rule themselves, however, came to an end with the rise of Cosimo de Medici in the year 1415. He inherited one of the largest banks in Florence from his father and set about increasing the institution's wealth by establishing branches in all major Italian cities, as well as London and Bruges, thus dwarfing the fortunes of all competing banks. By 1434, Cosimo had developed a sophisticated political machine. Although the Signory and Gonfalonier continued to be selected by lot, Medici wealth and influence insured that anyone selected to office supported the family. In turn, the councils made no decisions without first consulting Cosimo. Florentine society became intertwined with the interests of the Medici—the best jobs, offices, honors, lighter taxes, favor in the law courts, church benefices, and the most suitable marriage matches went to close Medici supporters.[302]

In 1464, Cosimo died, leaving his fortune and Florentine rule to his son Peiro. Five years later, however, Peiro died and his first son Lorenzo took over the Medici reins. Lorenzo had honed his diplomatic skills as early as fifteen years of age when his father had sent him on a mission to the pope to secure a monopoly on the lucrative mining and trade of alum, a mineral salt used to fix vivid dyes on cloth. The papacy controlled half of the proceeds from the entire industry and Lorenzo's success brought the Medici bank an unparalleled financial windfall.[303]

Lorenzo's education focused on the humanism that permeated Florence under Medici rule. The fifteenth century witnessed a re-birth in the knowledge of the Greek classical pagan literature with an emphasis on humanity's self-importance. With the fresh learning came a profound confidence in the potential achievements of mankind. Original ways of painting and architecture and knowledge of every kind exploded out of Florence and across the landscape of Italy.

Along with this classical education, Lorenzo also embraced and helped perpetuate the loosening of traditional, medieval moral values. The Medici had long been patrons of the visual arts, sponsoring and financially aiding promising young artists. Perhaps as early as the 1440's, the family commissioned Donatello to sculpt a statue of Florence's patron saint—King David. The work is remarkable in expressing an effeminate David. But Donatello's art simply reflected a city widespread with homosexual pedophilia.

In spite of laws against sodomy, by the year 1440, under Medici influence, Florentine society had become a protectorate and encourager of pedophilia. Parents actively persuaded their sons between the ages of ten to fourteen to become homosexual in the hopes that their availability would win them the good graces of financially and politically powerful pedophile patrons. It was said that "parents turned their boys into girls," so intent were they to win honors and offices for them. Cosimo de Medici in turn, protected his clientage. When officials arrested any patrons on sodomy charges, Cosimo made sure the courts released them. Related to such actions, political factions were held together by homosexual allegiances.[304]

By the year 1467, all of Italy knew the Florentines by a popular proverb: "If you want to have some fun, have sexual relations frequently with boys." As an example of the proverb in action, an anonymous informer in Florence pleaded with city officials to do something to limit the rampant pedophilia when he wrote, "Antonio de Michael keeps Jacobi Ciafferi for use as a woman. Please lord officials do something . . . he's only eleven years old." Generally speaking, the homosexual community considered it uncouth to have sex with adults, and adult unions rarely occurred. Sexual relations initiated by adult males with passive boys from the age of twelve were so common some historians have labeled Renaissance Florence as a city of pederasty.[305]

Lorenzo's own engagement in the arts included his writing of lewd ballads for pageants that he sponsored in order to keep the populace entertained. In his *Song of the Peasants,* he paid homage to oral sex when he wrote:

> We've all got cucumbers, and big ones too
> Use both hands to pluck them,
> Expose the top, peeling back the skin.
> Open wide your mouth and suck them in.

Lorenzo used such entertainments to pacify a populace that knew the Medici had stolen its form of government. While the city remained a republic in pretense, the citizens understood how the Medici worked to rule with bribery, graft, and corruption. They also knew that any resident that dared to speak out in public against the family would end up in banishment or prison.

While Lorenzo enjoyed personal power over the citizenry, he desired to leave even greater control to his family. Upon his death, he hoped to bequeath the city to his eldest son, Piero. For his second son, Giovanni, Lorenzo had even greater plans. His designs included installing Giovanni into one of the greatest seats of power in Christendom—the papacy itself.

The Ascendancy of Giovanni de Medici

Giovanni's rise to prominence began on December 10, 1475 when an omen seemed to suggest great things for him. On that night, Clarice Orsini dreamed she labored to deliver a docile lion, an animal exuding strength but also gentleness. About twenty-four hours later, she gave birth to Giovanni de Medici. She probably spent many nights pondering the mystical meaning of her vision. Years later, Giovanni would change his name in deference to the dream.[306]

Lorenzo worked to extend the family's power by forging connections with the papacy. He married his daughter to Pope Innocent III's illegitimate son. As the head of the Medici Bank, he accepted the mineral alum instead of cash for repayment on papal loans. He continually sent gifts directly to the pope through his papal couriers. With the seductions complete, in 1489 the pope lifted the age restrictions and made the thirteen-year-old Giovanni a Cardinal.[307]

With Giovanni's appointment, everything of which Lorenzo dreamed seemed to be coming to pass. The next step in his plan came in the year 1490 when he asked Savonarola to instruct Giovanni in theology. What he failed to discern, however, was the slow rumblings of an ideological earthquake that would shake the Medici family to its core. Unbeknown to the Medici patriarch, Savonarola had his own plans to remake Florence into the New Jerusalem. The ideal heavenly city included the destruction of Medici power and a return to a true republic.

Enter Savonarola

While the story of Lorenzo and Savonarola took a turn in the year 1490, the monk's plans had been brewing for some time. In 1482, the head of the Dominicans had ordered Savonarola to Florence's monastery of San Marcos where he would take up the position of chief lecturer in theology and Scripture. He found the friars in Florence and the monastery to be much different than in other towns. San Marcos came under the patronage of Lorenzo, and as such, vows of poverty were nonexistent. The Dominicans lived in opulence, wearing designer silk robes and enjoying the best food and wine. They lived off the money provided by Lorenzo, as well as rents from the lands that Cosimo had given the monastery. When Savonarola left the walls of the cloister to take walks among the poor, they showed him nothing but disdain. As far as they were concerned, he was a Dominican—one of Lorenzo's men.[308]

Savonarola's preaching during the first two years in Florence had little effect. Through the course of his sermons and lectures, he had shown a keen knowledge of medieval scholasticism and humanist philosophy, but he delivered the content in a dry and emotionless manner. Savonarola wrote of his own performance, "I had neither the voice, nor strength, nor the ability to preach: as a result everyone was bored when I delivered my sermons."[309]

When he wasn't offering his dull subject matter, Savonarola spent his time observing the workings of the Florentine society and government, as well as the condition of the city's clergy. By 1484, feelings about his own worthlessness coincided with the disgust he felt over the destitute state of the poor, the loss of liberty of the citizens, and the lust and greed that permeated the streets of Florence. One day in the latter part of that year, Savonarola's belief in his irrelevancy began to change as he accompanied a fellow monk to visit his sister at the convent at San Giorgio.

The Church's Scourge

Savonarola waited for his friend in the churchyard outside the convent. As he sat down to compose a sermon, a revelation struck him: God proclaimed several reasons to bring tribulation to the church. The monk's enlightenment gave him a new sense of purpose.

In the following year, Savonarola began a series of Lenten sermons in the town of San Gimignano based on his revelation. The orations had a three-point objective: first, that God would afflict the church, second, that He would then renew it, and third, that this would happen soon. The reasons for God's displeasure included a clergy corrupted by sexual lust and the desire to live a luxurious lifestyle.

For Savonarola, the greatest offense came by the way of simony—the selling of church offices out of personal ambition and financial gain. To hear the preacher mention simony must have awakened the sleeping congregation because it clearly challenged a practice that many people knew characterized the office of Pope Innocent VIII who had recently taken over for Sixtus IV. The monk composed a poem for one of these sermons that allegorized this particular vice: "When did I see that haughty woman enter Rome." The woman in the sonnet personified ecclesiastic ambition.[310]

In another poem he had written earlier, *De ruina Ecclesiae,* he described the Church as a virgin who took him by the hand and led him to a cavern. "When I beheld blind ambition invading Rome and contaminate all things," she tells the monk, "I sought refuge here." While never mentioning the pope by name, the poem echoed the feelings of many as it had been common knowledge that Pope Sixtus IV had bribed his way into office and continued to decimate it through nepotism. Long before he started his war with the Medici, Savonarola began an ideological conflict against the Vatican.[311]

In the course of the sermons, Savonarola explained to his audiences that through the biblical prophecies God had sent prophets to warn mankind of what would soon happen: wars, plagues, famines, and the coming of the Antichrist. The preacher was a man of his times, accepting the concepts of medieval postmillennialism and the historical interpretation of the book of Revelation begun by Tychonius and popularized by Joachim of Fiore. According to Savonarola, the book of Revelation foretold of seven ages in church history. For the Dominican, the fourth age, the period of indifference, was coming to a close. Tribulation would usher the church into the fifth age, a time of conversion and renewal.

While still not having honed his preaching skills, his sermons proved popular, for here was a man who did not fear speaking out against a corrupt power. By associating sections of the book of Revelation to describing the condition of the papacy, Savonarola entered dangerous territory. The monk, however, avoided any harsh reactions from the Vatican by never referring directly to the pope by name.

After finishing his sermons, Savonarola returned to Florence. The lectures expanded his reputation and several months later, the head of the Dominican order appointed him as Master of Studies at the theological school in his hometown of Bologna. In 1490, the monk returned to Florence at the request of Lorenzo to instruct Giovanni in theology. Lorenzo did not know, however, that the monk believed he had been given another vision. The scourge of God would include the city of Florence and its Medici-controlled government.

In Savonarola's dream state, he trekked up to paradise accompanied by four companions: Faith, Prayer, Patience, and Simplicity. The monk often referred to the poor as simple folk. Entering into the heavenly realm, he and his fellow pilgrims passed streams, trees, doors, and thrones until they stood before the bejeweled chair of the Virgin Mary.

"The city of Florence shall become more glorious, more powerful, and wealthier than it has ever been," Mary informed the Dominican. Before this could occur, however, the radiant woman described how the city needed to be chastised along with the church: "Therefore, let it not seem strange that Florence shall have her share of troubles, though she shall suffer less than the rest . . . The good citizens will be less afflicted, according to their conduct, and in particular according to how severely they pass laws against the blasphemers, the gamblers, the sodomites and other evil doers." With those words, the Virgin dismissed Savonarola from her presence.

Savonarola's vision took the idea of God's scourge beyond the renovation of the church. God's acts of purification would begin first and foremost with a reformation of Florence in both the personal morals of its people and the restructuring of its government. When the monk returned to the city and began preaching, the sermons eventually focused on the long-lost republic. Savonarola put forward his ideas for a democratic theocracy.

The monk preached his first sermons in the monastery of San Marcos and gained such a reaction that the monastic prior selected him to give the Lenten sermons for the following year in Florence's main church, the Cathedral of Santa Maria. As he stood in the pulpit, he no longer spoke sheepishly, but thundered on the themes from the book of Revelation and the tribulations that he believed would soon come. Bellowing for the city to repent, he included a reformation of the banking system and an end to "unjust taxes that are grinding down the poor." At such outbursts, the city's destitute flocked to the cathedral as they no longer considered the monk 'one of Lorenzo's men.'

On April 6, 1491, Savonarola preached to a private audience of government officials. "Everything that is good and everything that is evil in this city depends on the man who rules it." The words shocked the listeners as the monk continued. "Tyrants never change their ways . . . and refuse to return what they have stolen from the people. . . . They corrupt the voters, employ criminal tax collectors, and thus make it even worse for the poor." [312]

Lorenzo now regretted bringing the Dominican back to Florence and reacted by sending the young Giovanni to study theology in Pisa. He also worked to undermine Savonarola by pitting the city's Augustinian and Franciscan orders against him. Friar Mariano, the leader of the Augustinians, began attacking the Dominican in his sermons, labeling Savonarola as a false prophet. Savonarola fired back in one of his own lectures: "Who was it that suggested you should attack me?" The congregation understood the reference to mean that Lorenzo had Mariano under his thumb. The Augustinian left the city for Rome in disgrace and sought his revenge by working to influence the pope against Savonarola.[313]

In spite of Lorenzo's schemes against Savonarola, the monk's popularity continued to grow throughout the year of 1491. By mid-year, a contingent came to the Dominican warning him that if he did not change the content of his preaching, he would likely be banished. "Although I am a stranger in this city," answered Savonarola, "and Lorenzo is the most powerful man in Florence, it is I who will remain here and he who will depart. He will be gone long before me."

Shortly afterwards, Savonarola began preaching in front of large audiences at San Marcos describing great changes that awaited Florence and Italy. He prophesied before countless witnesses that Lorenzo, Pope Innocent VIII, and King Ferranti of Naples, would soon die. The city's populous murmured with talk of the prophecies.[314]

Lorenzo Breathes His Last

On April, 7, 1492, as the gout-ridden Lorenzo lay dying, he called for Savonarola. "I know no honest friar except this one," he muttered to his attendants. When the monk arrived, Lorenzo sought his absolution, confessing his sins.

Savonarola told Lorenzo there were three particular sins that needed forgiveness. "What things Father?" he replied.

"Firstly, you must have a great and living faith in God's mercy."

"I have the fullest faith in it, answered Lorenzo.

"Secondly, you must restore all your ill-gotten wealth, or at least charge your sons to restore it in your name." Lorenzo lay staring at the monk for a minute, but then nodded his assent. "Lastly, you must restore liberty to the people of Florence." Lorenzo spoke nothing and turned his head away from the cleric. The Medici patriarch could not bring himself to restore Florence to a true republic which would spell the end of his family rule. Savonarola left Lorenzo without granting absolution. On April 8, 1492, the Medici patriarch died.[315]

A New Leader for Florence

Wolves howled. Ghostly torches streamed down the hillside and into the Medici burial sanctuary where they flickered for awhile before disappearing. An unusually large, bright star glimmered over the house where Lorenzo the magnificent lay dying. At the moment of his death, the star fell toward the earth and extinguished. Such were the omens reported on April 8, when the Medici patriarch breathed his last. Everyone believed that calamities awaited Florence.

The eldest son, Piero de Medici, took over the reins of Florentine government. He soon ordered the assassination of his father's physician. In spite of the doctor doing all he could to save Lorenzo, the paranoid Piero suspected the poisoning of the patriarch.

On July 25, news reached Florence that Pope Innocent VIII had died in Rome. The city buzzed with discussions that the second part of the prediction had come true. Many now became convinced that Savonarola truly possessed the gift of prophecy. It is possible that at this time, the Renaissance artist Michelangelo came under the strong sway of the Dominican. A number of art historians believe that some of the frescos Michelangelo painted on the ceiling of the Sistine chapel reflect sermons preached by Savonarola on the subject of the creation and Genesis.

The fulfillment of the prophecies set the stage for Savonarola's Advent sermons in December of 1492. As he stood in the pulpit of the packed cathedral, a new prediction stunned his audience. A king was about to come from across the mountains and smite all of Italy.

Cyrus the Great

The sleepless Savonarola knelt beside his cot in his cell, praying for inspiration for his final Advent sermon. Then his mind's eye saw a hand brandishing a sword inscribed with the words, "The sword of God above the earth, striking and swift." A booming voice followed the vision: "The time is near when I shall unsheathe my sword. Repent before my wrath is vented upon you." Then angels descended from heaven offering crosses and white scarves to anyone who would accept them. Some did, but many did not as ecclesiastical prelates convinced them to reject the gifts. A voice then warned that the rulers of Florence would listen to sinners and reject God's counsel.

The next day, Savonarola explained the vision to the congregation, prophesying that a new Cyrus the Great was about to invade Italy as an instrument of God to reform both church and civil government. The Florentines knew Cyrus from the Old Testament—a pagan king that God used to return the Israelites to Jerusalem from their exile in Babylon.[316]

Although the prediction appears to echo the idea of the prophecy of the Last World Emperor, Savonarola never referred to this king in those terms. It seems likely, however, that this medieval prophecy informed the monk's interpretation of his own vision. It also appears he borrowed from one of the pseudo- Joachimist prophecies that emerged out of Spain,—this king would first reform the church before the world could be renovated. In this prediction, Savonarola stepped up his conflict with the papacy.

After the death of Innocent VIII, the new pope, Alexander VI, bribed his way into the papacy. His lifestyle and actions reflected a succession of mistresses, including the threat to excommunicate one of them for repenting and returning to her husband. This pope would become one of Savonarola's archenemies.

After the Advent sermons, the reform of the church became a primary concern for Savonarola. He focused on transforming the monastery of San Marcos by eliminating all Medici influence. He returned lands given to the monks by Cosimo de Medici, something welcomed by Piero. He also insisted on the monks' re-embracing the original ascetic lifestyle and practices of Saint Dominic. He then instructed the monks to learn the Turkish and Moorish languages. This action suggests that he merged the ideas of a last world emperor with the prophecies of Joachim of Fiore who believed that a monastic order would usher the world into the millennium. For Savonarola, his monks would follow the new Cyrus and convert the world to Christianity. The first step in this scenario was the conversion of San Marcos.[317]

While it was said already that Savonarola never proclaimed the French king as the last world emperor, Charles VIII believed he fit the role. The monarch dreamed of a glorious conquest to recapture Constantinople, which had fallen to the Turks, and then marching to Jerusalem to attain the Church of the Holy Sepulcher. Before he planned do this, however, his aspirations included an invasion of Italy to seize Naples, which he believed rightly belonged to him. On August of 1494, in what seemed to be the beginning of a remarkable fulfillment of Savonarola's prophecy, Charles VIII amassed his military in the foothills of the French Alps. In early September, 44,000 French troops and Swiss mercenaries advanced into Italy.

The French Invasion

"All Italians are dirty dogs, and the Holy Father is as bad as the worst of them." Charles VIII's cry preceded his march through Turin, Asti, Parma, and to the outskirts of Sarzana as the French cut through ancient fortresses.

With the news of the French successes, the terrified Florentines poured into the cathedral to hear Savonarola's sermons. The monk preached his oratory using the analogies of Noah's flood, proclaiming God would "destroy all flesh" if the gamblers, blasphemers, and sodomites did not repent. "The sword of God has descended," shrieked the monk from the pulpit. "I did not prophecy such a thing, but God himself. It is taking place before our very eyes." Even those who were the most loyal to the Medici rule felt awestruck, including the artist Botticelli.

In the meantime, Piero rode out to the French at Sarzana to try to cut a deal with Charles VIII. The negotiations proved disastrous as the Medici ruler gave up all towns and fortresses under Florentine control. Details of the arrangement reached Florence just as Savonarola began his Advent sermons. As French troops marched toward the city, the monk pleaded for the people to repent from their "pride, envy, thieving, and extortion."

Most of the government now turned against Piero and toward Savonarola. "It is time we stop being ruled by children," bellowed one of the Signoria. The statement referred not only to the twenty-three-year-old Piero, but also to the seventeen-year-old Cardinal Giovanni. The council decided to send Savonarola as the head of a delegation to speak to Charles VIII. As the mission approached the French, fear and discontentment enveloped the city.

When the Savonarola-led delegation reached the French king, the monarch came under the sway of the monk. In accordance with Savonarola's wishes, Charles VIII promised that he would allow the Florentines to set up a true republic. At Savonarola's request, he also agreed to march to Rome, depose the pope, and lead a renovation of the papacy. While these negotiations took place, Piero returned to Florence

The Fall of the Medici

The day after Piero arrived back in the city, the bell in the palazzo tower sounded the call and Florence erupted into rebellion. Cardinal Giovanni tried to rally support among Medici loyalists, marching some of them to the government building of the Signoria, but a larger mob of hostiles forced him to retreat to his family palace. Piero awaited him.

Barricaded inside, the cardinal knelt and prayed in the top-story window in view of the crowd. The show of piety, whether real or contrived, failed as cries for his death rang from the mob below. Knowing the time was short, Piero made his escape. Giovanni, however, stayed long enough to gather up all the Medici treasure he could conceal and carry. He disguised himself as a Franciscan monk and fled to the monastery of San Marcos. Soon the Medici brothers galloped across the Appenine Mountains toward the safety of Bologna. The rebellion brought Medici rule to an end, but Savonarola's reign was just beginning.

The New Jerusalem

On Palm Sunday, 1496, some ten thousand boys and girls, ranging in age from six to sixteen, marched through the streets of Florence while raising religious banners and singing a song to the New Jerusalem:

> Rise, O New Jerusalem and hear.
> See your glory, recognize and adore
> Your queen and her beloved son
> So that this may adorn not only you
> But the entire world.[318]

The boys, including four thousand under the age of nine, had their hair cut short above the ear to demonstrate they were no longer available for the pedophiles, long hair being a sign of homosexual accessibility.[319] They had flocked to Savonarola and embraced his message, no doubt feeling liberated and protected from the rapists and molesters that had long preyed upon them. Their pageant and song reflected the followers' belief that Florence had now emerged as the New Jerusalem, and they were on the verge of a renovation that would extend to the world and usher in the millennium of peace and righteousness.

The procession demonstrated a remarkable turnaround for a city that had been steeped in political and moral corruption. With the Medici gone, a true republic had returned to Florence. Taxation laws were reformed to favor the poor, and sodomites, thieves, and extorters now faced the death penalty if they continued their actions.

Two years earlier, Charles VIII left Florence after a short period of occupation. The French king kept his word to Savonarola during their meetings at Sarzana: he had held back the pillaging by his troops, as best he could, and agreed that the Florentines could form their own government.

During those November sermons, Savonarola outlined his vision for the Florentine republic. On November 28, 1494, the same day the French pulled out, Savonarola stood before the congregation. He focused on personal morality and caring for the city's poor. "Give yourselves to simplicity and let go of superfluous things and vanities. . . . Let go of your possessions, give them to the poor." He ended the sermon with a call to alms: "The first Sunday coming up there will be two collections—one will be for the poor in the city, the other will be for those outside."

On December 12, Savonarola concentrated primarily on a philosophy of government. He began by proclaiming that the best government is one which is ruled by a single leader, but only when that ruler is righteous and good. The Dominican, however, warned that human nature tends to produce the opposite effect. "Conversely, when that one leader is wicked, there is no worse government." The monk then explained that the situation in Florence dictated a true republic, as the Florentines possessed a high degree of intelligence and education and therefore, were well-suited to a democracy. Because of corrupt human nature, in most cases, "government by the majority is better than that of a single leader, and one could say that this is especially true in Florence."[320]

For the council, itself, Savonarola introduced to the people the idea of the Great Council consisting of one-fifth of the male population over twenty-nine-years of age. This figured to be 3200 people. All males over twenty-nine would be eligible to serve a term of six months. This would make Florence comparable to the great city sates of ancient Greece. The committee would be responsible to elect the smaller Signori.[321]

Savonarola envisioned a democratic theocracy for Florence, one in which the people would elect civic leaders who would enforce the laws he believed had been advocated by the Virgin Mary in his vision: "It is necessary that the Council pass laws against that accursed vice of sodomy, for which you know that Florence is infamous throughout the whole of Italy. . . . Pass a law, I say, and let it be without mercy; that is, let these people be stoned and burned." [322]

Although Savonarola believed in a rule of God instituted by way of a republic, his personal beliefs did not include the elimination of all opposition. While he hoped for a council made up primarily of his supporters, he believed that human nature dictated that opposition factions and individuals should be elected to the council as a way to mitigate a dictatorship of the majority which would likely occur if one faction had too much power. In this, the Dominican was ahead of his time. In the centuries to come, Democratic theocracies would emerge again, particularly in England and America under a group that would be known as the Puritans and a faction of the Puritans known as the Fifth Monarchy. In these forms, however, the idea of opposition would be less tolerated. [323]

On December 28, Savonarola returned to the same theme of civil government. During one part of the sermon, he focused on an example from the Old Testament: "But let yourselves be ruled by God, and do not behave as did those Jews who demanded a king from Samuel." The monk used a text from the eighth chapter of I Kings to explain how the Jews rejected God's warning and made Saul their regent, who, in turn, made himself a tyrant over the people.[324] Some two centuries after Savonarola, Thomas Paine would use the same Old Testament text in his tract *Common Sense* to help incite a revolution against what he believed was a British dictatorship.[325]

By the time of this final sermon of December, Florence had held elections and appointed the Great Council. In spite of Savonarola's popularity and new-found power, various factions grew in opposition. Some secularists resented his meddling in the secular government, although they supported a republic. Others desired the return of the Medici. Still others, including permissive priests and monks, longed for the days of libertine morality and the accumulation of wealth. The New Jerusalem had just begun, but Savonarola already had to walk with body guards to protect him from assassination. And the papacy soon awoke to the dangers of the Florentine prophet.

The Bonfire of the Vanities

The New Jerusalem was under full sway in 1496. Savonarola's boys roamed the streets in between their processions asking for alms for the poor and imploring people to give up their "vanities." These consisted of looking glasses, hair braids, pagan figurines and some other works of art, and anything associated with the fixation of one's self. Many people willingly and gladly gave up the items. But as their numbers grew, the boys began muscling their way into homes where the residents were less than compliant, and confiscated the illicit objects against their will. On several occasions Savonarola had to implore the youth to use more lenient tactics.

On February 7, 1497, Savonarola's supporters prepared the Bonfire of the Vanities. The ritual blaze took the place of the Medici Carnival day, which had resembled a pagan festival with lewd songs and street corner bonfires. In this fire, the blaze consumed all the vanities Savonarola's boys had collected. At the inferno's climax, flames rose to sixty feet. As the items incinerated, the crowd joined the youth in singing hymns, as well as songs mocking worldly luxuries. Some historians believe that Botticelli threw some of his own paintings in the fire. Others question this. However, it is true that at this time, the artist gave up painting his pagan beauties in favor of depicting scenes of Dante's Inferno.

While the sounds of joyous hymns flooded the air with the rising smoke of the vanities, Savonarola's followers also sang a song that rang with less optimism than their chants of the New Jerusalem.

> Stir up the Lord,
> Your might and come,
> Show that you are God:
> Lord why more suffering?
> Put bits in the mouths of this incurable mob,
> Which so-disturbs the well being of the city of flowers.

The hymn demonstrates the growing power of the various factions that opposed Savonarola. They appeared determined to disrupt the progression to the millennium. The bonfire itself further stirred emotions, causing splits among family members—sowing strife between brother and sister, wife and husband, and son against parents.[326]

Undaunted by the criticism, Savonarola stood in the cathedral pulpit overlooking the crowd of sixteen thousand. "I am here," he roared, "because the Lord appointed me to this place. . . . I send forth a mighty cry that shall resound throughout Christendom, and make the corpse of the Church tremble even as the body of Lazarus trembled at the voice of our Lord."[327]

Savonarola had predicted and hoped that Charles VIII would march to Rome and cleanse the church leading to the age of conversion. The French king, however, failed to fulfill the prophecy. The French marched to Rome but Charles chose not to depose the pope in favor of negotiations. Later, the pope had been able to assemble a confederacy of Italian rulers against the French monarch. The confederacy defeated the French at the Battle of Fornova, and Charles limped back to France. Savonarola, however, refused to lose hope in his prophecy, continuing to send encouragements to Charles to return to Italy to finish the job.

The pope fumed as he read the reports from his spies detailing the content of Savonarola's Lenten Sermons. The criticisms of the church from this "chattering monk," as his papal court referred to Savonarola, infuriated him to no end. In his address to a Florentine envoy, Alexander dispensed with diplomatic niceties. "He (Savonarola) vilifies us and makes mincemeat of our dignity—us the very occupiers of the Holy See." The envoy tried to pacify the pontiff but later wrote that it was in vain, "to calm the rage with which I saw him so inflamed." Even though the Dominican continued to avoid naming Alexander in his oratories, the pope knew very well that the monk's diatribes pointed to the corruption under his papacy.[328]

On May 13, 1497, Alexander VI issued a brief of excommunication to Savonarola for "sowing abroad a pernicious doctrine to the scandal and ruination of simple souls." Couriers delivered the Brief to Florence on June 18, and the government posted copies on the doors of the religious institutions. With Savonarola silenced, all moral restraint broke free throughout the city with gambling and sodomy freely practiced once again. Plague soon arrived in Florence. [329]

When reports reached the pope that Florentines lay dying in the streets, he grieved little. What drove him to deep sorrow, however, was the news that the authorities had dragged the body of one of his sons from the Tiber River. Rumors swirled that one of the pope's other sons perpetrated the murder out of jealousy. The Venetian ambassador proclaimed, "The wild wail of the old pontiff could be heard in the streets around the papal palace."[330]

The event caused Alexander VI to consider that God had sent him a message to repent. In confession he announced that he would end all favoritism in awarding church offices and push to end simony throughout the church. He also declared that he would reform his personal life. When Savonarola learned of the pope's commitment, he wrote to him, "May God console you in your tribulation."[331]

In spite of his new attitude, the pope remained conflicted toward Savonarola, refusing to lift the excommunication without a review. He appointed a commission of cardinals to evaluate the monk. Savonarola had written a number of tracts as well as a sizeable theological treatise entitled *The Triumph of the Cross*. The commission focused on these writings.[332]

Saved by Faith

"The third rule is to pray God grant you a true and living light to make you see that external ceremonies, although good in themselves, are worth nothing toward salvation if there is no spirit in them—because it is written that man is not justified by the works of the law, that is, by ceremonies and external works." Savonarola wrote this in a tract entitled *Ten Rules to Observe in Times of Tribulation*. Years later, the works of Savonarola would be read by another monk named Martin Luther who would use the concept of salvation by faith apart from external works to condemn the church practice of selling indulgences. Papal commissions would be set up by Pope Leo X to judge Luther just as Alexander VI had set one up to review Savonarola. Leo's commissions would not be kind to Luther. Alexander's commission, however, found nothing wrong with the tract.

The commission came back with the verdict—all the writings of Savonarola were orthodox. By this time, however, Alexander had another change of heart. It had not taken long for Alexander's feelings of shame to pass, and he once again followed the courses of self-indulgence and devious schemes. Despite the fact that Alexander could not accuse Savonarola of heresy, he refused to lift the Brief of Excommunication. As the months wore on, Savonarola learned that the pope had returned to his corrupt ways. He decided to challenge the pontiff directly.

Open Warfare

On Sunday, February 11, 1498, Savonarola once again stood in the pulpit viewing an overflowing crowd. "If anyone gives a command that opposes charity," cried the Dominican, "curse it. Were such a command issued by an angel or even by the Virgin Mary herself, or all the saints, curse it! And if any pope speaks contrary to this, let him be excommunicated." The monk proceeded to explain that the pope's excommunication did not come from God, but from the devil. Thus Savonarola threw down the gauntlet.[333]

With Savonarola's open confrontation with the papacy, a sense of dread descended upon the monk's followers, leading many to withhold public support. The Dominican knew he needed to act decisively or his New Jerusalem would collapse. The pope's personal, scandalous behavior and political conniving had outraged many of Europe's rulers. They would be only too happy to be rid of him. Savonarola sent letters to a number of kings calling for a church council to depose Alexander VI and replace him with someone more suitable.

History is unclear about what happened to all of the letters. What is known is that one reached Charles VIII of France and one fell into the hands of the pope. The council never occurred.

In the meantime, a Franciscan loyalist to the pope and an ardent enemy of Savonarola, Francesco de Puglia, challenged the Dominican to a trial by fire. Two stacks of wood soaked in oil would be laid out with a passage two feet wide in between. These piles would be set on fire, and then a chosen representative from the Franciscans and the Dominicans would walk between the two blazes. The onlookers would see who God chose to protect.

Francesco did not believe that God would protect either participant as he considered the ordeal to be superstitious. But in a sermon, Francesco declared, "I believe that I shall burn, but I am willing to do so for the sake of liberating the people of the city." A follower of Savonarola, Friar Pescia, believed he could survive the trial and convinced his master to let him try.[334]

On April 7, 1498, people crammed into the Plaza, salivating at the thought of the carnage they would witness. The Franciscans, however, deployed stall tactic after stall tactic to delay the beginning of the trial. Apparently, they had no intention of going through with the contest. As the hours wore on, the throng murmured and grumbled.

With patience running thin, Medici supporters decided to turn the event to their advantage as they caused a tumult. The crowd flew into a panic. Just then, a violent tempest rushed across the city, the weather dispersing the mob.

The Florentines felt robbed of their spectacle and they blamed Savonarola. As many of the monk's supporters abandoned him, Medici supporters stormed San Marcos. Some of the remaining followers were willing to fight to protect the Dominican. To save lives, however, Savonarola agreed to give himself up to the Signori, whose majority had turned against him. With the Florentine government against him and the pope yearning for an end to the monk, dark times lay ahead for Savonarola.

Torture and Interrogation

The jailer pulled Savonarola's arms behind the monk's back, fastened the chained manacles around his wrists and yanked on the pulley, lifting the victim off the ground by the handcuffs. Savonarola agonized as his shoulders separated from their sockets. The monk endured four such torture sessions before he broke. "Take me down," he told his torturer, "and I will tell you my life."

After a week of questioning, the interrogator read back the transcript to Savonarola. "If you publish this," the monk promised him, "you will die within six months." Savonarola objected to the obvious embellishments and falsifications in the document. The torturer responded that if he did not sign it he would be returned to the torture chamber. Savonarola signed.

The Signori sentenced Savonarola to death. When news of the verdict reached the pope, he sent back word that he agreed with the decision.

On May 23, 1498, the authorities led Savonarola and two of his followers to a gallows constructed in the plaza. A long ladder reached up to hangman's nooses with thickets of wood surrounding the bottom of the ladder. The sentence was death by hanging and burning. Once again, a crowd filed in with most of them hoping to see the death of the man who was the most responsible for giving them their political freedom. Some came longing for a miracle, yearning that God would save the prophet.

An official read the signed confession stating that Savonarola admitted he falsely prophesied, and that his main ambition for all he had done was for the sake of personal political power and worldly honors. One of his followers recorded what he felt at that moment: "I was there to hear the statement and I remained dumbfounded and bewildered. I was grief stricken to see such a grand edifice come crashing to earth because it had been built so wretchedly on a single lie. I was expecting Florence to become the New Jerusalem out of which would come the laws and splendor and example of the good life, and to see the renovation of the Church, the conversion of the infidels, and the consolation of the righteous. Instead, I realized, everything was just the opposite. So I had to swallow the medicine: 'All things, O Lord, are in thy will.'"[335]

Not everyone believed the confession. Another witness recorded the feelings of the crowd: "Many viewed him to be a charlatan, while on the other hand many were of the opinion that his confession was a simple forgery … or falsely extracted under torture."[336] The confession continues to be a source of debate with modern historians lining up on both sides. Lauro Martines notes that no original transcript survived, only secondary and completely unreliable pro-Medici documents. According to this historian, no truth can be ascertained from them. On the other hand, David Weinstein believes the Medici documents are reliable and Savonarola acted in his own self-interest, fabricating the prophecies for the sake of attaining worldly power. Paul Strathern takes a middle ground approach. He notes the unreliability of the confession and believes the overall sincerity of the monk, but also believes some of the confession may be true.

After the public reading of the confession, the authorities hanged and burned the three men. Ser Ceccone, Savonarola's interrogator, died six months later just as the monk predicted.[337]

The Ascendancy of Giovanni

Eight miles outside of Florence, Cardinal Giovanni de Medici's siege gun blasted through the fortified walls protecting the town of Prato. The Spanish infantry poured through the holes, pillaging, raping, and putting all to sword regardless of age or sex. They descended upon the monasteries and convents, decapitating the monks and nuns and violating the crucifixes and communion hosts. For the next two days they filled the town's water wells and streets with naked bodies. "Painful," commented Cardinal Giovanni when he learned of the massacre, "but at least it will serve as a message to all opposition." Florence understood the message.[338]

For sixteen years after the Florentine rebellion expulsed Giovanni, he plotted his revenge against Savonarola's followers, as well as those who continued to support Florence's republican government. During these years, a number of attempts to regain Florentine control ended in failure. Finally, in the year 1512, Pope Julius II gave the cardinal permission to use the Spanish army to conquer the city. The Medici clergyman bought the Spanish a siege gun to put an end to Prato, which had allied with Florence. The message of carnage from Prato caused the Florentines to give up without a fight. Cardinal Giovanni rode into Florence in triumph. As master of the city, Giovanni set about undoing all vestiges of republicanism created by Savonarola. He put an end to the Great Council and replaced the signori with men of his own choosing. He also reestablished Lorenzo's lewd street songs in the city's pageants.

One year later Pope Julius II died, and twenty-four cardinals met in the conclave of 1513. When one of the clergy nominated the name of Giovanni de Medici, the others met it with approval. Giovanni had few enemies among the cardinalship, and his seemingly celibate ways earned him the respect from the other members at a time when most of them kept their mistresses and prostitutes. Unknown to them, however, Giovanni simply had no attraction to women; he preferred homosexual relations.[339]

Cardinal Giovanni, himself, counted the votes and when he announced his name as the winner, he showed no emotion, impressing the conclave members. Remembering his mother's dream, he announced to them that he desired to take the name he had formed in his mind since childhood. They blessed it as the will of God. On March 11, the Sacred College announced to Rome that Giovanni de Medici had been elected Pope Leo X.

When the news reached Florence, the city erupted in chaotic celebration. Medici partisans poured out onto the streets yelling "Papa Leon," plundering shops owned by known Savonarola supporters and setting fire to their roofs. The frenzy lasted four days.

In Rome, Pope Leo X had his own celebration in mind. He called for his younger brother, Guiliano. "God has seen fit to give us the papacy," he said to his sibling, "now let us enjoy it." And enjoy it he did as he engaged in a lifestyle that even the wealthiest Italians envied.

In one of his first acts, Giovanni squandered almost a third of the papal treasury putting on a pageant called *Sacro Possesso*. In true Medici fashion, he had a taste for pageantry of a more lewd kind as he followed it with the plays *Candelaria* and *Mandragola*, productions interlaced with a variety of sexual intrigues. Between the spectacles, he held frequent sumptuous banquets of sixty courses. His love for hunting became legendary when he spent large sums of money on French hounds and Icelandic falcons. When money ran low, Leo X sought to replenish the funds through loans given by Florentine bankers who lent the money at forty percent interest. His own financial purse also ran low as a result of frequent gambling sessions. By the end of the first year of his reign, he had almost bankrupted papal coffers.[340] The pope responded to the financial emergency by cooking up a scheme worthy of the Medici heritage— take advantage of the doctrine of indulgences to replenish the papal treasury, as well as his own personal finances.

The Protestant Reformation

"Have mercy upon your dead parents," John Tetzel thundered to the congregation in the cathedral in Magdeburg, Germany. When he sensed the hesitation among some of the audience, he continued the theme. "Don't you hear the voices of your wailing dead parents and others who say, 'Have mercy upon me, have mercy upon me, because we are in severe punishment and pain. From this you could redeem us with small alms and yet you do not want to do so.'" Standing in the pulpit alongside the indulgence cross that was set up for the occasion, he made his final pitch, "Whoever has an indulgence has salvation; anything else is of no avail." At the end of the sermon, the people rushed to the front of the sanctuary where a table had been set up. They purchased the indulgence letters, which guaranteed the salvation of their loved ones suffering in Purgatory.[341]

When members of the parish at Wittenberg returned from Magdeburg, they brought their letters to Martin Luther. The Augustinian monk grimaced as he scrutinized them. On October 30, 1517, Luther penned a memo to Archbishop Albrecht of Mainz. "Oh great God," he wrote. "The souls committed to your care, excellent father, are directed to death." With his reading of the indulgences, it was as if the specter of Savonarola had entered and possessed the Augustinian, for a new round of conflict was about to begin between a monk and Giovanni de Medici.

At its earliest stage of development, the doctrine of Indulgences began as a public form of penance to demonstrate true sorrow for grievous sins such as denying Christ during times of persecution. Prayers, alms to the poor and to monasteries, and holy pilgrimages fulfilled the demands of the church for re-inclusion of the lapsed sinner. During the crusades, the idea of indulgences took a turn as Pope Urban II granted them to those who sought to win back the Holy Sepulcher, the journey taking the place of all penance.

Indulgences became intrinsically tied to the doctrine of Purgatory. While the church believed that Christ suffered in place of the Christian's eternal punishment, souls still needed to be purified or sanctified through affliction, such as suffering persecution as a strengthening of one's soul and faith. Furthermore, the church came to believe that some Christian souls after death needed to continue to be purged or sanctified from their sin nature through suffering, just as they did when they were still alive. In its original form, the doctrine responded to Gnostic views that said that the soul is perfected by leaving and being freed from the body, as the body corrupts the soul by its very nature of being physical. The church responded by claiming that the soul is not necessarily perfect just because its freed from the body, and it may have to continue to suffer for its perfection until the Day of Resurrection. Indulgences became a way in which the distressed soul's time in Purgatory could be shortened, allowing it to enter Paradise.[342]

During the reign of Pope Julius II, indulgences had been authorized for the construction of Saint Peter's Basilica and a crusade against the Muslims. Leo X renewed the pardon for the completion of the building project, but also extended it to replenish the papal treasury and his personal account. With the abuses of indulgences that had occurred in times past, much of northern Europe rejected Leo's pardon. The pope employed John Tetzel to breathe new life into the transactions. When the salesman finally reached Germany, his preaching set off what would become a firestorm of controversy with Luther.

Along with his memo to the Archbishop, Martin sent his *Disputation of the Power and Efface of Indulgences*. The ninety-five point thesis attacked indulgences as something inferior to true repentance for sin. Point fifty-two summed up the main assault on Tetzel's preaching: "The assurance of salvation by letters of pardon is vain, even though the commissary, nay, even though the pope himself, were to stake his soul upon it." In point eighty-six, Luther demonstrated ignorance in the nature of Leo and the pope's squandering of papal finances: "Why does not the pope, whose wealth is today greater than the riches of the richest, build just this one church of St. Peter with his own money, rather than with the money of poor believers?" When the archbishop read Luther's thesis he rejected it as the pope had promised him he could keep fifty percent of all money collected from the sale of the pardons.[343]

Those who agreed with Luther employed printing presses to reproduce his document in mass and distribution spread throughout Germany and beyond. Pope Leo responded slowly at first, employing a series of papal theologians and envoys to confront Luther, but these only hardened Luther in his resolve against the papacy. By 1521, the friar moved beyond indulgences to condemn or question a number of church practices and doctrines including the vow of celibacy by the clergy, Holy Orders, the Eucharist, and belief in Purgatory. Along with Luther's condemnation of celibacy, many cardinals saw his doctrine of salvation as particularly problematic.

Saved by Faith

By the time he wrote his thesis, Luther had already struggled with the theology of salvation. He wrote his commentary on Paul's Letter to the Romans in the year 1516. The monk's soul felt awakened by the seventeenth verse of the first chapter: "He who through faith is righteous shall live." Luther would write later, "I felt as though I had been reborn and entered paradise."

As he developed his theology, Luther coined the formula: "justification is by faith alone." In its most perfect context, the friar's phrase meant to emphasize that one could not earn salvation by doing good works such as donating to the church or buying indulgences. Salvation is a gift of God attained only by faith in Christ. In this, Luther had much in common with Savonarola's claim that salvation was by faith apart from engaging in rituals or external ceremonies. Luther eventually paid homage to Savonarola in his own writings.[344]

In time, Luther came to question the New Testament's book of James as overemphasizing good works in relation to faith and salvation. Luther correctly emphasized the context of Paul's letter to the Romans, but the "faith alone" seemed to disregard the overall framework of the Apostle's letters, as well as the second chapter of James. In First Corinthians 13, Paul indicated that a believer may have faith, but still not have salvation: "If I have faith to move mountains but have not love, I am as nothing." And again, "Of faith hope and love, the greatest of these is love." Luther might have softened some of the cardinals' reaction against him if he had included love as part of the salvation formula.[345]

Luther's reformation eventually spread to all parts of Europe. As many people adopted the "new Lutheranism," some of Luther's followers ignored the essential element of love as they propagated a number of his ideas. One of the most glaring examples came from a disciple named Thomas Muntzer. Muntzer preached salvation by faith, but his context failed to include love. He took the reformation beyond peaceful protest to violent rebellion.

The Muntzer Revolution

In the year 1524, Thomas Muntzer bellowed his sermon to nobles from Saxony. "Christ said in Matthew 10, 'I am not come to send peace, but the sword.' But what is one to do with the sword? Exactly this: sweep aside those evil men who obstruct the Gospel! Take them out of circulation!" The preacher came before the princes to espouse his own version of the Reformation, which included the use of force to eliminate the Church of Rome. "Because I say with Christ and with the guidance of the whole divine law, that one should kill the godless rulers and especially the monks and priests who denounce the Holy Gospel."

In his own preaching, Luther tried to calm the masses and keep the lid on violence, but it was too little too late. With Martin's reformation, peasants throughout Germany unleashed pent up frustrations with both civil government and Catholic clergy that had been brewing for decades. The German people had looked for a last world emperor who might emerge and bring the hoped-for era of peace and prosperity. But one by one, Germany's leaders had disappointed them: Fredrick II, Sigmund, Fredrick III, and Maximilian, all left the masses in poverty and despair. Now, violent uprisings dotted the landscape and magistrates responded with brute force by killing thousands. Some of the princes, however, gathered in Saxony to consider if Muntzer might be theologically correct in advocating violence against the Catholic Church.

Muntzer had read and admired the pseudo-Joachim document *Super Hieremiam*. The text railed against a corrupt clergy and prophesied that Joachim's third age of the Spirit was about to dawn. He claimed his own revelation advocating violence, however, came directly from God. The Divine instructed him that a Spirit-led time of violent revolution would usher in the third age, which preceded the return of Christ in the flesh. Muntzer believed that God called him to eliminate the Catholic Church to make the world ready for Christ's arrival.[346]

The princes at Saxony could not come to a conclusion about Muntzer, leaving him to continue his preaching and amassing his followers. The Muntzer rebellion came to a conclusion on the outskirts of Frankenhausen when he led some eight thousand peasants against overwhelming government forces. The promised divine intervention did not take place and the soldiers massacred Muntzers' followers while they captured and beheaded him. Muntzer's preaching led to the carnage of his supporters. When all the peasant uprisings were concluded, government authorities had killed over one hundred thousand.

Savonarola's Legacy

Savonarola influenced history on two fronts. One, he put forth an allegorical version of the New Jerusalem that dissociated the heavenly city from any connection to the Church of the Holy Sepulcher and placed it in a geographic location other than Palestine. Two, despite his ultimate failure, he enabled people to believe in the possibility of a successful challenge to the corruption of both church and state.

In the next chapter, we will set sail with a Genovese explorer named Christopher Columbus. In the year 1492, he would make a startling discovery of a new continent that would also help people rethink the concept of the New Jerusalem. Both Catholics and Protestants would associate America as the heavenly city that would shine as a millennial light to the rest of the world.

CHAPTER 11
A CLASH OF CIVILIZATIONS

AFTER THE CONQUISTADORS entered the landing boats, they paddled toward the two columns of smoke billowing from the island. After reaching the beach, the soldiers trekked in the direction of the fires. In a clearing beyond the trees, the party came upon two houses made of masonry, each with steps leading to altars. When they reached the top of the stairs of one of the houses, the sight dumbfounded the Spaniards. The table held a fierce looking monster made of stone. Blood covered the walls. To the side on the floor lay human body parts—arms, legs, and torsos with the areas covering the hearts slashed open. On a nearby spit smoldered the human hearts and entrails.

The mercenary soldiers returned to their boats and headed to the coast opposite the island. When they reached the shore a group of inhabitants welcomed them. The tribal natives brought the Spaniards what they had come for—gold. The Spaniards returned to their ship and traveled further up the seaboard. The natives had been supplying the Spanish with gold at many of the stops along their voyage, but in relatively small quantities. When the conquistadors pushed for more, the tribal leaders shook their heads and pointed up the coast. "Mexico, Mexico," the chiefs yelled. The Spaniards weren't sure what the word meant, but they understood that the enormity of the precious metal lay somewhere northeast.

At each stop, the elusive Mexico remained further north. The Spanish could not travel much longer for their food supply ran short and weevils invested the little bread they had left. They decided to return to Cuba.

Upon their arrival, the conquistadors had brought back some twenty-four thousand dollars' worth of gold. The amount of the precious metal wetted their appetite for a new expedition. To lead the next voyage, the governor of Cuba named a man of suspicious character—Hernan Cortes. The choice astounded the soldiers. Only recently, in a fiasco over a woman, the superintendent had promised to hang him. Now, however, the governor changed his mind on the basis that he believed his chosen man could bring back more gold than any other. At the last minute, however, the governor had another change of heart, but Cortes would not be denied. On February 19, 1519, Cortes set out for Mexico without the required charter.[347]

Brash, self-confident, and courageous, Cortes had joined other Spanish adventurers in crossing the Atlantic to find their fortunes in a newly discovered world. Many Spanish believed this new land would play an important part in fulfilling certain medieval prophecies which had permeated Christian Spain for over a century. It was the Spanish trust in these prophecies that had led to a chain of events that would eventually bring Cortes to the brink of his greatest adventure yet. In time his eleven ships would carry some five hundred soldiers, one hundred sailors, thirteen horses, and a small number of cannons. As he prepared for the journey, the Spaniard had no way of knowing that he would be the primary figure in leading Spain into one of history's greatest clashes of civilizations.

After leaving Cuba, Cortes's ships made first landfall at the island of Cozumel off the eastern coast of Yucatan. Some of the soldiers immediately embarked on an expedition to hunt wild pigs. While on the beach, several natives in a canoe paddled to meet them. "God and Saint Mary," cried one the men. If he had not spoken, the conquistadors could not have told him apart from the natives. They brought the Spaniard to meet Cortes. "I am Jeronimo de Aguilar from Ecija," he told the captain. Aguilar had learned from natives that enormous white-winged birds swam the waters off the coast. He knew his rescue had come.

Aguilar related the story of his origins in the new world. Ordained a priest, he traveled with seventeen others intending to reach Cuba. A strong current, however, brought them to this land where the Mayan Calthione tribe captured them. Some died of disease and others as human sacrifices to their gods. Only he and one other remained alive. He escaped from the Calthionenes and became a slave to the cacique tribe and learned the natives' language. The other captured Spaniard embraced his new life as a tribal warrior.

Cortes ransomed Aguilar with some of the green beads that he had brought as gifts for the natives. The beads were of little value to the Spanish, but the Mayans had never seen such items. With their new interpreter, the conquistadors set sail, hugging the coast until they reached the river Grijalva, which led to the city of Tabasco. The conquistadors anchored the larger boats and piled into the smaller ones to better navigate the river. At Tabasco, the Spaniards found twelve thousand native warriors amassed against them.

Through Aguilar, Cortes tried to tell the chiefs that they came in peace with gifts of beads. As an answer, arrows flew back at the Spanish and the natives cried "al calacheoni," meaning "kill the captain." With the initial battle, Cortes captured the city, but the warriors retreated to the countryside and regrouped with reinforcement.

Cortes understood warfare. He had studied the battles of the ancient Macedonians and the way Alexander the Great had defeated enemies who had larger numbers. The Tobascons played into the captain's hands with the inept native leadership that led many of their warriors into slaughter. The sheer numbers, however, began wearing down the Spanish. The horses turned the tide. Cortes brought the animals on shore and mounted a cavalry charge into the midst of the enemy. The natives had never seen a horse and believed the animal and its rider were one creature. Some of their gods were images of a half animal, half human. The natives fled in terror. At the end of the battle, eight hundred natives lay dead and only two Spaniards.

Cortes set sail again and under fair winds arrived at what is now the port of the city of Vera Cruz. As he scanned the shoreline from his ship, he spotted two canoes paddling towards him. The small boats contained what appeared to be high ranking priests and chieftains. Cortes motioned them aboard.

Cortes and the boarding party strained to communicate since the chiefs and priests could not speak coastal Mayan. Cortes, however, noticed one of the coastal slave girls they had recently picked up, conversing easily with one of the chiefs. The girl, Malinche, spoke fluent Nahuatl, the mountain Mayan tongue. She spoke to the party in Nahuatl and then translated to Aguilar in the lower coastal language. Malinche had a natural gift for learning language and would eventually pick up Spanish from Aguilar. Cortes learned from the girl that their native visitors came from a place they called Mexico.

The next day, the Spanish leader ordered a landing party ashore comprising two hundred soldiers, artillery, horses, and war hounds, making camp on the slope of a sand dune. The Spanish positioned some of the cannons on higher dunes.

A Message from Montezuma

The following days brought more native visitors. Cortes learned that they were ambassadors from a chieftain named Montezuma, a powerful man who ruled Mexico, a group of three city states: Tenochtitlan, Texcoco, and Tacuba. The peoples of this alliance were known as Aztecs. The Spanish leader also found out that Mexico contained an abundance of gold.

Through the course of their meetings, Cortes indicated that he planned to visit Montezuma. The ambassadors considered it an arrogant assertion. Cortez responded by demonstrating the power of his cannons. The explosive weapons amazed the Aztecs. Aztec painters created pictures of the military exercises and along with some gifts from Cortes, the ambassadors sent couriers to relay the news to Montezuma.

Ten days later, the couriers returned to the Spanish camp, bringing a message from the chief, as well as gifts of gold and silver. The message was cordial but direct: "Take the silver and gold back to your king and under no circumstance should you come to visit." Cortes replied with his own statement that it would displease his own king if he did not personally greet the Aztec leader.

When Montezuma learned of the correspondence, he met with his advisors who told him that the Spanish should be annihilated, for it had been reported that some of these foreigners had been destroying temples and replacing the idols with their own. These actions intrigued Montezuma for they spoke of the possibility that Cortes might be the return of the god Quetzalcoatl, who hated human sacrifice. According to the myth, the god had white skin. Centuries ago he had left, but vowed to one day return. In spite of this possibility that the god had come back, Montezuma began sacrificing young boys to the god of war.[348]

A Confrontation on the Pyramid

The ambassadors returned to Montezuma. Cortes and his men headed inland and north. They passed through thick foliage and tropical trees until they arrived at the town called Zempoala inhabited by the Totonac tribe. Envoys of the Totonac chief brought the Spanish to the center of the village which opened up to a large step pyramid with a temple on top. Cortes ordered some of his men to inspect the shrine. They returned with a report of the scene: blood covered portions of the walls from freshly sacrificed young boys, their hearts resting on a plate.

The Totonac chief met the Spanish and relayed the story of how the Aztecs recently conquered them, forcing them to pay tribute by providing boys and girls for the victors' sacrifices. The town was part of a Totonac confederacy of thirty villages, all unified by their hatred for Montezuma. Other tribes also despised these Aztec overlords, including one group in particular, the Tlaxcalans, who actively rebelled and remained unconquered. Cortes pledged his support for all tribes under the Aztec yoke.

With the possibility of attaining native warrior allies, the Spanish trudged further inland to various Totonac villages to solidify allegiances. Upon their return to Zempoalan, Cortes made a requirement of the natives if they were to expect Spanish help: they must give up human sacrifice. The explorers had become sickened by the practice. Conquistador, Bernal Diaz, gave an eyewitness account: "Every day they sacrificed before our eyes, three, four, or five Indians, whose hearts were offered to those idols and whose blood was plastered on the walls. The feet, arms, and legs of their victims were cut off and eaten, just as we eat beef from the butcher. I believe they even sold it in the markets."

Cortes called all the chiefs of the neighboring villages into an assembly where he laid out his conditions and preached a sermon on behalf of Christianity. He called them to give up their sacrifices and their practice of sodomy which the natives incorporated as part of their cultural way of life. After the meeting, Cortes had the chiefs bring all the people before the great pyramid.

At the base of the pyramid rested wooded cages containing four young men and women. The Zempoalans had prepared the fatted victims for sacrifice and ritual cannibalism. "If you give up these evil deeds," Cortes told the assembled natives, "not only will we be your friends, but we will make you lords over other provinces."

"It is not good that we give up our sacrifices," replied one of the priests, "for our gods give us health and good harvests, and everything we need to live."

Cortes turned to his men. "How can we accomplish anything worth doing if for the honor of God we do not abolish these sacrifices made to idols? Be prepared to fight."

Cortes commanded fifty of his troops up the stairs of the pyramid. As they began their ascent, the natives shrieked in horror. The chiefs cried out to the warriors to get ready to defend their gods. The conquistadors ignored the gestures. As they climbed the steps, the Zempoalan chief screamed, "Why do you want to destroy our images? If we dishonor our gods, we will all perish." As the natives continued to protest, the soldiers reached the pinnacle and began pushing the stone statues down the pyramid. The idols came crashing. The chiefs and the people wept and covered their eyes.

The warriors armed their bows. The conquistadors grabbed the Zempoalan chief and six priests, holding their swords to their throats. "All will be killed," shouted Cortes, "at the first hostile act." The chief commanded his combatants to put down their weapons.

Cortes ordered the shattered stones to be burned. Eight priests did as commanded and brought the pieces into a prayer house and burned them.

The next day, Cortes commanded all the native masons to whitewash the blood-encrusted walls in the temple. He ordered the priests to rinse their blood-caked and matted hair and thoroughly cleanse themselves. At the altar of one of the temples, he erected an image of the Virgin Mary and a plaster cross.

At the celebration of Mass, the chief and the most important town members attended. Afterwards, Cortes told them that he would help free them from the tyranny of Montezuma. The conquistadors left the town, bringing some of the warriors with them.[349]

Into the Mountains of Mexico

On August 16, 1519, Cortes and his men began their ascent to Tenochtitlan, the capital city ruled by Montezuma. On the way, they encountered towns where they forged alliances and picked up some warrior allies. When they reached the Tlaxcalans, however, the natives wanted no alliance and determined to make war against the intruders. The Tlaxcalans hated Montezuma but trusted no one but themselves.

The fiercely independent Traxcalans heavily outnumbered the Spanish. Through a series of battles fought over a number of days, however, the cunning Cortes defeated the enemy against all odds. Montezuma's spies sent word back of the battles and the Spaniards' incredible victory.

Montezuma sent a delegation with gifts of gold, promising to pay annual tribute to the king of Spain if Cortes would only turn back. The Spanish leader returned a message thanking Montezuma for the gifts and gesture, but he told the chief that he would continue the journey up the mountains. In the meantime, the leader of Traxcalans made a truce with Cortes and promised to help him wage war against Aztecs.

Cortes gave up his attempts to force the natives to denounce their religious beliefs. Father Olmedo, who accompanied the conquistadors, argued that education and patience were the best methods by which to convert the pagans. Cortes conceded and followed his pastor's advice. The Tlaxcalans made their own concession and offered one of their temples to the Spanish so they could erect a cross and hold their own religious services. Many native townspeople attended the daily masses.

Meanwhile, with the conquistadors getting closer and close, Montezuma spent days in deep meditation, casting spells, and sacrificing victims in a quest for an oracle to help him know what to do with the Spanish. He believed he received a vision that the Europeans would die in the city of Cholula, to the south of Traxcala. He sent couriers to Cortes with a message that he would meet with him in Cholula.

The Traxcalans urged Cortes to reject the idea and continue marching in a straight path to the Aztec capitol city. The conquistador, however, decided to allow the Aztec ambassadors to lead the way to Cholula. The Tlaxcalan chief offered Cortes one hundred thousand warriors to take with him. Cortes took only six thousand. He felt that was enough for whatever he might encounter.

When the forces reached the city, an ominous sign met the Spanish. Many of the inhabitants had left and the rest seemed to be on edge. Over the next few days, the female interpreter, Malenche, stayed with a native who told her that Aztec armies were waiting to ambush the Spanish whenever they left city. She reported the news to Cortes. He decided to make an example of Cholula.

Pretending to leave the city, Cortes invited the town's leaders to the court-yard of the temple to bid them farewell. In response, the city square overflowed with townspeople and chieftains. The Spanish military and warrior allies descended on the scene, massacring the mostly unarmed populace—women, children, priests, and town leaders. Cortes ordered the temple set on fire. It blazed for two days.

News of the massacre reached Montezuma. He increased the daily sacrifices. He remained alone in the temple, fasting and praying to his god of war. After a week, he made his decision. He relayed his plan to Cortes. He would formally receive the Spanish in the capital city.

After the final trek up the mountain, the Spanish began the descent down the other side, catching glimpses of an enormous city on a lake below. Finally they came into full view of Tenochtitlan. The soldiers had never seen anything like it. Amazed at the glistening metropolis before them, some of them asked if they were dreaming.[350]

The Spanish reached Tenochtitlan at the end of the year 1519. Thirteen years prior to this encounter, in April of 1505, a Genovese named Christopher Columbus died in Spain. The events which allowed Cortes to march to the city of Montezuma can be said to have begun when Columbus made his discovery of America in 1492. It is a well known fact to historians that the voyage would eventually bring Spain into contact with Montezuma's world. What is not well known, however, is the role that medieval European pseudo-prophecies played in creating an environment which made Columbus's journey possible. To understand how significant the idea of prophecy played out in the discovery of this new world, it's important to explore the life of the Genovese adventurer.

Columbus and the City of Granada

In the year 711, Muslim forces from Morocco crossed the Straits of Gibraltar, overrunning the area of southern Spain. By 1478, the Christian north had regained much of the territory and laid siege to Granada. The fighting continued for over ten years as the city's warriors stood their ground. At the end of 1491, Granada finally collapsed. On January 2, 1492, Muslim leader Boabdil handed the keys of the city to King Ferdinand. Christopher Columbus attended the ceremony. He did not, however, rejoice with the others.

Columbus had just failed for the last time in his long struggle in the Spanish court to win royal support for a journey to find a new, shorter passage to the Indies by crossing the Atlantic Ocean. During his twelve-year quest, he not only petitioned Spain, but also turned to various European monarchs only to be told his vision was impossible. Perhaps it would not have seemed so impossible had Columbus not insisted on attaining titles and honors following the success of his voyage. He had some supporters at the Spanish court, but a commission of experts in geography and navigation considered him "a despicable upstart and a contemptuous Italian." After several days of exclusion from the assembly, he rode out of Granada, feeling inconsolable, his final hopes dashed.

The next day, a royal messenger caught up with Columbus, entreating him to return to the city. The king and queen had a change of heart, for the fall of Grenada had altered the political landscape. Finances could now be directed toward maritime exploration, something the war with the Muslims had hindered, and which allowed the rival Portuguese to stay at the forefront of new discoveries. The possibility of finding another source of gold and locating a short passage to the spiceries of India also intrigued the Spanish monarchs. Above all, the new influx of material wealth could enable Ferdinand and Isabella to embark on a quest to recapture the Church of the Holy Sepulcher. For years, certain members of the Spanish Court had encouraged the royals to fulfill prophecy and take their rightful place as the King and Queen of Jerusalem. Upon the messenger's news, Columbus, immediately returned to Granada, riding on a mule.[351]

When Columbus arrived at court, Isabella blessed his enterprise. Nobody could believe it. The queen, however, had always liked the would-be adventurer, and her spiritual confessors had been intrigued with the idea that Columbus's scheme might open the door to fulfill prophecy.

"He who will restore the Ark of Zion will come from Spain." Arnold of Villanova, a follower of Joachim of Fiore and a diplomat at Aragon, included the prophecy in his work, *De Cymbalis Ecclesiae,* written in the early fourteenth century. This pseudo-Joachim prediction spoke of a Spanish last world emperor who would conquer Jerusalem before Christ returned. The prophecy circulated in Christian Spain throughout Arnold's lifetime.[352]

In 1492, Genoese legates sent the prophecy to King Ferdinand and Queen Isabella upon their victory at Granada. At the time Columbus won favor from the queen, he already knew of various prophecies relating to the end of the world, and he probably had been made aware of this one by certain Franciscan friends. Up until this time, he seemed motivated to embark upon his voyage by a sense of adventure and with the hope of attaining personal fame, fortune, and honor. With the abrupt turnaround in his fate, Columbus may have begun to believe he had a place in the fulfillment of the prophecy. Although the messenger declined to tell why the monarchs wanted him to return, he must have realized his fortunes might be changing. It appears that the news on the road outside Granada affected the beginnings of a deep conflict in Columbus's soul.[353]

In reading Columbus's works written after 1501, it is clear that in later years following a number of voyages, he became devoted to witnessing the conquest of Jerusalem and doing everything in his own power to help fulfill the Spanish prophecy. Recently, however, a debate has erupted between historians regarding Columbus's primary ambition for his first voyage. Was he motivated right from the beginning by a sincere spiritual quest to fulfill prophecy, or was he primarily driven by a desire for fame and fortune and only slowly converted to the idea of fulfilling prophecy in later years? Or is the truth found in a middle ground which views Columbus as a man of his time when personal achievement and glory could walk hand in hand with spiritual and religious quests? The following sections of this chapter will attempt to carve out evidence which supports the third option, but with some revision: his primary motivation changed on the way back to Granada in a kind of Damascus Road conversion. By the time he returned to the city and met with the royals, he became devoted to the quest to provide a crusader army for the Spanish monarchs to recapture the Church of the Holy Sepulcher.[354]

In one sense, which side is correct makes little difference to the overall thesis of this chapter's sections on Columbus—pseudo-prophecies of the fifteenth century helped create an environment which allowed the first voyage to take place. All historians studied for this chapter support such a thesis. The more intricate question of when Columbus become personally motivated by prophecy, however, is still an important inquiry for understanding how he viewed some of the details of what happened on his first voyage.

The struggle Columbus bore within himself can be said to exemplify the world into which he was born. An examination of what inspired the adventurer in his quest to win patronage for his expedition would help determine his sincerity about medieval prophecy. The world of the fifteenth century was a culture of struggle between spirituality, prophecy, and humanist glory, where humanism was often cloaked in religiosity.[355]

The World of Columbus

In 1485, Christopher Columbus arrived with his little son, Diego, at the gates of Rabida, a male Franciscan convent well known as a retreat center for famous shipbuilders and experienced sailors. He had sojourned from Portugal, where he tried and failed to win favor for his expedition to discover a passage to the Indies. By the time he reached Spain, he had exhausted his finances and entreated the convent for relief from his poverty. At this time, Columbus may have had one more reason to knock on the convent's doors—Queen Isabella employed two of the friars as her confessors. The friars warmly received him and the boy. In a little while, he entered a small cell on the south side of the convent where he met with the royal confessors, Juan Perez and Antonia Manchena. It is likely Columbus knew the prophecies of Joachim of Fiore and the pseudo-Joachim prophecies for they had been disseminated throughout Europe for several centuries. Here at Rabida, it is likely that the Franciscans discussed the prophecies with Columbus, as well as his own dreams of sailing the Atlantic.[356]

Columbus was born sometime around the year 1450, in the midst of the Renaissance in Europe. It may be said that he embodied some of the highest ideals of the humanist awakening—self-discovery, ambition, education, the hope for material prosperity and, above all, a desire for adventure and to discover new truths about the geography of the world.

Perez and Menchena, on the other hand, belonged to the Observant faction of the Franciscan order. The Observants reacted against the secular orientations of the Renaissance and its infiltrations they believed had occurred among the Franciscans. The Observants hoped to return the church clergy to a more devout, simpler, and humbler way of life. It is not known for sure, but it is possible the Observants also viewed themselves as members of Joachim's third order that the seer predicted would usher in the millennial age of peace.[357]

While the Renaissance incorporated humanist ideals, its principles were not always contradictory with the Christianity of the fifteenth century. Material affluence and the idea of opening doors to the outside world lent themselves to the post-millennial prophecies of the last world emperor and Joachim of Fiore. While the Observants embraced a vow of poverty for themselves, financial affluence and personal success could be used for the sake of bringing about the Kingdom of God. It is likely at Rabida, the Franciscans encouraged Columbus to use his ambitions in the service of fulfilling prophecy.[358]

Besides his encounter at Rabido, harder evidence exists that demonstrates that Columbus had encountered the prophecies of the return of Christ in years leading up to 1492. They are found in the writings that intrigued both the religious and the humanists alike.

The Education of Columbus

While his son claims Columbus studied at college for a time, most historians now believe that Columbus educated himself. The works he studied included Cardinal Pierre d'Ailly's *Imago Mundi* and Pope Pius II's *Historia rerum obique gesatrum*. He also read a letter written by Tosconelli advocating a lost continent. In his work, Pius laid open the possibility of unknown continents, although he had his own doubts about their existence.[359]

Imago Mundi, written in 1410, is a compendium of ancient cosmology and geography and incorporates a number of sources, including works by Roger Bacon. D'Ailly and Bacon advocated a short width of the western ocean. The copy of the *Mundi* that Columbus acquired also included a series of d'Ailly's smaller works. Columbus wrote explanatory notes in the margins of these writings.

These shorter documents, authored in the year 1414, discuss the interrelationships between astronomy, theology, history, and prophecy. The cardinal argued for the legitimacy of using astrology and astronomy for forecasting the fulfillment of biblical prophecy. He predicted the end of the world could be ascertained by observing planetary movements. In the compilation of his document, d'Ailly made references which included: Roger Bacon, astronomers, the sibylline prophecies, and Joachim of Fiore

In one of the smaller works entitled *De legibus et sectus*, d'Ailly applied the theories of Bacon, who mixed astrology with Christian eschatology. The cardinal professed the ability to determine the law, or age of the Muslims, when Jupiter is aligned with Venus. He followed that by postulating when Jupiter is aligned with the Moon it will demonstrate the age of the Antichrist. Later, the Cardinal proclaimed, "No sect comes after the law of Moses, only the Antichrist."[360] While d'Ailly makes no mention of a last world emperor, he shows an affinity with such prophecies by advocating a final age of Islam preceding the rise of the Antichrist.

It appears that Columbus read these works on prophecy sometime prior to 1492. In chapter 8 of his copy of *Imago Mundi*, Columbus made an explanatory note referring to a voyage made by Bartolomeu Dias in 1488. In d'Ailly's smaller work, *Of the Correct Calendar*, Columbus made a notation at the bottom of the page in chapter three claiming that the vernal equinox would occur in "this year, 1491 as the eleventh day of March."[361] Thus the evidence shows Columbus was aware of d'Ailly's writings on prophecy before 1492. But did he actually ascribe to the prophecies? At some point, the Genovese made notations in the margins which show his support for prophecy, but it is not known whether he wrote these particular notes before or after 1492. Prior to his first voyage, Columbus gleaned from these documents for his own understanding of the geography of the world. At the very least, he used the current understanding of geography and prophecy in attempting to win financial and political backing for his voyage.

The Spanish Court

Following his time at Rabida, Columbus began forging contacts with the Royal Court. No doubt aided by Friar Manchena, the Genovese made friends with a group of Isabella's ministers who had interests in overseas exploration and expansion, including Alfonso de Quintanilla and Francisco Pinalo. By May of 1486, Columbus won an audience with the monarchs to explain his grand scheme.[362]

Columbus made a favorable impression on Isabella, but less so on Ferdinand. Isabella, however, insisted Columbus should receive an audience before a committee of experts. Hernando de Talavera, a radical opponent of any idea that Asia could be reached by a short route across the Atlantic, headed the group. The commission did not reach a decision.

Columbus grappled with the commission for about two years until he finally lost patience and travelled to Lisbon. He sent his brother, Bartolomeo, on a journey to propose his Atlantic scheme to the kings of England and France. Bartolomeo spent the next three years pitching Columbus's idea, gaining some interest, but no confirmations of patronage.[363]

While it is possible that prophecy motivated Columbus during these years, the fact that he looked elsewhere from Spain shows that he did not have a great deal of faith in the pseudo-Joachim prophecy of a last world emperor from Spain or that Ferdinand was destined for the role. Or if the king of Spain was to be the object of the prophecy, Columbus must have reasoned, his own voyage had no part to play in it. It is likely, then, that prophecy was not his primary motivation. Soon, however, that would change.[364]

In 1489, Columbus returned to Spain and in 1490, his influence with Isabella grew. His supporters now included Diego Deza, a theologian, tutor to the monarchs' son, and the future Grand Inquisitor of the Spanish Inquisition. His greatest supporter, however, always remained Friar Manchena, whose own background in astronomy proved significant with Isabella and Columbus' other court supporters.[365]

As the Muslims stood on the brink of capitulation in late 1491, a new group of experts in navigation and geography assembled at Santa Fe, a village just outside the walls of Grenada. Once more, Isabella brought in Columbus to present his ideas before the commission. But again he failed to convince the professionals, his only supporter remaining Friar Manchena.

In January, a few days after the victory over the Muslims, Columbus left Granada having lost all hope. In what must have been the darkest days of his life, a light began to shine when Isabella's messenger caught up to him to entreat him to return to the city. Perhaps he thought God's hand beckoned him after all. Perhaps Ferdinand truly was the last world emperor. As Columbus engaged in new meetings with the monarchs, his thoughts turned to prophecy. The evidence for this is found in a journal entry he made while on his first voyage and in a letter he wrote at the end of that expedition.

The Voyage of Discovery

Sixty days after departing from Spain on the ship, Nina, the situation onboard turned toxic. The stench from all the rotting food below became unbearable and the crew had to sleep on deck. Finally, the sailors were at the end of their rope as they reasoned that they should have seen land by now. The shipmates lost all trust in Columbus. A band demanded the ship turn back to Spain. "Give me three more days," pleaded Columbus. He pointed to the fact that they had spotted vegetation in the water, indicating that they were close. On the last day, at midnight, October 11, 1492, the Nina's crew caught a glimpse of an island.[366]

At dawn, Columbus and crewmen went to shore with the ship's landing boats. As Columbus set foot on the beach, he unfurled the royal banner and planted the standard flags in honor of Ferdinand and Isabella who had finally granted him patronage for his voyage. He believed he had found his passage to India.

Columbus set sail again and on October 28, he reached what is known today as Cuba. Initially he believed the island to be part of the mainland of China. The captain viewed the natives on this land to be ripe for conversion to Christianity and to become an example of the ideal apostolic community. In spite of their peaceful ways, they made Columbus aware that a certain tribe was warring against them.[367] Eventually, Columbus understood that the warlike tribe was made up of cannibals.

On December 4 Columbus set sail again and a wind carried the ships to the island of Hispaniola. While ported off the island, he came in contact with the natives and, in particular, the king of the tribe. One of the most significant aspects of this sojourn, however, occurred on December 24. On this night, an event transpired that Columbus believed would help fulfill the prophecy of the Spanish last world emperor.

Shipwrecks, Gold, and the Quest for Jerusalem

At eleven o'clock on December 23, the calm winds and sea convinced Columbus that he could finally retire to his cabin. Worn out from sleep deprivation after being awake for two days, he plopped down in his cot. The seaman in charge of the tiller also felt confident, so much so that he handed the ship over to the ship's boy, something Columbus had forbidden. At midnight, the entire ship's crew went to bed. Soon, rising seas caused the ship to stray toward the rocks. The ship jolted as the rudder ground against one of them. The shaking and the screech from the wood's gnashing woke Columbus and the crew.

Columbus ordered the casting of the anchor to steady the ship, but part of the crew panicked and abandoned the craft in the landing boat. The Captain responded by commanding the mast to be chopped down in order to lighten the vessel. But nothing helped. When the seams gave way the waters flooded in. Giving up all hope in saving the vessel, Columbus ordered the crew to evacuate. Later, they returned with the natives to the stranded ship to retrieve the supplies still on board. Columbus then tore apart the wood from the ship to build a fort on the island.

The Captain usually wrote about himself in his journal in third person, but sometimes in the first.[368] On December 26, he made an entry blaming the treachery of certain crew members as the cause of the loss of the ship. He also reported, however, that the incident proved the providence of God, for now he could leave some of his crew behind at the fort. Columbus wrote, "It was a great blessing and the express will of God that his ship should run aground in order that he should leave behind some of his men. ... And he says that he hopes in God upon his return, he will find a barrel of gold, traded for by those he left behind and that they will have found the gold mine and the spices in such quantity that in three years time the king and queen could undertake to prepare to conquer the Holy House, for thus did I insist to your highnesses that all the profit from this enterprise of mine should be spent in the conquest of Jerusalem. And you highnesses laughed and said that it would please them, and that it was their desire even without this."[369]

The December 26 entry indicates that at the final meetings at Granada, Columbus vowed to give all the profits from his enterprise to the financing of a crusade to the Holy Land to capture the Church of the Holy Sepulcher. The Captain indicates he insisted this idea to the monarchs, demonstrating that he thought of this before the meeting. One may still argue, however that he used this as a propaganda ploy as one final pitch to win patronage. However, one more piece of evidence suggests a change in motivation leading to the meetings.

In returning from the voyage of discovery, on March 4, 1493, Columbus ported in Lisbon. There he met with the king of Portugal and showed him a letter he addressed to the king and the Spanish monarchs announcing his discovery. The letter had been lost to history until 1989 when professor Antonio Rumeu de Armas published an unsigned copy of the document from a manuscript of unknown origin that is believed to be from the sixteenth century. Since the copy's publication, scholars have argued for and against its authenticity. The majority, however, have favored its reliability.[370]

The remarkable part of the letter is found at the end where Columbus provided the reason for the voyage: "I conclude here: that through the divine grace of He who is the origin of all good and virtuous things, who favors and gives victory to all those who walk in His path, that in seven years from today I will be able to pay Your Highnesses for five thousand cavalry and fifty thousand foot soldiers for the war and conquest of Jerusalem, for which purpose this enterprise was undertaken."

At the final meetings at Granada, the sovereigns discussed with Columbus the details and the amount of gold that would be needed to launch a successful crusade for Jerusalem. The letter is similar to the December 26 journal entry. Agreed upon by both Columbus and the monarchs, the express purpose of the voyage was to finance the fulfillment of prophecy.

While Columbus did not abandon his motives of attaining honors and titles, his goals were reshaped by the experience on the road back to Granada and by the primary motive of fulfilling the pseudo-Joachim prophecy of a Spanish last world emperor. In the years to come, he would become completely devoted to the idea, even to the point that he began donning the garb of the Franciscan Observants.

In Columbus's future voyages, the new world would come to play an important role in the fulfillment of prophecy beyond simply providing the monetary means of a crusader army. In Columbus's mind, the conquering of the literal Jerusalem would spiritually walk hand in hand with the new earth spoken of by John in the book of Revelation. Columbus believed his discovery marked the beginning of the new earth and the paradise dwelling place of the faithful. In the Italian's mind, the conversion of the natives of the new world would parallel the crusade to the Holy Land.[371]

Columbus died in 1505. Some thirteen years later, Hernan Cortes played his part in what many Franciscans came to believe would be the fulfillment of Columbus's ideas on prophecy. This supposed new earth, however, would not come without bloodshed. As Cortes and his conquistadors entered the dream-like world of the city of Tenochtitlan, the clash was about to commence.

The City of Wonder

On November 8, 1519, Cortes and his party began entering the city of Tenochtitlan. The Aztecs built the metropolis in the middle of a great salt lake, with four main causeways leading over the water. Canals permeated the town with bridges crossing the channels to various districts. Conquistador Bernal Diaz described the scene: "The buildings rising from the water, all made of stone, seemed like an enchanted vision from the tale of Amadis. . . . It was all so wonderful that I do not know how to describe this first glimpse of things never heard of, seen or dreamed of before."

Within the various neighborhoods houses and temples were built to showcase the many stone idols. Among them, one stood out, according to Cortes, "whose great size and magnificence no human tongue could describe, for it is so large that within the precincts, which are surrounded by very high wall, a town of some five hundred inhabitants could easily be built."

As Cortes and his party crossed one of the causeways and moved into the city-proper, he marveled that such an advanced civilization could exist for the capital was built with remarkable architecture. It was larger than any city in Europe, yet in spite of its size, the streets and houses were uncommonly clean.

Soon Cortes met a long procession of nobles, and in their midst, attendants carried a litter. Setting down the transporter, the slaves laid their cloaks before the emerging king. Cortes beheld Montezuma dressed in a jewel-studded robe, jaguar-skinned sandals, and a quetzal-feathered headdress.

The conquistador presented the king with a pearl and cut glass necklace. In turn, Montezuma gave Cortes two necklaces of snail shells which the Aztecs held in high regard. After the initial cordial greetings, Montezuma spoke to Cortes, "You are weary, the journey has tired you . . . rest now." Attendants led the Spaniards to their quarters.[372]

The Aztec king housed the Spaniards in full view of the Great Temple. They instinctively knew the arrangement could be a tell-tale sign that Montezuma intended to sacrifice them. Cortes responded by positioning cannons, sentries, and guards around his compound. Then, in a show of force, he ordered a volley from cannons that he had moved into the central square. The blasts sent terror throughout the populace. Montezuma tried to ease tensions by letting Cortes know that he and his men had free access to go anywhere in the city to contemplate its splendor.

Over the next days as the conquistadors toured the city, they took in many wonderful sights, such as the many products in the market place, the beautiful gardens, and the cleanliness of the streets. One view, however, sickened them. They came upon what looked like a theatre that housed the bones of the sacrificial victims. They counted some 136,000 skulls held by poles supported by towers. They also witnessed a variety of ritual practices, including infants with their throats slit, the beheading of women, and teenagers dressing in recently flayed human skins.

One morning Cortes sought to investigate the Great Temple. Montezuma, fearing the Spaniards might desecrate the holy place, waited for them at the top of the pyramid where he had been sacrificing natives in anticipation of the meeting. As the Spanish and Melinche reached the top of the one hundred and fourteen steps, they beheld three burning human hearts in honor of the god of hell, who was also the deity of seed and harvest time. The Temple stank like a slaughterhouse.

Cortes spoke to the king in a half-hearted manner so as to emphasize the absurdity of what he witnessed. "Sir Montezuma, I don't understand how such a great prince and wise man has not come to the conclusion that these idols are not gods, but evil things and devils. Do me the favor of placing a cross at the top of this tower and an image of Our Lady so that you will see that these idols are deceiving you."

"If I had known that you were going to say such defamatory things, answered Montezuma, "I would have not shown you my gods; we consider them to be good, for they give us health and rains and good seed and many victories." Experiencing the emotions of Montezuma's anger, Cortes chose not to push his agenda and retreated down from the Temple.[373]

Cortes soon received a letter from a Totonic emissary that the fort he left behind had been attacked and six soldiers were killed. Juan de Ageulla had also been captured and sacrificed. The emissary indicated that he believed that Montezuma ordered the assault. Cortes had been scheming on how he could capture the city and find the Aztec gold mines, but now with the letter in hand he had the perfect excuse. He conspired to capture the Aztec king.

The next morning, with five of his captains and Malinche, the Spanish leader met with the Aztec ruler and accused him of the attack. Montezuma insisted he knew nothing about it, but he promised to make a full inquiry to find out the truth. Cortes responded that the native chief would have to come as his prisoner. At first Montezuma refused, but the female interpreter convinced him of the Spaniards' intent to kill him if he resisted. Cortes ordered the king to tell his attendants he was leaving of his own free will. At the Spanish quarters, Cortes placed him under guard.

Cortes allowed Montezuma to maintain the pretense of governorship, allowing him to govern while under captivity. Over time, however, Aztec leaders became suspicious that the king was simply a vassal under Cortes's thumb. After five months, Cortes offered to free him if he would agree that the two of them would rule Mexico together. Montezuma refused, preferring to remain in captivity. It may be that he believed his chieftains now viewed him to be a weak leader and would replace him by force if he returned to the palace. It is also possible that he believed he received a prophecy from the gods, ordering him to remain. More likely, however, he bided his time until he could find a way out of his situation.[374] In any case, Montezuma soon received news that heartened him. Aztec spies sent him word of a Spanish conspiracy against Cortes.

Gold Fever

Earlier in July of 1519, Cortes had ordered one of his ships containing a large amount of gold to return to Spain without making stops. When Valasquez, the governor of Cuba who had commissioned Cortes, heard of the ship he felt cheated. By now, the governor knew that precious metals permeated the new world and he wanted his share. He chose Lieutenant Narvaez to capture or kill Cortes with a contingency of nineteen ships. They set out for Vera Cruz on March 5, 1520. What was unknown at the time was that small pox infected a crew member on one of the ships under Narvaez's command.

Montezuma had withheld his knowledge of Narvaez from Cortes, but the Spaniard eventually learned of the conspiracy. The captain decided to return to Vera Cruz and strike at Narvaez, leaving a contingent of one hundred twenty conquistadors and the Tlaxcalans to guard the Aztec king. He worried that it might not be enough but he hoped the unit could do the job.

When Cortes reached Narvaez's defenses, he ordered a surprise night attack. Astonished at how quickly his enemy had made the long journey, Narvaez and his forces were caught off guard. As Cortes's troops surged through the camp, they heard Narvaez cry out: "Holy Mary protect me, they have killed me and destroyed my eye." Someone had speared him in his eye socket. After they seized Narvaez, the rest of the camp fell.[375]

While all this was going on, smallpox ravaged the native population. The Mayans had never encountered the disease before and had no immunity to it. They tried to cure it through ritual steam baths which worked to spread the illness like wild fire. The disease, however, would help speed the foreign conquest.

After Narvaez' defeat, Tlaxcalan messengers arrived from the capitol, bearing news that the Mexicans revolted against Alvarado. Cortes hastily set off for the return journey up the mountain. On the way, Aztec emissaries met the Spaniards claiming that Alvarado had attacked the city's leaders for no reason while they danced at the festival of Toaxcatl, the Aztecs most revered holiday. The atmosphere in the city remained charged with tension.

The Final Onslaught

Before Cortes had left to confront Narvaez, he agreed to allow the three-week festival to commence as usual. Although the holiday centered on human sacrifice, to refuse it would have caused the city's inhabitants to revolt. When Aztec priests approached Alvarado for permission to start preparations, he consented with the stipulation that they could not engage in the sacrifices. The priests remained silent.

When the preparations began, they disturbed Alvarado. All the arrangements suggested the city prepared for human sacrifice. What's more, he believed that his and his men's blood would be included in the rituals. His intuition proved right. He abducted two of Montezuma's relatives, torturing them for information. They confessed that the Aztecs planned on capturing the Spaniards and sacrificing them.[376]

While he kept Montezuma under guard, on the fourth day of the festival, Alvarado struck. As the nobles gyrated in the Serpent Dance in the main square, the Spaniards opened fire with their muskets. Foot soldiers then rushed at the crowd, slicing limbs and heads off with their swords. The Aztecs fled in terror, trampling one another as they tried to force their way through the patio gates. The Tlaxcalans waited for them, blockading their path as the swordsmen slashed away behind them. By the end of the attack, thousands of Aztecs lay dead on the patio floor.[377]

War drums pounded at the top of the Great Pyramid. At the sound, the populace responded. They besieged the patio area as the Spaniards fought their way to the palace where they barricaded the entrances. Alvarado commanded Montezuma to calm the masses, threatening to kill him if he refused. Alvarado took the king to the roof where he addressed the Aztecs. His words temporarily pacified the mob. From that point on, however, the conquistadors spent their nights listening to the constant beat of war drums and the cries of the city's natives pleading for their gods' revenge.

When Cortes finally arrived and rode into the city, it seemed deserted and ghostly quiet as the populace hid in their homes. They allowed Cortes to proceed to the palace. Once inside, all the Spaniards were surrounded.

The next morning, the Aztecs attacked. The battle stormed for days. Cortes' military cunning and prowess kept the Mexicans from overrunning the compound. However, he knew it was only a matter of time before thousands of the enemy would wear down the defenses. In desperation, Cortes ordered Montezuma to the roof to try to placate the attackers. When the king emerged in front of the throng, the Aztec chieftains called for silence and for the warriors to desist from hurling their darts, stones, and spears. Montezuma spoke affectionately, telling the people that the Spanish would leave. The crowd shouted back with such things as, "We have vowed to our gods to make war," and "we will not stop until all the Spanish are dead." Then a slew of rocks and arrows rained down on the king and conquistadors. Stones struck the king on the head, leg, and arm. The soldiers pulled him to cover.

The Spanish expected Montezuma to recover, but for three days he refused food and water. On the third day he died. Cortes wept for him.[378]

In desperation, Cortez ordered his carpenters to reconstruct large wooden towers on wheels, war machines by which the conquistadors might be protected inside as they fought their way out of the city. He had already employed the tactic once with his native allies pulling the machines through the thicket of enemy warriors and hurdling weapons. The ploy failed and the Spanish had to return to the compound. But now, he felt he had no choice but to try again. This time they made it as far as the Great Pyramid.

Cortez and his unit battled their way up the steps, dodging all the arrows, rocks, and darts the enemy could throw at them. Some Spanish and their allies fought at the pyramid's base, waging war in the patio for over three hours. When Cortes reached the summit, his men pushed down the idols as they set fire to the temple. The sight of the crashing gods demoralized the enemy, but left the conquistadors inspired. The Spanish knew, however, that they could go no further. They left the shrine ablaze as they fought their way back to the palace.

Cortes determined to try to break out again, but this time at night as the Aztecs were not adept at fighting in the dark. At midnight on July 1, 1520, under a torrent of summer showers, the Spanish began to flee the city. They moved as quietly as they could as many of the streets remained empty as a result of the rain. As the soldiers appeared to be heading to safety through the causeways, Aztec war cries rang out, and the city's canals flooded with enemy canoes. The battle raged through the night. Many conquistadors drowned as they fell into the canals, weighted down by Montezuma's gold that they had confiscated and stuffed into their uniforms. Bodies and horses saturated the water channels. However, Cortes and a contingent of Spanish and allied natives limped away from the city.

At daybreak, the Aztecs ceased the attack in order to celebrate their victory. They sacrificed and cannibalized captured conquistadors and natives. As they danced and feasted on human flesh, Cortes escaped. However, he was not done with Tenochtitlan. With small pox ravishing the Aztec population, Cortes returned with reinforcements and conquered the city in the year 1521.

In later decades, Cortes would be seen as a new Moses, a man whose conquest of Mexico opened the door to evangelization of the natives and ushering in the Kingdom of God on earth. The proponents of this vision believed themselves to the monastic order prophesied by Joachim of Fiore. Following in the tradition of the Franciscan Observants, the Spiritual Franciscans would move into the new world, claiming that the Spanish race under its kings had been chosen by God to undertake the final conversion of the Jews, Moslems, and pagan gentiles. They believed that Joachim's Third Order, or the millennium, was at hand.

CHAPTER 12
THE FRANCISCAN MILLENNIUM AND THE MAYAN INQUISITION

AT THREE O'CLOCK in the morning in the year 1514, Spanish soldiers stopped about one and a half miles from the native town. In a loud voice, the commander read the order given by the governor. "Indians of this land, hear ye! We notify you that there is but one God and one pope and the one king of Castile who is lord over these lands. Give heed and show obedience. And if not, be warned that we will wage war against you and will slay you or take you into captivity." Hearing no agreement to obey, the contingent moved toward the sleepy village, keeping the horses as quiet as possible. Once they arrived, the soldiers crept in among the huts. They flung their torches into the straw thatches. As the village blazed with the screams of men, women and children, the smell of burning flesh filled the air.

The Spaniards believed that the native village housed a store-load of gold so the soldiers didn't kill all the inhabitants. They took some prisoner so they could torture them to find out if other towns contained treasure. The following night they moved to the next community and carried out the same ritual of destruction. In similar manners the colonial Spanish in Nicaragua murdered some eight hundred thousand natives. Eventually, the message to convert to Christianity or suffer death or slavery reached many of the natives of the New World. Although they had never heard any preaching or been given any instructions in the faith, by the year 1524, the Indians of New Spain were ready to convert in mass.[379]

The Spanish monarchs hoped that the indigenous population could be peacefully integrated into the kingdom of New Spain. The crown passed a series of progressive laws with the intent of giving the natives some respect and proper treatment, while allowing the colonists and Spain to reap the benefits from the treasures unearthed in the silver and gold mines. The colonists, however, often manipulated the decrees in order to obtain as much financial profit as possible. The result of their greed was the enslavement and massive death of much of the native population.

The Franciscan friars, a Catholic order of religious men who accompanied or joined the conquistadors and secular colonists into the New World, eventually fell into three ideological camps. One camp opposed such treatment of the natives and believed they should be patient and try to peacefully convert the Indians. Another held the position that forced conversion was necessary for the natives own good. The third group entered the New World with a conviction that the natives possessed a nature which allowed them to instantly convert to Christianity in a way never before witnessed in the history of the Christian church. The last two groups followed Christopher Columbus's belief that the New World represented the paradise of the millennium and that they were on the threshold of Joachim of Fiore's third order.

The New World also witnessed a fourth way to convert the natives. This approach, it might be said, best mimicked the evangelization techniques of the earliest church of the first two centuries. Miracles, signs, and wonders accompanied the preaching to the natives. This method came from the most unlikely of sources. A conquistador named de Vaca, who explored the southern part of what is today the United States of America, was forced to rely on his faith alone for his own survival and in the process became a beacon for the presence of Jesus to the Indians.

The story of the Franciscans' attempt to bring the millennium to the New World begins in Spain in the town of Valencia de Don Juan. Several years before Martin de Valencia would journey across the Atlantic, he could be seen naked with a rope around his neck being pulled through the main street by one of his friends. The people laughed and cheered. But the friar got what he wanted—an experience in the humility of Christ's sufferings. Friar Martin believed that such ascetic practices helped him receive a vision from God. The vision changed his life and would help shape the history of the Americas.[380]

The Millennial Kingdom of the Franciscans

In the monastery at Estremadura, Spain, Friar Valencia fell into ecstasy. As he prayed in the spirit, an image permeated his mind—thousands of pagans came to him for baptism. Perhaps this, he thought, would be the sign that the millennium was at hand. The Franciscan sought a way to fulfill the prophecy. His opportunity arrived when Hernan Cortes sent a request for Franciscan Observants to come and convert the natives of the New World.[381]

In the year 1524, Cortes knelt down before the twelve ragged friars. Their bare feet oozed blood as he reached out to kiss Valencia's hand. Such an act of humility by the great conqueror of Mexico shocked the Franciscans.

The group of men, headed by Valencia, had just walked almost three hundred miles from Vera Cruz to the capital of New Spain which had been built on the ruins of the old Aztec empire. Other missionaries from a different Franciscan order had arrived earlier, but Cortes mistrusted them. On the other hand, he knew the reputation of the Observants, and he believed in their sincerity. They would not exploit the natives. For Cortes, this group reminded him of the twelve Apostles.

As a religious order, the Observants held to some of the apocalyptic notions of an earlier order known as the Spiritual Franciscans. The Spirituals had been outlawed by the pope in the thirteenth century for following the tenets of Joachim of Fiore too closely. Joachim had predicted that certain monastics would emerge, supplanting the Catholic hierarchy and bringing the world into the millennium. While earlier popes accepted Joachim as within orthodoxy, this pope deemed the theology as dangerous and seditious. The Spirituals saw themselves as Joachim's order. When the Observants emerged in the fourteenth century, they were careful to keep Joachim's ideas within the accepted orthodoxy of their day.

On the day the twelve Observants left Spain for the New World, the minister-general of the Franciscan order, Friar Francisco de Los Angeles, claimed their mission was the beginning of the last preaching of the Gospel on the eve of the end of the world. As he bade them farewell, he told them, 'The day of the world is already reaching the eleventh hour. You of the Father of the family are called to go to the vineyard."[382]

When the twelve arrived in New Spain, they brought Joachim's eschatology with them. One of the twelve in particular believed strongly in the millennial mission. Geronimo de Mendieta held that God had ordained Cortes as an instrument to bring about Joachim's third order.

The New Moses

Mendeita viewed the conquest of the Americas in apocalyptic terms in which its discovery heralded the end of the world. "Philip II of Spain," he would one day write in his history of the New World, "is the Promised one, the Messiah-Last World Ruler who is destined to convert all mankind on the eve of the Last Judgment." However, unlike Joachim who preached a peaceful transition to the millennium, this Franciscan supposed that the process would not always be nonviolent as false sects might have to be destroyed and opposition squashed. He was convinced that Hernan Cortes helped fulfill prophecy in conquering Mexico.

Mendieta believed Cortes' exploits against Montezuma copied Moses' confrontation with the Egyptian Pharaoh as described in the Old Testament. The Aztecs' human sacrifice and false religion represented the slavery of the Jews under the Egyptian priests. As Moses freed the Jews from bondage, Cortes freed the natives from spiritual oppression.

Cortes' greatest conquest, however, did not lay in his defeat of the Aztecs, but in his act of humility in welcoming the twelve Observants. Mendieta would write that in this gesture, Cortes acted "not as a human being, but as an angelic and divine being." The act of kneeling and kissing the hand of Valencia not only impressed the Franciscans but also the natives. The Franciscan made a point of including this event in his history because it gave an air of authority to his own religious order and to the millennial mission to the Indians.[383]

With Cortes establishing the stature of the twelve missionaries, they began carrying out their millennial task of converting the native population. The message went out to the surrounding villages—the twelve Franciscans had come to the New World to baptize the inhabitants. The response astounded the friars. Entire towns showed up. As the natives lined up, some dropped to their knees, raising and clasping their hands, while others moaned, wept, and sighed, all begging for the ceremony.

Over the following months, the twelve baptized thousands. The display convinced Friar Valencia that the natives had an innate spiritual nature which allowed them to respond to the call without preaching or the demonstration of signs and wonders. In such a situation, God did not need to perform such marvels. For Valencia and the other Franciscans, the miracle rested in the overwhelming numbers that responded to their call.[384]

Valencia proclaimed, "Now I see fulfilled what the Lord showed me in the spirit." The prolific baptisms convinced the friar that he witnessed the fulfillment of his own personal prophecy and it convinced the twelve more than ever that they stood on the verge of the millennium. The utopian mindset, however, blinded the Franciscans to the reality of the situation. The conversions proved to be a sham.

Deception

The native Indian snuck into the church yard and made his way into the empty chapel sanctuary. He began digging under the stones in the steps leading up to the large crucifix, burying an image from the traditional pantheon. On the next Sunday, he knelt before the crucifix and worshipped his pagan god.

That week, in a secret place in the jungle concealed from Spanish eyes, native worshipers stood before the pagan priest and his attendants. The servants laid a human victim on his back as the priest held up the knife over the heart. He slashed the instrument across the chest and plunged his hand into the cavity, pulling out the beating heart. He placed the organ on a heated barbeque spit and then cut off the victim's head. That practice was supposed to have ended with the mass conversions overseen by the Franciscans. Instead, pagan worship went underground. [385]

In the year 1526, Bernardo de Sahugan arrived in New Spain, studying under the tutelage of Friar Valencia. On his arrival, the Franciscans told him, "These people had come to the faith so sincerely that there was no need to preach against idolatry because they had abandoned it so truly." They further told him that the natives had come to be baptized with "little preaching and without any miracles." [386]

While on the voyage over from Spain, Sahagun gained a head-start on learning the native language from some Indians on board the ship. Once in the New World, he quickly became fluent in the foreign tongue. After interviewing a number of natives, the Franciscan suspected that the native population engaged in a dissident worship of its traditional pantheon. Sahugan learned that the Indians had duped the Franciscans with a "sly humility (with which) they quickly offered themselves to receive the faith."

In his recorded history, Friar Sahugan gives a number of reasons for the native's duplicity. One of his most telling explanations, however, was that the early Franciscans were blinded by their millenarianism and their belief that Hernan Cortes had been a new Moses who had set the native captives free from their spiritual bondage, paving the way for Joachim's third order. Under this scenario, the natives found a gullible group of men they could easily deceive. [387]

At the same time, the natives felt they had no choice but to pretend to be Christians. The Dominican missionary, Bartoleme de Las Casas, provided the motive. He wrote, "The Indians have been brought to embrace the faith…by threats of being slain or taken into captivity. . . . They are told they must embrace the Christian Faith immediately, without hearing any sermon preached and without any indoctrination." [388]

Missionaries such as Las Casas and Sahugan believed the tactics used by the Spanish evangelists needed serious reform. The Natives, the clergy advocated, required patience and in-depth teaching before baptism. They also heavily criticized the treatment of the Indians under the colonial system, which they equated with slavery and genocide. How could the indigenous population be expected to truly come to Christ while even the Christian Indians were exploited for their labor in the mines and treated as something less than human?

By the year 1561, the Franciscans found the New World church in complete disarray. Missionary Diego de Landa sought to change the situation. While critical of the greed of the secular colonials and their treatment of the natives, he still supported forced conversion. In his own quest for the millennium, De Landa set out to bring the Spanish Inquisition to the New World and root out paganism once and for all. The inquisition began after Mayan children seemed to vanish into thin air.

The Mayan Inquisition and the Millennium

What was happening to the smallest children of Mani? In 1562, the town's Spanish authorities wondered how and why they disappeared without a trace. The answer soon became evident.

Two Mayan boys stumbled into a cave on the outskirts of the village where they found a cache of ceramic sculptures and human skulls. An exploration of nearby caves by officials found the grisly remains of children that had been crucified. Apparently, certain members of the indigenous population had not given up the practice of human sacrifice; they just added crucifixion to the rites of heart extraction and beheading.

The leader of the Franciscan mission in the Yucatan, Friar de Landa, ordered an extensive investigation of the ritual murders and secret cult practices. The outcome revealed 196 human sacrifices deposited in various cave sites.[389]

De Landa began his examinations by arresting thousands of Mayans and questioning them under torture. He used various instruments and techniques, such as hanging the natives by their wrists and using the pulley and the "burro," which was a wooden rack that stretched the victim. Several hundred natives died in the interrogations while many others suffered permanent scars and disfigurements. De Landa also confiscated many Mayan religious texts and codices and burned them, an act that has helped stifle modern historical research into the ancient period.[390]

De Landa, however, did not simply wish to stop human sacrifice because of its unethical destruction of innocent human life. The friar was convinced that all the beliefs and practices of the native's indigenous religion threatened to keep the millennial kingdom from descending over the world.

Diego de Landa became a member of the Franciscan order in Spain at the age of sixteen. In 1549, he joined the mission to evangelize the natives of the Yucatan Province in the New World. In his early years in the region, de Landa was a protégé of Lorenzo de Bienvenida and Luis de Villalpando, both missionaries steeped in the Franciscan millenarian tradition. Like Mendieta, de Landa thought Spain had been called out by God when he wrote," May God glory in Spain when he chose her from so many nations to save so many people."

During his first year in the region, the friar became Assistant Guardian and built a monastery. He also erected a church building on top of the Great

Pyramid in the town of Itzmal. A look inside the church provides clues toward understanding de Landa's millennial beliefs. On the east wall of the chapel hangs a mural depicting the Virgin Mary that appears in keeping with John's description in the book of Revelation of "a woman clothed with the sun." In Catholic theology concerning the book, John's woman is representative of the Virgin Mary who further symbolizes the Catholic Church. The woman is an impending sign of missionary activity during the period of the Revelation.[391]

De Landa's own writings further clarify his beliefs in Franciscan eschatology. In his justification of the inquisition and his overall missionary work, he wrote of his understanding of the Yucatan in the light of the prophecies concerning Jerusalem, "that its enemies would encircle it and encompass it and press so hard against it." In his mind, if not for his own efforts and the efforts of his supporters, the New Jerusalem of the Yucatan would be destroyed. The march to Joachim's third order depended on the mass conversion of the natives of the New World and the purity of the Mayan church. De Landa's inquisition, therefore, had to be implemented in order to save the millennium. [392]

In spite of De Landa's belief that coercion was necessary, a counterpart to forced conversion had taken place some thirty years earlier in 1527. A conquistador, named Cabeza de Vaca, exploring the region that today is known as the southern part of the United States, lost his ability to wage war against the natives. Stripped down to slavery and on the brink of death, the Spanish adventurer turned to the power of the divine. The events that followed remain one of the most extraordinary stories in the annals of the New World. Cabeza de Vaca would demonstrate what could happen when one relies solely on faith to convert the natives, as well as for one's own survival.

The Journey into Darkness

The natives wept and had torn down their companion's lodge, the tribal way of indicating death. Conquistador Cabeza de Vaca leaned over the stiff body, finding its eyes open and staring up. He took the pulse on the wrist. No sign of life. De Vaca removed the blanket that draped the body. "Our Father who art in heaven," he began entreating. When he finished that prayer he recited the Hail Mary. He then spoke in his own words asking Christ to heal the lifeless native. He laid hands on the body and breathed on it a number of times. De Vaca then made the sign of the cross. With the ritual completed, the natives laid a basket of fish at the conquistador's feet and then escorted him to some others who suffered from vertigo. He prayed over all of them and then returned to his base camp.

That night, tribesmen burst into de Vaca's tent. Out of breath, they labored to described how after he had left, the dead man rose from his bed, had talked with them, and had eaten food. The others who suffered from vertigo had also been healed. The experience of the resurrection started a chain reaction that reverberated through the native populations of Texas and New Mexico. The event would help lead de Vaca out of his journey of darkness, a journey which started some years before when the Spanish believed gold could be found in the New World region of Florida.

In 1494, two years after Columbus made his voyage of discovery, Pope Alexander VI issued documents known as papal bulls that divided the new world into two regions. The eastern portion belonged to Portugal, while the pope gave the west to Spain. The pontiff believed that he had divided the land fairly. He based his decision, however, on the drawings of poorly-informed cartographers. The result was that Portugal had nearly nothing, while Castile was left as the ruler of two continents.

Spainish leaders, believing their country had been spiritually blessed, spent three decades plundering the riches of the Caribbean islands, and much of Central and South America. By 1527, however, regions north of the Gulf of Mexico remained mostly unexplored. Cabeza de Vaca signed-on to the expedition to discover what lay in the territory. His story begins in the Spanish colony of Santa Domingo.

Streams of Florida Gold

Rumors swirled throughout Santo Domingo—gold ran rife in the streams of Apalechen, a native village in the newly discovered area that is today called Florida. Ponce de Leon discovered Florida in 1512 and returned to establish a colony in 1521. He soon died, however, in a hail of native arrows. Five years later, Lucas de Ayllon attempted to found a settlement in North Carolina but suffered the same fate as Leon. The rumors of riches, however, meant that the Spanish monarchy could not ignore these northern territories because of potential violence.

Already a rich man from twenty years of conquests and enslaving the natives of the New World, Panfilo de Narveaz dreamed of even more adventure and wealth that awaited him in Florida. He journeyed to Spain to petition the king for the right to subdue and govern the northern territory. Charles V granted Narveaz the patent in 1526.

Although Charles allowed Narveaz to take command of the expedition, he knew of the adventurer's ruthlessness. The king hoped that he could establish peaceful relations with the natives and he established rules by which the colonists were to give proper treatment to the indigenous population. To this end, he appointed Cabeza de Vaca as treasurer. A hardened war veteran, de Vaca, nevertheless, displayed a sense of compassion, fair play, and honesty. The Spanish monarch could trust such a man to be his eyes and ears, as well as help mitigate Narveaz's worst impulses.[393]

In April of 1528, after a series of debilitating storms, the sailors of the expedition of four ships carrying some four-hundred men and eighty horses spotted land off the Florida coast. The ships anchored at what is today known as Saint Petersburg. Against de Vaca's better judgment, Narveaz decided to split the expedition in two, with two hundred men and forty horses trekking into the wilderness while the rest would remain on ships and sail up the coast. Narvaez planned to eventually meet up with the ships as the land expedition traveled north and then turned toward the coast again. Narveaz and de Vaca would never see the ships again.

Three hundred miles later, the land expedition reached the village of Apalachen. Weak from incessant mosquito bites and lack of food, the site of the native village made the conquistadors even more ill. Dilapidated and dirty, forty thatched huts made up the entire town. No gold or riches of any kind, only cowering native women and children. The men had fled into the jungle as they realized the approaching contingent.

Over the next course of days and weeks the native warriors fought a guerilla war of hit and run against the conquistadors, a tactic the Spaniards failed to effectively counteract. The number of Narveaz's troops slowly dwindled. After twenty days in Apalachen, the expedition left and traveled south. Everywhere the Spaniards went, however, they encountered the same impoverished communities, and the natives continued their jungle methods of battle.

Eventually, the Indians ceased their warfare, but fever became the expedition's new enemy. Despite the hardships, the tortured group reached the Gulf of Mexico. By the time they reached the coast, however, many of the men had perished.

As sick men continued to die, the contingent created make-shift rafts and they sailed south along the Gulf. After a series of misadventures with storms and hostile Indians, they landed at Galveston Island off the coast of Texas.[394] The natives on the island took the Spaniards as slaves.

What had started as a high adventure to find gold had been reduced to a constant struggle for survival. The men were reduced to depending on the natives' mercy for their continued existence. Throughout the ordeal of his slavery, de Vaca's religion became his only source of comfort. "When I was afflicted in this way," he wrote, "my only comfort and consolation was to think about the suffering of our redeemer Jesus Christ and the blood he shed for me, and to consider how much greater was the torment he suffered from the thorns than what I was suffering at that time."

The time of slavery and dependency on the natives also proved to be the fertile ground that would cause de Vaca's faith to grow. After a year, de Vaca and three other Spaniards escaped, finding shelter with another native tribe on the mainland. Even though the Indians treated them well, the Spaniards lived in fear of being sacrificed to the native gods.

One day, tribal members demanded the Spaniards heal their sick. "We have no degrees or diplomas in medicine," said de Vaca, making light of the situation. The answer did not amuse the natives. The chief responded by claiming that if the conquistadors had the power to travel from a distant land, they must have great power to heal. The natives withheld food from the Spaniards until they agreed to do as commanded.

The Children from the Sun

They had nothing to lose, so the Spaniards agreed to try to heal the sick natives. They began by emulating two of the techniques de Vaca had witnessed from the shaman medicine men: blowing and laying hands on the wound. Both methods had their precedents in the New Testament. In John's Gospel, Jesus blew on his disciples, telling them to receive the Holy Spirit, and there are many examples in the New Testament of the laying-on of hands for the sick for their healing. Next, the conquistadors turned to specifically Catholic customs by reciting the Our Father and the Hail Mary. Then they prayed in their own words. And finally, they completed the ritual by making the sign of the cross over the patients. To their amazement, the sick recovered.[395]

As a result of the healings, the natives treated the Spaniards with a little more kindness. Life, however, remained difficult with years of hard labor. Finally, de Vaca decided to travel inland to try to find other Spaniards. Of the original expedition, only four now remained alive. On September 23, 1534, the group set out to cross the region of Texas.

Hungry and burnt from the sun, the travelers first reached the camp of the Chavavares. The Indian tribe knew them. They were the famed white medicine men.

On the night of the Spaniards' arrival, sick Indians came to them complaining of what appeared to be migraine headaches. Castillo, one of the four, prayed and made the sign of the cross over the patients. The throbbing ceased. The natives paid the white men with so much venison they didn't know where to store it all. And then rejoicing began as the natives danced and chanted praises for the rest of the night.

Runners brought the news of the healings to neighboring villages and soon others arrived before the white men. The lame, the depressed, those with boils, cramps, hemorrhoids, indigestion, and all manner of affliction were brought by the throngs of patients waiting for prayer. Taking each person in turn, the Spaniards implored God and made the sign of the cross. As they experienced their healing, the ecstatic natives dropped to their knees and made the sign for themselves. In his journal, de Vaca wrote of the events, "We gave many thanks to God, for every day went on increasing His compassion and His gifts."[396]

All kinds of tribes came for healing: the Cultalchulches, the Maliacones, the Coayos, the Susolas, and Atoyas. De Vaca later wrote, "The Indians talked only of the wonders which God our Lord worked through us; people came from many parts to seek us that we might heal them."

One day, one of the Susolas pleaded with the healers to journey to his village as a man was near death and to too incapacitated to travel. The seriousness of the case frightened Castillo as he worried there was too great a chance for failure. De Vaca and the others, however, agreed to do what they could. When they reached the camp, the sound of weeping and crying told the healers they were too late. The two hesitated, but de Vaca had witnessed too many miracles to give up. In most of their healings, they had only to pray and make the sign of the cross to witness success. This time, however, the conquistador employed every ritual he could think of, including the shamans' practices of blowing and laying on of hands. Later, after de Vaca's village received the news the patient had risen from the dead, the natives told the four, "You are the children from the sun."

In the year 1535, de Vaca and the other three decided to leave the Chavavares' camp and continue their journey to find Spanish civilization. Each native village they encountered welcomed them. In a rare case when they reached a camp of natives who had never heard of them, the Spaniards quelled the indigenous peoples' fear by healing their sick. A number of natives came from another village and found healing. When the four once again set out on their travels, they were never alone again.

De Vaca reported that along the way, "We reached a hundred habitations." From village to village, contingents of natives followed along, sometimes numbering in the hundreds. Desiring to witness and experience healings, natives from each village joined the group. For the Indians, it became the trail of miracles.

The trail would lead to the various clans and tribes of the Comanche and Apache. As the group approached one village, the natives poured out, singing and dancing with men, women, and children fighting madly against each other to get close and touch the white healers. The natives presented them with medicine gourds– sacred rattles that only the holiest of men were allowed to touch. When the contingent left, all the people of the village followed.

Along the trail, de Vaca described the situation: "All these people came to us to be touched and blessed. They were so insistent that it was very difficult for us to deal with this. Everyone, sick or healthy, wanted to be blessed. It often happened that women who were traveling with us gave birth along the way. Once the child was born they would bring it to us to be touched and blessed. They always accompanied us until they turned us over to other people. All these people were certain that we had come from heaven."[397]

The conquistadors had learned six native languages, but along the trail, they encountered dialect unknown to them. In most cases, de Vaca had to communicate by sign language. In spite of the difficulties, de Vaca did the best he could to convey his religious beliefs: "We told them . . . that there was a man in heaven whom we called God, who had created heaven and earth . . . and that we did what he commanded us to do, and that from his hand came all good things; and that if they would do this they would be much better for it. And we found in them such a disposition to believe, that if there had been a language in which we could have understood each other perfectly we would have left them all Christians."

The group would eventually cross Texas into New Mexico and make its way to the Gulf of California before traveling down into Mexico and finding Spanish civilization. In spite of the linguistic obstacles, de Vaca left behind many in New Mexico who ascribed to his religion. Fifty years later, the natives of New Mexico remembered de Vaca. In his journey through the region, explorer Antonio de Espejo recorded that the teachings of Cabeza de Vaca and his companions were remembered: the sign of the cross, the doctrines of a Christian God, from which came all life and the blessings of the earth, all were not forgotten.[398]

Once they returned to civilization, the four men became spokesmen for better treatment of the Indians. For the most part, their pleas fell on deaf ears and the exploitation continued. De Vaca, however, did the best he could as he wrote: "We had many and great altercations with the Christians because they wanted to make slaves of the Indians." He even once addressed the King of Spain directly: "All these people, if they are to be brought to be Christians and into obedience of Your Imperial Majesty, must be led by good treatment . . . this is a very sure way, and no other will suffice"

Eventually, the Spanish herded the Indians of the southern United States into the mission system where many of them, particularly the Comanches, Apaches, and Wichitas rejected that way of life. Thus the colonials together with the religious orders of the Franciscans, Dominicans, and Jesuits spoiled de Vaca's spiritual advancements.

The Catholic Church rejected the accounts of the healings on the basis that the four were not ordained clergy and, therefore, the stories could not be true. The Protestants accepted the accounts as true, but since the healings took place at the hands of Catholics, they reasoned that they must have been done by the power of the Devil.[399]

Cabeza de Vaca proved that the natives of the New World would willingly embrace Christianity when faith in the power of the Spirit was coupled with concern for their welfare. Most of the various missionary groups, however, chose to try to force the millennial kingdom on earth by coercing the Indians to adopt their beliefs. A bishop would write: "The regular orders are now inflicting many mistreatments upon the Indians, with great haughtiness and cruelty, for when the Indians do not obey them, they insult and strike them, tear out their hair, have them stripped and cruelly flogged, and then throw them into prison in chains and cruel irons." In the years to come, the practices of the Dominicans, Franciscans, and Jesuits brought about violent rebellions against them, sometimes resulting in the friars' deaths.

Many of the natives' mistrust of the white man continued as people from England and France moved into the New World to stake their claim on the land and the riches it could provide. In England, pamphlets flooded the streets of London promising America as the land of profits, glory, adventure, and for the clergy, the assurance of new converts to Christianity. By the year 1607, English colonials arrived in Virginia. In the years to come, the natives would be exploited again, this time to work tobacco plantations. Eventually African slaves would be imported, as well.

By the year 1620, many of the English colonists known as the Puritans looked upon the New World as a New Jerusalem. Ninety years before this, however, at about the same time Cabeza de Vaca made his fateful journey into darkness, England would experience the first rumblings of a violent revolution that would reverberate through the British Isles and carry over to the Americas. The revolution and England's New Jerusalem can be said to have begun in 1529 when the King of England sought a divorce from his Spanish wife.

CHAPTER 13
MARY TUDOR AND THE REVELATION'S EXILES

"FAREWELL, MY DEAR CHILD, and pray for me, and I shall pray for you and all your friends, that we may merrily meet in heaven. . . . And the Lord bless Thomas and Austin, and all they shall have." After finishing the letter to his daughter, Margaret, Thomas More coupled it with his scourging whip and gave them to the jailer to send to his family.

Three days earlier, as guards led More from the hall where his trial had taken place, Margret had mixed with the crowd and waited for her chance to say her farewell. When her father passed by the spot where she stood, she pushed through the crowd and stormed past the sentries until she reached his side. Forgetting all the shyness and timidity that marked her nature, she fell upon his neck, pressing him to her bosom. "Oh, my father," she cried as she refused to give up her clasp. At last, the guards tore her away.

"Pray for my soul," More pleaded to his daughter as the guards led him back to his cell in the Tower.

The next morning, on July 6, AD 1535, More arrived at his place of execution. Once he made his way onto the scaffold, he expressed his desire to address the crowd, but the sheriff forbad it. He contented himself to make one quick statement. "I die a faithful servant of God and the king, and in the Catholic faith." At that he knelt down and recited the Psalm 50.

Then More thrust himself to his feet and in the customary fashion, the executioner begged his forgiveness. The condemned man responded by kissing him and saying, "On this day you shall give me a greater benefit that any other man can give me."

The executioner moved to bind a cloth around his eyes, but More held him back. "I have brought my own." He covered his eyes with the garment and then knelt, placing his head on the block. In one blow, the executioner did his duty. The crowd cheered as More's head dropped into the basket.

King Henry VIII rolled two dice on the table as Anne Boleyn sat by his side. The messenger broke into the room, interrupting the game. "Is Thomas dead, then?" asked Henry. The messenger replied that it was so. Henry burst from the table, pointing his finger at Anne. "You are the cause of that man's death," Henry bellowed. He stormed out of the room with tears streaming down his cheeks.[400]

The death of Thomas More was one of many executions that plagued England in the battle between freedom of conscience and religion and the advent of heresy laws disguised as political treason. More died as a heretic and traitor for opposing the king's marriage to Anne Boleyn. Ironically, during his life, Thomas More, this man for all seasons, advocated the burning of several Protestants for heresy.[401]

More's encouragement for the death penalty for religious conscience helped set the stage for a conflict that engulfed England's Catholics and Protestants. Eventually, the clash would involve two sisters, each one standing on different sides of the divide, with their bloody reigns remarkably alike. The clash, however, began with the event that started the argument between More and Henry. On the night of June 22, 1527, some fifteen years before More's execution, Henry entered the bed chamber of his wife, Katherine of Aragon.

A Queen's Broken Heart

The sounds of sobbing and wailing reverberated through the door and down the hallway. The sudden burst of tears shook Henry. He tried to pacify Katherine, telling her that he still loved her, but to no avail. The pronouncement struck her heart and nothing the king said now could alleviate the pain. When he first came to her she couldn't believe what he was saying—their marriage was a sham, an eighteen-year charade that defied God's Holy Scriptures.

Henry recited Leviticus chapter 20, verse 16: "If a man shall take his brother's wife, it is an impurity; he hath uncovered his brother's nakedness; they shall be childless." Katherine had been married to Henry's brother, Arthur, but she married Henry after Arthur died. In the midst of her sobs, Katherine protested that Arthur had been too sickly to consummate their marriage, and she had remained a virgin until she married Henry. But her reasoning fell on deaf ears. Later at her divorce trial she would reiterate her claim, "And when you had me at first, I take God as my judge, I was a virgin, without the touch of man. Whether this be true or not, I leave it to your own conscience."

For months leading up to his announcement to Katherine, Henry posed the question of Leviticus to England's scholars and theologians—did the passage refer to only a living brother or did it also refer to a deceased brother? And is this why so many of his children were born dead? The academics wrestled with the answer. Thomas More came down on the side that the passage referred only to a living brother and cited Deuteronomy which encouraged a man to marry his brother's widow. But More could not persuade the monarch. The king chose to listen to those scholars who told him what he wanted to hear.

For many years Katherine's marriage to Henry had been happy. For the last two years, however, they had slept apart. Now in her forties, the queen's youthful beauty had faded and some of her contemporaries claimed she looked grotesque compared to some of the women who lingered at the royal court, and in particular, one named Anne Boleyn. Despite their separation, Henry's announcement caught Katherine by surprise and her world crashed. And not only for her, but also for their royal daughter Mary, who would soon be proclaimed a bastard.

The Pearl of the World

Throughout the years of Henry's and Katherine's marriage the queen conceived eleven times. Ten children died with nine of them stillborn. Mary, however, was born on the eighteenth of February, 1516, and lived.

Two days later, at the Church of the Observant Friars, Mary's godfather, Cardinal Wolsey cradled the little princess in his arms as he held her over the baptismal font. He made the sign of the cross over her body before he poured the water over her head. Many of England's nobility looked on. The witnesses, however, did not include Henry or Katherine.[402]

Mary grew up having minimal contact with her royal parents, seeing them primarily on special occasions. Such a practice may seem odd today, but in the middle ages, daily contact was a luxury left for the less majestic of England's children. Mary spent much more time in the presence of her wet nurse and governess, Margret Pole, and her tutors, learning the theology of Augustine, Jerome, Aquinas, and reading the Bible in Latin.[403] Henry took pleasure in the little girl, though he seldom saw her, referring to her as his pearl of the world.

Through the years of her childhood, Mary cherished the infrequent visits with Henry and Katherine. At about age twelve she wrote to Wolsey thanking him for interceding on her behalf as "I have been allowed, for a month to enjoy, to my supreme delight, the society of the king and queen my parents."[404]

Time spent with her mother and father gradually increased and the princess must have appreciated those occasions. But after the night Henry announced his desire that his marriage to Katherine be annulled, Mary likely sensed the developing theological and cultural tempest that would tear her world apart. At the heart of the storm stood a raving black-haired Protestant named Anne Boleyn.[405]

The Other Woman

Attractive but not exceptional looking, Anne Boleyn, nonetheless, possessed a feminine charisma that enticed men. Equally important to Henry, she was young. The king believed she could provide him the male heir that Katherine could not.

The moment Henry fell in love with Anne is unknown. She had, however, frequented his court for some years before he voiced his affections in a note to her claiming that he had "been struck with the dart of love."[406]

Henry petitioned Pope Clement VII for the annulment. Clement was known to dispense annulments to heads of state at the drop of a hat, but with Katherine a Spanish princess, the political situation proved too volatile. Clement tried to find a way out by suggesting that Katherine commit herself to Holy Orders and chastity, thus freeing Henry to marry again. She refused and the pope vacillated in his decision.

The controversy dragged on and by the year 1531, an agitated Henry banished Katherine from court. Katherine never saw him or Mary again.[407] By 1532, it became clear to Henry that he would not win his case before the Vatican. In response to the pope's decision, a protestant theologian suggested to Henry to secede from the Catholic Church.

In earlier years the king had been defender of the Catholic faith and of the authority of the pope. On May 23, 1533, however, Henry broke from Rome and married Anne. At the time, she was one month pregnant.

Mary received a message from her father: "By order of the king, you, the present heir to the crown are required to witness the birth of the new heir. Leave for Greenwich Palace at once." Tradition required that Mary be present, not because Henry or Anne wanted her. The king had already stripped his daughter of the title of princess and now referred to her as Lady Mary. More humiliating than this, however, was the title of bastard, which the government placed upon her.

Mary arrived in the eight month of Anne's pregnancy. When the moment of delivery came on September 7, 1553, Anne was not worried about the baby's gender— the physicians, astrologers, and soothsayers all predicted a boy. A somber mood, however, accompanied the child's arrival. In spite of her tears, Anne remained confident. "A fine healthy girl this time," Anne proclaimed. "A lusty boy will be next." Eventually, the royal couple named the girl Elizabeth. Mary must have looked on with a certain satisfaction at Anne's inability to produce a male heir.

Three months after the birth, Henry established a house for the new princess in Hertfordshire with Ann Shelton, a relative to Anne Bolyn, as governess. The king also issued an order Mary was to join them immediately. When Mary heard she was to serve the new Princess of Wales, she balked. "That is a title which belongs to me by right and to no one else." But her words meant nothing. [408]

Humiliated by her decreased status and servitude to Elizabeth, Mary determined to hate the child. As the princess grew, however, the innocence and charm of the toddler won Mary's affection. Still, she refused to recognize the girl's elevated status. At times, she protested by throwing tantrums, and when expected to travel in a coach behind Elizabeth's, Mary stood her ground until picked up by servants and forced into the carriage.

By 1534, however, she knew she needed to be careful about how she acted or King Henry would fly into a rampage. In that year, Henry became intolerable to any who would defy his authority concerning the marriage. Even monks were not exempt from the king's vengeance.

The Oath of Loyalty

The Carthusian monk hung almost dead when the executioner brought him down from the walled shackles and laid him on a table. Still conscious, he felt the knife slit his stomach from one side to other. Then the abbot sensed the intestines and bowels being drawn through the opening. Horrified, he watched as his organs were placed on a hot spit. As the body parts cooked, the smell of his own burned flesh filled his nostrils. After a minute, the executioner cut the victim's body into four pieces.

Henry demanded an oath of loyalty that all citizens of England recognize him as the proper head of the Church of England rather than the pope. The Carthusians cloistered themselves away from society, preferring to spend most of their time in prayer and meditation. Many people, however, visited the monastery seeking advice. The monks refused to take the oath and voiced their support of Queen Katherine to their visitors. Henry responded by ordering the abbots hung, drawn, and quartered, a punishment reserved for the most hated of criminals. The pogrom continued with the execution of nuns and the confiscation of Catholic Church property.

Death of a Queen

Katherine lay dying. She mustered enough strength to write one more letter. "My utmost dear lord, king, and husband," she penned. "The hour of my death now drawing on, the tender love I owe you ... For my part I pardon you everything, and I wish to devoutly pray to God that He will pardon you also. . . . Lastly, I make this vow, that mine eyes desire you above all things."

Katherine died on January 7, 1536, by poisoning, according to rumors. After Henry heard the news he dressed in splendorous yellow garments and paraded Elizabeth before his courtiers. The king found joy not only in his first wife's death, but also in the fact that Anne was about to give birth again. The celebration was short lived. On January 29, the day of Katherine's funeral, Anne Boleyn miscarried. Once again, The king's eye began roving.

Anne of a Thousand Days [409]

The jailers waited for Ann at the top of the steps leading into the Tower of London. In shock and disbelief, she dropped to her knees and prayed for God to help her. She recovered her nerves and with the aid of Constable Kingston, she rose to her feet. "Will I go to a dungeon?"

No, madam, you shall go to the lodging where you laid at your coronation, answered Kingston.[410]

"Do you know why I am here?" she demanded.

Kingston replied that the three men she had committed adultery with were already in the Tower. Anne laughed and then fell into a panic, weeping. "My God bear witness," she exclaimed, "there is no truth in these charges. I am as clear from the company of men as from sin."[411]

Henry believed Anne had betrayed him. She promised a male heir and failed to deliver. The king also believed she had bewitched him, using black magic to make him fall in love with her. The charges of adultery were trumped up, a convenience Henry used to get out of the marriage. The final charges included incest with her brother.[412]

On May 18, 1536, Anne walked up the steps of the scaffold. On the platform she spoke to the crowd: "Good Christian people, I have not come here to preach a sermon; I have come here to die, for according to the Law and by the Law I am judged to die, and therefore I will speak nothing against it. . . . And I heartily desire you all to pray for me."[413]

Anne sank to her knees, praying, "Oh Lord have mercy on me. To God I commend my soul. To Jesus I commend my soul. Lord Jesus receive my soul." With those words, as one eyewitness described it, the executioner sliced off her head with one stroke of the sword.[414] Anne died on the one-thousandth day of her marriage to Henry.

Henry considered Anne's death a rightful act in payment for all the humiliation she had brought him. But even before any charges came against her, the king had already fallen in love with Jane Seymour. He married the woman eleven days after Anne's death, and she bore him a son named Edward on October 12, 1537. Twelve days later she died of an infection sustained during her pregnancy.

Before Henry Tudor's life ended, he would marry six times, with Edward the only male heir. The king died of diabetes on January 28, 1547. His death left Edward to ascend the throne at the age of fourteen. The boy was a committed Protestant and led an upheaval to unseat Catholicism within both the government and the populace. However, the religious revolution did not last long as the sickly boy died soon after becoming king. Following his death, a conspiracy to place his Protestant cousin, Jane Grey, on the throne ultimately failed. On July 19, 1553 Jane was arrested by troops devoted to Mary Tudor.

The Rightful Queen

On July 15, 1553, Catholic Church bells rang throughout the city of London as masses spilled onto the streets with cheers and celebration. Almost no one remained indoors. The jubilant throngs became so thick that the Lord Mayor had difficulty making his way to the cross at the Cheapside area to make his announcement. When he reached the cross he proclaimed Mary to be the queen of England. The crowd erupted into singing and dancing and authorities worked to run the city's fountains with wine. Most of the people in England had always considered Mary the true heir.

Those of the nobility that had supported the conspiracy to crown Jane Grey did an about face, switching their allegiance to Mary. The queen pardoned most of them, but not Jane. Her fate would be the scaffold and the executioner's ax. Many Protestants looked upon the occasion with bitterness.[415]

Early in her monarchy, Mary dealt with religion. She burned with the desire to return England to the authority of the pope and all the people to Roman Catholicism. The sacrament of the Eucharist and the real physical presence of Christ stood at the heart of her belief. Mary couldn't understand why anyone held a different view of communion. For her, rejection of transubstantiation, the belief that during communion, the bread and wine turn into the physical body and blood of Jesus, was the deepest of heresies.[416]

Mary moved quickly to re-establish the Catholic Mass as the official celebration in the churches in London, ending Edward's banishment of the practice. Many Protestants in the government had to step down, and were replaced by Catholics. The queen moved slowly in attempting to bring the nation back under the authority of the pope. Her father had established the Monarchy as head of the church, so why not use her ecclesiastical supremacy to completely reform the English church and government under Catholic law?

While the queen instituted reforms around Catholicism in society, she determined that she would not force Protestants to recant. In spite of this, many Protestants reacted strongly against her actions, taking to the street corners and parks to openly condemn her. Another of her actions, perhaps the most reviled of all, inspired a strong Protestant reaction. Mary brought an alliance that convinced many Protestants that England would eventually subject itself to Catholic Spain. No doubt the violent response against her would play an important part in eventually turning Mary away from religious tolerance. Her marriage to a Spanish prince would help spin the wheels of religious persecution.

Philip of Spain

Mary entered the room at Whitehall and walked to a corner where the Sacrament hung from a rope. She flung herself to her knees before the Host and cried to God that she did not desire marriage out of lust or carnal desires, but only out of her sense of duty to her country and its people.

Philip arrived in England from Spain on July 20, 1554. Three days later he met Mary for the first time. Two days after that, he entered the Episcopal Church in Winchester. Mary had kept him waiting for more than an hour. When she finally appeared, she dazzled the onlookers with a dress that shone with gold. Together, Philip and Mary walked up the aisle to the altar where the wedding ceremony commenced and finished three hours later.

Philip did not love Mary, and he never would. The marriage was politically expedient—a Catholic England could keep this part of Britain out of alliances with Spain's rebellious subjects in Germany. Before they met, Mary knew him only from a portrait and information given about him from couriers. Three months before the marriage, while in prayer, she made a choice to love him. What started as an act of the will ended in a deep emotion of the heart. Mary always loved Philip even though he would break her heart time and time again.

After the ceremony, as the couple made their way through the streets of London, Philip's Spanish attendants could sense the hostility in the faces of the people. Few English favored the marriage to a Spaniard, and the Protestants, in particular, were livid.[417]

Prior to the marriage, a protestant named Thomas Wyatt had hatched an elaborate plot to stop the betrothal from taking place. Several thousand Protestants joined in, but the rebellion collapsed and Wyatt was arrested. With hostility toward all the Catholic reforms running high among the Protestants, Parliament's and Mary's mood for tolerance ended.

On November 24, Cardinal Pole addressed Parliament, encouraging it to take strong actions against the Protestants. The Assembly complied on November 29, restoring England to papal authority. By Christmas it passed an act against heresy. The law gave Catholic bishops the right to investigate those suspected of heresy and hand them over to the civil authorities for prosecution. The writ of each execution was to be signed by the Queen, giving her direct responsibility. However, at first, heretics were allowed to recant their position and make their peace with the Catholic Church, and thus be set free.

Bonfires lit up the streets and once again, church bells rang throughout London. The rumors ran rampant— Mary had given birth to a son. When the announcement reached Spain, Philip's sister sent him a letter of congratulations. However, no child appeared and soon everyone realized the report was false. Mary swore that the swelling in her womb indicated pregnancy, even though her midwife doubted it and believed the doctors to be either very ignorant or content in telling Mary what she wanted to hear.

The realization that she was not pregnant struck Mary profoundly. Not only had she misdiagnosed her condition but Philip was nowhere near. He felt stifled by the marriage and he desired adventure. The Spaniard believed he had done his duty in providing an heir and so left for the Low Countries on a campaign against the French. Under the persuasion of Cardinal Pole, Mary had already started a pogrom against Protestants.

The Queen's personal life was now spinning out of control. Questions as to why had permeated her mind. Had she been devout enough to her faith? Had she acted too slowly to purify England from Protestantism? Despite all she had done, perhaps God was angry with her. In any case, the failures in her personal life did not deter her from continuing to persecute the Protestants and may have convinced her to show little mercy. The burnings had started earlier in February of 1555. Now they would continue unabated for the next three years.

Bloody Mary

As the sheriffs brought John Rogers out of his cell to be transferred to his place of execution at Smithfield, Sheriff Woodroofe asked him if he would repent of his doctrines and evil opinion of the sacrament of the altar. "That which I have preached," answered Rogers, "I will seal with my blood."

"You are a heretic," Woodroofe accused.

"That shall be determined at the day of Judgment."

"I will never pray for you," rejoined Woodroofe.

"But I will pray for you," responded Rogers.

At Smithfield, just before the sheriffs lit the fire, they brought a pardon from the queen and offered Rogers one more chance to recant. Once again, he refused. As Rogers' body burned at the stake, French Ambassador Noailles commented how the crowd sympathized with Rogers. "Even his children assisted at comforting him in such a manner that it seemed as if he had been led to a wedding rather than an execution," wrote Noailles.[418] John Rogers died on the morning of February 4, 1555, the first of many Protestants to burn.

John Hooper was next. Accused of denying the physical presence at communion, among other things, he took three-fourths of an hour to completely burn as his executioner bungled the job. When the flames finally engulfed his flesh, he cried out," Lord Jesus have mercy, Lord Jesus receive my spirit." As he slowly burned, he pleaded with the crowd to fan the flames to hasten his death.[419]

Authorities arrested Thomas Bennet for distributing tracts that claimed the pope to be the Antichrist. A monk visited Bennet in his cell, trying to persuade him to recant. "My life is not dear to me," he answered the friar. "I would rather die than partake in the detestable idolatries and superstitions, or be subject to the Antichrist, your pope." The sheriff of Devonshire burned Bennet on January 15, 1531.[420]

As is often the case with persecution, the first few deaths led to sympathy from the population, having the opposite effect Mary envisioned. Protestants became more devout and some Catholics converted after witnessing the faith of the ill-fated. Mary failed to discern the real reason for the conversions, believing instead that she needed to intensify the persecution.

The burnings included people from all walks of life, including the most uneducated and ignorant, including those who could not even define the differences between Catholic and Protestant theology. At the end of three years, some three hundred people died in the fiery trials.

The burnings convinced many English Protestants they lived in days of the Great Tribulation described by the book of Revelation. Some Protestant leaders who were able to flee the country before they were captured began developing a system of eschatology to help make sense of their predicament. In the midst of their exile, they taught that the book of Revelation proclaimed the pope to be the Antichrist.

John Bale and the Marian Exiles

John Bale escaped Mary's persecutions, fleeing the country and eventually finding his way to Basil in Switzerland where he joined other Marian exiles. He wrote a history of the English church based on his understanding of the Book of Revelation. In Bale's *The Two Churches,* the history of the English church spanned seven ages as revealed by the seven seals of Revelation.[421] The exile believed he lived in the time of the sixth seal with the upheaval of Catholic attacks upon Protestants representing the persecution of martyrs as described in Revelation, chapter six and with the papacy representing the Antichrist. The future seventh seal represented the final time period when the teaching of the true gospel and true church would permeate the world and an age of peace would ensue.

Eventually, certain exiles added the concept of equating days with years, symbolizing the 1260 days as expounded in the books of Daniel and Revelation and claiming the period represented the span of church history—1260 days equaled 1260 years. [422] The exiles used this periodization of church history to connect the papacy with the dragon in Revelation, chapter twelve, who persecuted the woman in the wilderness for 1260 days. The woman symbolized the true church through the centuries. This historical interpretation of John's Revelation, as it has become known, would one day be combined with post-millennial concepts to inspire war against Catholic Europe. In the meantime, however, Mary's bloody reign was coming to an end as her half-sister waited in the wings.

With the stench of the smoke from Protestant flesh filling their nostrils even many Catholics ended their support for Mary. The joy the population had heaped upon her at her coronation turned to scorn as she became one of the most hated monarchs in English history. On November 17, 1556, Mary died childless, and with her the dream of a united Catholic England. Upon Mary's death, Anne Boleyn's Protestant daughter ascended the throne.

In this next chapter, we'll become acquainted with Elizabeth as queen, and experience a fierce ideological battle that takes place as certain Catholics challenged the Protestants' historical interpretation of the book of Revelation. In Spain, a Jesuit priest would launch a re-birth and re-popularizing of a literal interpretation of the book of Revelation. The competing eschatologies would try to win the hearts of Europeans as the new queen of England brought her own brand of torture to religious opponents. In this way, Elizabeth's reign would resemble the reign of her sister Mary, and the Protestant interpretations of Revelation would help form the background of the new sufferings and killings.

A HOODED FIGURE left his studies and entered the seminary's dining room in the town of Douai, France, in the year 1576. He exposed his flesh by cutting a hole in the back of his robe. As the pupil walked up and down the area, he swung the leather handle of the cat of forty chords back and forth over his head, striking his back. The crooked wires at the end of the cords ripped through his skin. As blood streamed down his robe, he mumbled a prayer confessing that his sins caused his country to fall into heresy.

The next morning William Allen met his students in the classroom of the seminary. The professor founded the school with a twofold aim: to win back the Catholic community in England to a devout Catholicism and to ultimately turn all of England to the traditional Catholic religion. The Institute would accomplish this goal by training the exiled English students in the art of debate and apology against Protestants. Since the Protestant cry had been "Scripture only," the school took up the challenge by making the Bible the sole source of the debate. Catholic interpretation of Scripture would lie at the heart of the contention.

After Mary Tudor died in the year 1559, radical changes had taken place for England's Catholics. Under Mary, Catholic leaders enjoyed prestige and admiration and their churches flourished. Now the church buildings were empty, their altars smashed, and their holy water stoups destroyed. One could no longer find any representation of the Blessed Virgin Mary, the mother of Jesus, or any images representing the Trinity.

The English government passed a new round of heresy laws, but instead of targeting Protestants, as did the edicts under Mary Tudor, they now aimed at Catholics. A number of Catholic leaders fled the country to avoid prison, but some left of their own accord. Many Catholics responded to the defacing of churches with apathy and joined the new Church of England with its emphasis on merging Catholic and Protestant forms of worship. The Douai students intended to win them back and by the year 1774, a contingent had left France and stepped onto the shores of England. News soon reached Allen about how the English government treated these first missionaries. He understood that when he sent these current students back to their home county, it would be like they were stepping into a lion's den.

Along with classroom studies, self-flogging was an integral part of the Douai program. To Allen, it increased the student's discipline and tolerance for pain. The professor believed that soon they'd be ready to infiltrate England and cope with the greater tortures he knew awaited them.[423]

The seminary professor and students would help launch a new chapter in the history of religious persecution and in the interpretation of the book of Revelation. Protestants would justify the torture of Catholics by applying the historical interpretation of Revelation and claiming that the seat of the papacy had always been Antichrist. Eventually, certain Catholic Jesuit priests would respond with a more literal interpretation of the book. In a twist of irony, their understanding would help instigate an upheaval in eschatology and eventually usher in a resurgence of futurist premillennial interpretations among Protestants that continues to this day.

Allen founded the seminary in 1568. By 1576, the second group of missionaries embarked on the secret journey back to England. The toxic atmosphere these priests faced, however, began some fifteen years earlier, when Mary Tudor's half-sister, Elizabeth, took the throne of England.

A New Queen for England

On the morning of January 14, 1559, Crowds of onlookers filled the sidelines as a golden litter paraded Elizabeth through the streets of London. At different points in the procession, she would stop for a series of five pageants played out before her. Each play, in turn, stressed an important element by which Elizabeth intended to hallmark her regime. The first established Elizabeth's "Englishness" as opposed to Mary's "Spanishness." In the second play, the actor portrayed herself as the true religion that would stamp out superstition and ignorance. In the third, the mayor presented Elizabeth with a gift of gold representing the city's alliance with the crown. The fourth showcased an actress portraying Truth who presented Elizabeth with a Bible. The final play depicted Elizabeth as the Old Testament Deborah, who rescued Israel and went on to rule for forty years.

The next day in Westminster Abbey, a Catholic bishop spoke out in Latin as he crowned Elizabeth. Following the ritual, several parts of the service were read in both Latin and English. The clever compromise foretold what Elizabeth planned regarding the Church of England. She intended to strike a balance.

Elizabeth's Hybrid Church

On January 25, 1559, Nicholas Bacon gave the opening speech to Parliament. "The purpose of this government," he bellowed, "is to unite the people of this realm into a uniform order of religion." Bacon laid out part of the plan on how to reach this goal. "Frivolous and nitpicking theological arguments are for scholars, not government councilors . . . and members of the council are not to insult each other with terms such as 'papist,' 'heretic' or 'schismatic.'"

While the rhetoric suggested compromise, Elizabeth miscalculated her opposition with her first act proclaiming herself as supreme head of the church. The Catholic-dominated House of Lords soundly rejected the bill. Even some Protestants had an issue with a woman in such a role. With the second bill, however, Elizabeth employed her art for compromise by replacing the term "supreme head" with "supreme governor." The bill passed.

In April 1559, the Elizabethan government passed the Act of Uniformity. On one hand, it continued the queen's flair for cooperation and laid the groundwork for the Elizabethan church. She reinstated Edward's Protestant prayer book but also instilled two interpretations for communion: "and grant that we, receiving these thy creatures of bread and wine, according to thy Son our Savior

Jesus Christ's holy institution, in remembrance of his death and passion, may be partakers of his most blessed body and blood." The language suggested a physical presence of Christ, thus hoping to appease Catholics, but the language also suggested that communion represented a commemoration of Christ's death, thus hoping to appease Protestants. On the other hand, the Act struck a stringent chord of confrontation in that all of the clergy had to adopt the prayer book or suffer penalties.

In many respects the hybrid church resembled Catholicism in worship but its beliefs were mostly protestant. The church encouraged the English Bible to be read by parishioners in both church and privately in the homes, a practice frowned upon by traditional Catholics, who believed the clergy should always interpret the Scriptures. It was the Act's celebration of the Eucharist, however, that most assaulted the traditionalists' sensibilities. Staunch conservatives on both sides refused to accept it.[424]

Catholic Londoners, in particular, gravitated to the new church. The stench of burnt Protestants under Mary still lingered in their memories and they welcomed the compromise. In the country side, however, priests ignored the new service, holding on to the traditional form of communion and prayers. The government responded with a slow, methodical destruction of Catholic vestiges within the churches.

By 1561, the government whitewashed church walls of any paintings and images that smacked of the former religion. Crucifixes and altars were smashed and removed, and wooden figures of Christ and the saints were burned or used to poke vestry fires.[425] Elizabeth, however, did not strongly enforce the imprisonment of priests, preferring a strategy of continual persuasion. By 1563, the queen knew her policy of toleration would be difficult to maintain.

The Council of Trent

On December 4, 1563, the Council of Trent held its last session. At its conclusion, the Cardinal of Loraine rose to speak. "All heretics," he declared, "be anathema." Everyone shouted back, "Amen," and in unison sang *Te Deum*. During the assembly, the council had made it clear—those English Catholics who frequented the new church were to do so no longer.[426]

The Council, which initially convened in 1559, had also made provisions for the establishment of new seminaries devoted to a counter-reformation against the Protestants. These schools aimed to reconvert Catholics who had turned to Protestantism.

England's Privy Council responded to Trent by demanding the execution of those who refused the Oath of Uniformity. Elizabeth resisted such a notion and continued a position of compromise. Trent, however, stoked the fires of fear and by the year 1567, the government banished some of the more troublesome priests. A number of the most learned clergy left voluntarily. They eventually made their way to Douai to study under William Allen.

While many of the remaining Catholic clergy complained of Elizabeth's church, some Protestants found the new religion just as repugnant. For them, Elizabeth's church was too popish.

Small bands met in secret throughout England to preach separation from the Church of England. For these separatists, mixing Catholicism and Protestantism comingled the church of God with the synagogue of Satan. They often cited passages from John Bale's commentary on Revelation proclaiming the pope to be the Antichrist.

In London, on June 19, 1667, at a place called Plumber's Hall, a small congregation met and opened with prayers. "Look, Lord and Judge most just, on the proud bragging and boasting of the Antichrist, your enemy. . . . And, for your name's sake, wash away all dregs of popery that trouble the state of your church."[427]

Government spies had learned of the meeting and authorities barged in. They arrested the shocked leaders, conscripting them to Bidwell Prison. The incident highlighted the growing tide of the movement that would become known as Puritanism, which broke into two factions—one that wanted complete separation from the Church of England, while the other believed in reforming the church and abolishing all vestiges of Catholicism.

Both Puritans and Catholics worked to undermine Elizabeth's work for a unified church and country. She still believed, however, that the relatively minimal laws against religious dissent could persuade her opponents. Three years later, Rome made a pronouncement that all but dashed the queen's hopes.

Excommunication and Treason

In the year 1570, the pope published *Regnans in Excelsis*, a bull of excommunication. It read: "We do out of the fullness of our apostolic power declare the foresaid Elizabeth to be a heretic and in favor of heretics, and her adherents in the matters aforesaid to have incurred the sentence of excommunication and to be cut off from the unity of the body of Christ. . . . We charge and command all—the nobles, subjects, and peoples that they dare not obey her orders, mandates and laws. Those who shall act to the contrary we include in the like sentence of excommunication."

On the night of May 24, John Felton, a Catholic priest, fixed the bull to the gate of Saint Paul's in London.[428] Under torture he admitted he received it from the Spanish ambassador.

The English government took the bull of excommunication as an act of national sedition. The English Council responded with a fresh set of laws proclaiming that if any subjects accused the queen of heresy, they were to be charged with treason. Even saying mass in the traditional manner became an act of treason. Anyone carrying a papal bull of any type directed at England or not, would suffer the death penalty.[429] Suspicion began reigning over the country's Catholics, and in the minds of government officials, every Catholic traditionalist might be guilty of plotting assassination.

By 1674, the first Douai missionaries embarked for England. Most of them had no wish to mix religion with politics and desired only to convert lapsed Catholics back to the true faith. They hoped that if captured they would simply be imprisoned or banished. However, their hope proved to be in vain. In 1577, the English authorities captured, hung, drew, and quartered Douai missionary, Cuthbert Mayne. Just months later, archaeologists discovered the catacombs beneath Rome. The seminarians still waiting in Douai became convinced that the two events signaled their martyrdom.[430]

By 1580, a new group of Douai graduates prepared to embark on England. They belonged to an organization that Protestants hated the most. Edmund Campion would be the first of a contingent of Jesuits.[431]

Edmund Campion

A rising star in the Anglican Church, Campion had impressed Queen Elizabeth with his keen intellect and debating skills. At the age of twenty-six, the Oxford professor had Londoners buzzing. But just before his ordination, he had a crisis of conscience. In the year 1572, he threw away all his prestige and entered the seminary at Douai. He later joined the order of Jesuits and in 1580, Catholic authorities hailed him back to England.[432]

A comet of blood hovered over London with its tail looking like a hand brandishing a sword. A pack of ghostly vicious hounds barked in the skies above Wiltshire. A hostile fleet floated off the shores of the village of Bodmin. Such were the omens people reported seeing in England in the early part of 1580. The signs convinced many Catholics that the arrival of the Jesuits heralded the end of Protestant rule. Once more Campion had become a star, but this time on behalf of the Catholics.

News of Campion's arrival spread quickly among both Catholics and the government. Elizabeth's spies tried to cover every part of London, hoping to track him down. The Jesuit stayed away from the city and with the help of designated, trustworthy laymen, Campion ferried from one safe house to another through the various towns in the countryside.

While on the run from the authorities and while preaching from village to village, Campion wrote his *challenge* to the authorities for he knew it was only matter of time before they caught up to him. He wanted to make sure they understood his intent was only spiritual and not political: "I never had any mind, and am strictly forbidden by our Father that sent me, to deal in any respect with matter of state or policy of this realm, and to those things which do not pertain to my vocation, and from which I gladly restrain and sequester my thoughts."[433]

Campion must have sensed the rising political storm for in December of 1580, two English Catholic lords asked the pope if God sanctioned the assassination of Elizabeth. "This guilty woman," answered the pope, "who is the cause of so much intrigue and loss of so many million souls . . . there is no doubt that whoever sends her out of the world with the pious intention of doing God's service, not only does no sin but gains merit." The reply, which became known throughout England, dismayed the government.[434]

In April of 1581, secret Jesuit printing presses pumped out Campion's apology entitled *Ten Reasons for the confidence with which Edmund Campion offered his adversaries to dispute on behalf of the Faith*. In the document, he appealed to the more evangelical of his opponents by pointing out Martin Luther's rejection of the New Testament's book of James, but he also must have inflamed the government with accusations that Luther would inspire the rise of the Antichrist: "The Church Father, Hypollytus pointed out beforehand the power of the Antichrist in the times of Luther."[435]

On June 27, Oxford students found several hundred copies of the *Ten Reasons* waiting for them on the benches at their commencement ceremony. For Campion, however, it would be his last writing for soon he would have little use of his extremities and putting pen to paper would be almost impossible.

The Rack

On July 27, 1581, the authorities finally caught up with Campion in Berkshire and transferred him to the Tower of London. His *Charge* made little difference to them. The papal bull of excommunication and the pope's sanctioning of assassination had made separating the spiritual from the political virtually impossible for them. At the same time, rumors of Catholic-backed foreign invasions abounded. The government brought in torturers to get all the information they could from Campion.

The jailers laid Campion on a bed-like wooden frame with rollers on each end. They tied his hands and feet with ropes connected to the rollers. As they turned the rollers, Campion's body stretched until his tendons and ligaments cracked and popped. Several of his muscles elongated beyond the ability to contract with Campion losing the use of his right arm. After the third and final racking, the jailer asked him how his hands and feet felt. "They do not feel bad," he answered, "because I have no feeling in them at all." [436] In spite of the torture, he refused to recant or give up the names of other Catholic missionaries.

The government tried Campion on November 20, 1581 and pronounced him guilty of treason. On December 1, the authorities drove him in a cart to Tyburn, the place of hanging. Some in the crowd derided him and someone asked him what he thought of Elizabeth. "I have and do pray for her," he answered. "Yes, for Elizabeth, your queen and my queen, to whom I wish a long and quiet prosperity."[437]

While Campion remained on the carriage, the executioner placed the noose around Campion's neck, the other end of the rope tied to an overhanging wooden beam. The hired killer lashed the horses and the cart pulled away from under the Jesuit's feet. As he strangled, the executioner began to take him down alive as was the custom for drawing and quartering, but the authorities stopped him and allowed Campion to finish dying by the rope, sparing him the final torture. Once dead, they took him down and completed drawing out his organs and cutting him into four pieces.

As they dissected him, the Protestant Henry Walpole watched. Some of the blood splashed upon his clothes. He would later recount that as soon as the spray hit his body, he felt he should become Catholic. Eventually Walpole joined the mission and Campion in martyrdom. But it was his brother who left a more lasting legacy. Michael Walpole continued the English mission into the 1600's and wrote a defense against the historical interpretation of the book of Revelation and the Protestants' claim that the pope sat in the throne of the Antichrist.

Michael Walpole published his *A Treatise of Antichrist* in the year 1613. The work was a translation in English of some of French Jesuit Robert Bellarmine's arguments written in Latin some years before. Bellarmine, himself, gleaned off an even earlier writing from Spanish Jesuit, Francisco Ribera. At the heart of these writings lay an attack against the Protestant reformers interpretation of the books of Daniel and Revelation. Keeping with the theological principles of symbolization by Tychonius and Joachim of Fiore, the reformers symbolized the two books' portrayal of 1260 days to mean 1260 years. Starting in the year AD 300, or AD 606, (different reformers used different dates) the papal Antichrist would reign for 1260 years. Thus every pope sat on the throne of Antichrist. The Jesuits countered this by insisting on a literal time frame put forward by the second century church father Irenaeus—Daniel and John wrote exactly what they intended—the Antichrist would rule for a literal 1260 days or three-and-a-half years before the return of Christ at the end of the world. Therefore most of the book of Revelation remained in the future, and the Antichrist had yet to appear. This position is known to us today as futurism.

The first Jesuit writings appeared four years after the execution of Campion when the rhetoric by both Protestants and Catholics concerning the Antichrist reached a peak. For years the accusation helped fuel persecutions on both sides. The most important futurist writing that tried to mitigate the inflammatory speech by Protestants was by the Spanish Jesuit Ribera. He sought to convince the Christian church to return to more literal interpretation of Revelation.

Ribera and the Futurist Interpretation

Francisco Ribera joined the Jesuit order in 1570 and became the confessor for the Carmelite nun and famous mystic, Teresa of Avila. The Council of Trent had ordered the Counter-Reformation to answer the charges made against Catholicism by the Protestants. Ribera answered Trent's call by seeking to convince Catholics that the pope was not the Antichrist. In 1585 he prepared his commentary on the book of Revelation.

Ribera proposed that the first few chapters referred to John's own time period. The rest of the book, however, described events that would occur over the last three and a half years before the return of Christ. For Ribera, the Antichrist would be a single individual who would rebuild Solomon's Temple in Jerusalem, abolish the Christian religion, deny Christ, be received by the Jews, proclaim himself God, and conquer the world.[438]

This literal understanding rejected the Protestants claim that much of Revelation had already occurred and that the book covered the entire span of church history. Ribera, however, wrote in the confines of Augustine's amillennial position. The Jesuit still believed that the church existed in the midst of the millennium and that Christ would return at the end of it.

Over time, Bellarmine and Walpole latched onto Ribera's commentary with Walpole writing in English. Neither the Latin nor the English, however, made much of an impression with the Protestants. At the beginning of the seventeenth century, certain Puritans began writing apologies against Bellarmine, although some would put forward a futurist premillenial understanding of Revelation chapter twenty while holding to a historicist view of the chapters that preceded the twentieth. Apart from these Puritans, it's probable that most Protestants did not bother to read Ribera, Bellarmine, or Walpole. They might have taken the position that arguments originating with the Jesuits couldn't possibly be correct. Another Jesuit, however, wrote a commentary in 1791, but this time under a pseudonym that hid his Catholic identity. It proved to be a stroke of genius.

Mannnel de Lacunza's manuscript portrayed itself to be written by a Jewish Christian convert. Using many of the same arguments that came before him, Lacunza, however, differed from Ribera and other Jesuits on certain key points and proposed a return to premillennial theology. He made a particular point in emphasizing Paul's letter to the Thessalonians and an event that eventually became known as the rapture.[439]

Lacunza used the pseudonym to hide his identity from the Catholic hierarchy because he felt he would come under scrutiny from criticizing the official Catholic position of amillennialism. But because of the alias, the influential Protestant clergyman Edward Erving was persuaded to read the work. Before he realized the true identity of the author, he was already infatuated with Lacunza's Scriptural interpretations. In 1827, he would use this manuscript to start a theological revolution in eschatology that reverberates to our own day. [440]

Revelation's Third Vial

While the Jesuits busied themselves proclaiming the futurist view through the latter half of the sixteenth century, the Puritans did not shy from giving a response. In the year 1600, Thomas Brightman refuted Robert Bellarmine in his *A Revelation of the Revelation*, a work he claimed he received in an experience from God.[441] His eschatology continued to fuel the antagonism between Protestants and Catholics and justified the heresy laws perpetrated against the English mission and the torture of the Jesuits.[442]

Brightman declared that three of the vials of judgment foretold in Revelation chapter sixteen, had already occurred as God used Elizabeth to punish the Catholics. The fist vial began in 1560 when Elizabeth exiled troublesome priests who left and became part of the Douai mission. The second vial exposed the errors of the Council of Trent. The third vial was composed of England's judgments against the Jesuit order and God's support of the tortures and executions of its missionaries. According to the commentary, the final four vials would be revealed in the future.

Brightman set his vials in the midst of an amillennial/postmillennial view of the church and world. Revelation, according to Brightman, was actually comprised of two millenniums. The first began in the fourth century and the second began in the fourteenth with the preaching of early reformers.[443]

Writing in 1600, Brightman looked to the past when England's actions against the Jesuits became progressively harsh. The steps leading up to the most violent period against the missionaries began in the 1580's. The political events of this decade all but doomed the English mission.

The Road to War

While Francisco Ribera worked on his commentary, the 1580s witnessed the rise of tensions between Spain and England. For years, Philip of Spain had been the object of ridicule by English pamphleteers portraying him as the Antichrist.[444] For his part, the Spanish king grew incensed at the torture and execution of Campion and other missionary priests. From the political and economic side, English privateers attacked Spanish shipping off the West Indies, resulting in the loss of huge amounts of cargo and precious metals. Elizabeth also supported Holland in its desire for independence from Spain. In March of 1586, Philip wrote to the pope, asking for the blessing to invade England. The pope readily gave it.

In August of 1586, English spies broke up a plot to assassinate Elizabeth by a group led by the wealthy Catholic lord, Anthony Babington and the Catholic priest, John Ballard. The assassins had hoped to put Elizabeth's cousin, the Catholic, Mary Queen of Scotts on the throne in conjunction with the Spanish invasion. Mary had already been in house arrest when she and the conspirators were executed.[445] The English now knew the invasion was imminent. Elizabeth spent the next year trying to find a diplomatic solution with Spain. Mary's death, however, had hardened Philip's resolve.

On May 30, 1588, the Spanish Armada of 130 war ships set sail from Lisbon bound for England. The ships held thousands of copies of a papal bull, blessing the operation, reaffirming Elizabeth's excommunication, and calling on her subjects to rebel and aid the invasion. The invading forces planned to distribute the document on the shores of England.[446]

On July 27, the Armada anchored off Calais, not far from Dunkirk, where it picked up 16,000 troops to ferry across the English Channel. The English Navy, however, had shadowed the Spanish and geared up to intercept them. The English prepared five hell-burners, or fire ships by filling them with wood and covering them with pitch. At midnight the hell-burners slammed into the heart of the Armada, causing panic and chaos in the midst of the wind-fanned inferno. The Spanish ships could not regroup and the morale of the invaders sunk.

A final battle ensued on July 29, with the Spanish losing eleven ships and 2000 men, and the English only fifty men. The battle ended when both sides ran out of ammunition. On July 30, a "protestant wind," as the English named it, scattered the remainder of the Armada causing further damage. The Spanish Navy limped back to Spain with a mere 50 ships intact.[447]

The invasion had been an unmitigated disaster. It also proved to be a debacle for the English missionaries. Even English Catholics turned against the mission, their hatred for the Spanish and their nationalistic pride rising in support of the queen. The Monarch celebrated her victory by executing twenty priests, ten layman and one woman, all of whom had been imprisoned prior to the Armada.

The political situation through the decade of the 1580s had made Elizabeth's attitude of tolerance and compromise difficult to maintain. She needed to alleviate the Privy Counsel's desire to punish all Catholics with strict enforcement and strengthening of the heresy laws. The Queen found that striking hard at the English mission kept the Council pacified. Toward this end, she increasingly came to rely on master torturer, Richard Topcliffe.

The Pressure Increases

"Do you know me? I am Topcliffe of which I have no doubt you have heard." He laid his sword on the table near his hand to give the impression that he intended to use it. Father John Gerard gave no answer.

Topcliffe wrote a few sentences on a piece of paper and handed it to Gerard. The paper read: "The prisoner has been sent by the pope on a political errand to beguile the Queen's subjects and lure them from obedience to the Sovereign." Gerard told Topcliffe that he wished to answer in writing: "I am forbidden to meddle in matters of state; I have never done, and never will do so."

"I'll put you in my power," said Topcliffe after he read Gerard's reply, "and hang you in the air and show you no mercy. And then I will see if God will rescue you out of my hands." The guards took Gerard back to his jail cell.

Eventually the authorities transferred Gerard to the Tower of London and proceeded to take him to the torture room. The guards held candles to illumine the pitch-black corridor leading into the chamber. The lights flickered across the walls of the crypt, revealing various racks and other instruments of pain. They told Gerard he would experience them all before they were through with him. The attendants then led him to a large pillar of wood where hung chained manacles. They slipped his wrists into the manacles and ordered the prisoner to walk up three wicker steps. They raised his wrists and arms above his head and stapled the manacles to the pillar. When they pulled away the steps, Gerard's body dangled in air, suspended by his fastened wrists.

Gerard fainted several times from the pain. Each time, the guards took him down long enough for him to revive and then hung him again. During the interrogations, the prisoner refused to recant or answer any of their questions. "Hang there, then," said one of the torturers, "until you rot."

Later that night, they brought him down and returned him to his cell. He would go through three such torture sessions. Eventually, a sympathetic jailer had to feed him by putting the food into his mouth because he lost the use of his hands. Finally, Father Gerard escaped prison. After much exercise, he regained the use of his hands and wrote his autobiography.[448]

Richard Topcliffe relished in the physical and emotional suffering of Catholics. Although he left Gerard to attendants in the Tower, he engaged in torturing most of his victims in his own house, in a room he transformed into a torture chamber. While Gerard lived to tell his tale, most of Topcliffe's victims either died under his procedures, or were hung, drawn and quartered after the tortures.

Elizabeth strongly depended on Topcliffe through the 1590's to keep the missionaries at bay. By the time she died in 1603, over one hundred and fifty Catholic priests had been tortured and executed. Upon her death, James ascended the throne. With Elizabeth never having married and leaving no heirs, James the First, son of Mary Queen of Scotts, gave hope to the Catholics by way of his background. In spite of the Catholicism of James's parents, however, he proved less than friendly and maintained heresy laws against the papists. This led some Catholics to scheme to take down the entire English government with one terrorist act.

The Gunpowder Plot and the Growth of the Puritans

On May 20, 1604, the Catholic plotters met to discuss their plan to blow up the House of Parliament. In March the conspirators leased a cellar that ran under the House of Lords and filled it with thirty-six barrels of gun powder. In October, they planned the final details—blowup King James along with all members of Parliament, kidnap James's daughter, Elizabeth, and install her as a puppet queen.

An anonymous letter on October 26, however, tipped off the government authorities that something was afoot, and eventually the plot and plotters were uncovered before they could act. James responded with a set of fresh laws against Catholics including forbidding them from serving in the military.

The plot blacked the eye of English Catholicism at a time when the government worked toward peaceful relations with Spain, healing the long rift caused by the Armada. While Catholicism kept losing prestige, however, the Puritans gained. Previously having been seen as extremists, now the Puritans made great strides among the merchant class and by 1609, the charter for the Virginia Company's new Jamestown Colony in America included the words: "We would be loathe that any person should be permitted to pass that we suspect to affect the superstitions of the Church of Rome, so we do hereby declare that it is our will and pleasure that none be permitted to pass in any voyage from time to time to be made into the said country but such as first shall have taken the oath of supremacy." Puritans dominated the Virginia Company.[449]

While James disappointed the Catholics, he also frustrated the Puritans. He passed a few minor reforms favorable to them, but dashed their greater expectations. Not only was James leery of the reforms they pushed for in the Church of England, but the Puritans sparked suspicions that they supported an end of the Monarchy in favor of a republican form of government.[450]

Brightman's Final Vials

While the first three vials lauded Elizabeth for correctly punishing the Jesuits, Thomas Brightman, nonetheless, believed the final four vials would bring judgment on the Church of England for its continued flirtations with papal doctrines. For Brightman, the Anglican Church paralleled Revelation's church of Laodicea with its attitude of being spiritually lukewarm and Jesus promising to spit it out of His mouth if it didn't reform. At the same time, Brightman wrote a number of passages against the idea of separating from the Anglican Church. He remained hopeful of purifying the Church.

The commentary would have an effect on both factions of the Puritan movement. It convinced the separatists that the wrath of God would soon fall on England. At the same time, they ignored the anti-separatist passages, and in some cases, wrote critically of Brightman on that point.[451] For this wing of the Puritans, it would be better to leave England before God's judgment struck. For the other faction, however, Brightman convinced them of the possibility of reform in both church and nation.

Elizabeth's Legacy

Elizabeth's ambitions helped lead England to be respected as a world power. She also united many Catholics and Protestants into one church. Most of the Catholic and Protestant world, however, could not accept such a compromise. Those two entities would continue to clash, both theologically and with physical force.

Elizabeth's England witnessed the emergence of two competing eschatologies. In the next several chapters, as the reader of this book, you will observe the consequences of these two views of the end times. By the early nineteenth century, Jesuit eschatology would eventually find its way into Protestantism and lead many to embrace a more pacifistic and apolitical mentality. The Puritan eschatology of Thomas Brightman, on the other hand, would embrace the notion that the Kingdom of God needed to be ushered in by way of war. In time, the separatists would engage in a mass exodus to the new world while the other Puritans would combine the notions of Brightman and the eschatology of Joseph Mede and launch a violent revolution against the English Monarchy.

CHAPTER 15
STUART, CROMWELL, AND THE PURITAN REVOLUTION

THE TROOPS THAT ASSEMBLED at Bristol quivered when they heard the news—by the time they reach Dublin, 30,000 enemy combatants might be mustered against them. Many in the battalion refused to embark upon the invasion. Colonel Oliver Cromwell appeared before them, and the murmuring stopped. The army chaplains took the opportunity to encourage the soldiers. Remember, they told them, the Israelites destroyed the idolatrous Canaanites. The words calmed the soldiers as the ministers spoke in turn. Babylon will fall, they prompted them, and the New Jerusalem will rise out of the ashes.[452]

Two years before, Dublin fell to British rebel parliamentary forces fighting against the king of England who had allied himself with Ireland. Now, in July of 1649, the English Civil War had come to an end with the king's defeat and his execution. The rest of Ireland, however, still remained in opposition to the English Parliament. Maintaining the port of Dublin was necessary for an all-out invasion of the Emerald Island. Thirty thousand Irish troops moved to recapture the city in order to stop the English landing.

The day after the chaplains' addresses, reports reached Cromwell: the Irish failed to recapture the city. Upon hearing the information, he exclaimed, "an astonishing mercy, so great and seasonable that we are like them that dreamed." Cromwell had the port-city he needed to bring Ireland to its knees.[453]

On August 15, the colonel and some 15,000 troops landed at Ringside, a port village in the suburb of Dublin. Upon stepping from the ship, he took a moment to lecture the Irish nation. "You Are part of the Antichrist, who's kingdom the Scripture so expressively speaks shall be laid in blood. The fury and the wrath of God will be poured out to you"[454]

When all his troops had assembled from the ships, he instructed them. "Show no mercy to the Irish." He then took a cue from the chaplains, reminding the soldiers of their sermons. "Treat the Irish as Joshua treated the Canaanites." The example was not lost on the Puritans in the army, for they knew their Bible well. Joshua had killed every man, woman and child, except one, when he conquered the city of Jericho.[455]

After his speech, Cromwell rode his carriage toward the heart of the greater city. Cannon shots echoed in salute. When he reached his destination, he stopped the horses and stood to speak to the crowds thronging to see him. "In his providence, God has brought me safely here so I can restore liberty to all whose hearts are devoted to work against the bloodthirsty Irish and for the propagation of the Gospel of Christ." When the speech concluded, the crowds erupted in applause and shouts, "We will live with you and die with you."[456]

Atrocity at Drogheda

Several days later, Cromwell marched ten thousand of his best soldiers up the coast toward the village of Drogheda, some twenty-three miles north of Dublin.

The seaport town lay as a strategic gateway to Northern Ireland, and he needed it for a supply route from England. On the way, they camped near a churchyard where they saw a large crucifix in the center. In disgust, some of the troops tore down the icon. They considered it the mark of the Beast.[457]

They arrived at Drogheda on September 3, 1649, and laid siege two days later. Two thousand, two hundred troops defended the town.[458] After the English breached Drogheda's walls, about two thousand of the Irish soldiers surrendered and laid down their arms. The rest did not trust the English and kept their weapons. According to one eye witness account by an English officer, Cromwell ordered that no man, woman or child be spared. The English remembered Jericho. The slaughter began.

In the midst of the carnage, some one hundred Irish soldiers fled and sought sanctuary in Saint Peter's Cathedral. The move didn't save them, for the church represented the theological system of the Antichrist. The English set it on fire. Soon the smell of burning flesh permeated the air and a scream rang from the Cathedral. "God confound me, I burn, I burn." Those who chose to rush out of the flames were immediately cut to pieces in the street leading from the church. The blood flowed so freely that later generations of Irish would remember the route as 'Bloody Street.'[459]

The blood of the Catholics flowed from the houses, the streets and the open fields. The English butchered soldiers, women, children, and priests. The massacre continued over five days. As Cromwell walked along one street, he looked down at one of the corpses. An infant struggled to suck from the breast of its dead mother.[460]

What led to the onslaught was a history rooted in Puritan theology. In particular, certain eschatologies played their part in bringing about the mentality of hostility and conflict with the Emerald Island. To understand those theologies and the part they played, however, one must travel back to the beginning of the Puritans' influence in English government, an influence which began in earnest in the decade of the 1630's.

The Exodus to America and the Puritan Revolution

The year 1630 proved pivotal in the history of both England and the New World of America as a major debate erupted among the Puritans. Could the nation and the Church of England be reformed along the lines of what they considered to be the true religion? Most of them hoped for the dawning of a new day in England, but pessimism pervaded a large minority. For them, their country was Babylon, a nation hopelessly corrupt by the vestiges of Catholicism and the pope, a man the Puritans fervently believed to be the Antichrist. The destruction of England was imminent as God would pour his wrath on all who flirted with the policies of the papal Antichrist. They responded with a mass migration to the New World where they hoped to forge the Kingdom of God in the wilderness of America.[461]

In 1633, a crisis emerged fueling the debate even further when King Charles Stuart I installed William Laud as Archbishop of Canterbury. Laud instituted a sequence of reforms aimed at moving the Church of England towards a heavier sacramental theology. The Puritans also believed he supported free will over predestination. Puritan theology held that the papal Antichrist instituted the philosophy of free will.

While the exodus to the New World continued throughout the 1630s, the majority of remaining Puritans moved up into the middle class which allowed them to become influential in politics. In 1640, Charles called the Long Parliament into existence to deal with an impending invasion by the Scotts. According to charter, he needed consent to raise the funds for an adequate army. A number of Puritans won election. Although a minority in membership, they quickly became a vocal force in speeches and debates, often embarrassing the royalist majority. For many Puritans, the existence of this hostile element in the Assembly confirmed their decision to stay in England. And just as important to them, it signaled an end to the Antichrist.

The Theology of Brightman and Knollys

The news of the election of Puritans to the Long Parliament traveled across the ocean to the New World. In 1641, Hanserd Knollys, who had fled to America after experiencing imprisonment for preaching without a license, returned to address Parliament and the people of London. As he stood to preach to his new congregation, the new-found jubilation of the Puritans could be found in his sermon titled *A Glimpse of Zion's Glory*: "…there was a voice saying: Babylon is fallen, is fallen. … Babylon's falling is Zion's rising. Babylon's destruction is Jerusalem's salvation."[462]

In the Puritans' thinking, the changes occurring in England heralded the beginning of the collapse of the Antichrist's kingdom. Knollys grounded his sermon in the theology of Thomas Brightman, who followed a number of Protestant reformers proclaiming the pope the Antichrist. He also followed the historical interpretation of the book of Revelation which stated that certain events described in Revelation had already happened within church history. According to this theology, throughout the Revelation, the kingdom of God was progressing through the centuries towards fulfillment of the Kingdom.

Based on Brightman and his own understanding of the eleventh chapter of the book of Daniel, Knollys sermon included his own time frame by which the Antichrist's kingdom would come to an end. "Now reckon so many years according to the number of the days, it comes to 1650; and it is now 1641. … in 1650 they shall begin; but it shall be 45 years before it comes to full head, and blessed is he that comes to this day. … The light that I have from this, I acknowledge to be from that worthy instrument of God, Mr. Brightman." He believed the millennium would begin in 1686. Eventually, he revised this to 1688.[463]

Like Brightman, he believed that Christ's return would be spiritual and the millennium would be ruled by Christians endowed with Christ's Spirit. Christ's return in the flesh would occur at the end of the millennium.[464]

In 1642, debates raged between Puritans and the king's Loyalists in both Parliament and the military revolving around the legitimacy of monarchy. "If hierarchy be Antichrist, or monarchy or superiority, then antichrist is in Heaven," bellowed the royalist Edward Symmons. He argued that the concept of monarchy cannot logically equal the concept of Antichrist since God is a lone monarch. In his rebuttal to parliament, however, Henry Burton accepted the idea of a heavenly monarch but not an earthly one and proclaimed, "The hierarchy of Antichrist has been in England since the Reformation." Burton's response shook the royalists in parliament as it linked the very concept of monarchy with the Antichrist.[465] Such ramblings from sermons and debates, laid the foundation for war.

The king reacted to these criticisms believing that his adversaries operated outside the will of God. He began his reign stating that the rights of the people were vested solely in the king. He alleged this right had been given to him by God, and parliament had no business questioning his authority or actions. With this right in mind, he levied a series of taxes without parliament's consent, further inflaming the Puritans.

Even worse in the minds of parliamentary Puritans, Charles' wife belonged to the Catholic Church. Henrietta may have influenced Charles to install Laud as Archbishop. In any case, they judged that with her influence, the pope pulled the strings of a puppet monarchy and church hierarchy.

Archbishop Laud and the Publications of Joseph Mede

In 1637, in response to criticisms, Laud forbade the publication of any documents which proclaimed the pope the Antichrist. He followed this with the arrest of several Puritans and had their ears cut off. In 1640, at the convening of the Long Parliament, the assembly arrested him and published Joseph Mede's *Clavis Apocalyptica* in English.

The author originally wrote his work in Latin. As early as 1633, scholars in Leyden, an English city that become a hot-bed of anti-monarchy sentiment, sought after the work. It is, perhaps, ironic that Mede supported the Anglicans on most issues. However, Mede's view of the end times put him at odds with the Archbishop.

Mede incorporated the historical interpretation of Revelation with classical premillennial thinking. Parts of the Revelation occurred in the past but the millennium occurs in the future after Christ returns in the flesh. But his discussion of the vials described in Revelation particularly troubled Laud. The first vial described the judgment pronounced against the papacy by the early reformers who came before Luther: "This was fulfilled, when the lower orders of Christians, whether known by the names of the Waldensians, Albigensians, Wicliffites, Hussites, or by any other names, began everywhere to renounce the authority of the beast, crying out, that Rome was the apocalyptical Babylon, and that the pope was Antichrist."[466]

In Apocalyptica, the pope was the ten horned beast of Revelation and the Roman bishops his demon minions. The Puritans did not find the idea novel, of course, for Brightman had already raved against the pope in his own writings. But the publication of Mede's commentary on the book of Daniel in 1642 laid the real theological bombshell that eventually shook the foundations of England.

Sections 34 through 48 of the commentary implied that nations that had anything to do with Catholicism corrupted themselves with idolatry. Mede mixed Daniel with the discussion of the time of the gentiles found in the Gospel of Luke, and equated the gentiles with these idolatrous nations. In section 49, he associated monarchy with the time of the gentiles and the seventieth week of Daniel. The week represented an indefinite time period which would witness the end of all world monarchies: "That is, as was said before, until the Monarchies of the Gentiles should be finished. For these times of the Gentiles are that last period of the fourth Kingdome prophesied."[467]

When taken in conjunction with the Apocalyptica, at the end of the seventieth week, the day of resurrection occurs with the final battle of Armageddon waged against the papal antichrist. Then the millennium begins. Here in Mede is a combination of premillennial and post-millennial ideas. The destruction of world monarchies progresses through an indefinite period of time until Christ returns in the flesh. In the politics of the day, certain Puritans believed the final week was at hand and soon all Catholic monarchies would end.[468]

Discord in Zion

At the arrest of Laud, speeches against him peppered Parliament. Members claimed his rule instituted the church with bits and pieces of the Antichrist.[469] For example, Lewis Hughes told Parliament that the use of the sign of the cross during baptism was the very mark of the Beast, thus the children were baptized into the Antichrist.[470]

Many of the elder Puritans took the most radical approach concerning Bishop Laud and the Church of England. They believed in an extreme congregational form of church government: The Church of England should be ruled by an eldership elected by the congregation rather than by bishops. They also attacked the system of tithing and the mixing of civil and ecclesiastical offices. For these members, the dawn of the Long Parliament was the first step to weeding out the "root and branch" of the Antichrist. They advocated a completely new nation and spearheaded the drive to end the monarchy.

Some of the younger Puritans, however, known as National Presbyterians, differed with their elder members in that they believed that both king and Church could be reformed. Oliver Cromwell stood at the center of the dispute.

He rose from peasantry to the ranks of Parliament. Since the days of his conversion to a devout Christianity and the theology of John Calvin, Cromwell painted his life with scripture and predestination. He tried to devote every aspect of his existence to God's will. He came to believe that not only was his salvation predestined, but God preordained him for a seat in the assembly and eventually to become commander of the Army. In the embracing of Calvinism, he particularly came to hate the idea of free will. This in turn caused him to side with the "root and branch" element in eliminating every vestige of Catholicism he believed Laud had snuck into the Church of England. At the same time, he opposed the complete elimination of the monarchy, at least early on, thus siding with the National Presbyterians.

Henrietta and the Rumblings of War

Laud's arrest initiated the first reform the Puritans desired. On the heels of the arrest, a rumor circulated that the queen would join the Archbishop in the Tower of London. Charles believed the rumor for he knew Cromwell and the other Puritans utterly despised the idea of a Catholic queen ruling England.

Henrietta was the love of Charles' life. With such a passion, what would life be without her? More to the point, what would his reign have been without her? The answer to that question is that civil war might have been averted, the monarchy maintained, and the king die of old age. But history is full of powerful men who made fateful decisions over the love of women. Perhaps if he had simply been less impetuous where Henrietta was concerned, the past may have turned out differently. If he had waited before acting on the rumors, they may have proved false. The king's burning for Henrietta, however, would change England's history forever.

Charles quickly responded to the rumors and urgently moved to arrest Cromwell and certain other members of Parliament. As the dreaded news reached Parliament that the king dispatched the soldiers, all of the accused fled except one. Cromwell remained fixed in his seat. His stance emboldened the majority of Parliament. Upon their arrival, the militia did not dare carry out the task. Cromwell won the day, but the victory left Charles furious. He summoned and raised an army of mercenaries. England stood on the brink of civil war.

The Battle against Antichrist

In keeping with medieval gestures, Charles raised the royal standard in Nottingham on August 22, 1642. He then set up his court at Oxford, with his government controlling most of the north and west of England. On the other side, Parliament was popular in the cities were Puritanism was at its strongest. As a result, Parliament controlled London and most of England's south and east.

Even though most of the English cities hated Charles, when war finally broke out, Parliament initially found it was a tough sell, as the people hesitated to support a war against their rightful king. To be successful, the assemblymen needed to hammer-home just who it was fighting. The propaganda cry against Babylon provided the impetus. When one nobleman took up arms in behalf of Parliament, many in London believed him to be John the Baptist who would lead the way for Christ to return and destroy Charles.[471] With pamphlets supporting such ideas, the masses no longer hated Charles just because of his policies, but because they believed he allied himself with the Beast of Revelation. With the proclamation that the war against the monarchy was a war against the Antichrist's form of political government, the people's revulsion broke. The successful propaganda provided an important first step to ultimate victory.

But this war against the Antichrist proved costly. By the end of the struggle, historians believe that up to two hundred thousand people died from battles, skirmishes and diseases caused by the conflict. The death toll did not just involve the militias and militaries, but civilians are believed to have been massacred by the scores.

With the death toll mounting and royalist armies winning most of the battles, some within Parliament were willing to strike a compromise, with a deal almost reached in 1643. However, with the theology of the Civil War swaying toward eschatology, the cities and the Puritans would not stand for it. Once again anonymous pamphlets were distributed to make sure the people understood who they were fighting. One such tract, *England's Alarm to War against the Beast* spelled out in no uncertain terms that one could not compromise with the Antichrist.[472] The bloodshed continued.

The Trial of Laud

With the Civil War teetering, parliament took the opportunity in the spring of 1644 to bring the Archbishop to trial on charges of treason. Other formal charges against him included subverting the true religion with Catholic superstition, his refusal to call the pope the Antichrist, his rebuff to abolishing the Office of Bishop within the Church of England, and the belief that he advocated free will over predestination.

As he addressed Parliament in his own defense, he claimed he never denied predestination. As far as refusing to call the pope the Antichrist, he repeated his position that he did not believe in using foul language against others, nor did he believe that calling the pope the Antichrist ever converted one Catholic to the true religion. He did admit, however, to the charge that he refused to abolish bishops, and in this he refused to admit his error.

In 1637, Laud had already made his defense of the Anglican church government in a speech delivered to the Star Chamber, a court of inquisition, when he stated, "And I say farther, That from the Apostles' times, in all ages, in all places, the Church of Christ was governed by Bishops: And Lay-Elders I never heard of, till Calvin's new-fangled device at Geneva." Calvin put forward a congregational form of government on his supposition that all letters associated with Ignatius of Antioch were fraudulent. In reaction to the Catholic abuses that led to the Protestant Reformation, the Puritans believed that congregations should be ruled by a council of elders with the pastor just one more elder. Perhaps because of his spirited defense, Parliament could not come to a final decision against him and so returned him to prison.

This unwillingness to compromise finally paid off when the war turned in 1644 as Royal forces failed to press home a final victory at the Second Battle of Newbury. The reprieve allowed parliamentary forces to regroup under the leadership of Cromwell, who wrested sole control from the more inept leaders.

He formed the New Model Army. Nepotism and one's nobility ruled the old army. Now one's pure ability to lead troops in battle was all that mattered. At the same time, this army would be better trained and more professional than its predecessor. Perhaps more importantly, Puritans solely made up the leadership. These leaders fought to the death for they didn't simply fight against high taxes or for a more democratic form of government, they battled against the Antichrist. This army became known as the "saints in arms."

With victory in sight, the Root and Branch component of Parliament took the opportunity to call for Laud's head. They pronounced him guilty on the 10th of January, 1645 and paraded him to Tower Hill. Just before he laid his head on the block he addressed the crowd, "I will die with these words in my mouth that I never intended much less endeavored the subversion of the laws of England nor the bringing in of popish superstition upon the true Protestant religion established by law in this kingdom." He then prayed that England would be ruled by love and charity and that Christians no longer shed the blood of other Christians. With that, he placed his head on the block, and the ax spilled the blood of one more believer.

Fueled with the combination of better training and eschatological fervor, the New Model Army won battles at the towns of Naseby, Northampton, Shire, Langport, Bridgewater, Bristol, Exeter, Turo, and Chester. Of all the battles won, perhaps the most important was Naseby, in 1645. In just three hours, the rebels killed most of the royalists and butchered the rest as they tried to escape to the town of Leicester. They finished the gruesome battle by hacking to death some one hundred prostitute camp followers. The king lost five hundred officers and all his artillery. He also lost secret letters showing he intended to raise military support from Catholic countries. The publicity led many of his supporters to turn against him. The war ended within a year, and the king fled to Scotland.

The End of the Monarchy

In January of 1647, Scotland handed Charles back to the English Parliament. The king pledged to work out a deal in which Presbyterianism would rule both church and state. The final agreement witnessed a further pledge to suppress the more factional Root and Branch independents.[473] The National Presbyterians seemed to have won the day. The peace, however, did not last long.

In July of that year, a royalist insurgency broke out in several cities with the Scots invading England under the blessing of Charles. This became known as the Second Civil War. The New Model Army quickly put down the uprising, dashing the king's hope to reestablish his full authority. The final war put Stuart's rule to an end and established a parliamentary democracy. Moreover, it was the opportunity that a group of independents waited for. Their own brand of postmillennial, democratic theology began to bubble to the surface.

The postmillennial type eschatologies of Brightman, Knollys, and Mede fueled the English Civil Wars and brought parliamentary rule in place of the monarchy. But this was only the beginning. The execution of Stuart and the invasions of Ireland and Scotland lay ahead for the future of England. And an independent movement that would become known as the Fifth Monarchy would be the driving force behind it all as it tried to establish England as the hub from which the millennial kingdom descends over the world.

CHAPTER 16
MEN OF BLOOD: THE FIFTH MONARCHISTS

IN THE EARLY MORNING of January 30, 1649, King Charles Stuart climbed the steps to the top of the scaffold, faced the crowd, and spoke. "I am the martyr of the people. I go from a corruptible to an incorruptible crown, where no disturbance can be, no disturbance in the world."

After kneeling and praying for a few minutes, the king lay down his neck on the block. With the crowd in a hush, Stuart thrust his arms behind his back, the customary sign that the victim was ready. The executioner raised the ax, holding the blade for a moment to aim the deadly instrument. In a second the blade fell. With one blow on the neck, the man that some declared to be the arm of the Antichrist died. For those same critics, the Fifth Monarchy could now begin.

Throughout the 1640s, the Root and Branch faction of Parliament argued that a monarchy was the political form of the Antichrist's government. This helped fuel the First English Civil War. Out of this faction emerged a group of men even more severe in their thinking: If they could eliminate the monarchy and get rid of Stuart, his death would herald an end of what they considered the Fourth Monarchy and pave the way for the Fifth. But no one mortal man would rule. The Spirit of King Jesus would rule through the men of the Fifth Monarchy.

Some historians place the rise of the Fifth Monarchy in 1653, well after the execution of Charles. However, the rudimentary concepts of the movement can be traced to the preaching of certain members of Parliament in 1641 and the publication in English of Joseph Mede's *Clavis Apocalyptica* in 1640 and *Daniel's Weeks* in 1642. The bridge between 1642 and 1653 was laid in 1646 when Christopher Feake denounced monarchy and aristocracy as antichristian.[474] He became one of the most important members of the Fifth Monarchy Movement and a powerful inspiration to Thomas Harrison.

The Trial of Charles and the Rise of the Fifth Monarchy

Major-General Thomas Harrison surfaced as the most influential of the men who comprised the Fifth Monarchy. Born to a middle class family, Harrison became noted for his bravery and keen military mind, which enabled him to rise quickly in the ranks of the New Model Army. Based on his military honors, the Major-General was elected to Parliament in 1645 where he came under the sway of Feake. While his courage in battle and victorious strategy brought him honors in his own time, historians mostly remember Harrison for his theological thinking.

Harrison's heroics in war made him a natural rallying point for officers sympathetic to concepts similar to the Fifth Monarchy. As early as October of 1647, some of the highest ranking officers gave speeches proclaiming that it was their duty to destroy the rule of the Antichrist, fully abolish the monarchy, and initiate the millennial kingdom. All of this molded Harrison as he rose in political stature. By November of 47 it became clear that Fifth Monarchy philosophy dominated his beliefs. At a conference of officers, he did his best to convince Cromwell that the king was a "man of blood" who should be brought to trial. Cromwell considered Harrison's arguments to be without proper Christian compassion and determined to provide clemency for the king.[475] In contrast, Harrison believed Christian compassion meant eliminating that which stood in the way of the Kingdom of God, and in keeping with Mede's theology, Charles stood in the way.

After the Second Civil War and the king's treachery in hiring Irish catholic troops, Cromwell no longer needed convincing: Charles Stuart was, indeed, a man of blood. In December, Cromwell and the army purged Parliament, leaving only those with sympathies to the military and with Fifth Monarchy leanings. On December 15th, 1648, Cromwell sent Harrison to bring Charles to Windsor Castle. Royalist sympathizers relayed to the king that Harrison intended to kill him.

Before arriving at Windsor, the army brought Stuart to a private house in Farnham. That night, as Stuart sat before a fire in a large parlor room, many officers crowded around to get a glimpse of the king. Stuart spotted Harrison at the other end of the parlor and beckoned with his hand for the major to come over to him. Harrison hurried with due reverence. They conversed for over half an hour. Among other subjects, the king asked him if he intended to murder him, as was reported to him earlier. Harrison denied the charge. But he reminded the king that true justice did not favor the rich over the poor or nobility over the peasants. In spite of the response, the king displayed a cheerful disposition throughout the rest of the evening, hiding his anxiety.[476]

From Farnham, they transported the king to Windsor and then to St. James for his trial. While riding in a coach to St. James, he sat with Harrison. The king asked him point blank, "What do they intend to do with me? Do they intend to kill me or not?"

"We have no such thought," replied Harrison. "But God has reserved you as a public example of Justice."[477]

On the 20th of January, the trial of Stuart took place in Westminster Hall with Harrison among the seventy members of the High Court of Justice. They charged him with treason and other crimes. When given his opportunity to defend himself, the king refused to accept the authority of the Court and spoke only of the divine right given him by God: "I am your lawful king, and what sins you bring upon your heads, and the judgment of God upon this land. ... Let me see a legal authority warranted by the Word of God, the Scriptures." The Court declared him a tyrant, traitor, murderer, and public enemy to people of the nation.

Many of the army officers debated on what to do with him. Some thought that the king should simply be removed from his throne. Others pushed for him to be poisoned in private. Harrison growled that his sentence should be carried out in the full light of the sun in front of all the people. He and fifty-seven other commissioners signed his death warrant.

With the king's execution on January 22, the Kingdom of God could now arrive. In February a petition was distributed among the officials in the army predicting the Fifth Monarchy was about to follow the end of the Fourth, whereby the people of God would rule the world "until Christ came in person." [478] The statement, *until Christ came in person*, is an extraordinarily revealing declaration indicating the theology underpinning the Fifth Monarchy

Invasion of the British Isles and the Barebones Parliament

The end of the Second Civil War in 1648 fired-up many army chaplains, and their leanings toward Fifth Monarchist principles became evident. Chaplain Thomas Collier exemplifies this attitude: "When Christ as King of the saints reigned in the army, then the army would rule the world."[479] Once the Spirit of King Jesus came to fully indwell the army, the troops could move to abolish all world monarchies.

By April of 1649, the House of Commons had been purged and the king had been tried and beheaded. But for those who held the mentality of the Fifth Monarchy, the revolution was only beginning. In that same month, John Owen stood and addressed Parliament: "The influence of papal Antichristian Rome runs through all the nations of the western world. Unless all nations are so shaken as to have every nook and cranny searched and brushed, the world will not be safe for Lord Christ and his people."[480] Many in Parliament understood. Before Christ returned in the flesh, England's revolution needed to spread to all the nations of Europe.

The British turned their eyes on the closest nation. England freed itself of the Antichrist's control, but across the Irish Channel, the power of his demon minions was just a short boat ride away. Owen's speech continued the verbal propaganda influencing England toward invasion.

Owen addressed Parliament in April. By August, Parliament called for the subjugation of the Emerald Island and the Irish Catholic rebels who aligned themselves with English royalist forces loyal to Charles' son. Cromwell eagerly took up the cause. He still remembered a slaughter carried out by Irish forces in 1641 and it was time to pay back the Antichrist's army with some spilt blood of their own.

The invasion on Irish soil began in Dublin and moved through Drogheda where Cromwell ordered the massacre of the town after most Irish forces surrendered. He put an end to the slaughter after encountering an infant lying in the street trying to suck from its dead mother's breast.[481] About thirty Irish managed to surrender and survive. The British sent them into slavery at Barbados. In his address to Parliament on September 17, Cromwell admitted to executing some of the soldiers captured from one of the churches: "Their officers were knocked on their head, and every tenth man of the soldiers killed, and the rest shipped to Barbados."[482]

On November 1, Parliament called for a special day of thanksgiving for the victory at Drogheda. The English Army went on to massacre another Irish town, but evidence suggests it did so this time without the consent of Cromwell. England subdued the rest of Ireland and then carried war to Scotland and engaged in a sea war with Holland. The Fifth Monarchist, Christopher Feake wrote in support of the campaigns.

By 1653, however, disputes broke out between Parliament and the Fifth Monarchists in the army. Parliament's ineptness in carrying out Monarchist principles soured the army as early as 1651. In early April of '53, Cromwell proposed that Parliament be disbanded in favor of a council of "Godly men." Fifth Monarchy men embraced the proposition, as one of their chief tenants was that the country should be ruled by a council of seventy members based on Old Testament examples. The moderates among Parliament balked at such an idea.

On April 20, Cromwell led a contingent of soldiers to Westminster Hall. He addressed the members telling them that they must leave. They leered and refused. Cromwell gave the order and the soldiers stormed the chamber with Major-General Harrison pulling the Speaker of the House from his chair.

On April 29, Cromwell and army officers chose the council after asking churches throughout England, Ireland, and Scotland to recommend candidates. They followed Fifth Monarchist recommendations in everything except the number of council members, choosing one hundred forty instead of seventy.[483] Fifteen members of the Fifth Monarchy made up part of the Assembly. The rest of the council had varying degrees of moderate to radical religious views. Praise-God Barebone, the name of one of the Fifth Monarchists, was one of the new members. Critics named the council the Barebone Parliament, believing that the Fifth Monarchists held too much power and influence on Cromwell.

By July 13, cracks emerged in this new Assembly of the Saints, as some referred to it. The issue of tithes caused the first disruption. Fifth Monarchists insisted that tithes paid by the state to support the clergy should be abolished. They argued that government tithes belonged to the system of the papal anti-christ and the clergy should be self-supporting or exist only by free-will offerings from congregations. Many in the rest of Parliament sympathized with their abolishment but could not agree on how to replace them.

Another contentious issue revolved around the legal system and the very existence of lawyers. Charlatans and money grubbers infested the legal system, so went the Monarchist cry: "Law should stream down like a river freely, as for twenty shillings what formerly cost twenty pounds."[484] One Fifth Monarchist published a book claiming that lawyers were the locusts described in the book of Revelation and part of the remaining vestige of the Antichrist in England. [485]

A tipping point came when the Fifth Monarchists insisted on replacing the office of the Chancery with the Law of Moses and certain laws derived from the Gospels. Moderates responded with disdain. Fifth Monarchists shouted that the moderates belonged to the Fourth Monarchy and were not fit to rule.[486]

In spite of their best efforts, moderates lost ground and the Fifth Monarchy men influenced the majority to back their proposals, including passing the act to abolish tithes. It seemed Monarchy men were on the verge of taking complete control of Parliament. The moderates, however, had one feather in their cap. The Fifth Monarchy movement began to sour on Cromwell's foreign policy and in turn, Cromwell felt the Monarchy men moved too quickly to achieve their goals.

The Fifth Monarchy's Quest to Rule the World

For some time, conflict brewed between England and Holland over the Dutch trading with colonies sympathetic to the royalist cause. In 1652 hostilities broke out between the two nations as warships battled each other in the North Sea. By April of 1653, however, rumors circulated that Cromwell desired an end to the hostilities. The news dismayed the Fifth Monarchists.

The Fifth Monarchy's mentality towards foreign policy is best seen in the writings of John Rogers. Cromwell appointed Rogers minister of Saint Patrick's Cathedral in Dublin during the Irish invasion. After about a year, Rogers became disenchanted with doctrinal squabbles in the church, which included debates concerning infant versus adult baptism. He returned to England and fervently worked towards converting others to the doctrines of the Fifth Monarchy.

Cromwell's desire for peace with Holland particularly displeased him. In response, he addressed a letter to Cromwell. On April 3, he wrote: "Every tongue is now tipped with the talk of a treaty with the Hollanders and other nations. But if you make leagues let Christ not be forgotten. ... Oh, a peace on account of Christ, to engage together against Antichrist, Rome and all enemies in all nations- to stand and fall together, to live and die in one cause, for the bare and very interest of Christ, would be a blessed peace indeed.... For in Judges it says that you will make no league with them but pull down their altars."

The Fifth Monarchists were not interested in peace with Holland. In spite of its Protestantism, the Dutch Nation did not ascribe to Monarchist principles and conspired with Catholic monarchies. Rogers insisted peace with Holland was peace with the Antichrist.

In September, with the Barebones Parliament in full force, Rogers wrote a 200-page book entitled, *Sagir*, which included another letter to Cromwell.[487] Along with attacks on tithes and the lawyers, the book addresses the characteristics of foreign policy that represented the Fifth Monarchy. The call to love our neighbors as ourselves lies at the heart of a plea to invade Europe: "We are bound to help our neighbor as well as ourselves, and to aid the subjects of other princes that are either persecuted for true religion or oppressed under tyranny. . . . How can our army be still with so much work to do abroad? . . . Are there no Protestants in France or Germany even under persecution? . . . For it is the Lord who sends us forth and calls for at least part of our army into France and Holland, . . . And let not men dispute whether it is lawful to strike for another's liberty and deliverance, if it were lawful to do so for our own, seeing that we must love our neighbors as ourselves."[488]

Rogers goes on to describe the ultimate goal of the Fifth Monarchy which began with the execution of the King Charles in 1648: ". . . in the year 1648 in the High Court of Judicature erected for the king's trial. After this comes the Fifth Monarchy. By 1660 the work of this monarchy is to get as far as Rome, and by 1666, is to be visible in all the earth. It will come mysteriously, suddenly, and terribly, and will redeem the people from ecclesiastical bondage, and from the decrees, councils, orders, and ordinances of the pope."[489]

For Rogers and the Fifth Monarchists, Cromwell and the English Army should continue the military invasion past the British Islands into Holland and beyond. The next seven years should see significant success and by 1660, the Army should reach Rome. Christ then returns in the flesh to carry out the final battle. All of this reflects Joseph Mede's seventieth week of Daniel which envisions the collapse of all monarchies prior to Christ's return.

In Rogers' thinking, God's implementing of the Barebones Parliament was the next step to this ultimate conclusion of God's Kingdom on earth. But Cromwell seemed to be backing out of the plan by seeking peace with Holland. Cromwell took note of the criticisms of Roger's and other Fifth Monarchists.

On December 8, 1553, two days after their defeat concerning tithes, about forty moderates approached Cromwell and pleaded for the dissolution of the Parliament. Cromwell concurred. Troops marched into the Assembly and demanded the members to leave. Thus Cromwell extinguished the theological hopes of the radicals in the Barebones Parliament

The move infuriated the Fifth Monarchists. They felt betrayed by the man they trusted most. Cromwell knew their rage and immediately summoned Major Harrison and two other Fifth Monarchists from the army and requested a pledge that they would not act against him. They refused and he arrested them.

On December 16, a moderate in the army, John lambert mustered the army in behalf of a new constitution naming Cromwell as Lord Protectorate over the British Islands. The Office gave Cromwell the right to dissolve Parliament and established him as leader for life.

Ministers Rogers, Feake, and Simpson reacted strongly by railing against Cromwell in their sermons preached to their congregations. In response, Cromwell arrested Feake and Simpson. Rogers continued to preach and write against Cromwell until his arrest in 1654. He was released in 1657, and although still active among the Fifth Monarchists, prison appeared to soften his stand. As others involved themselves with various conspiracies against the government, no evidence suggests he approved. While Rogers might have moved away from advocating violence, another Fifth Monarchist led plots that would lead to gunfights on the streets of London.

Thomas Venner and a Door of Hope

Thomas Venner immigrated to New England in 1637 and held various jobs, some more legal than others according to critics, while trying to raise a family. He returned to London in 1651, a few steps ahead of the Boston police. He came under the influence of the Fifth Monarchists, including PraiseGod Barebone. By 1656, he became leader of a large Fifth Monarchist congregation.[490] Government spies kept a close watch on the church, and reported a growing excitement in the congregation.

In early April of 57, a meeting took place on Coleman Street between some independent Baptist congregations and followers of Venner. Many believed the time had come to take down the government. They elected Venner as leader of the group. He decided to move ammunition to various areas throughout the city. They determined to strike on April 9.

When the night came, the spies reported a suspicious gathering in Shoreditch. Troops surrounded the house and arrested Venner and twenty other armed men. Eventually, he was released. While some of the Fifth Monarchy Men, including Harrison, gave up advocating violence by this time, Venner was just getting started.

Cromwell died in 1658 and his son became leader of the nation. By 1660 England yearned for a return to the Stuart Monarchy, and Charles II, took the throne. In response, Venner played one last hand to bring about the Fifth Monarchy.

In late December of '60 or early January of '61, Venner published and disseminated a pamphlet entitled *A Door of Hope*, promising that the saints would not put away their swords until the Fifth Monarchy ruled the entire earth.

The tract begins with due respect to Joseph Mede and his *Clavis Apocalyptica* and then turns its attention to the king: "And now Charles Stuart, the son of that murderer, is proclaimed king of England, whose throne of iniquity is built on the blood of precious saints."[491]

The tract continues to lay out the Fifth Monarchist agenda concerning the nations: "For we are not purposed to sit down under our vines and fig trees, but to go on to France, Spain, Germany, and Rome, to destroy the Beast and Whore and burn her flesh with fire. To bring not only these, but all the nations in subjection to Christ." [492]

In terms of the exact eschatology, however, the pamphlet sheds light on the nature of the Fifth Monarchy's postmillennial leanings: "…some may be ready simply and ignorantly, and others willfully, to mistake and misunderstand us, some to malicious ends, not knowing what we mean by the Kingdom of Christ, …as that Christ should immediately appear to head an army." The author clears up misunderstandings about Monarchist theology and explains to the readers that they are not intended to wait for Christ to return in the flesh before waging war against the English Monarchy.[493]

As the tract continues, the author pleads for the readers to come join the insurrection: "And whoso loves God, his Country, or his own rights which Christ purchased for him by his blood . . . must now take up the sword against this beastly crew."[494]

On Sunday evening of January 6, Venner, a comrade named William Parsons, and fifty armed men emerged onto the streets of London. They convinced themselves that once fighting began the city would flock to their cause. Nobody did. Nonetheless, they managed to terrorize the city for several days as they engaged in gunfights and holding government troops at bay. Finally, on Wednesday, the king's troops gained the upper hand. With most of his comrades dead, Parsons dashed down Coleman Street, jumped a small wall, and narrowly escaped a contingent of soldiers chasing him. He found safety as he mixed with the crowd. Venner was not so lucky. One week later, Parsons watched as the executioners hanged him in front of the old Fifth Monarchy meeting house on Swan Alley. Parsons knew his chance of living a long life was unlikely if he stayed in London. As soon as he could, he boarded a boat to New England. Although conspiracies and plots continued for several more years, the Movement no longer posed a major threat to the government.[495]

The Fifth Monarchy movement began with the optimistic, postmillennial theology that helped usher in the English Revolution and democratic rule and ended with a small group battling government troops on the streets of London. Some of the basic ideas of the Monarchist theology, however, would continue to have influence across the Atlantic. In the next chapter, you will step into the English Colonies of America where you will experience a religious revival that will stir men's hearts. And the revival's theological remnants will help lead men's minds, once more, in waging war against the British Monarchy.

ON FEBRUARY 14, 1766, The Sons of Liberty congregated near the liberty tree in Boston to hear preaching on prophecy. The group that had been founded and spearheaded by Samuel Adams anticipated the speaker's subject matter. Relying on the historical interpretation of the book of Revelation, the preacher opened his speech by expounding that the current struggle with Britain was but a microcosm of an age old conflict between the two Beasts from chapter thirteen and the humanity they sought to enslave. As the orator continued, he described how the Beasts had currently revealed themselves as the Earl of Bute and England's Prime Minister, George Greenville. He portrayed that the second Beast, Greenville, who was particularly loathsome, "Ordered that none amongst us shall buy or sell a piece of land, except his mark be put on the deed, and when it is delivered, the hands of both buyer and seller must be branded with the odious impression." The lecturer then implored the Sons. "Beware for fear that by touching any paper with this impression you receive the mark of the Beast."[496]

Six months earlier, the Sons began their insurgent activities by setting up an effigy of Andrew Oliver hanging on Newbury Street along with a large boot with the devil peeking out of the top. Later that day, a large crowd carried the effigy to the Stamp Office and ransacked it. Oliver had been commissioned to enforce the Stamp Act in Massachusetts, a desperate attempt by Britain to raise money from the American colonies to help pay down on the mushrooming financial debt incurred as a result of the French and Indian War in the colonies and the greater war with the French on the European continent. Now, on this day in February, the Sons anticipated that their deeds were not only supported by Scripture, but that they were in direct accord with the fulfillment of prophecy.

Originally printed and distributed from Rhode Island, a colony founded by postmillennialist, Roger Williams, the sermon encouraged the kind of secret rituals and exploits the radical Sons had become famous for. The last six months had witnessed the growth of the group throughout the colonies as they ransacked homes, threatened the merchants willing to import British goods, and put fear in the royal governors to the point that many of them went into hiding.[497] However, the speaker's intent with this sermon went far beyond encouraging violence to put an end to an act that had required publications and legal deeds to be given a stamp before distribution. The preacher designed the symbolism of this particular discourse to imply that by resisting tyranny they might very well begin the implementation of God's millennium on earth.

The sermon reflected a theology that had percolated throughout Massachusetts and Rhode Island for decades. It had crossed the Atlantic in the 1630's with certain Puritans who followed the quasi-postmillennial teachings of Thomas Brightman and the combined postmillennial and premillennial traditions of Joseph Mede. By 1740, it incorporated the clearly defined postmillennial beliefs of Daniel Whitby. Along with these tenets, this eschatology employed much of the democratic-republican revolutionary rhetoric of the Fifth Monarchy Movement.

By 1765, this theology preached by colonial ministers would inspire Samuel Adams to confront British taxation policies with civil disobedience. In time, Adams would write a proclamation which included his postmillennial viewpoint when he jotted down a prayer: "The rod of tyrants may be broken into pieces, and the oppressed made free: that wars may cease in all the earth, and that the confusions that are and have been among the nations may be overruled by the promoting and speedily bringing on that holy and happy period when the kingdom or our Lord and Savior Jesus Christ may be everywhere established, and all the people willingly bow to the scepter of Him who is the Prince of Peace." [498]

Adams grounded his postmillennialism in a long tradition born out of the Puritan cross-migration from England to New England and back again to England. Radical millennial-republicanism permeated New England in the Puritan religious-political experiment that has become known as the Errand in the Wilderness. This ideal would eventually migrate back to London with a number of colonists sympathetic with the Fifth Monarchy Movement, spurring a last ditch effort by the Fifth Monarchists to topple Britain's government. For the most part, the Fifth Monarchy ended in a bloody shootout with government troops on the streets of London in 1653. An exploration into the history of this cross-emigration demonstrates the connection between Fifth Monarchy leaders, Massachusetts, and the civil disobedience of the Sons of Liberty.

The Fifth Monarchy and Massachusetts

After the judge asked Thomas Venner if he was guilty or not guilty, the rebel raised his hand to give one last defense of his Fifth Monarchy philosophy. Venner had been one of twenty survivors of an attempted coup to topple the kingship of Charles Stuart II. Venner's arrest came after a bloody hand-to-hand, house-to-house battle with government troops on the streets of London. "Twenty-two years in New England," Venner proclaimed to the court, had forged his beliefs in a coming spiritual Fifth Monarchy that would replace the Stuart regime. When he continued to provide a rambling discourse on his theology, the agitated judge finally interrupted him. "Are you guilty or not guilty?"

"Not guilty."

The court sentenced the revolutionary to death.

Shortly afterwards, remaining Fifth Monarchists distributed a pamphlet in honor of Venner. The Movement was not meant for England alone, declared the manifesto, but God gave the wilderness of America as a gift to England and the wider world. In the minds of these rebels, the eschatology that gave rise to the Puritan Revolution under Cromwell in England had also permeated the colonies of New England.[499]

The theology of Thomas Brightman had given momentum to the Puritan exodus of 1630 with both his postmillennial concepts and his prediction of England's coming destruction under the wrath of God. For Brightman, the millennium was already under way: "Not that He (Jesus) will personally reign upon the earth . . . but his powerful presence shall not only spiritually cause his churches to grow without number . . . but also the whole civil government of people upon earth shall become his."[500] The Puritans migrating to America believed they would forge a New Jerusalem in the wilderness that would take England's place as the light that would shine to the rest of the world. As the Puritan Revolution under Cromwell got under way, however, Massachusetts came to share in the optimism of their Puritan brothers and sisters in the homeland that England might indeed be reformed.

By 1650, many in New England embraced Cromwell's invasion of Ireland and Scotland as well as the Fifth Monarchist call to arms to overthrow the Catholic monarchies. A tract printed in Massachusetts exhorted all God's people to equip themselves with "swords, rapiers, and all other piercing weapons."[501]

William Aspinwall, a one-time member of the church at Boston and then Rhode Island, emigrated from New England to London in 1653 and wrote six pamphlets published by the Fifth Monarchy Press, Including *A Brief Description of the Fifth Monarchy*. In his works, he advocated that English government should adopt some of the practices of magistrates in New England, such as opening in prayer in the courts and counsels.[502] In *A Brief Description*, Aspinwall also echoed Joseph Mede when he advocated that "for a season and a time" before the Fifth Monarchy begins, there will advance the destruction of all kings.[503]

It is probable that Thomas Venner sat under John Cotton's ministry in Boston for seven years. As early as 1636, the pastor called for instituting the Law of Moses as a standard for Massachusetts law. Such a view would have appealed to Venner, Aspinwall, and others infatuated with Fifth Monarchy ideals. In 1655, Aspinwall republished Cotton's *Abstract of Laws and Government*.[504]

In 1647, Cotton endorsed Joseph Mede's eschatology when he wrote to Roger Williams instructing him that praying for the coming of Christ's kingdom involved praying for the "coming down of all opposite kingdoms."[505] Roger Williams, in turn, reflected Mede's antimonarchy mentality when he proclaimed King Charles Stuart I "a friend of the Beast and an enemy of Jesus Christ."[506] Mede, whose overall theological framework was premillennial, had written a commentary on the book of Daniel that proposed an indefinite period of time that would experience the collapse of all world monarchies prior to the return of Christ in the flesh. Thus Mede incorporated a postmillennial concept within his premillennialism. Fifth Monarchy tracts often lauded Mede as a prophet.

The traditions of Brightman and Mede would continue to influence the culture of English societies long after most of the Fifth Monarchists had been killed or captured during the 1653 uprising. Postmillennial theology would persist through The Glorious Revolution of William of Orange in England, as well as during the early decades of the eighteenth century in New England.

The Millennium and the Glorious Revolution

In the autumn of 1688, the English monarchy reached its crisis point. The

Catholic king, James II, who took over England after his brother Charles died, tried to pacify his opposition by reversing his policies concerning church and state, and easing his persecution of certain Protestants. However, it was too late—William of Orange had already set his invasion plans in motion. By November 5, his ships landed at Torbay. In early December, James sent envoys to negotiate with William, but once again, the king acted one step behind. On December 15, William's forces captured James. Soon after, James escaped to France. William and his wife, Mary, now sat on the English throne. In May of 1689, Parliament passed the Act of Toleration ending the harassment of Protestant dissenters.[507]

Anglican authors interpreted the Glorious Revolution of William of Orange in Apocalyptic terms.[508] Ministers preached sermons in front of William using the book of Revelation to proclaim a glorious age. One minister predicted that the "Church of Rome would be thrown down . . . and with the destruction of Mystical Babylon, the Christian world would be renewed. A New Jerusalem would come down from heaven." Often the sermons mixed apocalyptic scenarios with individual rights and freedom of conscience, although only for Protestants, not Catholics.[509]

Throughout the decade of the 1690's, England observed a number of Anglicans and independents who published a variety of apocalyptic works, with many giving reference to Joseph Mede. Some were premillennial in nature, keeping in mind Mede's overall eschatological framework. They were keen to advocate waiting for Christ to return in the flesh rather than radically strike out on one's own to inaugurate the millennium. Clearly, their warnings had in mind those who still followed the Fifth Monarchy interpretation of Mede. Those others, however, followed Brightman's postmillennialism and Mede's claim of a period of world-monarchial collapse. One such tract written by these radicals predicted, "God will have an army to cut down Babylon prior to Christ's appearance."[510]

Meanwhile, as Brightman's and Mede's eschatology continued to influence England to the end of the century, New England also maintained a doctrine and conviction in an emerging millennium. During the early 1690s, Benjamin Harris published his *New England Primer*, a textbook for children to learn to read. The book included a catechism by which students learned that the pope occupied the seat of the Antichrist and the Whore of Babylon portrayed the city of Rome. Harrison's publication had a profound effect upon New England as millions of colonials learned to read from his textbook.[511]

At the beginning of the eighteenth century, Reverend Increase Mather proclaimed that the New Age "Has ever been received as a truth in the churches of New England."[512] Mather's theology incorporated a doctrine of personal sanctification and holiness. Without individual obedience and goodness, the millennial kingdom could not dawn.[513]

Mather had played a pivotal role for the American Colonies as their representative to Britain after the Glorious Revolution. As a result of the reverend's influence, William of Orange granted the colonies a charter guaranteeing their right to vote for their own representatives, a privilege that had been removed under King James. Thus at this time, New England embraced patriotism towards the government of William of Orange as a generator of civil liberties.

Although some historians have noted a scarcity of apocalyptic writings from the early decades of the eighteenth century, some evidence shows that civil Liberty and millennial thought appeared to comingle in the colonies. Along with Mather's example and Harrison's textbook, Benjamin Coleman wrote that he was worried that a recent earthquake in New England might be a bad omen that would spell the end of civil liberties in Britain.[514]

For decades prior to the reign of William of Orange, New England had ignored Anglican theology, but on the heels of the Glorious Revolution, writings by Anglican authors appeared on the library shelves of Harvard and Yale. One of the results of this influence was that Congregationalism born out of the Puritan tradition began embracing theories which celebrated representative government.[515]Continuing the trend of a Fifth Monarchy mentality, in the early eighteenth century, New England experienced republican strains of millennial beliefs.

While an earthquake in 1727 helped bring about some apocalyptic speculation in New England, the appointment of a certain minister to the senior pastorate of Northampton would help cause a sea-change in the influence of millennial theology in the American colonies. Jonathon Edwards would help inspire one of the greatest Christian revivals in history as well as a postmillennial eschatology that would eventually bring America into conflict with Britain.

The Great Awakening and the Millennium

Nathan Cole dropped his tool and ran from the field. A messenger had brought him news. "Make ready to go," Cole told his wife, "Mr. Whitfield is preaching in Middletown this morning at ten o'clock." When they reached about three miles from town, they encountered a steady stream of people and horses making their way toward the meeting house. Some four thousand people crammed the area. Cole glared toward the river and witnessed overloaded boats ferrying toward the house.

George Whitfield climbed the scaffold. "He looked," Cole later wrote, "like he was clothed with the authority of the Great God. And when he began preaching, he wounded my heart. And I realized my own righteousness would not save me."

While in times of prayer, Cole spent the next two years arguing with God over the revelation. Then one day in the year 1742, while working in his field, he envisioned a gate by which sinners were saved by Christ. "I saw," Cole wrote, "I was saved by Christ."[516]

In that year of 1742, thoughts of the millennium stirred Jonathon Edwards. In 1729, he had been appointed to the senior pastorate of Northampton. Through the next decade, Edwards would record that his congregation experienced periods of deeper spiritual awakening. "There were some instances of awakening and deep concern about the things of another world, even in the deadest of occasions."[517]

In 1740, Pastor Edwards invited George Whitefield to preach in the church for a period of time. The twenty-four year old Whitefield had already attained a reputation for preaching in front of large crowds in the southern colonies. Edwards hoped that Whitefield could spark a revival in his congregation that would spill out from Northampton to the rest of Connecticut and throughout New England.

About a month later, Edwards dream became a reality as the entire town experienced an awakening. Whitefield went on to preach in other areas, and with the distribution of tracts Edwards had written, a religious revival exploded across the American colonies.

This spiritual renewal cut across diverse ethnic lines to enlist settlers from the Dutch to the German to the Irish, as well as the English. Small farmers, traders, servants, laborers and African slaves grabbed-hold and embraced the message of the evangelists. As historian Ruth Bloch put it, "The Great Awakening was the first real mass movement in American history."[518]

Edwards looked upon the movement as the beginning of the transformation of the world.[519] Throughout the period of the Awakening, the Northampton pastor preached on the millennium with his sermons drawing heavily from the book of Revelation. So amazed by the extent of the spiritual outpouring in the colonies, Edwards announced that the millennium would probably begin in America.[520]

He was not the only one proposing that the Awakening heralded the beginning of the millennium. In 1743, some seventy New England pastors signed a document promoting their view that the revivals had confirmed expectations regarding "the coming of the latter days."[521]

Along with Whitefield, Edwards followed the theology of Daniel Whitby, who in the year 1702 originated a formal definition of postmillennialism. The concept, which had passed through the centuries in latent form, now had been given a distinct theological expression as Whitby proclaimed that Christ would return at the end of a one-thousand year period, an age which had yet to begin.

Edwards viewed the millennium as a nonviolent progression. In his thinking, as true Christianity grew throughout the world, monarchies would peacefully melt away, replaced by the rule of the saints. "The saints have for the most part been kept under, and wicked men have governed. But now (in the millennium) they will be uppermost. The kingdom shall be given into the hands of the saints."[522] In a certain sense, Edwards' theology echoed that of Joseph Mede, but in formal postmillennial and pacifist garb.

Despite Edwards' nonaggressive eschatology, the Great Awakening also stimulated a more aggressive theology mimicking the Fifth Monarchy. A militant postmillennial eschatology emerged in the colonies when the French teamed up with Indian tribes to lay claim to the disputed territory of the Ohio Valley.

The French and Indian War

The inhabitants of the little French village endeavored to stay out of the war. They had sworn allegiance to Britain, but they also vowed that they would not take up arms against the French military. On September 2, 1755, they peacefully worked their fields when they noticed three ships sailing up the bay. The townspeople were curious. Who were on these ships and what did they want? Their inquisitiveness intensified as a curator arrived reading a notice that had been posted on the church door: "All inhabitants of the village of Cobequid are to meet in the church tomorrow at three P.M." When the residents arrived the following day, British soldiers with raised bayonets astonished them.

Over the next few days, the British army ordered the confiscation of all property and the deportation of all inhabitants. The villagers embarked upon two of the ships. As they sailed away, soldiers burned the church and their houses. [523]

The same scenario took place throughout the Minas Basin of British controlled Nova Scotia. The British planned to disperse some six thousand Cajuns into the thirteen American Colonies. The English believed they could not risk the villagers joining up with the French forces. For many colonists, the incident known as the Acadian Exile was one of the urgent and justified acts that would help inaugurate the millennium.

Back in the summer of 1753, reports alarmed colonists that French and Indian forces had invaded the outskirts of Pennsylvania and Virginia with the goal of securing the profitable fur trade of the Ohio Valley. The following year, further information incited a near panic—Jesuit priests provoked Indian tribes to rise up against New England. In response to the perceived threat, Reverend Samuel Checkly of Boston echoed the sentiments of many congregations when he preached that "French Catholics were members of the Antichristian Roman Church spoken of in the book of Revelation." During the Great Awakening, Edwards had preached that the French Catholics were "members of the kingdom of Antichrist." Many colonists believed God was calling them to action. [524]

By the 1750's, The Great Awakening had all but fizzled out with the churches experiencing a spiritual lethargy. Edwards' and other evangelists' optimism of a peaceful beginning to the new age was soon replaced by views that the millennium needed British military victories against the papal Antichrist and his French Allies.

The war began as French troops moved down from Canada and infiltrated the Ohio valley, effectively ending a 100-year peaceful coexistence in the territory between France and Britain. The British responded by declaring war on France in 1756.

The French claims on the territory caused anxiety among the churches of the Great Awakening. At the outset of the war, Reverend Samuel Davis of Virginia exclaimed, "Now who can tell, but the present war is the commencement of the grand decisive conflict between the Lamb (Christ) and the Beast." A more militant attitude about the millennium permeated the preachers from the Awakening revivals. As the tide of the war turned in favor of the British, ministers embraced an optimism of an imminent collapse of the papacy. Robert Smith of Pennsylvania thundered from his pulpit that providence would soon "tumble Antichrist from his usurped seat and give the Whore of Babylon her double cup." [525]

As the Colonies entered the decade of the 1760's, after the defeat of the French, certain characteristics in the eschatology of Thomas Brightman, Joseph Mede, and George Whitby continued to find fertile ground. This time, however, combative postmillennialists transferred their wrath from France to Britain and incorporated a radical republicanism not witnessed since the days of the Fifth Monarchy Movement.

Taxation and the Republican Millennium

"For if our trade may be taxed why not our Lands? Why not the produce of our lands and everything we possess or make use of? This we apprehend annihilates our Charter Right to govern & tax ourselves." Many local newspapers reprinted these words by Samuel Adams. In spite of his protests, Britain implemented the Sugar Act in the year 1764.

While the Colonies refused to appreciate the need for Britain to raise new revenue, only sporadic incidents of violent protest occurred in the one Colony of Rhode Island. Things would change the next year, however, as England tried to enact the Stamp Act. In the same year, Massachusetts elected Samuel Adams to the legislature.

In reaction to the Stamp Act, Adams and James Otis founded the Sons of Liberty in Boston. Violent street protests became the Sons' hallmark. After the sermon given to the Sons at the Liberty Tree on February of 1765 depicting the Act as the Mark of the Beast, the association of Britain with the Devil became a standard feature of colonial dispute leading into the early 1770's. [526] That protest would reach its zenith as Britain tried to control the colonies by way of the Tea Act.

The Boston Tea Party and the Advent of War

At evening, George Hewes dressed himself in the costume of an Indian and painted his face with coal dust. He made his way toward Griffin's Warf, meeting up with others dressed as he was. Together they marched to the three ships that contained the cargo of tea. The group split into three in order to board all the boats. Once on his ship, Hewes sought the captain and ordered him to give him the keys to the hatches. The captain gave him the articles, only requesting he do no harm to the boat and the riggings. After Hewes opened the hatches, he and the others carried out the chests of tea to the side of the vessel, split them open with hatchets and poured the tea into Boston Harbor. In three hours, the Sons of Liberty disposed of all the tea from each ship. British warships surrounded the three vessels, but made no attempt to stop the Sons.

In 1773, Britain passed the Tea Act in the latest effort to raise revenue in the Thirteen Colonies. While it raised no new tax and would actually reduce the cost of tea, the colonists viewed it as another attempt by Britain to control local merchants and the economy of the colonies.

Upset by the Boston Tea Party, Britain enacted the Coercive Acts in order to punish Massachusetts. The Acts included a provision that gave Catholics in Quebec the freedom to worship. Many colonists now looked upon King George and the English Parliament as shills for the pope, reinforcing their belief that Britain was in league with the Antichrist. Both secular journals and printed religious sermons distributed throughout New England combined millennial fervency with republican ideals. The colonies responded by forming militias and new alternative forms of governments. These efforts allowed for a quick mobilization of military forces when hostilities finally broke out.[527] By April 19, 1775, the Massachusetts Militia prepared for battle at Lexington.

"Lay down your arms, you damned rebels, or you are all dead men." Then, the British officer yelled, "Fire." A volley of guns burst forth from the royal line, but no colonials were injured. The British fired a second volley and several militia men collapsed and died. The rebels fell back with the royals in pursuit.

The Battle of Lexington represented the first outbreak of war between the American colonies and England. On the eruption of hostilities, a surge of sermons from colonial clergymen depicted the enemy as the dragon, the serpent, or the antichristian Beast of biblical prophecy.[528] One preacher proclaimed that the tyranny that came forth from London incorporated the "rage and fury of the horrible wild beast of John's Revelation," and another minister claimed that the Beast of Revelation applied to British tyranny rather than to the pope in Rome.[529] During the French and Indian War, France and the pope had been the target of the American clergies' apocalyptic zeal. Now, Britain primarily took their place and the cause of liberty from English tyranny became intertwined with the cause of God.

Printed patriotic sermons and poetry proclaiming a dawning new age appeared throughout New England as colonists took an optimistic view in their struggle with the enemy. One example occurred in November of 1775. Ebenezer Baldwin predicted that the American colonies would be "the principle seat of that glorious Kingdom which Christ shall erect upon the earth in the latter days." [530] As historian Ruth Bloch put it, "So intense were these millennial expectations during the early years of the revolutionary war that numerous patriots foresaw the final destruction of the Antichrist and the establishment of the Kingdom of God within the immediate future."[531] So pervasive were expectations that even secularists jumped on board the millennial train. Thomas Paine would become one of the great secular apostles for the dawning of a new age.

Thomas Paine and the Secular Millennium

"We have it in our power to begin the world over again." The words published as part of a tract called *Common Sense* echoed the millennial hopes permeating the American colonies in 1776. Written in sermonic style and relying on biblical references, the document proclaimed "a situation, similar to the present, hath not happened since the days of Noah. The Birthday of a new world is at hand."

The pamphlet written by Thomas Paine was an immediate success with the largest sale and circulation of any book published in America at that time. Paine claimed that he sold 120,000 copies in three months. He donated his royalties from the publication to George Washington's Continental Army.

In 1759, popular colonial authors used analogies from the Old Testament in their writings using Israel's King David as an example of loyalty to the monarchy. Even though King Saul had pursued David with evil intentions, David steadfastly maintained a commitment to Saul as his master. By 1777, however, sermons reinterpreted David as one who confronted Saul as a cruel tyrant. Thomas Paine had led the way in the transformation. He pointed out in *Common Sense* that the Jews rebelled against God by demanding Saul as their King. Sermons that followed Pain's tract portrayed David as a revolutionary hero.[532]

Paine used millennial biblical imagery and a hint of Fifth Monarchy sentiments to explain to his audience that independence offered them a chance to "start government at the right end." Just as Noah's flood washed away all corruption and offered mankind a new start, the colonies could reformulate republican rule that could remake the world with the end of all monarchies.[533]

Today, historians debate the sincerity of Paine's millennial and biblical thought. Some believe he used the imagery to rouse an audience steeped in biblical tradition, while he, himself, was devoted to secularism. In contrast, some Evangelical historians claim that Paine sincerely believed what he wrote and only later became devoted to completely secular ideas when he penned his *Age of Reason* in 1794. It must be noted that even *Age of Reason* has a smattering of millennial thought, although clearly in a secular sense. In any case, the popularity of *Common Sense*, at the very least, indicated an American colonial period entrenched with apocalyptic and millennial beliefs.

Paine did not stand alone in his conviction in a secular, deist-oriented millennium. In John Adams' 1765 "Dissertation on the Canon and Feudal Law," he contended that the British colonization of America was "the opening of a grand scene and design in providence for the illumination of the ignorant, and the emancipation of the slavish part of mankind all over the earth." He later translated his millennial euphoria to the revolutionary colonies. The evidence of this change came on the heels of the final battle of the Revolutionary War.

On September 28, 1781, colonial general George Washington moved his troops close to British-held Yorktown. A turning point in the war had been churning since 1778 when Britain declared war on France. The French king responded by sending troops to aid the colonials. The American and French allies now amassed 17, 600 troops against some 8000 British forces defending Yorktown. After laying siege for some three weeks, the British surrendered, bringing an end to the war.

While the news shocked London, celebrations broke out throughout the colonies. The victory gave John Adams a renewed optimism for the world's millennial future. "The great designs of providence must be accomplished," he wrote. "The progress of society will be accelerated by centuries by this revolution. . . . Light spreads from the day spring in the west, and may it shine more and more until the perfect day."[534]

While Adams and Paine reflected a millennial belief among the more secular-minded revolutionaries, Samuel Adams, the original instigator of civil disobedience against Britain, mirrored the devout religious belief in a coming millennium. One day before he signed the Declaration of Independence, he spoke before the Continental Congress. He recounted how providence had blessed the revolutionary colonies with a large enough army to now resist tyrannical Britain and play their part in helping to implement the coming millennium: "The hand of Heaven appears to have led us on to be, perhaps, humble instruments and means in *the great providential dispensation, which is completing*. We have fled from the political Sodom; let us not look back, lest we perish and become a monument of infamy and derision to the world."[535]

From the 1770s through the 1780s, millennial ecstasy ran deep throughout the colonies. In the last commemoration of the Boston Massacre in 1783, Doctor Thomas Welsh spoke of his belief in the coming millennium: "Soon all nations will beat their swords into ploughshares and their spears into pruning hooks." From Baltimore to Richmond, Virginia, both religious and secular social groups echoed Welsh as they rejoiced in the American victory with millennial-minded speeches and sermons.

The ensuing republican democratization of the colonies left many religiously devout people believing in the possibility that democracy alone could bring about the kingdom of God on earth. Even the staunch religious postmillennialist, Yale president Timothy Dwight, flirted with the idea that God might bring about a secular millennium. Such notions began to turn sour when the ultimate secular-minded millennial experiment turned bloody. The French Revolution would turn many of these men back to proposing a specifically religious postmillennial view, while others would abandon both postmillennialism and the historical interpretation of Revelation altogether and switch to a futurist-premillennial eschatology.

Horror in France

The mob opened the prison cell and pulled out the two priests. Those in the throng mocked the Catholics as they slashed open the clerics' throats. They brought the next two out and continued the ritual, going from cell to cell until all two hundred and twenty priests lay dead along the road known as the Rue Vaugerard.

Mangled carcasses littered the streets of Paris. The crazed included as many women as men. The hordes swept through the city looking for anyone resembling a gentleman, or what they would call an aristocrat. When they came across someone wearing a new coat, or a shiny pair of shoes, or perhaps a ring or watch, anyone who fit their description of a criminal, they left the victim's body on a pike and lifted up for all to see. Thus in the year 1792, Paris became a scene of bloody carnage and violence. The brutality was the opening salvo in what would eventually become known as the Reign of Terror in the following year.[536]

For a number of centuries, numerous expositors had predicted the downfall of the papacy. Some of these commentators also predicted that France would play a pivotal role. In 1701, Thomas Fleming predicted that France would be the progenitor of a revolution that would destroy the papal Antichrist. Thomas Newton, prior to the year 1782, predicted that the French would demolish Rome. When initial hostilities broke out, many Protestants compiled and distributed these and other prophecies concerning the Frankish country.[537]

By the year 1794, an anonymous commentator on biblical prophecy wrote about the conditions in France: "A universal fraternity of tolerance, liberty, and equality," would soon emerge from the French skirmish against European tyranny.[538] The optimism displayed by the author had resounded throughout the new country of the United States ever since 1789 when reports of a French revolution sparked fresh millennial fervency.

As the 1780s drew to a close, France lay in crises. The cost of having provided the American colonies with supplies and troops coupled with the extravagant spending of King Louis XVI left the country near bankruptcy. Drought and Cattle diseases added to the peasants' growing unrest. On July 14, 1789, Parisians stormed the Bastille fortress to secure weapons and gunpowder.

On August 4, a new government constitution emerged promising liberty and human rights for all. Among other things, the charter swept away the special privileges enjoyed by the Catholic Church. On that night, a number of aristocrats, both secular and clerical, renounced their feudal rights for the sake of an equality of the masses. The ecstasy generated by that event created high hopes for a millennial transformation of France that would spread to the entire world. As Robespierre put it, "Eternal providence has called you forth, only you since the beginning of the world, to re-establish on earth the empire of justice and freedom."[539]

The initial euphoria that rocked the masses in a coming new age, devolved into hysteria when the government failed to live up to expectations. The constitution had provided for a constitutional monarchy—power to be shared by both the king and the Legislative Assembly. By 1791, the Assembly degenerated into chaos with a depleted treasury and an undisciplined army and navy. The disappointment in the Assembly's ability led to the mobs taking things into their own hands.[540]

On August 10, 1792, radical republicans stormed the palace and arrested the king. The September massacres followed in the streets of Paris. On January 21, 1793, the extremists initiated the Reign of Terror by beheading the king on the guillotine. Over the next two years, authorities attempted to eliminate all political opposition through beheadings and mob actions.

While Protestants throughout America and Europe, including France, hoped for a religious-based democratic millennium, the Revolution soon exposed a radical humanism born from enlightenment philosophers. In Paris, the leaders of the rebellion closed all churches and replaced the Christian God with the idol of human reason. On November, 24, 1793, the Parisian committee had passed the following resolution: "whereas the People of Paris have declared that it will recognize no other religion than that of Truth and Reason, the Council General of the Commune orders: That whosoever shall demand that either church or temple shall be opened shall be arrested as a suspect."[541]

In spite of the violence that left up to 40,000 people dead, as the nation moved into the latter 1790s, something even more ominous was in the making. By 1792, a movement that promised liberty and equality for all, devolved into further chaos with runaway inflation, high unemployment, and famine. The time was ripe for the rise of a war monger with dictatorial ambitions named Napoleon Bonaparte.

With the failures of the French government to provide the secular millennium, street riots broke out in the summer of 1797. By November, General Napoleon staged a coup that toppled and dispersed the weak rulers. In spite of Napoleon abolishing the constitution, the people were ready to follow a strong man, a military man. By 1802, France proclaimed him emperor.

In time, Napoleon would engage in wars of conquest and an attempt to force the Continental System on Europe in order to control the economy. When his wars were ended, some three-and-a-half million people throughout the continent were dead. As a result of his actions and policies, many in England and Russia became convinced he was the Antichrist.

In America and England, people in the early to mid-nineteenth century would look back upon America's, France's, and Napoleon's failure to bring about the millennium and begin to entertain different eschatologies from post-millennialism. In the next pages, we will meet some who will advocate a theology not experienced by the Christian church since the days of the early apostolic fathers. In the nineteenth century, certain Catholics and Protestants will support different versions of a futurist premillennialism that will help spawn a movement that permeates today's Protestant evangelicalism.

CHAPTER 18
THE WHORE OF BABYLON AND THE RAPTURE OF THE CHURCH

Tis not the pope,
Or the popish priest,
Nor yet Tom Paine;
But Bonaparte,
He is the beast
That is to be slain.[542]

IN 1798, the French monarch, Napoleon Bonaparte, invaded Egypt and Syria to protect his country's trade interests and to undermine Britain's access to India. On March 20, 1799, French troops laid siege to the city of Acre as a stepping stone to capturing Jerusalem. As Napoleon amassed his troops against Acre, he believed the city would fall quickly. As the battle got underway, however, the townspeople stiffened their defenses. Earlier, French troops had conquered Jaffa and massacred thousands of prisoners of war. Acre refused to give in to the French.

Just before the siege, Napoleon had prepared a proclamation that he intended to read once he conquered Jerusalem. In the title, he addressed it *To the Rightful Heirs of Palestine*. "Arise with gladness, ye exiled! . . . A war unexampled in the annals of history . . . offers to you at this very time, and contrary to all expectations, Israel's patrimony!" He dated the document April 20.[543]

After weeks of intense fighting in Acre, the city still stood. In the meantime, the British blocked French ports, thus cutting off Napoleon's supply lines. Plague began ravaging the malnourished French troops. On May 20, Napoleon finally gave up and withdrew his forces to Egypt.

Later, in the year 1800, Napoleon reflected on his failed attempt to conquer Jerusalem and his proclamation *To the Rightful Heirs of Palestine*. "If I governed a nation of Jews," he wrote, "I should reestablish the Temple of Solomon."

The above poem, "The Beast, a Sure Word of Prophecy," written in the year 1803, reflected a growing belief throughout Europe that the French emperor, Napoleon, cloaked himself in the flesh of the Antichrist. In England, in particular, pamphleteers tried to point to wars of conquest and the economic policies under Bonaparte to prove he mimicked the Beast from the book of Revelation. The French king had sought to unite all of Europe under one currency and tried to exclude British trade from the European continent. For many, such aspirations replicated the claim from the Revelation that no one could buy or sell without the mark of the Beast. One other policy aided Britain's prophetic outlook on Napoleon—his desire for the Jews to return to Palestine.[544]

Some two centuries before Napoleon, the Jesuits Francisco Ribera and Robert Bellarmine wrote that the Antichrist would someday restore the Jews to Palestine and rebuild Solomon's Temple. Some of the early Puritans also claimed that God would restore and redeem the Jews. In spite of Napoleon's failure to reestablish the Jews in their ancestral homeland, his quest fueled speculations about the Jews and the Antichrist's role in prophecy. Such speculation would help lead to a renewed interest in the literal interpretation of the book of Revelation and a re-popularizing of a futurist, pre-millennial eschatology not experienced since the first few centuries of the Christian church. Napoleon's mimicking of the Antichrist led some Protestants to look for someone other than the pope to fulfill the role of the man of sin.

With the failures of the French Revolution and the rise of Napoleon, a number of European scholars of prophecy began to question the symbolic interpretations of postmillennialism and amillennialism and entertain the idea that the early Jesuits correctly put forward a futurist view of certain aspects of the book of Revelation. What many had thought pertained to the past through the historic interpretation of Revelation now began to rethink their positions and came to believe that much of what the Revelation describes had yet to take place. Figures such as Manual Lacunza, Thomas Maitland, and John Nelson Darby would inspire many Americans and Britons to not only abandon postmillennialism and historicism but embrace the doctrine of the rapture, a belief which continues to be popular in today's evangelicalism. The earliest of these commentators on the Apocalypse, the Jesuit Manual Lucunza, would stand-out as the forerunner in inspiring modern evangelical eschatology.

Lacunza and the Coming of the Messiah

"I held the Bible to be insipid, even dangerous, as if bread given to children hid poison within it." As Manuel Lacunza opened the Scriptures, one could almost sense him fumbling with the pages. By his own admission, he had never read much of the book. It's true he had heard short homilies preached on certain passages and read other people's interpretations, but he never before considered interpreting the Bible for himself. With caution, the Jesuit priest Lacunza began reading the biblical prophesies and considered the literal interpretation of Christ's return. The Catholic theologian had been trained in the long-standing tradition of symbolism and the historical interpretation of the book of Revelation put forward by the likes of Origen, Eusebius, Tychonius, Augustine, and Joachim of Fiore. To consider the plain sense of the Scripture seemed to him to be a venture into the hazardous territory that led to false and carnal interpretations from ancient heretics like Cerinthus. And even if he came up with a less extreme position from the early church schismatics, he may still end up with an interpretation that defied the Catholic Church's official position. But despite the dangers, "I intended," wrote the Jesuit, "to separate the true from the false, the precious from the vile."[545]

In the year 1800, most Protestants believed in the historical interpretation, a highly symbolic understanding of the book of Revelation which claimed that much of what the book describes had already taken place within the past history of the Christian church. Protestants used the interpretation to rail against the pope as one who sits on the throne of the Antichrist, a seat that many of them claimed began under the Emperor Constantine in the fourth century. Thus the Protestant reformers reasoned that all popes throughout history were Antichrists.

A majority of both Protestant and Catholics accepted the Augustinian view of Revelation, chapter twenty which redefined the millennium as the church age. Symbolizing Scripture, Augustine put forth the idea that the church already occupied the millennium. The Catholic Church adopted this amillennialism as its authorized doctrine. Within this eschatological framework, many Catholics also adopted the historical interpretation of Revelation.

Starting in the sixteenth century, certain Jesuit scholars began questioning the historical interpretation as they sought to undermine the Protestant accusation that the pope inhabited the seat of the Antichrist. Francisco Ribera wrote that most of what the book of Revelation prophesied remained in the future and, therefore, the pope could not be the antichrist because the apostate had yet to arrive. Robert Bellarmine followed Ribera with similar views. This futurist interpretation, as it became known, caused concern among the church hierarchy, but because both Ribera and Bellarmine kept Revelation within an amillennial framework, the popes deemed the writings as acceptable.

The Protestants successfully attacked the Jesuits' futurist viewpoint, keeping the Reformation church from adopting futurism. Many of the Protestants who later embraced premillennial theology, such as Joseph Mede and the Fifth Monarchy, maintained a historical interpretation of Revelation up to chapter twenty while also incorporating postmillennial concepts within a premillennial context. The controversy and attacks on the Jesuits, however, helped spread the seed germ of futurism throughout Europe.

During most of the eighteenth century, the embryo of futurism remained dormant until after the French Revolution and the Napoleonic invasions. The bloodshed that occurred under the Revolution caused many to question the idealism of postmillennialism. With Napoleon's attack on England, a number of English Protestants converted from postmillennialism to something similar to Joseph Mede's historicist premillennialism, a combination of the historical interpretation with premillennialism. Toward the close of the century, the kernel of futurism also began to awaken and sprout. This time, however, it harkened back to the eschatology of the earliest apostolic fathers and took root in the context of premillennialism. The impetus arrived with the distribution of *The Coming of the Messiah in Glory and Majesty*.

By the year 1775, Lacunza had overcome his fear of taking a literal reading of the biblical prophecies and began writing *The Coming of the Messiah in Glory and Majesty*. He toiled on the document for some sixteen years. Sometime before he finished the manuscript, someone smuggled out the incomplete version where it crossed the ocean and caused a stir in South America. On page twelve of the preface of the completed document, Lacunza lamented the copying and distribution of the partial document because it led many to misunderstand his true viewpoints.[546] Lacunza finally finished *The Messiah* in 1791.

The completed work soon reached Spain and South America. Despite laborious hand copying, the manuscript exploded in circulation where it won both ardent friends and bitter opponents. The discussions of the document spilled throughout Europe.[547]

One of the first printed versions in Spanish appeared from Cardiz, Spain in the year 1812. In 1816, fifteen hundred copies in Spanish were published in London.[548] A number of European countries soon published the book in their native languages, including Italian. In 1824, after reviewing the book, the pope forbade the *Messiah* from any further translations and publications. The book displeased the pope, as Lacunza criticized Augustine and insisted on a premillennial theology. While the pope's actions helped impede Lacunza's growing effect on Catholics, they helped encourage Protestants to investigate the work. Once again, the controversy helped spread Lacunza's popularity.[549]

The Rapture in Focus

"And I saw the souls of those who had been beheaded because of their testimony about Jesus and because of the word of God. They had not worshiped the beast or its image and had not received its mark on their foreheads or their hands. They came to life and reigned with Christ a thousand years. The rest of the dead did not come to life until the thousand years were ended."[550] Most commentators in Lacunza's time symbolized Revelation, chapter twenty's proclamation of two resurrections. The literal reading states that the righteous dead shall be raised at the beginning of the millennium with the unrighteous dead resurrected at the end of the thousand years. Following Augustine's analysis of the passage, these commentators believed there would be only one resurrection with both the righteous and unrighteous rising at the same time. Some of these scholars kept a distinction in time between the two resurrections but instead of a thousand years between them, the dead in Christ would be raised first, and then "five or six minutes later" the unrighteous dead. Lacunza rejected this symbolizing of the two resurrections.[551]

Within Lacunza's insistence on the literal interpretation of a thousand-year difference between the two resurrections, he introduced Paul's letter to the Thessalonians: "The dead in Christ shall rise first. Then we which are alive and remain shall be caught up together with them in the clouds, to meet the Lord in the air." In his description of Christ's return and the first resurrection, the Jesuit declared a compelling notion—this "being caught up" or rapture, as it will eventually be called by others, occurs "much before" Christ's actual arrival on earth.[552]

In the second volume of his work, Lacunza defined the "much before." The rapture takes place in the context of a forty-five-day-period that occurs at the end of the Great Tribulation period. He appeared to borrow from his fellow Jesuit Bellarmine in claiming that the Antichrist would be destroyed over a literal forty-five days. In this, both Lacunza and Bellarmine attempted to harmonize the Prophet Daniel's claim that the Antichrist would persecute God's people for 1260 days, but the persecuted saints who hold out for 1335 days would receive a blessing.[553] For the Catholic theologians, this extra forty-five-day period represented the time in which the destruction of the Antichrist will take place. The beginning of the end of the Antichrist's rule effectively starts at the end of the 1260 days when God's final judgment commences. The Prophets Malachi and Isaiah in the Old Testament predicted a "day of the Lord's wrath" that will take place at the end of time as we know it, putting an end to evil on earth. Lacunza symbolized this "day" as taking place over a period of multiple days, as opposed to one 24 hour period.[554]

Lacunza proclaimed the beginning of the forty-five days as the moment of the rapture. This idea mimics the modern-day notions of the pre-wrath and seventh trumpet raptures. In these contemporary scenarios, the rapture occurs somewhere near the end of the Antichrist's reign when the wrath of God falls on the Antichrist. Lacunza, who studied Irenaeus, followed the second century church father in placing the day of resurrection of the righteous at the end of the Antichrist's reign.[555]

Lacunza was not the first to emphasize the rapture. *Pseudo-Ephraem* in the eighth century, the fourteenth century text, *The History of Brother Doicino,* and Morgan Edwards in the middle of the eighteenth century all put forward a rapture that occurred at the beginning of a three-and-a-half year tribulation period.[556] While these texts demonstrate that some discussion swirled around the idea of a rapture during their time periods, none of the documents generated any lasting enthusiasm for the doctrine. The Jesuit's version would change that.

Although an English rendition of Lacunza's work did not appear until 1826 under the translation of Edward Irving, a number of ideas from Ribera, Bellarmine, and Lacunza surfaced in Britain in earlier years. In 1808, Thomas Witherby put forward a defense of futurism based on both Catholic and Protestant opinion.

The Emergence of British Futurism

"There is, I am persuaded, no act of piety that can be performed by a Christian, more acceptable to God, than administering to the necessities and comfort to the Jewish nation. When Messiah shall come to the deliverance of his people, then will the promise be accomplished: And Jehovah thy God shall circumcise your heart." With these words at the core of his defense, the lawyer by trade, Thomas Witherby argued that the prophecies of both the Old and New Testament foretell a day when the Jews will be reestablished in their homeland of Palestine, and Israel will be reborn.[557]

Most Protestants and Catholics of Witherby's day argued that such prophecies had already occurred, for God had meant for the Christian church to replace Israel in the prophetic Scriptures after the Jews rejected Jesus as their messiah. The attorney's book, *A Vindication of the Jews,* attacked this "replacement theology," as it became known, and put forth a literal and futurist view of the book of Revelation. The book, written in the year 1809, followed earlier tomes on the same subject by the lawyer, which included *An Attempt to Remove Prejudices Concerning the Jewish Nation: By Way of Dialogue,* written in 1804, and *Observations on Mr. Bicheno's Book,* written in 1800.

In his work, *Observations,* Witherby argued against Bicheno, a Baptist minister from Newbury, who symbolized the earthquake of the book of Revelation, chapter eleven, to refer to the political upheaval that began with the French Revolution. Witherby countered that the earthquake would be literal and take place in Jerusalem, and the Antichrist was yet to come.[558]

In *An Attempt to Remove Prejudices,* Witherby answered his critics that claimed he attempted to convert Protestants to Catholicism because he relied on the futurist views of certain Catholics. The apologist asserted that he followed an eschatology common to some Christians from all denominations. "All these,

Papists, Protestants, Roman Catholics, Lutherans, Calvinists, Churchmen, Methodists, and their many divisions, all agree with me in opinion concerning the Jews. I follow in a beaten path, in which all these have walked before me." He then declared that he could make his points from Scripture alone and not have to rely on Catholic exegesis. [559]

William Witherby followed Thomas Witherby with treatises appearing in 1818 and 1822. Apparently, no immediate family connection existed between the two, but William shared Thomas's futurist views and attacked the symbolizing of Daniel's 1260 days into years popularized by those holding the historical view. Neither of the Witherbys made strong headway in convincing high numbers of people to convert to futurism. Samuel Maitland, however, would prove to be a more significant figure in imparting the futurist position in England. [560]

Samuel Maitland took priestly orders in the Church of England in 1821. He desired to see Jews convert to Christianity and had long-held sympathies for the return of Jews to Palestine. The priest would eventually embark on a journey to visit Jews throughout Europe. At some point, Maitland came in contact with Francisco Ribera's work and developed grave doubts about the historical interpretation. [561]

In the year 1826, Maitland wrote a pamphlet attacking the symbolizing of Daniel's 1260 days. At the time of the writing, however, Maitland was unaware of William Witherby's work. Critics immediately accused him of plagiarism, for several ideas expressed in the pamphlet resembled arguments made by Witherby. In a response he wrote in the preface of a follow-up pamphlet, Maitland apologized for the consistencies between the two authors, but claimed they were unintentional. The Anglican priest pointed out that he stood in a long line of commentators through the centuries who held to the literal, futurist interpretation and, therefore, his arguments were bound to be similar. [562]

Maitland's first pamphlet caused an immediate commotion as critics waged a paper war against it. A number of journals aimed at prophetic studies weighed in against Maitland's defenses. *The Christian Examiner* emerged as one of the first publications to come out in opposition at the end of 1826. *The Christian Guardian* followed in 1827 and *The Christian Observer* in 1828. By 1829, *The Morning Watch* could no longer ignore Maitland's arguments, acknowledging the popularity of the two pamphlets while entering in with its own criticisms. By 1830 futurism gained a stronghold among a number of Anglican clergy. At about the same time Maitland wrote his first pamphlet in 1826, Lacunza's treatise was making headway with Anglicans, Baptists, and Independents through the promotion by the Scottish clergyman Edward Irving.

Edward Irving and Albury Park

On the first day of Advent in the year 1826, Edward Irving and eighteen other men filed into Henry Drummond's residence known as Albury Park. Most of them belonged to the Anglican Church, but a few of them claimed Baptist affiliation, and at least one other claimed himself as a Dissenter, an independent from mainstream membership. Although the name of Lady Powerscourt, an

Anglican, does not exist in the official register, she also joined the group.[563] They were historicist premillennialists, believing that most of the book of Revelation had already been fulfilled, but they also held to a future, literal fulfillment of the twentieth chapter of Revelation. They came to discuss remaining prophesies that had yet to occur. The conference lasted six days.[564]

In order to attend the conference, Irving had put off publishing his translation of Lacunza's book. He had come in contact with the book while sojourning through Spain and brought back a copy so he and some friends could work on rendering the document in English. Although he followed the historical interpretation, Lacunza's futurist work fascinated the Scott. It's not clear if he introduced Lacunza ideas to the 1826 gathering, but it is likely that he did, for one of the members, Joseph Wolf, claimed that by the end of the conference, all adopted the futurist notion that the pope was not the Antichrist, but that person was still to come in the future.[565]

As a result of the excitement generated by the first conference, a second gathering took place at Albury in 1827. According to Henry Drummond, Lacunza's book became the primary topic of discussion. Although all the members at the conference agreed that Daniel's and John's 1260 days had already been fulfilled, Drummond encouraged the group not to overlook the possibility that Maitland and Lacunza might be correct in claiming that the 1260 days could find a future, literal fulfillment. He reconciled the futurist and historicist approaches by suggesting that prophecy could be interpreted both symbolically and literally, and the same prophecy could have a past and future fulfillment.[566]

Several more conferences took place in succeeding years. Out of these meetings emerged Edward Irving's acceptance of Lacunza's rapture, although Irving's timing of it in relation to the Tribulation period is still a point of debate among historians.[567]

After the first conference, Lady Powerscourt attended several more of the Albury meetings. So enthralled with the idea of the Second Coming of Christ, she decided to continue such conferences in her own estate in Ireland. The Albury Park and Powerscourt conferences proved to be the crossroads in the eventual widespread belief in the doctrine of the Rapture.

The Powerscourt Conferences

"May we not, by taking the beast into our bosom, thrust out God; and blasphemy being found on our forehead, have to take our lot with Babylon." Lady Powerscourt's letter, written in 1830, decried the current state of the church. In the correspondence, she reflects on her association with Edward Irving: "The way that Mr. Howard's and Mr. Irving's petitions are handled with ridicule, shows that the Word is still foolishness to the Greek." [568]

Born Theodosia Howard, Lady Powerscourt became a devoted convert to Christianity at the age of nineteen. At age twenty-two, in 1822, she married Richard Wingfield, fifth Viscount Powerscourt. His death the following year, however, cut short their marriage.

In spite of her love for the Anglican Church, Theodosia became disenchanted with nominal and lukewarm Christianity. She became particularly incensed at the reception of the Catholic Emancipation of 1829 in Ireland, which effectively made the Anglican and Catholic creeds one and the same.

Believing that the time of the Second Coming was soon at hand, Lady Powerscourt invited Edward Irving to hold a prophecy meeting at her house in September of 1830. The small gathering gave way to a larger meeting the following year. In October of 1831, seventy men and women attended the Powerscourt Conference. The number of people present included Irving and an Irish Anglican priest named John Nelson Darby.

John Nelson Darby

One day in October of 1826, the Reverend John Nelson Darby rode his horse along the paths of Dublin. As something frightened the animal, Darby's body hurled through the air, crashing into a doorpost. Seriously injured and unable to care for himself, his sister, Susan, took John into her home.

Over a number of months, Darby convalesced, spending the occasion in prayer and Bible study. Years later, the Irishman would reflect on this period. During his convalescence, he came to a conclusion about the state of the Anglican Church. For Darby, the mainstream church was in danger of becoming Mystery Babylon: "The union of church and state I held to be Babylonish, that the church ought to govern itself, and that she was in bondage but was (still) the church."[569]

One other thought occupied his mind—an imminent return of Christ: "I saw that the Christian, having his place in Christ in heaven, has nothing to wait for except for the coming of the Savior, in order to be set, in fact, in the glory which is already his portion in Christ."

During this time of reflection and scriptural study, Darby evolved from a position of postmillennialism to premillennial historicism. In 1827, another event occurred that further solidified Darby's view of church and state and helped ground his position in an imminent return of Christ in the flesh.

The Oath of Supremacy

"I hear you have obtained a chaplaincy of 300 pounds a year, a fine thing, a capitol price for an old traitor." But the satirical Catholic article gave advice to the converted priest. "These are fat things that Protestants want for themselves. Enjoy yourself for awhile . . . you will one day be likely to seek refuge in the church you have abandoned."[570] The article made its message clear—someday, when the Catholic majority attains their independence from Britain, those who converted to the Anglican state church would find themselves in trouble.

The Protestant crusade to convert Irish Catholics, known as the Second Reformation, ran full throttle through the 1820s. In spite of the attempts by the Catholic hierarchy to minimize the effects, by 1826, six to eight-hundred Catholics a week converted to the Anglican Irish Church. Such conversions, however, were fraught with political overtones, for the Protestant church was tied to British nationalism. Many Protestants believed that if Catholics remained the majority, separation from Britain would follow.[571]

In 1827, the Archbishop of Dublin further fanned the flames of controversy for both Protestants and Catholics. Believing that it was crucial to turn the converts from Catholicism into proper British subjects, William Magee required all those entering the Anglican Church within his jurisdiction to take the Oath of Allegiance and Supremacy to Britain. Many evangelicals within the mainstream church objected to the requirement, for they feared it would stop the high number of conversions.

John Neslon Darby wrote his petition against the Oath. "What is the Church of Christ in its purpose and perfection? It is a congregation of souls redeemed out of 'this naughty world' by God manifest in the flesh. . . . As a people, their King is in heaven, their interests and constitution heavenly." [572] The political situations leading to 1828 would increasingly lead Darby to believe that the mix of church and state lay at the heart of Revelation's Mystery Babylon. This in turn would progressively inform his overall theology of the Second Coming of Christ.

In 1828, Darby penned a tract attacking the Protestant national churches. "These observations are in some measure applicable to all the great national Protestant bodies since the outward form and constitution became so prominent a matter, which was not the case originally while deliverance from Babylon was in question."[573]

Although a member of the Anglican Church, Darby's treatise demonstrated how disenchanted he had become with any denominationalism. "He is an enemy to the work of the Spirit of God who seeks the interests of any particular denomination. . . . So far as men pride themselves on being Established, Presbyterian, Baptist, Independent, or anything else, they are antichristian." The Irishman proclaimed that such people would suffer in the Day of the Lord's Wrath. "In that day a man shall cast his idols . . . to the bats; to go into the clefts of the rocks, and into the tops of the ragged rocks, for fear of the Lord."[574] By the next year, the Anglican appeared to borrow from Lacunza in placing the rapture before this day of wrath.

Historicism and the Rapture

Darby came to believe in an imminent return of Christ during the period of his convalescence. The concept emerged as a consequence of his conversion from postmillennialism to historicist premillennialism. A debate has emerged between historians over Darby's recollections that he came to believe in an imminent return as early as 1826. Some believe that Darby later exaggerated that he believed in this doctrine at that date in time because he did not write about a pre-tribulation rapture until after he attended the Powerscourt Conferences. Others take his word for it concerning an imminent return and assume he believed in a pretribulation rapture as a result of a direct enlightenment at his sister's home. However, both sides demonstrate a misunderstanding of Darby's developing theology from 1826 to 1831.[575]

During this period in his life, Darby came to believe in the historical interpretation along with premillennialism. As with most historicists, he understood John's and Daniel's 1260 days to mean "years." Later in 1829, Darby authored a tract attacking Maitland's futurism entitled, *On Days Signifying 'Years' in Prophetic Language.* In the treatise, the Irishman refused futurism on the basis that it projected Mystery Babylon and the Antichrist as entities that are still in the future instead of existing in Darby's own day. For Darby, only the historical interpretation was safe to declare that prophecy has proclaimed the pope as the Antichrist and the current mainstream church as Mystery Babylon: "The mystery of Babylon and the papacy have no place in the prophets unless the 1260 days mean years."

In 1826, it is likely that he agreed with most other historicists that the 1260 years had found their fulfillment in the late 1700s, and the Great Tribulation period was over. For Darby, then, since the Tribulation was over, nothing remained to be fulfilled in prophecy before Christ returned to set up his millennial kingdom on earth. However, some three years after his riding accident, it appears that Manual Lacunza's concept of the rapture made its mark on the Irishman.

In 1829, Darby penned a tract mixing his historicist beliefs with the idea of Christ's Second Coming. In the seventh section of *Reflections upon the Prophetic Inquiry and the Views Advanced in It*, the Anglican revealed his knowledge of Lacunza's book. Throughout the work, Darby disclosed his familiarity with First Thessalonians and the gathering in the air of those alive on the Day of Resurrection. In section twenty-nine, however, he discloses a connection with Lacunza's theology of the "Day of the Lord's Wrath." "The Son manifested to tread the winepress of wrath is not the Spirit subduing willing souls by the gospel. The operation, everywhere given, of the gospel, is the gathering out of souls before the wrath come."

As with Lacunza, Darby believed in a pre-wrath gathering of Christians in the air. And like the Jesuit, in 1829, the Anglican believed in a post-tribulation rapture. The difference between the two theologies is that for Lacunza, the Great Tribulation still remained in the future, while Darby believed the Tribulation was already finished, and he made no point of portraying the wrath as a forty-five-day-phase. Eventually, Darby transformed his belief into a pre-tribulation rapture. At the Powerscourt Conferences, Darby began embracing futurism.[576]

Darby's Turn to Futurism

Along with Darby, thirty-four clergy men, twenty women, and fifteen laymen attended the conference at the Powerscourt House in 1831. Prior to this, Darby had been meeting with a group of prophecy students in Dublin for several years. Several members from Dublin accompanied Darby to Powerscourt. This inner circle would eventually grow and become known as the Plymouth Brethren.

The attendees devoted the second day of the meetings to the question of whether the 1260 days means days or years. Only one person argued for the literal, futurist position, apparently with little success. On the third day of the gathering, the discussions included the topic of the rapture. [577]

One year later, by the end of 1832, Darby began to rethink his position on historicism. At this conference, futurist arguments swayed many to change their minds regarding a future Antichrist. By the 1833 conference, the Irish priest had made a complete transition to futurism while adopting a rapture that occurs before a future three-and-a-half-year-tribulation period.[578]

Although Darby slowly adopted Maitland's futurism, what might have been the ultimate catalyst that turned the Irishman against historicism? The answer may be found in his exposure to an Anglican missionary from London named Thomas Tweedy.

Of Jews and Gentiles

In reminiscences, John Darby claimed that Thomas Tweedy opened his eyes to the doctrine of the rapture. Tweedy appeared to believe the concept along the lines of Lacunza, advocating that the rapture would occur before the Day of the Lord, thus probably receiving some of his teaching from the Jesuit's book.[579] This alone, however, would probably not have been enough to convince the Irishman, since he had already been exposed to the Jesuit's writings as early as 1829. It may be that Tweedy taught one other interpretation of Scripture that turned Darby's head.

In 1833, Darby held a meeting in Dublin with his Brethren men. The group allowed a visiting Anglican missionary from London to speak. The missionary opened his New Testament to Mathew 24. The first fourteen verses, he explained, belonged to the gentile church. But then he read verse fifteen and sixteen: "When you see standing in the holy place, the abomination that causes desolation, spoken of through the prophet Daniel—let the reader understand—then let those who are in Judea flee to the mountains." According to the missionary, these and the following verses belong to the Jews only. By the time the Antichrist commits the abomination of desolation in Solomon's Temple, proclaiming himself to be God, the gentiles will have been taken up in the rapture. The gentile church belongs to heaven, chimed the missionary, and the Jews are to inherit the earth. The interpretation struck Darby—he had "found the key never discovered before." At least one Darby-biographer speculated that the missionary was Thomas tweedy.[580]

At the Powerscourt Conference of 1832, the Irishman considered the idea that the rise of the Antichrist might, indeed, pertain to the future. By the 1833 conference, the attending members witnessed Darby's complete conversion to futurism with the literal 1260 days of tribulation a forthcoming event.

During the time of his convalescence, Darby held the view similar to Irenaeus that the millennium would inaugurate the dispensation for the conversion of the Jews. With Darby's growing belief in futurism, however, and the influence of Tweedy's hermeneutic, the Anglican turned away from the church father and professed that the dispensation of the Jews would begin with the Great Tribulation. Certain passages of the New Testament, then, belonged to the Gentiles, while other passages belonged to the Jews. For example, the Irishman believed that when Jesus prophesied that the meek would inherit the earth in his Sermon on the Mount from the Gospel of Matthew, Christ spoke specifically about the Jews. The gentile church would be raptured to heaven, and the Jews would be left to inherit the earth. This "Jewish interpretation" fit well into Darby's outlook toward his denomination—the Irish Anglican Church had degenerated into the Whore of Babylon.

Mystery Babylon

As the evening meeting concluded, Lady Powerscourt burst into tears. According to one witness, she suffered in heart and conscience, feeling a "wrench that was worse than death." One of the discussions of the 1833 conference centered on the question of whether Christians should continue to belong to the Anglican Church. Darby was of one opinion while others disagreed. One of the Irishman's best friends, Mr. Bellett, told Darby he meant to stick to the old ship, a reference to the national church. "The old ship," answered Darby, "is going to Rome." At Darby's insistence, Lady Powerscourt renounced her membership as an Anglican, although it caused her immense grief. Although she lamented the amount of nominal Christians in its association, she loved the organization where she first became a convert to Christ. But the Lady had recently become engaged to Darby, and for the Irishman, his fiancé should not turn back, for as far as he was concerned, the national church had become Mystery Babylon and was becoming thoroughly political and popish.[581]

"I saw a woman sitting on a scarlet beast that was covered with blasphemous names and had seven heads and ten horns. And upon her forehead *was* a name written, Mystery, Babylon the Great, The Mother of Harlots and Abominations of The Earth." [582] The Apostle John's vision of Mystery Babylon surfaced as one of the important subjects discussed at the 1833 meeting. Darby was convinced that the national churches could not be reformed. The Irishman recommended that the gentile church should have nothing to do with politics and the church of Christ should withdraw from any association with nationalism and popery. The Gentiles belonged to heaven, not the earth, and so should wait for Christ's return, which could happen at any moment, rather than become embroiled in the policies of the world.

Darby believed that the Roman Church exerted a cunning influence in the political life of Protestant nations thus leading them into heresy and was becoming Mystery Babylon in the time of the Great Tribulation. "Popery is re-assuming its control of the civil power, though in a gentler, more subtle way as yet; while Protestantism is more completely subject to it than ever, viewed as national churches." [583]

Lady Powerscourt's engagement lasted little longer than her earlier marriage. John Nelson Darby broke off the arrangement in 1836. "I turned down a marriage," pondered Darby some years later, "and broke a heart." The Lady died soon after in December of that year.

Darby and Democracy

In later years, Darby argued in tracts that Christians should be apolitical. "I need hardly assure your readers that I have no desire that they should meddle in politics; I do not do so myself, nor do I think that a Christian ought. Parties are all alike to me; they are all alike guilty, and have all alike had their part in what is going on . . . the Babylonish or idolatrous power, with which the kings of the earth had committed fornication, will be utterly destroyed."

Darby would not even accept simple democratic participation, such as voting. "But is it not true that this voting . . . ought to be avoided as a snare by all Christians who understood the will of God and their position in Christ?" When a certain election came up in 1848, Darby wrote a letter to his brother. "Very Dear Brother, it seems to me so simple that the Christian, not being at all of this world, but united to Him who died and rose again, has no business to mix himself up with the most declared activity of the world."

While Darby always insisted on the Doctrine of Imminent Return and an apolitical position, after 1845, he found that once again he had to alter his view on the rapture. When he first proposed it, the pre-tribulation rapture caused a certain controversy within the Plymouth Brethren. One leading member, Benjamin Willis Newton, attacked the doctrine as un-scriptural fiction. One of the problems became immediately apparent—Scripture simply didn't proclaim an imminent return of Christ.

Starting from the period of his convalescence, Darby sought to convince the Christian church that it should avoid the national churches and wait for an imminent return of Christ in the flesh. The Irishman adopted a futurist view with a pre-tribulation rapture after he believed he had found a way to reconcile futurism with an imminent return. When he presented the doctrine of the rapture at the Powerscourt Conference of 1832, one of Darby's pupils among the Plymouth Brethren, Benjamin Willis Newton, remained unconvinced.

By the 1833 Powerscourt Conference, Darby had emerged as the primary leader of the Plymouth Brethren. The Irishman's viewpoints dominated the meeting's subject matter. Later, Newton, who attended, wrote of the proceedings, "I was never more disappointed."[584]

In the few years following the conference, Darby developed more fully his "Jewish" hermeneutic in relation to the rapture. In those same days, Newton became an ardent opponent. Among other disagreements, the former pupil's opposition included three points of doctrinal dispute: the pre-tribulation rapture, Darby's insistence that certain passages of the New Testament were primarily meant for the Jews rather than the gentile church, and an imminent return of Christ. Newton argued in favor of a post-tribulation rapture.

From 1833 to 1845, Newton and Darby confronted each other's theology in tracts and letters. Newton attacked Darby's doctrine of the Imminent return of Christ by citing biblical events such as Jesus giving a prophecy to Peter that he would grow old before he died and Paul receiving prophecies that he was going to suffer as he conducted his mission to the Gentiles. The pre-tribulation rapture proved equally difficult to reconcile with a number of passages. As a result, Darby often waffled in his commitment to his doctrines. After 1845, however, Darby hardened his conviction, as he believed he had solved at least one of the contradictions. He stretched the Great Tribulation from a three-and-a-half-year-period to a period of seven years.[585]

This action allowed the rebuilding of Solomon's Temple, one of the sticking points in trying to advocate that no other prophecies needed to be fulfilled before the rapture. The prophet Daniel predicted that the Antichrist would commit the abomination of desolation in the Temple three-and-a-half-years after signing a peace agreement with Israel, thus initiating the time of distress that would last another 1260 days. By stretching the Great Tribulation back to the beginning of the peace accord, Darby could answer at least one contradiction to his views. Prior to this, no one throughout the history of the church had ever proposed a seven-year time period for the Great Tribulation, as there is no indication in Scripture of distress occurring during the three-and-a-half-years immediately following the peace accord, only after the abomination of desolation. The new time interval did nothing to assuage Newton.[586]

By 1848, the Plymouth Brethren had dissolved into two divisions: one following Newton and one following Darby. Eventually, six factions emerged over various doctrinal and social disputes. Today, some of the Brethren function nearly as a cult status, rejecting and blackballing family members who convert from one faction to another.[587]

Zionism and the Pretribulation Rapture

Throughout decades of the nineteenth century, optimistic views of progressive postmillennial theology continued to drift into decline. Pacifism and apolitical stances became acceptable among theological conservatives. Many Evangelicals found solace in the idea of an imminent return of Christ.

In the late 1800's, the growth of the Zionist Movement, the hope for an imminent return of Christ, and the pre-tribulation rapture merged together in the writings and actions of William Blackstone. Despite many evangelicals moving toward an apolitical stance on most issues, he helped convince them to embrace the Zionist Movement in America and turn it into a political force. In the years 1890-91, Blackstone's work coincided with the anti-Semitic laws and exodus of hundreds of thousands of Jews from Russia, with many of them moving to America and Palestine.[588]

The Scofield Reference Bible, published in 1909, further popularized Darby's pre-tribulation rapture. The Bible coined the term "rapture" to describe the Greek word used in 1 Thessalonians that is normally translated as "caught up." As the word evolved, it became associated with the idea that Christians will one day vanish or instantly disappear before the Great Tribulation. However, John also used the word in Revelation 12:5 to describe Jesus' ascension to heaven that was witnessed by the Apostles. Most commentators do not believe Jesus instantly disappeared when he ascended, so the current popular theology of associating the rapture with instant vanishing is questionable.[589]

John Nelson Darby used the book of Revelation and insisted on a pre-tribulation rapture as a means to keep Christians from becoming involved with politics and national churches. Although this helped move the church away from post-millennialism and the backing of religious wars, it encouraged the opposite extreme of Christians refusing any involvement at all in democracy. In spite of this theology's growth, another violent conflict brewed as a result of postmillennialism. Beginning as early as the 1830's, the southern part of the

United States would advocate succession from the nation thus bringing the country to the brink of civil war.

CHAPTER 19
THE SOUTHERN NEW ISRAEL

ONE MORNING in June of 1860, the residents of Charleston, South Carolina woke up to an astounding news report in the *Charleston Mercury*. The popular paper described the situation relating to New York: "In two hours, the great rich city, with 1, 200,000 residents, was so covered with flames, that no possible human means could have prevented the full consummation of the calamity." But not just New York, chaos engulfed Philadelphia and Boston as well. The report also included the capture of Washington D.C. by Confederate forces. The city was proclaimed the new capitol of the Southern Federal Government.

A few days later, the *Mercury* printed a follow-up story concerning the condition of the southern states. "The commercial prosperity of the southern confederacy is growing with a force and swiftness unimagined by the most ardent advocates for the independence of the south. The business of ship building is pursued actively. Factories are thriving. The devastated northern capitalists, manufacturers, and merchants are seeking investment or employment in the south. . . . New York will remain, as now, overspread by the ruins left by the inferno." The information given by the *Mercury* described how the south now rested on the verge of unparalleled prosperity. A golden age had dawned on Dixieland.

The newspaper dated the stories to March, 1869. Written in the past and present tenses, the clever narratives played on the sentiments of southern readers by appearing as if they were current news accounts. The predictions, penned by Edmund Ruffin, helped stir up nationalistic passions throughout Dixieland as the Carolina Legislature debated whether the state should break away from the United States of America.

Ruffin had been traveling through Florida, Georgia, and South Carolina preaching his version of the future, publicly debating on behalf of secession, and circulating tracts and pamphlets. While he did not proclaim that he had any supernatural powers of prophecy—only human reason—Carolinians hailed him as the prophet of disunion.[590]

Ruffin's forecasts lay in a long line of secessionist predictions by both northern and southern postmillennial prophets, of which many believed that the way to reach the millennium depended on the separation of the south and the north. At the heart of the debate on disunion lay the question over the legality of slavery. In time, postmillennial theology in relation to slavery would help bring the United States to the brink of civil war. To understand how, one must explore the history of how the churches of America reacted to the institution of African bondage and servitude.

Prophecy and Ebbing Toward Secession

Despite Bourbon County's support of slavery, residents elected David Purviance to the House of Representatives of Kentucky in the year 1799. The congressman authored an amendment to the state constitution calling for the slow emancipation of slaves. The bill found no support among the other members. If it had, it would have altered the history of Kentucky, and perhaps, the southern states at large.

An evangelical elder with the church at Caneridge, Purviance preached that Christians should treat slaves as they, themselves, wished to be treated. In a poem he wrote,

> He pities the opprest;
> He knows the many thousands
> Thus burden'd and distrest;
> He sees immortal creatures
> Converted into herds,
> Abus'd by proud oppressors,
> Who fancy they are Lords.

Most congregation members of his church converted to his view and liberated their slaves.[591]

In 1801, Purviance and his son, Levi, witnessed a revival that swept over parts of Kentucky and careened into Tennessee. Presbyterians, Methodists, and Baptists came to camp meetings in Bourbon County by the thousands. Levi, who was eleven at the time, would later recollect, "Such were the glories of the times that many good people thought that the millennium had began to dawn upon the world." As the revival continued to grow in strength, so too, continued the belief that the world had entered the final period. People flowed into Kentucky from Ohio and Tennessee, taking back with them the persuasion "that the glorious millennial day had commenced, and that the world would soon become the Kingdom of our Lord Jesus Christ."[592]

While southerners viewed the revival optimistically and that the south was progressing into the Kingdom of God, many felt that a cataclysmic event needed to occur to thrust the millennium onward. From the Great Awakening in the eighteenth century, evangelical congregations felt their churches floated on the edge of this prophetic eruption. One explosive event might bring about the anticipated age of peace. They believed the south itself would be the harbinger of this coming visionary episode. They hoped that when it occurred, the nation would be prepared.[593]

In early nineteenth century, the predominate eschatology in both the north and the south was postmillennialism. Within this framework, many evangelicals throughout the south sided with Purviance in supporting emancipation. Some ministers and laymen dealt with the problem by purchasing slaves and releasing them to Liberia on the western part of Africa. As the century progressed into the third decade, however, attitudes of the southern clergy began to change.

Beginning in the 1830s, northern postmillennialists started a barrage of criticism toward the south over the slavery issue. Some of these abolitionists advocated separating from the south as a means of purifying the north so it could better carry out the millennial mandate. Southerners reacted strongly and pushed for their own isolationism.[594]

In Dixieland, people who supported slavery began to persecute and sometimes kill clergymen who spoke out in favor of emancipation. The harassment drove many of these ministers to leave the south.[595] Those who remained began to alter their opinion on slavery and support the isolationist mentality.

The southern clergy, both evangelical and orthodox, initiated a counter theology to the abolitionists and proclaimed that it was the north that worked to inhibit the millennium. In this eschatology, slavery played an integral part in establishing the golden age. Instead of slowly passing away, as the earlier southern emancipationists envisioned, many alleged that slavery would remain throughout the millennial period. Such a mentality would help lead the nation to the cataclysmic event that many postmillennial evangelicals had waited for.

The Road to Armageddon

In 1854, Methodist ministers Samuel Baldwin and Fountain E. Pitts toured Tennessee giving lectures claiming the book of Revelation's battle of Armageddon would detonate in the Mississippi Valley. The skirmish would involve Great Britain whom many still believed was the second Beast of Revelation.

The lectures proved so popular that Baldwin published a book on the subject. The *Nashville Christian Advocate* gave it a positive review which helped expose the work throughout the south. The document instilled in many southerners the idea that their homeland would be the scene of the great skirmish.[596]

Baldwin helped reinforce one more tenet of white southern ideology—the superiority of the white race. In the millennial empire, the Japhetic, or white race, would rule over Asians and Blacks: "The position of the three races will be, Japheth (Caucasian) first and head; Shem (Asian) second; and Ham (Black) third. Equality of political rights will not be held in common by the three races during the Millennium. . . . This arrangement and no other will be endorsed by Providence."[597]

Baldwin's theology of the black race became standard with the southern clergy—God had cursed the Africans and subjugated them under the white race. "Japheth received the highest blessings from God; . . . but Ham received no blessing; . . . to be unblessed of God is to be subject to his curse." The blight would remain until the end of the millennium.[598]

In 1857, Baldwin followed up with a second book, continuing the diatribes he started in the first. "Degradation and infamy have been the actual lot assigned, by Providence, to the Hamitic race." For Baldwin, God designed and resigned the black race to slavery under the whites.[599]

Although the sectional divide between north and south deepened during the 1850s, both Baldwin and Pitts did not believe that the United States would separate, but instead, held the view that the Union would still lead the world into the millennium following the battle of Armageddon. However, toward the end of the decade, the southern clergy at large dug in with their theology of Japheth and Ham and the apologies defending slavery were in full force in church pulpits. At the same time, northern postmillennial abolitionists began to silence pacifists within their own ranks, arguing that violence was needed to end the violence of slavery. In the year 1860, southern periodicals published articles detailing how the current north/south conflict played into the apocalyptic scenario, indicating an end to the present dispensation.[600] For the southern ministers, it was southern secession that would lead the world into the millennium. The cataclysm was about to begin.

War and the New Israel

In November of 1860, a convention to discuss secession convened in South Carolina upon the election of President Abraham Lincoln. While the delegates argued, preachers throughout the south thundered to packed churches on behalf of separation. On December 17, Carolina representatives met in the Baptist Church of Columbia. As one member later recalled about the mood of the members, "The winds of secession could not be held back." On December 18, the convention moved to Charleston's Institute Hall as the result of a small pox infestation in Columbia. At seven o'clock on the evening of the twentieth, the convention pronounced a declaration of secession from the United States.[601] The statement followed a sermon by W.C. Dana delivered in the Central Presbyterian Church. "Would South Carolina," he asked, "allow a foreign and hostile government to rule over them?" He told his congregation that the immediate future is dark, but the prospects beyond are bright. After South Carolina, four more states joined it and broke free from the Union.

For southern evangelicals, secession came at a critical moment as they quickly rose up to support the decision with millennial rhetoric and theology. William Sasnett wrote in the *Southern Christian Advocate* that it had always been part of God's design for the American Union to divide. Methodist Joseph Cross, likewise, claimed that God desired to create two independent and separate states in which the south would become "the restored Israel of God."[602] In Cross's mind, if southerners followed the precepts that God established, then an everlasting covenant of a Confederate New Israel would dawn upon the world.[603]

From this New Israel, God would bring salvation to the world. N.R. Sled preached, "God has chosen us to be the repository of His will and a light to the nations. . . . His majesty is despised by those idolatrous northern ammonites! . . . Let us be valiant for Israel (the south) and for Israel's God."[604]

Following Carolina's secession, U.S. Major Robert Anderson's soldiers occupied Fort Sumter, a battlement that was built in 1829 to protect Charleston's harbor. On April 12, 1861 Carolinian forces responded by firing on the fortification. With Anderson's surrender on the 13th, northerners rallied to Lincoln's call to send troops into the south to preserve the Union. Believing the war would be of a short duration, the president conscripted volunteers to only a ninety-day enlistment.

In July of 1861, throngs lined the streets of Washington D.C. shouting and clapping as General Irving McDowell's 35,000 troops marched off to capture Richmond, Virginia and bring a swift end to the war. As the enthusiasm intensified, many citizens and congressmen followed the army's advance to watch the destruction of the Confederates.

On July 21, McDowell's first order of business was to capture the railway junction at Manassas, which led west to the Shenandoah Valley and Richmond. As Union forces clashed with the Southern Army, the lack of training and experience of the federals became obvious as the more disciplined Virginia militia began to route its enemy. Panic set in as the retreating unionists collided with the citizen-mobs that come to watch.

In the spring of 1862, the Union, once again, tried to capture Richmond, but, once again, failed when Confederate General Robert E. Lee turned back General George McClellan. Upon the victory, the Confederate president Jefferson Davis called for a day of fasting and prayer in thanksgiving.

For this special day of fasting on Tuesday, September 18, Anglican Bishop Stephan Elliot gave the sermon in his church in Savannah, Georgia. Within the delivery of his address, he made what today may seem like a strange declaration: "African slavery, upon this continent, had its origin in an act of mercy." For Elliot, God intended slavery to bring about the Kingdom of God.

In his speech, the Anglican made a particular reference to the history of slavery as it related to the first English colony in Virginia. American slavery of Africans began in 1619 when a Dutch naval vessel took over a Portuguese slave ship, the San Juan Batista, and transported its cargo to Jamestown, Virginia. The Dutch traded twenty slaves to the English colony for tobacco and arms. The saga of that fateful day had commenced two years earlier in 1617 when a Portuguese adventurer named Mendez dreamed of conquering Africa.

Portugal, Witches, and Slavery

Brimming with confidence, Luis Mendez de Vasconcelos landed in the port town of Luanda in the Portuguese colony of Angola. He had written a treatise on war and intended to conquer the lands of Africa from one coast to the other, thus opening a new route to India. The immigrant, however, had very few Portuguese soldiers at his command. Only the strange Imbangala tribe lay at his disposal.[605]

The Imbangala, a quasi-religious group, murdered all new born babies in their camp by burying them alive. They replaced them by capturing adolescent boys and grooming them for war. On behalf of their religious beliefs, which resembled witchcraft, they often ate the captured adults as part of their human-sacrificial rituals. They kept some of their victims alive, however, so they could sell them as slaves to Portuguese colonists. Initially repulsed by the Imbangala, Mendez quickly learned he needed the witches as his allies.[606]

Over the course of two years, Mendez waged a war of attrition. A Portuguese bishop wrote in 1619 that the dead from the campaign had infected all the rivers and a "great multitude had been captured without cause."[607] The Portuguese commander, with the aid of his witchy allies, seized so many slaves that the number often overwhelmed Luanda.[608]

The thirty-six slave ships that left the port in 1619 included the San Juan Batista. Portuguese law required that all slaves be baptized and made Christians before they reached their final port. Jesuit priests noted that the slaves had an adequate fundamental understanding of the Christian religion by the time they arrived. It is likely then that the twenty slaves that reached Jamestown had already been introduced to the faith.[609]

Bishop Elliot probably never knew the history of Mendez and the Imbangala, but even if he had, it likely would not have changed the nature of his sermon. He and the southern clergy had become convinced that the prophecies of the coming millennium included, and depended upon, the preservation of slavery. In their millennial model, they believed that slaves would bring the gospel to Africa.

The Southern Mission to the Slaves

As Bishop Elliot looked over his congregation on that day of fasting and prayer, he opened with a reference from a speech he had given at the beginning of summer. "In my opinion the real troubles of our enemies are just about to begin." The bishop claimed he had not spoken under prophetic inspiration but only from reason and deduction from the Scriptures.[610]

While he claimed he was not a prophet, much of what he was now telling his congregation came from the written prophecies: "As the world draws towards its end, the hand of God becomes more visible in its affairs. . . . The period approaches when God's economy of grace is to be consummated."[611]

Elliot then went through a litany of how various missionaries through different time periods had tried and failed to evangelize Africa. In no small part, the reason for their lack of success had to do with their race and skin color. "They too have failed, because the Caucasian blood has not been able to bear the enervating heats and destructive fevers of the torrid zone." The fulfillment of prophecy, therefore, could only come from the black race: "In God's own time, to plant the Gospel in their Father-land, after they themselves shall have been prepared, through a proper discipline, for the performance of this duty. He has caused the African race to be planted here under our political protection and under our Christian nurture, for his own ultimate designs."[612]

In a former address in 1861, Elliot defended the institution of slavery in a similar manner: "However the world may judge us in regard to the institution of slavery, we regard it to be a great missionary institution—one arranged by God. . . . We believe we are educating these people as they are educated nowhere else; that we are elevating them in every generation; that we are working out God's purposes; whose consummation we are quite willing to leave in His hands."[613]

The bishop echoed the theology of other southern ministers, such as I. R. Finley and Throton Stringfellow—God instituted slavery in America as a means to convert the African Continent to Christianity. This conversion would take place before the consummation of the millennium. However, none of these preachers explained how the slaves were to be set free so they could travel back to Africa. One assumes that they believed that some kind of reform would take place. They never made this clear, though, for to have done so would have upset the slave industry and brought criticism down upon them.

Apart from millennial theology, the southern clergy advocated that both the Old and New Testaments advocated slavery. According to these ministers, the abolitionists undermined the authority of the Bible by criticizing and desiring to end the institution. In fact, a number of historians today claim that the southerners made the more honest biblical argument, while the abolitionists allegorized passages and engaged in a faulty hermeneutic. However, in a modern study of the Ancient Near East, the context for most slavery that took place was that it was primarily on behalf of the poor and, in most cases, was voluntary by those who were sold as slaves. They chose to become slaves in order to escape extreme poverty. The rules guiding slavery in the Old Testament, in particular, appear designed to protect the slave.[614]

The southern clergy might be forgiven for not having access to the documents now available to current authorities in ancient history. The abolitionists, however, made one biblically based argument against slavery that the pro-slavery ministers dealt with dishonestly. An illustration of their argument may be best demonstrated by the story of an eleven-year-old African named Olaudah.

Slavery, Kidnapping and the Bible

One day in 1756, in the region now known as Nigeria, two men and one woman snuck over the walls of a residence and grabbed eleven-year-old Olaudah Equiano and his sister. The abduction was swift. At that hour, the children's parents worked their fields and had no clue that they would never see their offspring again.

The group traveled for several days. At night Olaudah and his sister would sleep in each other's arms, trying to give one another what comfort they could. On the third day, the thieves separated the children. The siblings grasped at each other, pleading with their captors. They tore the boy's sister away, nonetheless, and one of the men carried her off. The boy cried for several days, and his subjugators had to to force-feed him.

They soon arrived at the coast. The slave ship awaited them. Once on board, Olaudah's rough handling convinced him he resided in a world of bad spirits and death expected him. After he was put below deck, the stench filled his nostrils to the point that he fell ill. The white men flogged him for refusing to eat. While out at sea, some of the blacks who were chained together jumped overboard when they had the opportunity, preferring drowning to the conditions the whites had subjected them to.

The ship anchored at Bridgetown at the island of Barbados. The Captain ordered the Africans to be brought up on deck. The sailors shoved Olaudah and the other prisoners into parcels where they could be examined. Merchants and planters came on board and sized up the captives, ordering them to jump up and down. Using their knowledge of some of the indigenous tribal customs as a point of reference to determine what this all meant, the Africans feared these men planned to eat them. After the captors herded the Africans back below deck, shrieks bellowed from the bowls of the ship throughout the night as the prisoners dreaded the future they thought awaited them. The next day, however, they learned they were to be made slaves, not food.

Once on land, the captors packed the Africans into the merchants' yard. The beat of a drum signaled that the sale was on, and merchants rushed into the place of confinement. The excitement from the buyers and the noise and clamor from the scene struck fear and apprehension in the hearts of the captives. The dread turned to grief as brothers, sisters, mothers, sons, daughters, husbands, and wives realized they were going to be separated as the merchants took no care in keeping family members together as they took the slaves into owner-ship.[615]

Such was the typical scene that the southern clergy argued was biblical and necessary in bringing about the millennium. Exodus 21:16 says, "Anyone who kidnaps someone is to be put to death, whether the victim has been sold or is still in the kidnapper's possession." Paul wrote to Timothy in 1 Timothy 1:9-10, "Knowing this: that the law is not made for a righteous person, but for the lawless and insubordinate, for the ungodly and for sinners, . . . for kidnappers, for liars, for perjurers, and if there is any other thing that is contrary to sound doctrine." The best argument the southern clergy could come up with to answer these passages was to claim that the offspring of kidnapped slaves could be legitimately bought and sold while the kidnapped could not be. Such a washing of the hands from the stain of kidnapping cannot be seen as honestly dealing with Scripture, and such a line of reasoning did nothing but help perpetuate the industry of abduction. The faulty hermeneutic rested with the southern clergy.

Perhaps Olaudah summed up the worst aspect of slavery as it related to the American south when he wrote: "O, ye nominal Christians! Might not an African ask you—learned you this from your God, who says unto you, do unto all men as you would have men do unto you? Is it not enough that we are torn from our country and friends, to toil for your luxury and lust of gain? Must every tender feeling be likewise sacrificed to your avarice? Are the dearest friends and relations, now rendered dearer by their separation from their kindred, still to be parted from each other, and thus prevented from cheering the gloom of slavery, with the small comfort of being together, and mingling their sufferings and sorrows? Why are parents to lose their children, brothers their sisters, or husbands their wives? Surely, this is a new refinement in cruelty, which, while it has no advantage to atone for it, thus aggravates distress, and adds fresh horrors even to the wretchedness of slavery."

While the southern clergy ranted how the Confederates' early victories proved God to be on their side, the year 1863 proved to be a turning point in the war. Lookout Mountain and Missionary Ridge would give the northern clergy their own new fodder to predict the fulfillment of the millennium.

The Northern Millennium

Without orders, George Thomas's Union soldiers stormed up the ridge. "Who ordered that charge?" bellowed General Grant.

"I didn't," replied Thomas, fearful of his men's gung-ho exuberance.

The charge initiated a contagious fervor as more federals followed the initial wave. "Chickamuaga, Chicamauga!" The blue coats' battle cry rose in remembrance of their commander Thomas' courageous stand in the face of defeat at the Tennessee creek several days before.

The stunned rebel forces tried to stop the onslaught with their artillery, but the poor placement of the cannons made them almost useless. The Confederates retreated as the Yankees poured over the Confederate line. Missionary Ridge now belonged to the Union, the second victory in two days, with Lookout Mountain being the first. For many clergymen in the Northern States, these triumphs represented a turning point in the United States Civil War and heralded the beginning of God's millennial kingdom on earth.

Gilbert Haven climbed into his pulpit in Boston and gazed over his congregation. Until just a few days before, northern congregations must have felt there was little to be thankful for. During the first few years of the war, Union officers had proven to be inept and Confederate victory after victory had left thousands of young union soldiers dead on the battlefields. On this Thanksgiving Day of November 26, 1863, however, the parishioners' mood must have been heightened from the reports of the Battles of Lookout Mountain and Missionary Ridge that had just filtered in. Haven used the opportunity to speak of the millennium.

"What relation does the present conflict have with the millennium?" Haven asked his congregation. "A very distant relationship you may answer. Can the bloody feet of battle be reconciled with the Gospel of peace? But such is the doctrine and providence of God. War is the forerunner of the Gospel, the one who cries, 'prepare ye the way of the Lord.'"

Haven then described the struggles that have come with the emerging millennium "The principle of the equality and fraternity of man carried us through the first days of our disastrous defeats when the riotous rebels built their campfires on the bones of our slain heroes in the site of our capitol. . . . Then McClellan removed, Burnside defeated, Hooker routed, Fremont cashiered, how thick the darkness, how faint the national heart. . . . But God is pushing us toward His, not our millennium.

After the minister described the necessity of calamities and defeat in testing a nation, he explained how the righteous quest for the end of slavery has turned the tide of the war: "Slavery is doomed by the proclamation of the nation and the arm of (General) Grant. The rebels have fought against the lamb and the Lamb has overcome." Haven ended the sermon by predicting the millennium would follow the final victory by the north over the southern states: "the glory of the Lord shall cover the earth as the waters cover the sea."[616]

The Millennium Postponed

On August 20, 1866, President Andrew Johnson proclaimed an official end to the American Civil War. The declaration came after a series of battles incapacitating the south, including the surrender of Robert E. Lee's Army of Northern Virginia in 1865. The expected millennium, however, failed to begin.

The initial euphoria many northern postmillennialists experienced with the surrender of General Lee became muted with the assassination of President

Lincoln on April 14, 1865. During the war 620, 000 soldiers died in total, more Americans than any other war before it or since. Throughout the south, property damage was extensive and the economy became a shambles. The war cost untold billions and tended to nourish rather than eliminate many old prejudices and hatreds. With the carnage of the campaign, many postmillennialists and historicist premillennialists began to look anew at futurist premillennialism.[617]

In the 1840's, futurist premillennialism began attaining large numbers of adherents in England and began crossing over to the United States. With the end of the Civil War, followers of the eschatology plowed fertile theological ground in many evangelical churches, particularly in the south. Dwight L. Moody became one of the first popular American evangelists to support premillennialism, and his conferences at the end of the 1870's helped thrust the movement forward. Although Moody may not have supported the dispensational form brought forth by John Nelson Darby, his disciple, C. I. Scofield, pushed Darby's scheme through the Scofield Reference Bible published in 1909, which explained dispensationalism in the footnotes of the biblical text.

While postmillennialism fell in to retreat during the later part of the nineteenth century, it temporarily resurged in the early twentieth century through various progressive reform movements, such as the prohibition against alcohol. World War I and the Great Depression helped put it back in decline in America. In other parts of the world, however, theologies similar to Christian postmillennialism were just getting started. In the next section, we will first march with the Japanese in their quest for a final apocalyptic battle with the United States. Then we will analyze Islamic prophecy and come to understand what is driving global Islamic terrorism. A millennial-type eschatology grounded in Japanese Shinto/Buddhist theology as well as Islamic apocalypticism will help thrust the mid-to-late twentieth century into chaos and turmoil.

CHAPTER 20
ON THE THRESHOLD OF THE NUCLEAR MILLENNIUM

THE PILOTS FROM the Special Attack Force lined up around a table and drank Sake in one last toast to their officers and country. In the next step of the ritual, they waved the flags of their homeland, cheering in celebration. The officers presented them with strips of cloth portraying the rising sun. Then the smiling pilots climbed upon the wings of their Zero fighter planes and hoisted themselves into the cockpits. This depiction, which can now be viewed in photographs and YouTube videos, seems to suggest the airmen felt a sense of honor, pride, patriotism, and without hesitation, had embraced the destiny that the Japanese Navy had prearranged for them. Pilot Hayashi Ichizo, however, told a different story.

The night before the flight, Hayashi had written to his brother: "The time has come, Elder Brother. I am sorry that I cannot see you. Elder Brother, do survive the war. . . . Please tell my friends how hard it is to terminate my life."

The traditional farewell party held for the pilots the preceding night may also have betrayed a different attitude on the part of the rest of the airmen. A steward in charge of looking after the meals described a typical scene at gatherings that had taken place before other flights: "The whole place turned into mayhem. Some of the pilots lifted chairs to break the windows and tore white tablecloths. Some sang military songs, while others filled the air with curses. Some shouted in rage, others sobbed aloud."

In the midst of the party chaos, some of the pilots meditated. No doubt this included Hayashi. As he climbed into the cockpit that morning, he carried with him a Bible and Christian existentialist philosopher Soren Kierkegaard's *Sickness unto Death*. Born and raised in a Christian family, the young pilot had grown up under the influence of the teacher Uchimura Kanzo, who was noted for refusing to bow to the emperor as a deity. Navy Vice-Admiral Onishi Takijiro's Special Attack Force included a number of Christians.

The Japanese government graduated Hayashi from college two years early so he could be drafted into the military. The navy conscripted him into the Attack Force on February 22, 1945. On February 23, the young pilot tried desperately to believe in the mission that the Navy had assigned him. In his diary he wrote: "I know my country is beautiful. . . . My earnest hope is that my country will overcome this crisis and prosper. I can't bear the thought of our land being stomped by the dirty enemy." But further in the entry, he penned, "To be honest, I cannot say that the wish to die for the emperor is a genuine one coming from my heart."

In Hayashi's goodbye to his brother, he echoed the words of Saint Paul: "Elder Brother, 'For me to live is Christ. To die is also gain.' This is for the memory when we drank sweet wine." According to his diary, the pilot planned to sing hymns and his dormitory song as he flew his plane into combat.

Perhaps Paul's words filled Hayashi's mind as he pulled back on the rudder and lifted the plane into the air. Navy munitions experts and mechanics had reconfigured the Zero's fuselage to wrap around a five-hundred pound explosive. On April 25, 1945, the airman steered his flying bomb to confront the United Sates war ships anchored off the island of Okinawa.[618]

The pilots of the Special Attack Force are known to us today as the kamikazes. In October of 1944, the Japanese government "volunteered" recruits for suicide missions—to slam their Mitsubishi-built Zeros into U.S. ships as a last ditch effort to work a miracle and turn the tide of the war back in Japan's favor. Vice-Admiral Takijiro intended to use the kamikazes as the primary weapon in what he believed would be one final apocalyptic battle with the United States. The pilots conscripted into the Force had no choice but to agree to the objective. If they refused, they would be shot and their families punished in disgrace.[619]

College age men made up the majority of pilots for the Attack Force. In their diaries, some of them reflected a longing for a new era, a golden age they hoped would ascend on Japan and the world at large. Kamikaze Miyazawa Kinji wrote, "I pray that we will see the day as soon as possible when we welcome a world in which we do not have to kill enemies whom we cannot hate. For this I would not mind my body being ripped apart innumerable times."[620] Such hopes reflected a number of the Japanese military that believed that one day Japan would herald its own millennium.

The decades of the twentieth century leading up to the 1940s witnessed a variety of philosophies that mimicked concepts from postmillennial theology. Members of the Republican Party in the United States, both secular and religious, rushed to support the progressive reforms under President Theodore Roosevelt. The movement would prove to be a precursor for the utopian–minded, secular progressive movement of today. Russia experienced the atheist-undergirded and utopian philosophy of Karl Marx. Adolph Hitler professed that his fascist and racial political movement would usher in a thousand years of Arian perfection for Germany. In the latter part of the century, a movement of apocalyptic Islam would borrow on Christian concepts to try to funnel in its version of the Kingdom of God on earth. These movements imitated postmillennialism in that they attempted, and attempt, to force in an era of peace and prosperity by human means. As for Japan, its version of a golden age of peace and prosperity began in 1901 when Buddhist philosopher Chigaku Tanaka promised a fifty-year-timeline in which Japan would establish the age of Buddhahood over the earth.[621]

The Lotus Millennium

In 1931, Lieutenant Colonel Kanji Ishiwara considered Manchuria, in the northeast part of China, to be the perfect experimental proving ground for his belief that Japan needed to liberate all of Asia from western influence. The army officer submitted an invasion plan to Tokyo. Japanese civilian authorities rejected the plan on the basis that the region had to antagonize Japan before the government would act. Ishiwara reacted by fabricating a Manchurian hostility.

On September 18, Japanese Lieutenant Suemori Komoto snuck along the

Japanese controlled part of the Manchurian railway line north of Mukden, China. When the bomb he planted detonated, it caused little damage to the rails. Nonetheless, Ishiwara responded by ordering his troops to occupy Mukden. Within days, the Japanese military captured Manchurian cities all along the 730 miles of railway. Back in Tokyo, the Lieutenant Colonel's actions outraged top government officials. With victory after victory being reported, however, the authorities became powerless to stop the army. When Ishiwara returned home, right-wing army officers, ultranationalists, and the Japanese people as a whole hailed him as a hero.

In 1935, the military brass appointed Ishiwara to the Chief of Operations. This gave him the opportunity to articulate his vision of his Japanese millennium. In his battle plan, Japan would align with China and attack the Soviet Union. With Russia defeated, the military would move to liberate all of Southeast Asia from European colonialism. This would set up a final apocalyptic war to conquer the United States. With the decadent and corrupt west defeated, a spiritual birth would descend over the world. Ishiwara's inspiration for this plan came from Chigaku Tanaka.

Tanaka followed the thought of Japanese Buddhist monk Nichiren who, in the thirteenth century, believed that one could only reach Buddhahood by reading the Scriptures of the Lotus Sutra and chanting its title. While the Sutra did not portend to be a millennial or apocalyptic text, Nichiren wrote interpretations that lent themselves to a millennial reading.

In Nichiren's belief system, wherever the Lotus is embraced, the territory will become a Buddha land where pestilence and disasters would cease to be: "When all the people throughout the land enter the Buddha vehicle . . . the wind will not thrash the branches nor the rain fall hard enough to break the dirt clods. . . . There can be no doubt of the Sutra's promise of peace and security in the present world."[622]

Nichiren merged his concept of the Buddha land and transformed it into a nationalistic notion with Japan at its center. In his writings, he would portray this Buddhism as emanating from a Japan that would rise like the sun, moving from east to west, and illuminating the world. This millennial vision would begin to captivate his later followers at the turn of the twentieth century and persist until the end of World War II.[623]

In the early twentieth century, Tanaka combined Nichiren's millennial thought with the traditional pagan Shinto creed that the emperor had descended from the sun goddess. This new mix of millennial Buddhism with the Shinto religion attracted military officers, politicians, and ultranationalists. Tanaka's greatest appeal was that his apocalyptic vision depended on Japan's territorial expansion.[624] Two of his converts, Ikki Kita and Colonel Ishiwara, advocated that strong imperial rule and military invasion would create the Lotus millennium.

Shinto-Buddhism and World Conquest

Ikki Kita has been viewed as a kind of second Nichiren. Borrowing on the earlier philosophers's concepts, he sought to inspire Japan to help Asia overthrow all western influence. To achieve this end, he linked military conquest with the Lotus millennium. Once Japan conquered the world, the Japanese would rule over a league of nations. World peace would then descend as all people converted to Shinto-Buddhism.[625]

In 1916, Kita wrote *A history of the Chinese Revolution* where he first revealed his millennial beliefs. "The flag bearing the sun, of the nation of the rising sun, is about to illuminate the darkness of the entire world. . . . I am a disciple of the Lotus Sutra, Nichiren, my elder brother. . . . He preached the doctrine of world unification, but it has yet to reach China or India."[626]

Another of Kita's books, *An Outline Plan for the Reorganization of Japan,* published in 1919, called for the country to take the lead in liberating China and India from the west. The book became a primer for young military officers.[627]

Ishiwara, the man who inspired the invasion of Manchuria, found his military calling in the perception of the Lotus Millennium. A convert to Nichiren and Tanaka, the military officer believed that war acted as a driving force for progress. In his philosophy, current societies aligned themselves along two competing polar axes: the west, led by the United States, incorporated the "way of dominance," while the east, spearheaded by Japan, pursued the "way of righteousness." The final war between Japan and the United States would lead to a Japanese victory which would usher in an everlasting peace. In 1939, he predicted that this last battle would take place within seventy years.[628]

Eventually, Ishiwara became disgusted with the army's war crimes in Manchuria and the corruption under General Hideki Tojo. He opposed the attack on Pearl Harbor as the army had neglected a true spirituality and had not yet peacefully aligned Japan with China according to his plan. After the war, he witnessed at the war crimes tribunal, arguing against the prosecutor and claiming that U. S. President Truman was a criminal for purposely targeting Japanese civilians in bombing campaigns and for using atomic weapons against the cities of Hiroshima and Nagasaki.

Some historians, such as Walter A. Skya, have argued that Ishiwara could not have effectively contended for his doctrine combining principles of Shinto and Buddhism, for the two religions contradict each other. Furthermore, because he ultimately failed in his propositions, he must have had little effect in influencing the military to engage in expansionism based on his version of Buddhism. Skya contends that Japanese imperialism was based wholly on Shintoism apart from any influence from Buddhism.[629] However, scholars have shown that Shintoism was intrinsically part of the imported Chinese Buddhism and was not originally indigenous to Japan. Also, according to the wartime memoirs of Imperial soldier Hiroshi Funasaka, most Japanese households during WW2 had altars to both Shinto and and Buddhism. Thus the combination of Shinto and Buddhism permeated Japanese society. In addition, it should be noted that Skya's description of Shinto cosmology incorporated the idea of a coming world order of harmony based on state-emperor worship. Therefore, it does not seem farfetched to think that many strict Shintoists in the military could sympathize with Tanaka's and Ishiwara's eschatology.

Whatever may be true in Skya's position, certain things about Ishiwara's impact cannot be disputed. Ishiwara's model of the Buddhist-Shinto millennium caused the officer to initiate the invasion of Manchuria which then started the wheels of history spinning toward Japan's place in World War II. It led to the war crimes against the Manchurians and other civilians with a total of sixteen million civilian deaths in China alone.

As the war progressed, Ishiwara's mentality of a final apocalyptic battle influenced a number of high ranking Japanese officers, including Onisha Takijiro and Captain Minoru Genda. Takijiro, the architect of the kamikaze strategy, believed that the final clash should either end in a Japanese victory, or Japan should commit national suicide rather that surrender.[630] And Captain Genda dreamed of dying a glorious death as a fighter pilot in the final apocalypse.[631]

The end result of the Manchurian invasion led to a devastation of Japan with a total of just under three million dead including the senseless deaths of the kamikaze pilots. It also led to millions of total dead from the rest of Asia, Britain, Australia, and America. And Ishiwar's attempt to establish the millennium helped lead to one more event of historical significance: the advent of nuclear weapons. With the atomic explosions over Nagasaki and Hiroshima, it now became possible for a particular vision from Jesus to come true. Jesus foresaw a time in the future in which, if God does not cut short the days, "no flesh on earth would survive." The prophecy was given in the context of both natural disasters and "wars and rumors of wars."[632] Such a scenario suggests the use of modern weapons of mass destruction.

The Apostle John predicted a development in which nations gather for battle at the hills of Megiddo, a site in Israel that in ancient times sat at the heart of a road that linked Egypt and Damascus. Along with nuclear weapons, the occurrences of World War II appeared to have helped initiate another situation which will assist the fulfillment of New Testament prophecy—the Battle of Armageddon.[633] The failure in implementing the Japanese millennium echoed the failed attempt by Adolph Hitler in establishing his thousand year Reich for Germany, a state which included the elimination of the Jewish race. The effort to create the Nazi millennium, with the devastation committed by the Nazis against the European Jewry, led to a mass migration of surviving Jews to Palestine and the establishment of the State of Israel in 1948.

The Jewish immigration to Palestine produced conflicts with Israel's neighbors and eventually gave birth to another ideological apocalyptic model. Similar to Adolph Hitler's desire to wipe out Jewry, this 'end times' scenario would target the Israeli nation and the Jewish race. In the decades ahead it would cause many to engage in terrorism and prepare the weapons of war for the appearance of the Islamic messiah.

Egypt and the Islamic Apocalypse

In 1970, starting with the election of Anwar Sadat to the presidency, a chain of events occurred in Egypt that would lead many in the Middle East to predict an Islamic apocalypse. First, President Sadat allowed the exiled Muslim Brotherhood organization back into Egypt. Second, In the midst of economic unrest among the poorer class, Sadat began peace negotiations with Israel, ending with a peace treaty signed in March. Every Arab leader in the Middle East condemned the accord and a fatwa by an Egyptian cleric condemned the president to death. Third, Sadat gave the ousted Shah of Iran refuge. Fourth, Mossad, the Israeli Intelligence Department, warned Sadat of assassination attempts planned against him. Fifth, in response, Sadat purged fundamentalists from the government. However, he made the mistake of leaving the army untouched.

At ten o'clock on the morning of October 6, 1981, Sadat took his place on the viewing stand occupied by more than a thousand guests, including politicians, journalists, and diplomats. They had come to witness a military parade in celebration of Egypt's independence from Great Britain achieved in 1922. Soon the celebration began with jets streaming overhead while trucks and mechanized armaments convoyed past. Unknown to the President as he watched the procession was that a trusted member of the military had engaged in a conspiracy against him.

Earlier, before the parade, Officer Khalid Islambuli gave three men from his detachment a leave of absence and replaced them with members of a fundamentalist sect known as the Egyptian Islamic Jihad. An hour and a half into the parade, Islambuli's truck reached the stand where it stopped directly in front of the president. The officer ran from the truck hurtling three grenades at the platform, while the other three opened fire with assault rifles at the crowd. In the midst of the chaos, one of the bullets struck Sadat.

With the president dead, Egypt fell into confusion and turmoil for the next five years. The newly elected Mubarak did what he could to quell the tempest. But by 1986, the unrest had culminated with terrorist attacks, including one on Israeli tourists, as well as rebellion in the police force. In the midst of such bedlam, journalist Said Ayyub composed his tract entitled *The Antichrist*.

"The Jews have placed themselves in the hands of the Antichrist. They have considered him as one of their princes; they have forged a strategy for carrying out his purposes. . . . They have infiltrated political and diplomatic activity in many places in the world." In August of 1986, Ayyub completed his document outlining human history. The journalist portrayed the past as one event unfolding after another that was manipulated by the Jewish Antichrist in a conspiracy to take control of the world. The pages of *The Antichrist* included denials of the Holocaust.

The popularity of *The Antichrist* on the Arab street led to a wave of similar tracts and books. By 1990, this fashionable street literature had devolved into crass sensationalism. *Beware: The Antichrist Has Invaded the World from the Bermuda Triangle* and *The Hidden Links between the Antichrist, the Secrets of the Bermuda Triangle, and Flying Saucers* were among the titles advocating that the Antichrist commandeers flying saucers and will one day rule Jerusalem. Underpinning most of such writings was the use of *The Protocols of the Elders of Zion,* a forged document from the early twentieth century alleging that Jewish leaders were conspiring to take over the world. In a 1905 version of *The Protocols*, the elders acted in conjunction with the Antichrist.[634]

In the *Antichrist*, Ayyub accused Israel of conspiring to bring about a third world war for the purpose of eliminating the Muslim world. The Antichrist will manifest with armies in both Jerusalem and the ancient region of Khurasan, which included Afghanistan and parts of Iran.[635]

In 1991, a Beirut company that had published a later work by Ayyub, sought to capitalize on such apocalyptic literature for the Shia community. The organization began distributing works from other authors that emphasized the reappearing of the Mahdi, an Islamic messianic figure whom Shia believe disappeared in the ninth century and will reappear at the end of time to lead the world into an era of peace and prosperity. The titles included *The march of Time up Until the master of the Age*, a document that claims that the Mahdi will not appear until the ruin of Israel along with the collapse of America.[636] This was followed by the publishing of a similar ancient Shia document that had recently been found in a Library in the Iranian province of Khorasan.

By the beginning of the twenty-first century, the Shia-dominated Republic of Iran experienced a surge in apocalyptic fervor centering on the emergence of the Mahdi. The eschatology rested upon an ancient Islamic prophecy promising a deliverer from Khurasan (Khorasan) that would liberate Jerusalem. The theology eerily mimicked the aberrant medieval Christian prediction of a last world emperor that had influenced the Crusaders to wage war in the Middle East. In one of the modern interpretations of the prophecy, Iran is destined to march to Jerusalem and hand it over to the messianic Mahdi.

Iran and the Conquest of Jerusalem

In March of 2011, high ranking officers of the Revolutionary Guard and senior clerics gathered to view a video that had just been completed. The movie had taken several months to put together. The production values could have been better, but there was no time to waste in putting out the message of an imminent arrival of the Mahdi.

The motion picture opened with a montage of celebrations of the Iranian Revolution, including a large gathering of cheering partisans before the current Supreme Leader of Iran, Ali Khomenei. "Greetings to the Mahdi," the narration begins. "And greetings to all those who are preparing for the reappearance and to all those awaiting the rising of the sun."

The voice-over continued, describing Islamic apocalyptic prophecies known as hadiths. The hadiths are sayings ascribed to Muhammed and other prominent ancient Muslim figures, but are not in the Koran. Photos of George W. Bush, Barak Obama, Benjamin Netanyahu, and German Chancellor Angela Merkel flashed across the screen. Muhammed was quoted from the Koran: "The worst kind of humans will become leaders." Later in the movie, these politicians will be accused of belonging to the Freemasons, a secretive group that mixes ancient Egyptian Pagan religion with Judaism and Christianity. The makers of the film accused the Freemasons as having set up Jerusalem as their capital.

The presentation continued with a quote from a hadith: "Whoever guarantees the death of King Abdullah of Saudi Arabia, I will guarantee the imminent appearance of the Mahdi." The narrator also commented on the prediction while describing the existing situation in Saudi Arabia. He explained that it has been over one hundred years since there has been a king in Arabia named Abdullah. Sunni Arabia is the chief rival to Shia Iran for power in the region. The film goes on to imply that the current King Abdullah will be in league with the Sufyani, an evil person described in the prophecies as one who acts to impede the rise of the Mahdi.

Iranian war ships glided through the waters of the Persian Gulf. The Iranian Army marched past Supreme leader Ali Khomenei. Ballistic missiles streamed from their launching pads. Frame by frame, these images filled the screen as hadith proclaims that a leader will arise from the east to march his army to Jerusalem. The current conflicts in Iraq, Afghanistan, and Yemen are all portrayed as fulfilling the scenario that the Islamic prophecies predict. In the midst of this turmoil, a nation will arise out of the east which will march to liberate Palestine. According to the makers of the film, the army will carry and plant black flags in Jerusalem. The black flags are considered a sign of the Mahdi's imminence.

Within Islam, there are a number of hadiths with variations on the black flags and Jerusalem. One claims that the army of the black flags will "defeat the companions of the Sufyani until he (the army's leader) comes to the house of Jerusalem." Another foretells that "Armies carrying black flags will come from Khurasan. No power will be able to stop them and they will finally reach Jerusalem where they will erect their flags."

The film incorporated other hadiths about the conquering of Jerusalem and the leader of this army of the black flags. The sign of the Mahdi's appearance will be war banners led by a man with a disability known in the prophecies as Seyed Khurasani. Iran's Supreme Leader Ali Khamenei has a paralyzed right hand. The narrator was careful not to make an absolute statement declaring Khamenei as the commander of the black flags, but, nonetheless, claimed that "some scholars believe" that he is the one.

The same is said about two other leaders that the prophecies associate with the army of the black flags. Then President Ahmendinejab and the current head of Hezbollah, Hasan Nasrallah, are believed "by some scholars" to be those who will fulfill the hadiths. The movie ends the segment with Ahmendinajab giving one of his speeches: "Palestine with the full strength of resistance and power of faith will become free. Justice will come. The oppressed will be saved."

In the midst of these discussions of the Shia prophecies, the producers of the film featured a commentary from one of the Iranian newspapers. "The establishment of the state of Israel ruined the unification of Muslims, and the time of The Coming will be heralded by the conquering of Palestine from the Jews with forces by Iraq and Iran." The paper's diatribe is, of course, false as the Shia and Sunnis have been at odds with each other for centuries.

The film ends with a call to arms: "The sun of Imamat is about to rise. Come forth in praising God and with jihad of faith to be part of the governance of the pious on earth." The final frames show a statement by the Supreme Khamenei describing his belief in the coming Mahdi: "I can tell you with confidence, the promise of Allah for The Coming and the establishment of a new Islamic civilization is on its way."[637]

As soon as the video aired over the internet, moderate Muslims reacted with criticisms of the movie. TV Station A9, broadcasting out of Istanbul, Turkey, cited a number of errors in the Iranian presentation. The disapproval stemmed around the rejection of the Shia-recognized hadiths in favor of a

Sunni-accepted prophecy that the Mahdi will come in peace. A9's mission is to peacefully convert the world to the moral principles of Islam.

On March 28, 2011, a former double agent who had worked in Iran for the CIA, Reza Kahlili, wrote that his contacts in the Iranian Revolutionary Guard informed him that the Supreme Leader Ayatollah Ali Khamenei and the Iranian President Mahmoud Ahmadinejad had approved of a project by the Basij, the Iranian Parliamentary force, in conjunction with a group known as The Conductors of The Coming. Reports indicate that Esfandiar Rahim Mashaei, President Amadinejad's top adviser and chief of staff, was directly involved with this project. The finished product is the video just described entitled *The Coming is Upon Us*.[638]

At the time of his writing, Kahlili claimed that the video was being disseminated for screening throughout the Basij and Revolutionary Guard bases. The producers were in the process of translating it from Farsi into Arabic for mass distribution throughout the Middle East. The former CIA agent gave his own thoughts about the producers' mission: "Their intention is to incite further uprisings with the hopes of motivating Arabs to overthrow U.S. backed governments with the final goal of the annihilation of Israel and Allah's governance of the world!"

At the heart of Iran's grievance against Israel and the west is the belief that it must fulfill the prophecies of the black banners. The Iranians, however, are not the only ones who seek to fulfill the apocalyptic predictions. While they latched onto the black banner prophecy with its emphasis upon Khurasan, some Sunnis came to believe that the hadith spoke to them as Khurasan also included the region that is now Afghanistan. The Taliban and Al-Qaeda also found their purpose in life by trying to light the match they believe will usher in the Islamic Kingdom of Allah.

Islamic Prophecy and World Terrorism

FBI agent Ali Soufan sat across the interrogation table from Al-Qaida member Abu Jandul, the man who had served as Osama Bin laden's most trusted aide. The Yemeni terrorist prepared for the interview by going on the offensive. "We will be victorious," proclaimed the prisoner with a sneer.

"Why do you think you'll win?" Soufan asked.

"You want to know why? If you see the black banners coming from Khurasan, join that army, even if you have to crawl over ice; no power will be able to stop them . . . ."

"And they will finally reach Jerusalem," Soufan finished the prophecy, "where they will erect their flags."

Jandul's eyes widened. "You're aware of the prophecy?"

Soufan had interviewed many of Al-Qaida who quoted the ancient hadith. In 2002, Bin Laden's propaganda specialist, Ali al-Bahulu, confessed that the terrorist organization's black flags announced the Islamic apocalypse. [639]

Taliban leader Mullah Muhammad Umar had given Bin Laden's terrorist organization safe haven. Their common interests were not simply the same form of government employed by the Taliban over Afghanistan, but they included their shared ultimate goal. In the midst of the conflict with the United States, Umar stated, "First we will see America's end and then the black flags will march to Palestine."[640]

The new generation of Taliban commanders put forward a global agenda: first to free Afghanistan, and then liberate Jerusalem from the Jews. According to an anonymous Jihadist apologist, "This trend is not limited to only the Taliban, but occurs around the world and around the different affiliates of Al-Qaida." These associates operate in Yemen, Morrocco, Algeria, Tunisai Somalia, Nigeria, Mali, Syria, and France.[641]

The apologist continued: "The distinct line between Al-Qaida and Taliban is becoming increasingly blurry, and the new generations of Taliban are pledging allegiance to the Al-Qaida ideology of a global struggle. They are all uniting under one flag—a black flag. This trend is not limited to Afghanistan. In fact all groups suspected of being associated with Al-Qaida have black flags."[642]

Now, the influence of the hadiths of the black banners has moved beyond the Middle East and France to the middle of Boston in America. The Tsarnaev brothers bombed the Boston Marathon on April 15, 2103. The case perplexed many U.S. authorities and media commentators. In particular, many asked how the younger brother, who attended college, liked to smoke pot, and seemed to be assimilated into the American youth culture, could turn into a jihadist. The underreported answer was found on his brother's YouTube page. There, the site linked to a video entitled, "*The Emergence of Prophecy: Black Flags from Khurasan.*[643]

Besides the prophecies of the black flags, the video includes another apocalyptic hadith: "The last hour will not come until 70,000 from Bani Ishaq (children of Issac) will attack and conquer Constantinople." The movie relates that these are Jews who had relocated to Khurasan at some point and converted to Islam. "After the city falls, the Antichrist will be killed by Jesus." For some Sunnis, Jesus and the Mahdi is one and the same person. In Shia theology, the Mahdi arrives first and then Jesus. The hadith appears to have been gleaned from John's description in the Revelation of 144,000 Jews selected from the twelve tribes of Israel who follow Jesus and are attacked by the Antichrist.

At the time of the writing of the hadith, Turkish Constantinople belonged to the Christians while today the city is Muslim and has been renamed Istanbul. However, the current view of the Turks tends to favor moderation and a positive relationship with the west. Some extremists consider this a heresy and believe they must conquer Istanbul. Others believe "Constantinople" is merely symbolic for the west or Christianity. Thus for the terrorists, the hadith about Constantinople is still relevant and will still prove true.

All of these incidents, from Iran to Afghanistan to Boston, demonstrate that the shared goal of all the jihadists, both Sunni and Shia, is the fall of Israel and the United States. They also reveal that this aim is directly influenced by Islamic prophecy. This hatred for the Israeli government does not stem from its treatment of the Palestinians, however right or wrong that might be. The terrorists view America's involvement with Israel as intrinsically linked by the prophecies, and the hadiths call the militants to action.

"It is not the manner of the Islamic State to throw empty, dry, and hypocritical words of condemnation and condolences. . . . Rather, its actions speak louder than its words and it is only a matter of time and patience before it reaches Palestine to fight the barbaric Jews and kill those of them hiding behind the gharqad trees – the trees of the Jews." These are the words printed in the second and latest edition of *Dabiq*, the propaganda magazine of the Islamic State, also known as ISIS or ISIL. The organization does not focus on hadiths of the black banners from Khurasan. However other ancient hadiths concerning Israel, the area of the Levant, and the west spur these particular terrorists to action, and the group shares in parading the black flags that announce the apocalypse.

"You will invade the Arabian Peninsula, and Allah will enable you to conquer it. You will then invade Persia, and Allah will enable you to conquer it. You will then invade Rome, and Allah will enable you to conquer it. Then you will fight the Dajjal (the Antichrist), and Allah will enable you to conquer him." The final hadith printed in the magazine predicts the final battles that lead to emergence of the Mahdi.[644]

The title of the magazine refers to an area currently under control of Syrian forces. The town is believed by Muslims to be the site where Armeggedon will take place. The ultimate goals of ISIS are the liberation of Mecca from control by the Saudi monarchy, the conquering of Jerusalem, and the defeat of the Crusaders (the west) at Armageddon. The final object of the Islamic State is the conquering of the world.[645]

Although there are differences in some of the details of the eschatologies between the various Islamic Shia and Sunni terrorist groups, what unites and fuels the movements is the desire to conquer Jerusalem and hand the city over to the reappearing Mahdi. In this, the jihadists mimic the Christian Crusaders of the middle ages, who sought to conquer Jerusalem from the Muslims and hand it over to Jesus at his return. Apart from the chilling call to war against Israel, one of the most striking features of the hadiths of the black flags is their resemblance to the prophecy of the Last World Emperor.

Islamic Prophecy and the Last World Emperor

"I am he of the black banners." When the governor of Khurasan heard that his opponent, the rebel al-Harith Ibn Surayj, had made such a claim, he sent him a message. "If you are who you claim," wrote Governor Nasr, "you will tear down the walls of Damascus and bring the rule of the Umayyads to an end. If you are the one you mention then my life is in your hands. If you are not that one, then you have destroyed your tribe."

Al-Harith replied to the governor, "I have learned that this claim is true."[646]

In the year AD 746, al-Harith revolted against the Umayyaud Caliphate, which covered most of the Middle East, Spain, and parts of India. The heart of the grievance centered on the rebel's opposition to a tax imposed by the Umayyad family upon non-Arab Muslims in the region of Khurasan. The ever-growing unrest was spearheaded by the Koran's call for equality under Islam and the sense of injustice felt by the mixed tribes of the region.[647] Along with the injustice experienced by the Khurasans, prophecy also played its part in spurring the revolt.

According to the messages sent between al-Harith and Nasr, the rebel believed he was the prophetic figure predicted to end the Umayyad dynasty. The Islamic historian al-Tabari recorded the correspondence in his work written in the ninth century. One of the most interesting aspects of the communications, as indicated by Tabari, is that they imply that Damascus was the goal of the prophecy of the black banners, rather than Jerusalem.

Al-Harith's insurgency ended in disaster for the rebels, but the Khurasans continued to despise the Umayyads. The next uprising occurred in about the year 750. The family of the Abbasids sought to install its own rival caliphate over the Umayyad region. They recruited Abu Muslim to lead the Khurasans to Syria, the seat of Umayyad power. Mustering more support than Al-Harith, Muslim successfully marched his troops from Khurasan to Damascus and Bagdad where he planted the black banners of victory.

Once the Abbasids took power, they claimed the prophecy of the black banners had been handed down to the Prophet Muhammad's cousin, Ali B. Abu Talib and eventually to the Abbasids. Some modern historians, however, believe it was a legend fabricated by the family to justify their authority. One historian places the origins of the predictions at about the year AD 700, when a number of people in the Khurasan region had finally become fed up with the Umayyad Caliphate. In the midst of revolutionary fervor, war banners were adopted as the revolutionary symbol, as history records that the Prophet Muhammad waived a black flag when he attacked Mecca.[648]

The Umayyads considered Jerusalem an important spiritual center within their empire and built the Dome of the Rock and the Al-Aqsa Mosque on what is believed to be the Temple Mount. However, Mecca remained the most important religious hub for the family, and for Islam, in general. The most crucial political city of the Caliphate was Damascus from which the family ruled. As indicated by Tabari, Damascus, rather than Jerusalem, was the original aim of the army of the black banners. Abu Muslim needed to take the city to undo the Umayyad dynasty. Conquering Jerusalem alone would have failed to unseat the power at Damascus. But if that's true, why and when did Jerusalem displace the Syrian city in the hadith?

In the year AD 660, a Christian abbot from Syria penned *Pseudo-Methodius* which claimed a last world emperor would conquer Islam. The prophecy found its final form in the year 691 when the Coptic Christians suffered extreme taxation by the Umayyad regime. Over time, the prophecy percolated throughout the Middle East and a number of similar predictions were written in Syria and Europe. At the heart of these imitating predictions lay a last world emperor who would siege Jerusalem, rescue the Church of the Holy Sepulcher from Muslim occupation, and hand the city over to Jesus at his Second Coming. From the historical evidence at hand, throughout the later 700s and early 800s, Muslim hadiths emerged that put an emphasis on Jerusalem. [649] In what appears to have been a reaction against *Pseudo-Methodius* and like-minded prophecies, the city and the al-Aqsa Mosque began taking center stage as the place where

Muslims could find refuge from the Antichrist.

After the Christian crusaders captured Jerusalem in about 1099, the hadiths needed to be updated, for Jerusalem had now passed out of Muslim hands. In the prophecies, a commander who would be an arch-type of Abu Muslim would lead the army of the black banners from Khurasan. In the final version, he would become known as Seyed Khurasani. He would re-conquer Jerusalem and hand the city over to the Mahdi at his reappearing. In the hadith, Seyed takes the place of the last Christian king, and the Mahdi replaces Jesus. The prediction of the Black Banners became the Islamic counter-response to the prophecy of the Last World Emperor.[650]

Some Sunni scholars have repudiated all the predictions of the black banners as inauthentic.[651] This has done nothing, however, to dissuade much of Islam from believing in the prophecies, including many Shia. In the late 1980's, a document of apocalyptic hadiths, known as "The Return of Al-Mahdi," was discovered in a library in the modern Iranian province of Khorasan. It appears to have helped fuel the fervor that brought Ahmadinejad to power in 2005. Published in an Iranian academic journal in 1994, one of the prophecies portend that the army of black flags from Khurasan, led by a Shia leader from Uzbekistan, will do battle with the Sufyani, an evil apocalyptic tyrant that will control Palestine. "The Return of Al-Mahdi" claims that the Sufyani will be killed prior to the arrival of the Mahdi. Many in the Iranian government appear bent on preparing a military that can fulfill the prophecy.

In 2013, Ahmadinejad had to leave office as he completed his two terms. His claim to have had mystical experiences with the Mahdi made many of his supporters in the government uncomfortable with him. The ruling clerics also became disenchanted with him as he began to swing toward a traditional Shia theology that criticized clerical rule in place of lay leaders. A man believed to be a moderate, Rouhani, won the election for president. However, while one hard-line Mahdist lost power, another had been working for years to consolidate his authority. The current speaker of Parliament, Ali Larijani, has toiled to successfully infuse family members into high positions in the Iranian government. Larijani's eschatological beliefs can be understood by peering into Iran's Mahdi Conferences.

Jihad and the Mahdi Conferences

"Each one of you must prepare your weapons for the advent of al-Qa'im (the Mahdi) . . . even if it be as little as an arrow. When Allah the High knows that a person has this intention, then He will give him longer life." This Mahdi hadith is one of many that Muslims memorize. Apparently, this particular saying underpinned a paper presented by Mariam Tabor at the Mahdi Conference held in Tehran in the year 2008. Tabor declared, "The military capabilities of the future Mahdist state depend on Islamic governments in the here and now acquiring abilities to stand against the enemies of the imam."[652] The inference was clear. Since Tabor would consider the enemies as having weapons of mass destruction, Islamic governments should possess the same.

The keynote speaker at the closing session was Ali Larijani. "The Islamic Republic and other Islamic governments need to prepare for the Mahdi's governance by promoting justice and development and, although we have long-distance missiles, we are not war-like." The last part of the speaker's statement could hardly assuage fears of Iran's intentions, especially as he finished his speech by quoting a famous scholar from early Islamic history: "There must be bloodshed and jihad to establish Imam Mahdi's rule." [653]

Larijani and his brothers rose to power by forging a strong relationship with the Supreme Khomenei. The family has risen above most in their quest for influence. "What distinguishes the Larijanis is the number of brothers and the direction they are moving in, whether it is ideological consistency or their ability to place themselves in opportunistic situations," said Farideh Farhi, an independent researcher when she spoke to the Arab news agency *Al Jazeera*. "There are so many of them, and they have clearly used their relations for power."

Marsha B. Cohen, an independent scholar and news analyst specializing in US foreign policy with Iran, concurred and added, "What makes them fascinating is their pragmatic ability to shift with the winds and switch on a dime. By doing so, the Larijanis put themselves in a position where they could be useful no matter what." Cohen went on to describe how the power held by the siblings currently places them above the president: "As president you have to present yourself to a public vote and be subject to a campaign where you come out as either a winner or loser," Cohen said. "But to get a position in which you are appointed, or elected by political insiders, can actually be more influential." Evidence of this is found in their relations with Khamenei, who has played a consistent role in their elevation through the ranks. [654]

At the same time, former president Ahmadinejad is not going away quietly. The Supreme Council of the Cultural Revolution has granted him a license to establish a private technical university in the capital, Tehran. The university will specialize in high-tech fields including nanotechnology, aerospace and, interestingly enough, nuclear engineering. He has also invited the current president to a debate on allegations that his former administration misused government oil funds. President Rouhani has accepted the challenge thus helping to keep Ahmadinejad at the forefront of the Iranian media and politics.

In the latest conference held in 2013, Larijani reiterated his beliefs in the imminent arrival of the Mahdi: "It has been stated in the Islamic hadith that a wave of uprisings (such as the current upheavals in the Arab world) … takes place before the main uprising and that the righteous government (takes place) before the coming, which I hope (Iran's) Islamic Revolution is that."

The parliamentary leader went on to emphasize the popular Iranian view of the corruption of the west: "All mental crises are rooted in hopelessness and despair in life," Larijani said, "and from a societal point of view, this is because the big powers of the world are pushing for a culture that has no identity and with their power give their illicit desires a legal aspect. With the help of their media, they explain away the biggest corruption."

While certain members of the Iranian government continue to beat the drums of war as a result of the black banner eschatology, Muslims across the Middle East agitate over the Haram al-Sharif, the Muslim name for Jerusalem's Temple Mount. The Mahdi hadiths and the Jewish/Christian beliefs about the rebuilding of Solomon's Temple threaten to bring about war in the Middle East.

The Battle for the Temple Mount

The Popular Resistance Committees organization threatened Israel on Tuesday, August 21, 2012 warning it that if any harm comes to the Al-Aqsa Mosque it would "open the gates of hell against the Zionist enemy." At the center of the controversy is a renewed interest by orthodox Jews to be allowed to pray on the Temple Mount, something currently forbidden by law.[655]

"Settler groups, backed by the Israeli army, announced earlier they would storm Al-Aqsa Mosque on Sunday and Monday, to establish a Jewish synagogue, followed by laying the foundation for constructing the alleged Temple on Tuesday." The story reported by the Palestine telegraph, set off a wave of activity on Muslim websites and message boards. One board ran with the opening line: "Its official, its going to be destroyed soon (the Mosque). When will Muslims wake up?" The projected storming never took place, but the report demonstrated the quagmire encircling the Temple Mount in Jerusalem and the heated temperaments from many orthodox Jews, Muslims, and Christian Zionists.

As explained above, ninth century hadiths concerning the Mahdi developed, to some extent, in reaction to medieval Christian prophecy concerning Jerusalem and the Church of the Holy Sepulchre. The Muslim counterparts began to emphasize Jerusalem and the Al-Aqsa Mosque which sits upon what many people today believe is the Temple Mount, that is, the foundation of Solomon's and King Herod's Temple. In their final form, the black banner hadiths predict the conquering of Jerusalem, paving the way for the Mahdi. As a result, the Temple Mount has become a constant source of friction between Muslims and orthodox Jews, and Christian Zionists.

The book of Daniel and Saint Paul indicated that the Temple will be in existence during the reign of the Antichrist. Many historians and archaeologists believe the foundation for Solomon's Temple lay under the Muslim Dome of the Rock. Any rebuilding of the Temple would infringe on Muslim territory in relation to the Dome and Al-Aqsa Mosque. The result of this belief has caused all parties to take a defensive posture toward the Temple Mount.

In 2011, Jeremy Gimpel turned in his Bible to the book of Ezra. Speaking in front of the congregation of Fellowship Church in Winter Springs, Florida, he had been lecturing on biblical prophecy concerning the return of Jews to Palestine from the Babylonian exile. Referencing the books of Jeremiah, Ezekiel, and Isaiah, the religious Zionist explained that Ezra described the fulfilment of prophecy concerning the rebuilding of Solomon's Temple by the returning exiles. He quoted Ezra, chapter three, "And they laid the cornerstone of the Temple in Jerusalem." Gimpel then created a hypothetical situation in the minds of his listeners concerning the Dome of the Rock. "Imagine if the Golden Dome—I'm being recorded so I can't say 'blown up'—but let's say the Dome was blown up, right? And we laid the cornerstone of the Temple in Jerusalem. Can you imagine? None of you would be here. All of you would be like, 'I'm going to Israel, right?' No one would be here, it would be incredible!"

On January 15, 2013 Jerusalem TV station channel 2 broadcast the video of the Florida speech, causing an outbreak of criticism towards Gimpel. The media firestorm endangered his bid to win election to the Israeli parliament known as the Knesset. The political candidate quickly denied that he supported destroying the Dome. He had made past statements, however, that the Dome does not belong on the Temple Mount for it is, "The holiest place in the World." [656] The controversy ended up causing the candidate to lose some of his support, and he lost his bid for the Israeli legislature.

But the question has to be asked, what would happen if Jewish militants, with the financial backing of some Christian Zionists, successfully blew up the Dome and/or the al-Aqsa Mosque? And what if, after all, archaeologists find out afterwards that the Temple Mount was not the original site of Solomon's Temple? The final chapter of this book will investigate that question with the evidence for and against the Temple Mount and the possible counter-site of Solomon's Temple.

CHAPTER 21
INTO THE LAST DAYS

THE INTERNAL BLAST from the missile rained the liquid over Jerusalem's Bayit V'gan suburb. The Israeli government had issued gas masks to its citizens and warned them to remain clothed from head to toe. When the missile arrived, however, many were outside the shelters and less than fully clad. In the area home to the Holocaust Museum, hundreds lay dead from a nerve agent ten times more potent than VX.

Even though ancient Islamic prophecy allowed them to work to delay the onset of the apocalypse, Iranian officials cursed themselves for postponing their nuclear weapons program. Now the trigger devices in nuclear warheads failed to detonate during tests. But all was not lost as they had other effective weapons of mass destruction. Ever since the collapse of the Soviet Union, the Persians had been working on binary delivery systems for chemical weapons. Rogue Russian agents had supplied the Iranians with classified documents on how to build ballistic missiles that could combine two chemicals into one deadly agent and deliver the substance in mid-flight over a target region.[657] Stealth technology stolen from the United States by the Chinese and fed to Iran made the missiles impervious to radar detection. The first covert missiles avoided Israel's Iron Dome missile defense system.

Jewish militants had struck the match the Persians had been waiting for, and they believed the time had come to fulfill the Islamic prophecies. Just when the chemical weapons wreaked havoc on Jerusalem and other Israeli cities, half a million Iranian troops swooped into Iraq. At the head of the military procession, black flags whipped in the wind. The Army from Khurasan readied its march to Jerusalem.

As fighter squadrons from the Nevatim Israeli Air Force Base streamed toward the northern border, they passed over the top of Jerusalem's Temple Mount. One building was conspicuously absent. One week before, Jewish militants blew up the Dome of the Rock.

There had always been a question as to whether Israel had nuclear weapons. Most people believed they possessed them, but the Israelis had refused to give a definite answer. With the Iranian attack, however, there would be no more ambiguity. Hebrew officials gave the order. Air Force ordinance men armed the F-15s and F-16s with Jericho-11 missiles carrying nuclear payloads. The Middle East was about to be set on radioactive fire.

Obviously, the above scenario is fictional. But while no one could predict precisely what would happen if the Muslim buildings on the Temple Mount were actually destroyed, it's a certainty that major conflicts would erupt and probably lead to World War III. What if, in the aftermath of such a war, archaeologists were able to do the work on the Temple platform and find out there is no evidence that Solomon's Temple once stood there?

"The Temple faces the east and its back is toward the west. The whole of the floor is paved with stones and slopes down to the appointed places, so that water may be conveyed to wash away the blood from the sacrifices, for many thousand beasts are sacrificed there on the feast days. And there is an inexhaustible supply of water, because an abundant natural spring gushes up from within the temple area." These were the words of the gentile Aristeas describing the Jewish Temple in Jerusalem. According to the correspondence to his brother in Alexandria, Aristeas had been sent by the king of Egypt to bring back seventy-two Hebrew scholars to translate the Bible into Greek in the year 281 BC.[658]

Continuing his travelogue, Aristeas explained more of the water structure in the Temple. "There are, moreover, wonderful and indescribable cisterns underground, as they pointed out to me, at a distance of five furlongs all round the site of the temple, and each of them has countless pipes so that the different streams converge together. ... There are many openings for water at the base of the altar which are invisible to all except to those who are engaged in the ministration, so that all the blood of the sacrifices which is collected in great quantities is washed away in the twinkling of an eye."

The passage has perplexed modern archaeologists. While cisterns have been shown to have existed in the Temple Mount, the extensiveness of the system described by Aristeas seems implausible. Furthermore, no evidence exists that a natural spring gushed up from the Temple platform. Many historians and commentators have preferred to believe that the Egyptian was simply mistaken and, perhaps, unknowingly viewed water being supplied to the Temple by a Solomon-built aqueduct pouring down from the north of Jerusalem. And the canal was later updated by the Maccabees.

The biggest problem with the Maccabean canal theory, however, is that it is undercut by Tacitus. The Roman senator and historian, writing in the latter part of first century, gave his own description of the edifice: "The Temple was like a citadel and had its own walls, which had been even more laboriously and skillfully constructed than the rest. The porticoes around it constituted in themselves an excellent defensive position. To these advantages must be added a spring of never-failing water, chambers cut in the living rock, and tanks and cisterns for the storage of rainwater. Its builders had foreseen only too well that the strange practices of the Jews would lead to continual fighting. Hence everything was available for a siege." [659] In his description of Jerusalem, Tacitus writes about the city's fortifications but never mentions an aqueduct streaming from outside.

Tacitus pens his account in his history of Vespasian's siege and eventual attack against Jerusalem in AD 70. Thus the senator described the Temple as having been built with a defense against enemies. Modern commentators are not sure what sources the historian used, but it is likely he relied on Roman military reports. Not only did the senator verify the Egyptian courtier concerning a natural spring, he also debunks the aqueduct hypothesis by claiming the Jews constructed the Temple to withstand a siege. If an aqueduct was the main source of water, enemies surrounding Jerusalem could have easily cut off the water flowing down from Bethlehem. Tacitus described how the Romans cut off the city's food supply but mentions nothing of an aqueduct by which Vespasian could shut down the water. The siege took about two years to complete.

Remains of an ancient aqueduct do exist extending from Bethlehem to the Temple Mount. However, its dating is under dispute. Some have appointed it to the Maccabees, while some orthodox rabbis and Christians believe it goes back to King Solomon's time. Others, however, have dated it to the late first century AD, after the Jewish/Roman War, and believe the emperor Hadrian built it. The archaeological evidence, though, shows that the canal empties twenty meters below the Temple platform, too low to be used for most of the Temple's purposes.

This problem has been noted by Tuvia Sigev and Ralph Martin, who have put forward alternative theories. Accepting the Maccabean canal theory, Sagiv, nonetheless, believes the Temple existed to the South of the Dome of the Rock, twenty meters below, and in between, the Dome and the Al Aqsa Mosque.

Martin bases his theory on Tacitus and Aristeas. He places the Temple over the Gihon Springs, which is in the City of David, below and completely off the Temple Mount. Historians believe the Gihon is the only natural spring to have existed in Jerusalem. Martin's is the lone view in line with Aristeas and Tacitus. If Martin is correct, hypothetically, the Temple could be rebuilt without violating any part of the Muslim Holy space.[660]

In the year 2001, Temple scholar, Leen Ritmeyer responded to the book written by Martin on the subject of the Temple location. Most of the scholar's criticisms could be answered by Martin's overall thesis. However, Ritmeyer made one salient point—1 Kings 8 suggests that after Solomon built the Temple, the Ark of the Covenant was brought up out of the City of David, which according to the Scripture was called Zion, and placed in the Temple. Martin never adequately answered the criticism, only pointing out that King David had at one time placed the Tent of the Tabernacle and Ark of the Covenant over the Gihon Springs. However, some of Martin's followers on the subject have attempted to provide a response. The fortress conquered by David was originally called Zion and is located below the Gihon. Upon his domination of the stronghold and Jerusalem, the citadel went by both names—Zion and the City of David. 1 Kings, then, refers to the fortress and not to the area around the citadel built up by David after he occupied the fort. These commentators speculate that Solomon housed the Ark of the Covenant in the fortress while construction was under way and brought it up to the Gihon upon the Temple's completion.

Another problem associated with the water system and Tacitus is that the Gihon Springs exist outside the known walls of the City of David, making it vulnerable to siege. There are two towers nearby which might have been used to defend the Springs, but one has to wonder why the ancients didn't build their fortifications with the Gihon inside the city proper. However, some believe the area known today as the City of David had been misidentified by archaeologists. The first century Jewish Historian Josephus placed the City of David in an area west of where modern historians believe it exists today. A number of Orthodox rabbis have tried to build a Scriptural case that Josephus was right. If further digs ever prove them correct, then the archaeologically-determined site of the location of the Gihon would be thrown open to dispute.[661]

In his criticism of Martin, Ritmeyer never answered the question of the "natural spring" and the water problems associated with the Temple. Chuck Pitts, however, did respond by speculating that Aristeas and Tacitus may have been using the term "natural spring" as metaphorically and spiritually to describe God's dwelling place. One wonders, however, why a Roman would be describing a Jewish building's construct against a siege in spiritual terms, particularly when he believed the religious practices of the Jews to be "strange." If one reads Tacitus's entire account, it's clear he is describing the Temple in literal, geographic terms.[662]

The apparent contradictions in the ancient sources and current archaeology remain a mystery. With less than ten percent of ancient Jerusalem uncovered by archaeologists, making absolute claims about the Temple Mount are probably not wise, especially in light of the current conflicts with the Palestinians. However, one thing is clear from Scripture and the early church fathers. Wherever Solomon's Temple rested, whether in the place of the Dome of the Rock, somewhere beside it, or over the Gihon Springs, Scriptural prophecy does, indeed, indicate the Temple will be rebuilt.

The Temple and the Antichrist

In about AD 180, Irenaeus, the pastor of Lyons and disciple of Polycarp, wrote his commentary on chapter two of Paul's second letter to the Thessalonians—"When this Antichrist shall have devastated all things in this world, he will reign for three years and six months, and sit in the temple at Jerusalem."[663] At the time he wrote this in the second century, the Jerusalem Temple had already been destroyed. Irenaeus, then, held a literal understanding of the passage and understood that the Temple would be rebuilt at some point in the future. As explained in the early chapters of this book, his eschatology stood in line with the futurist premillennial thinking of the likes of Justin Martyr, the author of the Didache, and other church fathers from Asia Minor and the west.

Historicists and preterists have disputed this understanding of Paul's passage, preferring to follow the fourth century symbolic interpretations of the fourth century teacher Tychonius. The Donatist's eschatology implied that things that Revelation describes and appear to happen in the future could have occurred in the past. The historicists follow Tychonius in his view that Paul symbolized the Temple to refer to the Christian church. For the historicists, the abomination of desolation in the Temple (the church) has been committed by the popes throughout history. The preterists similarly consider that the passage refers to the past when Roman soldiers put up banners at the eastern gate area of the Temple after they destroyed the edifice in AD 70. The soldiers made sacrifices to the banners and proclaimed Titus as imperator, which indicated they wanted him to become emperor. They also claim the book of Revelation was written before the Jewish war of AD 70.

While the preterists take a more literal interpretation of Paul's passage, the problems with their approach are twofold. One, the Apostle indicated that this man of lawlessness will proclaim himself God. While the Roman standards may have had an image of the emperor blazoned on them, and the soldiers made sacrifices to them, neither Josephus nor any other historical reference maintain that Titus or the emperor Vespasian declared themselves God or deities in the Temple, or at any other time for that matter. In general, preterists assume Titus proclaimed himself God in the Temple before the soldiers burned it, but there is no historical evidence to back up this conjecture. The second problem is that there is no evidence that the earliest church believed in the preterist position—neither the orthodox nor the Gnostics. The preterists point to Eusebius of Caesarea as the most primitive person that might be associated with preterism. Besides being late in history, Eusebius, while believing the millennium was all but in the past, demonstrated little faith in the book of Revelation and only grudgingly accepted it as canonical. The bishop of Caesarea also claimed that he had at his disposal pagan writings supporting Irenaeus's claim that John had been exiled to Patmos during the reign of Domitian.[664] The truth of the matter is that there is no evidence that anyone believed in preterism until AD 1614 when the Jesuit Alcazar concocted the eschatology to answer the Protestants' claim that the pope was the Antichrist. Alcazar posited his view as an alternative to Francisco Ribera's futurism.

Likewise, the historicists' position reveals a number of problems. To this author's knowledge, no pope has ever been known to have proclaimed himself God. Certainly it has not been the practice of every pope since the fourth century. Another difficulty with their position is that the Antichrist's heresy will not be the current doctrines of Roman Catholicism.

One of the purposes of this book is to build a case for the literal interpretation of Irenaeus and to put forward an eschatology that is more in line with his thinking. As one who was a disciple of Polycarp, and Polycarp a disciple of the Apostle John, Irenaeus stood as a link in the apostolic tradition and interpretation. As this church father indicated that the rebuilding of the Temple remains in the future and that the Antichrist will not come until that rebuilding occurs, it is important to summarize the first two chapters of this book in order to correct some more modern notions of the Revelation and the emergence of the man of sin, as Paul calls him.

Portrait of the Antichrist

"You have heard that antichrist is coming. I tell you antichrist is already here." The Apostle John's words in his first letter referred to the spirit of Antichrist which raged against the churches of Asia Minor in the later first century. As detailed in the early chapters of this book, Irenaeus claimed John wrote his Gospel in response to the Gnostic teachings of the Nicolaitans.

Gleaning from the Gospel, the book of Revelation, First Timothy, and the sketch of the Nicolaitans outlined by Irenaeus, the group taught a variety of heresies: They believed the resurrection of both Jesus and the church was meant to be only spiritual, rather than physical, and occurs when one has faith. The sect held to an open sexuality similar to what's emerged out of the sexual revolution of the 1960's in the United States. They also taught that it was permissible for Christians to deny the name of Christ rather than suffer persecution and martyrdom. Adding to these, the Gnostic faction believed in a prosperity doctrine, holding to the idea that with faith all Christians could become materially wealthy. Furthermore, the Nicolaitans embraced the Christology of the Gnostic teacher Cerinthus.

According to Irenaeus, Cerinthus opposed John while the Apostle lived in Ephesus. The Gnostic taught that Christ and Jesus were two different beings. The Christ, as a spiritual entity, came upon Jesus at his water baptism. As Christ should not suffer, he then left Jesus just before his crucifixion. Within the teaching of classic Gnosticism, with the enlightenment from the Christ, anyone could obtain godhood.

In his first letter, it became clear that John dealt with the doctrines of Cerinthus. "Every spirit that confesses that Jesus Christ has come in the flesh is of God. Any spirit that does not confess Jesus Christ in the flesh . . . this is that of the Antichrist. . . . Everyone believing Jesus is the Christ is of God.[665] By studying these and other passages from the letter carefully, we can understand that the Antichrist will teach that Jesus and Christ are two separate beings, just as Cerinthus advocated.

The religious teachings of the Antichrist, then, will mimic the Gnosticism of the Nicolaitans and Cerinthus. For the pope to be the Antichrist, he would have to fundamentally change the Christology of the Roman Catholic Church, as well as liberalize the organization's moral teachings.

Other viewpoints have been put forth recently and garnered a fair amount of attention in evangelical circles. These include Joel Robinson's book proclaiming that the Antichrist will be the Islamic Mahdi. The author makes a case that the Antichrist will portray himself as a traditional Muslim and hide his true beliefs until he commits the Abomination of Desolation in the rebuilt Temple. While this is hypothetically possible, it is unlikely. Robinson makes his case primarily from similarities between Muslim and Christian eschatologies. As demonstrated in chapter twenty above, however, it is clear that Islam borrowed much of its eschatology from Christian sources and reconfigured it to answer Christian prophecies and criticisms.[666]

Another view that has become popular on Internet message boards is that of a Middle Ages prediction proclaimed in a document known as *Prophecies of the Popes*, which was attributed to the Irish Saint Malachy. The document, like those of the predictions of Nostradamus, has its detractors and supporters. Its supporters believe that the current Pope Francis will be the final pope that will rule during the Tribulation Period. Some evangelicals believe that the document is proof that Francis will be the false prophet that will lead many in the church to worship the Antichrist. However, even if the prophecy proves correct, there is nothing in it that defines the final pope in this way, only that he will preside over the Catholic Church in the time of John's Revelation. For Francis to be the false prophet or the Antichrist, as indicated above, he will have to radically alter the Catholic Church's Christology and viewpoint on human sexuality.

Some evangelicals claim that Francis will fulfill the role of Malachy's prediction, but they also admit that the pope will have to radically change Catholicism. They claim he will do this by calling for an ecumenical council to embrace a more universalist doctrine. But if Francis has to alter Catholicism, what makes the Catholic Church the prime target of these evangelicals to begin with? Are the existing Church and its teachings Antichrist or not? If the Roman organization is Antichrist in its current condition, why will Francis need to change it? [667]

The present reality suggests that Irenaeus was correct in his assertion that the Antichrist and the false prophet will teach the theology of Cerinthus and the Nicolatians. At present, there is no shortage of biblical commentators pushing a Gnostic reinvention of Jesus Christ in both Catholic and Protestant circles. The Jesus Seminar, a liberal think tank based in Santa Rosa, California is made of scholars with an agenda to change the mainline Protestant and Catholic churches' Christology and traditional morality. The Seminar leaders make no bones about wanting to rewrite Christian history. Authors such as Karen King and Elaine Pagels have been part of the seminar and they currently push the Gnostic reinterpretation of Christianity. In fact, popular writers, such as Dan Brown, and scholars from around the world are unknowingly setting the stage for the arrival and acceptance of the Gnostic Antichrist.

Along with Gnosticism, the Apostle John paints a picture of the Antichrist in the Revelation that duplicates the traits of the first century's three Flavian family emperors, along with the Roman ruler Nero: The man of lawlessness will persecute the church as Nero hounded the Christians in the city of Rome after the Great Fire. He will wage war as effectively as Vespasian and Titus conducted the battle against Israel. And he will merge all aspects of society and culture under emperor worship as Domitian attempted to do in the latter part of the century. He ruled so brutally that the Roman Senate secretly derided him with a term that meant "Nero back again." or "Nero has returned." With these attributes, combined with Gnostic religion, we are given an overall portrait of the Antichrist that reflects John's own cultural milieu, but one that will reemerge in the last days.

Besides the question of the criteria for determining the identity of the Antichrist, another controversy occupies the evangelical church—the place and timing of the rapture in relation to the Revelation and the Great Tribulation period. The majority of Evangelicals favor John Darby's rapture that occurs just before, or at the beginning of a seven-year Tribulation. Others hold to a gathering that takes place in the middle of the Tribulation. Still others argue for raptures at the end of either a seven or a three-and-a-half year period.

In recent years, Marvin Rosenthal has resurrected the pre-wrath rapture favored by the Jesuit Manuel Lacunza, but with some revisions. While Lacunza argued for a day of wrath that occurs at the end of the Tribulation, Rosenthal posits a period of wrath within, and somewhere toward the end of the time of the Tribulation. The wrath begins with John's discussion of the sixth and seventh seals as recorded in Revelation, chapter 6. The rapture occurs just before the opening of the seventh seal. One might call this position a revised post-tribulation rapture, as it occurs at an indeterminate point near the close of the Tribulation, but not precisely at the end.

While Rosenthal's doctrine has much to commend it, another revised post-tribulation view has emerged that still further modifies Rosenthal's teaching. It can be introduced by reading Paul's words in 1 Corinthians 15:51-52: "Behold, I show you a mystery; we shall not all sleep, but we shall all be changed in a moment, in the twinkling of an eye, at the last trump: for the trumpet shall sound, and the dead shall be raised incorruptible, and we shall be changed." For Paul, then, the day of resurrection would occur at the blowing of the last trumpet. The last trumpet recorded in prophetic Scripture was Revelation's seventh trumpet. To help explore this most recent of rapture viewpoints, it becomes necessary to turn back to the history of the Temple just before an invasion of Jerusalem by Babylon in 587 BC.

The Last Days and the Rapture

The Babylonians appeared on Judah's horizon. Invasion was imminent. Jerusalem was about to be sacked and the Temple defiled. Jeremiah went up to the mountain where Moses had ascended centuries before, and there he found a hallow cave. Inside, he placed the Ark of the Covenant and the Tent of the Lord's Presence. Then he sealed the entrance. As he descended, the prophet encountered some who had tried to follow him and mark his path, but they could not find the precise way. Jeremiah reacted with anger, "No one must know about this place until God gathers his people together again and shows them mercy. At that time, he will reveal where these things are hidden."[668]

The words of Jeremiah recorded in the apocryphal book Second Maccabees demonstrates a similarity to the Apostle Paul's description of the rapture in Second Thessalonians, chapter two—"Now we beseech you, brethren, by the coming of our Lord Jesus Christ, and by our gathering together unto him."[669] Both passages refer to a gathering of God's people in an eschatological sense. Interestingly, followers of both a pretribulation rapture and a posttribulation rapture agree that Paul here refers to the rapture. However, both groups dispute other elements in the rest of the passage.[670] Apart from Paul, another correlation between Maccabees and prophetic Scripture may also exist—the blowing of the seventh trumpet.

John's description of the blowing of the seventh and last trumpet in the eleventh chapter of his Revelation tied together a number of events using the Greek aorist tense: "The seventh angel sounded his trumpet and there were loud voices in heaven, which said: 'The kingdom of the world has become the kingdom of our Lord and of his Messiah. . . . The time has come for judging the dead. . . . Then God's temple in heaven was opened, and within his temple was seen the ark of his covenant." The use of the past tense in each verse binds the blowing of the trumpet with the announcement of God's rule of the kingdom of the earth, the judgment of the righteous dead, and the revealing of the Ark of the Covenant in heaven. This is the heart of the argument for the Seventh Trumpet Rapture—when God gathers his people in the rapture, the Ark of the Covenant is revealed from Jeremiah's hiding place and brought up with them.

Rosenthal's Pre-Wrath Rapture and the revised pre-wrath seventh trumpet rapture were devised with the idea of reconciling a number of apparent contradictions that Scripture has with the traditional views of the rapture—pretribulation, midtribulation and posttribulation. For example, in a pretribulation rapture, how does one reconcile the claim by Paul in 1 Corinthians that the day of resurrection (and therefore the rapture) occurs at the blowing of the last trumpet if there are seven more trumpet blasts to come as described in the Revelation? And how does one resolve the modern notion of an imminent return of Christ with the fact that Jesus told Peter he would grow old before he died. Or, in a traditional posttribulation view, how does one answer the riddle of a rapture that is supposed to occur on the final day of the Great Tribulation with the idea of a wedding feast that is supposed to take place in heaven. There doesn't seem to be enough time for the ceremony.

Besides the ability of the pre-wrath and seventh trumpet raptures to resolve a number of passages, these two viewpoints have the added benefit of harmonizing with Irenaeus's eschatology. The pastor from Lyons claimed the day of resurrection will occur at the end of the Antichrist's reign. In both modern scenarios, the rapture occurs just before the final judgments that are aimed to bring the Beast's rule to a close. In other words, the rapture marks the beginning of the end of the Antichrist.

When God is All in All

Throughout this book, we have seen how the history of western civilization has been shaped by false interpretations of the book of Revelation. The chronicles of war after war and violent revolution after violent revolution can be explained by the quest to bring about a utopian millennial age. Even John Nelson Darby's theology, which was essentially apolitical and pacifist, has the potential to cause war in the future as some of its adherents have been known to support activities in behalf of the desire to rebuild Solomon's Temple in place of, or in the Muslim sacred space of, the Dome of the Rock—a potentially aberrant reconstruction that could result in large scale armed conflict.

As has been shown throughout these pages, some liberal biblical commentators and historians have responded to this by advocating the elimination of John's Revelation altogether, arguing that it is the book itself that is the root of the problem. This answer denies the truths found in the book. In the midst of the visions on the island of Patmos, John witnessed the corrupt condition of human nature. The following of the Antichrist as described in the Revelation is something history has witnessed time and time again. From the faith that ancient Romans put in some of the emperors to the following of despots, such as Napoleon, Adolph Hitler, Joseph Stalin, Moa se Tung, or various last world emperors, mankind, whether religious or secular, has embraced the spirit of the Antichrist in believing that humanity can create its own utopia.

History witnesses to the reality of the book of Revelation. Throughout the centuries, the spirit of the Antichrist, that is, Satan, has worked feverishly to bring about the scenario of what Revelation describes, except in Satan's mind, he wins over God in the end. The evil archangel inspires humanity to believe in the goodness of its own nature and to imagine that political and religious leaders can solve mankind's problems and bring about the era of peace and prosperity. We've seen this play out in our own time with the giddiness that many people display over politicians who promise to bring us back to mythical Camelot or democratic movements that assure an era of worldwide harmony and serenity. And time and time again, people are left disappointed in the reality of their failures.

Historicists and preterists throughout the centuries have witnessed this working of Satan and mistakenly believed that the book of Revelation has already been fulfilled or portions of it have been fulfilled. But these efforts from the spirit of the Antichrist only foreshadow what is to emerge in the future. The despots of the past and present are merely forerunners of the Antichrist who is yet to come. These tyrants witness to the reality of the future Antichrist but never accomplish his role completely. Someday the Holy Spirit will remove his hand from holding back the full force of evil, and the Antichrist will come forward and fulfill the entire role of what the Revelation claims.

In spite of mankind's prolific failures to bring about utopia, humanity will someday experience the age of peace when Jesus Christ returns in the flesh to literally transform the earth. In some of his parting words, Irenaeus warned Gnostics not to allegorize away this apostolic doctrine of the faith when he wrote: "If, however, any shall endeavor to allegorize [prophecies] of this kind, they shall not be found consistent with themselves. . . . For there shall be a new heaven and a new earth; and there shall be no remembrance of the former, neither shall the heart think about them, but they shall find in it joy and exultation. . . . For as it is God truly who raises up man, so also does man truly rise from the dead, and not allegorically. . . . And this is the truth of the matter. . . . For He (Christ) must reign till He has put all enemies under His feet. The last enemy that shall be destroyed is death. . . . And when all things shall be subdued unto Christ, then shall the Son also Himself be subject unto God, that God may be all in all." [671]

Glossary

Amillennialism holds that the thousand years mentioned in Revelation 20 is a symbolic number, not a literal description; it proposes that the millennium has already begun and is identical with the current church age. It more rightly should be termed **nunc-millennialism** (that is, now-millennialism) because the millennium, or church age, has already begun. The doctrine was Augustine's attempt at finding a middle ground between premillennialism and postmillennialism.

Coptic Church traces its religious lineage back to Saint Mark, who wrote the Gospel of Mark. Ancient church documents claim Mark evangelized in Egypt and was martyred in Alexandria.

Eschatology: theology referring to the end of the world as we know it.

Futurism claims that most of the prophetic events recorded in the Book of Revelation remain in the future and have yet to be fulfilled.

Historicism proposes the opposite of futurism. Many of the events recorded in Revelation are associated with past historical events and most, if not all of the Revelation, has already occurred. Many historians claim the eschatology originated with Joachim of Fiore in the twelfth century AD. Its origin should more-rightly be linked to the rules of prophetic interpretation by Tychonius in the fifth century as it highly symbolizes events and numbers associated with the Book of Daniel and the Revelation.

Historicist premillennialism combines historicism with a literal futurist interpretation of Revelation, chapter 20.

Historic Premillennialism is a modern term given to the particular futurist, premillennial eschatology of the second century church fathers from the west and Asia Minor. It should be understood as distinct from historicist Premillennialism. The church fathers proposed that the Christian church would suffer during a three-and-and-half year period known as the Great Tribulation, and the day of resurrection would occur toward the end of the Antichrist's reign.

Premillennialism is the belief that Jesus will return to the earth in the flesh before a literal thousand-year era of peace and prosperity. The doctrine is called "premillennialism" because it holds that Jesus' physical return to earth will occur prior to the inauguration of the millennium.

Dispensational Premillenialism: a modern form of premillenialism that claims the rapture and day of resurrection occurs before the Tribulation.

Postmillennialism is a symbolic interpretation of chapter 20 of the Revelation which sees Christ's return as occurring at the end of the millennium. In latent form, the doctrine can be traced back to the early fourth century AD. It found its popular formal definition in the seventeenth century.

Preterism. A system of eschatology formulated during the CounterReformation by the Jesuit Luis de Alcazar in response to the futurism of other Jesuits and the historicism of the Protestant Reformers. It claims that the book of Revelation has already been completely fulfilled.

----

[1]Dio Chrisostom, Oration 56. Chrisostom describes political clubs causing strife in the city of Prusa.

[2]Trajan's paranoia can be seen in his correspondence with Pliny, the governor of Bithynia, in about A.D. 111. Pliny wrote asking the emperor's opinion of starting a fire department in the city of Nicomedia. Trajan replied as follows: "You are of opinion it would be proper to establish a company of firemen in Nicomedia, agreeably to what has been practiced in several other cities. But it is to be remembered that societies of this sort have greatly disturbed the peace of the province, in general, and of those cities in particular. Whatever name we give them, and for whatever purposes they may be founded, they will not fail to form themselves into factious assemblies." *(Letters of Pliny, 43).*

[3]Eusebius, *Ecclesiastical History*, book 3, 36:4. On the background of Eusebius see chapter seven below.

[4]Ignatius wrote to the church at Smyrna: "They abstain from the Eucharist and from prayer because they do not confess that the Eucharist is the flesh of our Savior Jesus Christ, flesh which suffered for our sins..." *Smyrneans* 6:2. The schismatics Ignatius refers to became known as Gnostics. Apparently, at this time, the mainstream churches in Asia Minor held to the physical presence of Christ in the Eucharist. In light of this, it made sense that early Gnostics refused the ceremony since they believed that evil was intrinsic to physicality. The recently discovered *Gospel of Judas* was written as a Gnostic-oriented condemnation of the orthodox theology of communion. For more about Gnosticism, see below in this chapter and in chapter 3 below.

[5]The precise reason for the arrest of Ignatius is a hotly debated topic of modern Ignatian scholars and is open to speculation. The theory above is based on Chrystosom's Oration and Trajan's reply to Pliny about associations. In a further correspondence by Pliny concerning how to deal with Christians, Pliny discusses arresting two Christian deaconesses with the following description: "It was their custom to disperse and reassemble later to take food of a common and innocuous type; but they had in fact given up this practice since my edict, issued on your instructions, which banned all associations." Christine Trevett, and a number of other scholars have put forth a competing theory that Ignatius was arrested because he could not control factions in his own congregation and they were causing public disturbances. This theory is based on a later statement by Ignatius after his arrest that he is pleased that the Antiochan church is at peace. This theory implies that the authorities had a legitimate reason to arrest Ignatius and he was not being persecuted for Christian practices. The weakness of this theory is seen in that Ignatius was not explicit in mentioning any schisms existing in his church, while he does mention factions and schisms in other churches in Asia Minor. His own letter to the Romans implies he was persecuted for his Christianity, "I am writing to all the Churches and I enjoin all, that I am dying willingly for God's sake." Eusebius wrote in his *Ecclesiastical History* that Ignatius was arrested, for *his testimony for Christ*

(Book 3, 36). Second century church father Irenaeus quotes *Romans*: "As a certain man of ours said, when he was condemned to the wild beasts because of his testimony with respect to God: 'I am the wheat of Christ, and am ground by the teeth of the wild beasts, that I may be found the pure bread of God.'" *Against Heresies*, 5, 28, 4. Concerning the "peace," the more traditional view was put forth by J.B Lightfoot who believed that the peace that returned to the church was the end of persecution. This is likely in that the authorities probably returned to business as usual once Trajan left the region as they probably had no initial desire to arrest Ignatius in the first place. This is verified by the fact that there is no evidence that any others were arrested but Ignatius. The "peace" is probably a return to normal worship and Communion that the Antiochans had refrained from until after Trajan left the area.

[6]According to Eusebius. See note 48 below on the year of Ignatius's death.

[7]According to Tertullian, the Apostle John appointed Polycarp to the pastorate. See *Against Heresies* book 32. Irenaeus claimed Polycarp was instructed and appointed by apostles in Asia Minor and was a disciple of the Apostle John. See Irenaeus *Against Heresies* Book 3, Chapter 4, Verse 3 and Chapter 3, Verse 4. On the background of Irenaeus see chapter 3 below.

[8]See the website for the Izmir-Agora Museum.

[9]See the letter addressed to the church in Smyrna in the book of Revelation, 2:8-11, "I know your poverty, yet you are rich."

[10]Here we receive a glimpse of Ignatius's theology of suffering. One becomes a disciple by faith Christ, but one becomes the more perfect disciple by suffering for Christ. Ignatius's Letter to the Romans, Chapter 5:1. The translation of all passages is by Kenneth J. Howell except where otherwise noted. *Ignatius of Antioch and Polycarp of Smyrna: A New Translation and Theological Commentary*, p.115.

[11]As recounted in his letter to the Smyneans that he wrote after arriving later in the city of Troas. Burrhus, a church deacon, was allowed to accompany Ignatius to Troas.

[12]On the authenticity of the Ignatian writings, see note 26 below.

[13]*Romans*, chapters 1, 2, and 5.

[14]*Romans* chapters 6 and 4.

[15]*Ephesians* chapter 1:1-5.

[16]Revelation, 2:4.

[17]1st John, 3:17-18. Two primary themes in both the 1st Letter of John and the Revelation in regard to the Ephesians are the struggle with love for one another and the church's rejection of a certain heresy that developed in the later part of the first century.

[18]The Greek word "anazopuresantes," translates as "you rekindled." According to *The Analytical Greek Lexicon of the Greek New Testament*, it literally means to kindle or revive a dormant fire. This is one indication that Ignatius was familiar with the book of Revelation. See more on Ignatius and Revelation below in this chapter.

[19]*Ephesians*, 10:1.

[20]Howell, p. 9.

[21]From the time of the Protestant Reformation, the issue of church govern-

ment has been hotly debated. John Calvin claimed the early church operated by way of a "congregational" model—the congregation was ruled by an eldership elected by the congregation and no one person stood in authority. He based this on letters of the New Testament written while Peter and Paul were still alive. Patristic writings, however, suggest that just prior to their deaths, the Apostles set in motion the Episcopal form of government with the term "episcopos" made distinct as the designation for lead elder/pastor and taking authority in the congregation as a way of taking the place of the Apostles. See chapter 3 below, on the succession of bishops (English translation from the Latin of episcopoi) from the Church of Rome. Also see Clement of Alexandria, as quoted by Eusebius in *Ecclesiastical History*, 3:23, who claimed that after John was released from exile on Patmos, he appointed certain individual bishops over some of the churches in Asia Minor. One Patristic writing known as the *Didache* is in line with New Testament writings claiming no distinction between episcopoi and presbyteroi. But this document was probably written when most Apostles were still alive, with some scholars believing it was written by Matthew. This debate between congregational and Episcopal government became one of the hot-button issues leading up to the English Revolution under Oliver Cromwell. See chapter 15 below.

[22]According to the *Actum Martyrium*. The *Actum* is of a late period and most scholars reject its reliability. However, a few of its details may be correct.

[23]The translation is literal and my own.

[24]Revelation 3:12.

[25]See more on this point in chapter 3 below.

[26]John David Michaelis, in 1832, was one of the first scholars to claim that Ignatius had no knowledge of John's Revelation. In 1842, John Collyer Knight responded to Michaelis with the forceful counterargument concerning Ignatius's knowledge of Revelation based on the letter to the Philadelphians. Unfortunately, however, Michaelis's argument has stuck. In her conclusion that the Apostle John did not write the Revelation, Adela Yarbro Collins ignored Ignatius when she discussed the early church's knowledge of the book. Commentators Bernard McGinn, Elizabeth Fiorenza, and Jonathon Kirsch are in agreement with her arguments. See Collins, *Crisis and Catharsis: The Power of the Apocalypse*, p.25.

[27]See also, note 29 below. The lack of direct quotes helps establish authenticity of the letters.

[28]After Domitian's assassination in September of 96, Emperor Minerva released Domitian's exiles.

[29]There are a number of other letters attributed to Ignatius. These have been rejected by almost all scholars as having been forged centuries after Ignatius. Seven core letters, however, have been accepted as authentic by the Protestant Scholar, J.B. Lightfoot, and most modern scholars have accepted Lightfoot's arguments. These letters are: *Ephesians, Smynaeans, Trallians, Philidelphians, Romans, Magnesians,* and to *Polycarp*. Eusebius recounts that Ignatius wrote the seven letters as listed above. Irenaeus quotes from the letter to the *Romans*. The third century teacher, Origen, quotes from

Romans and Ephesians and claims that Ignatius wrote them. Lightfoot and others compared these three letters to the other four in style and composition and determined their authenticity. Three versions of the letters are extant: the short and long versions and heavily abridged versions of *Romans, Polycarp,* and *Magnesians*. Most Scholars accept the short version. The long versions of the letters contain extensive quotes from both the Old and New Testaments. In my opinion, this speaks against their authenticity as Ignatius probably did not have access to these writings while incarcerated. The relative few quotes in the short versions make more historical sense as he would have had to rely on memory.

[30]1 John 2:22 and 1:7.

[31]The doctrines of Cerinthus evolved out of earlier Gnosticism that taught that an evil god was responsible for all the physical creation, while a good god created only soul or spirit.

[32]According to Irenaeus, John wrote his Gospel as a direct reaction to the theology of the Nicolaitans.

[33]The basis for Nicolaitan theology is taken from several sources besides Irenaeus. Gnostic writings dating to the Second Century that were found in Nag Hammadi, Egypt, portray some Gnostics as anti-martyrdom, particularly the Gospel of Mary. While not all Gnostics may have shared this view, it seems that most did. The Nicolaitans certainly fell into this category. See more on this below.

[34]According to Irenaeus, the Nicolaitans descended from heretics discussed in 1st and 2nd Timothy, where Paul writes that there were those who taught the Resurrection had already occurred, and some of them followed a prosperity doctrine as Paul explained in 1Tim, chapter 6. This idea that the Resurrection has already occurred is also found in the Nag Hammadi document *The Treatise on the Resurrection*, authored by the Gnostic Valentinus or one his followers.

[35]The Greek word for paracleat encompasses both ideas of comfort and counsel.

[36]Adela Yarbro Colins repeats a long standing criticism that the Gospel contradicts the Revelation of John as she claims the Gospel teaches a realized eschatology. That is, the Gospel teaches there is no future return of Christ or resurrection of the body of the saints. Full salvation can be attained in the here and now by the giving of the Holy Spirit, as opposed to the future eschatology of the Revelation. This viewpoint demonstrates a fundamental misunderstanding of the Gospel as it relates and reacts to the theology of Cerinthus and the Nicolaitans. As recounted above, the primary purpose of the giving of the Holy Spirit in John's Gospel is to help the followers endure the coming persecution, a persecution that finds its ultimate fulfillment in the Revelation.

[37]Revelation 6:18. Irenaeus claims John was exiled to Patmos by the Emperor Domitian.

[38]Revelation 6. The proclamation that the martyrs come from every tribe and tongue runs counter to the modern, predominant evangelical view that only Jewish Christians will exist during the Great Tribulation, with the time of the gentiles having come to an end prior to the start of the Tribulation

period. The idea is that the gentile Christians will have been "raptured" or removed from the earth and only Jews are left to convert to Christianity. In Revelation six, however, John describes the scene in the present tense, indicating that as he watched it unfold, both Jewish and gentile Christians are being murdered and increasing the overall number of martyrs. For the origins of the pre-tribulation rapture, see chapter 18 below.

[39]Revelation 13:10. The translation above is according to the ancient Greek text of Revelation known as Sinaiticus which dates to between AD 325 and 360. Many scholars prefer the variant reading found in the text known as Alexandrinus which dates to the fifth century. Alexandrinus reads: "If anyone is to be killed with the sword, with the sword he will be killed." However, Irenaeus quoted this passage. According to the Latin translation, it reads: "If anyone will have killed with the sword, with the sword he himself should be killed." *Against Heresies*, Book 5, chapter 28. Irenaeus's rendering is the earliest version we have of 13:10. The original Greek of Irenaeus has been lost. However, the Latin translation of Irenaeus from the Greek dates to between AD 180 and 240 as Tertullian quoted from it verbatim in his *Adversus Valeninianos*. Some scholars date the Latin to the late fourth century, but they ignore the evidence from Tertullian. There also exists an Armenian version of Irenaeus that dates to the fifth century, but I have failed to attain an English translation for comparison. However, an article citing and explaining variants between the Armenian and Latin written by Armatage Robinson does not include this passage, leading me to believe there is no variation. An English translation of Armenian *Against Heresies* books 4 and 5 would be a welcome edition. Also see chapter 2, note 75.

[40]Revelation 6:6: "A measure of wheat for a penny, and three measures of barley for a penny; and see thou hurt not the oil and the wine." According to Michael Rostovtzeff, *The Social and Economic History of the Roman Empire*, Biblo & Tannen Publishers, 1926, p.528, John used this slogan that appears to mimic what had happened during the famine of Galatia when a measure of wheat cost one day's wages. This helps date the Revelation to after AD 92. Irenaeus's indication that the Revelation was authored in A.D. 96 fits quite well.

[41]Revelation, 17:6.

[42]Revelation, 17 And 18 portrays the Whore as one who sits on the city of seven hills-a classical description of Rome, and the woman is responsible for the city's wealth. The Whore and the city fall under God's judgment for shedding the blood of the saints. The wrath of God is in direct response to the unjust persecution of the Christians.

[43]Paul Trebilco, *The Early Christians in Ephesus from Paul to Ignatius*, p. 437. See also the discussion in Adela Yarbro Collins, *Crisis and Catharsis* p.89.

[44]1Peter 1:7 and Revelation 6:6.

[45]This prophecy, as well as a prophecy Jesus gave Peter concerning Peter's death, as recorded at the end of the Gospel of John, is problematic for those who believe that Jesus taught that the Christian church is to expect an imminent return of Jesus. This doctrine teaches that Jesus can return in the flesh at any moment. However, if Smyrna was to undergo persecution

for ten days, whether the period is meant to be literal or figurative, then logically Christ could not have returned until after the persecution ended. Early church evidence demonstrates that the prophecy was not fulfilled until A.D.155. On this point, see chapter 2 below. Likewise, the passage in the Gospel claims that Jesus told Peter he would die when he became old. According to early church evidence, this prophecy was not fulfilled until A.D. 65, when Peter was crucified on Vatican Hill, some 30 years after the prophecy was given.

[46]Trallians chapter 10.

[47]Romans chapters 5 and 6.

[48]This was according to Jerome. He visited Antioch and the Daphne Gate some three hundred years after the martyrdom. Eusebius tells us Ignatius died in the tenth year of Trajan's reign. This places his death in the year A.D. 108.

[49]Later, the Montanists would teach that Christians should in no way resist persecution and always allow themselves to be arrested, and in some cases, even volunteer for martyrdom. On the Montanists, see chapter three below.

[50]The above narrative of Polycarp's arrest and dialogue is recorded in *The Martyrdom of Polycarp*, written by congregants from the church of Smyrna and, according to the Moscow Manuscript, preserved by Irenaeus. The events of the martyrdom recorded in this chapter are abridged from the Moscow but are consistent with the text as recorded by Eusebius in his *Ecclesiastical history*, which some scholars consider the earliest and most reliable account. I make note where there are differences from Eusebius. I have also slightly paraphrased the dialogue for the sake of readability and clarity.

[51]While it is hypothetically possible persecution could have been visited upon Smyrna before Polycarp became pastor, no direct evidence of persecution exists between AD 96 and AD155. As indicated in chapter one above, according to patristic evidence, Polycarp ruled the Smyrneans from just before or very soon after the writing of the Revelation. And again, as indicated in the above chapter, this speaks against the modern doctrine of an imminent return of Christ. Hypothetically, even if the prophecy began to come true the day after the writing of Revelation, the fact that it had to take place over a ten day period still contradicts the doctrine of Imminent Return.

[52]Polycarp's Letter to the Philippians 2:1, 6:3-7:2. The date of the letter is a matter of scholarly speculation. Most place the letter anytime between AD 110 and 140.

[53]*Philipians*, chapter 11. The word translated "avarice" is from the Latin and means greed or love of material wealth. The Greek text of Philippians ends at chapter nine and only the Latin remains of the remaining chapters.

[54]See chapter one above for the beliefs of the Nicolaitans and their similarities with the Gnostic teacher Cerinthus. For differing scholars' views on who the heretics were in the letter, see Paul Hartog, *Polycarp and the New Testament: the occasion, rhetoric, theme, and unity of the Epistle to the Philippians and its allusions to New Testament literature*, chapter 6. While some believe Polycarp had Marcion in mind, who held to a combination of

Gnostic and orthodox doctrines, Hartog believes they were probably followers of Cerinthus or a group with similar beliefs. Hartog also mentions differing opinions on whether avarice and heresy are linked in the letter. But as shown in chapter one above, the study of Gnosticism shows the connection between heresy and the prosperity doctrine as practiced by the Nicolaitans, and the connection in Philippi is likely by evidence in the letter. It's also possible Polycarp had a variety of false teachers and teachings in mind, including, Cerinthus, the Nicolaitans, and Marcion.

[55]Within the imperial cult, the act of swearing to the genius of Caesar was to accord divine honors to the emperor and considered an act of worship by both pagans and Christians. As historian George Hyman indicated, in the first century, the imperial cult had evolved as part of the" peace of the gods" by which order and balance would be maintained in the cosmos, and by which the emperor could be ritually present throughout the empire. To refuse to swear to the genius could upset the tranquility and peace of Roman society and undermine the emperor's authority. See *The Power of Sacrifice: Roman and Christian Discourse in Conflict*, CUA Press, 2007, with particular emphasis on pp. 83-90.

[56]This is according to the Moscow Manuscript version of *The Martyrdom of Polycarp*. The narrative about Irenaeus is believed to have been from his own testimony, but is not recorded in Eusebius.

[57]The idea that Irenaeus was the pastor of Vienna at the time of this journey to Rome is speculation by scholar Eric Francis Osborne to explain how Irenaeus avoided the persecutions that eventually struck many in the church at Lyons. *Irenaeus of Lyons*, p.4. However, how Irenaeus avoided persecution is a matter of conjecture. The letter describing the persecutions is recorded by Eusebius, *Ecclesiastical History*, 5. 1. 3. On the New Prophecy, see chapter three below.

[58]Letter is recorded by Eusebius, *Eccl. History*, 5. J.B. Lightfoot dates the letter to somewhere between 130 and 150.

[59]In his seminal work, *From the Lost Teachings of Polycarp: Identifying Irenaeus's Apostolic Presbyter and the Author of Ad Diognetum*, Charles Hill gives a convincing argument that Polycarp influenced large portions of Irenaeus's theology and his knowledge of the various factions and teachers within Gnosticism.

[60]The following story is based on the account by Irenaeus and supplemented with material by Hypollytus that is complementary.

[61]Early Christianity followed the theology of *First Enoch* that taught that rebellious angels had sexual intercourse with human women, giving birth to giants. Demons are the spirits of the giants who died in Noah's flood, thus half angel, half human beings. Old Testament evidence for this is found in the Septuagint version of Genesis which reads that angels came down and had sex with women. New Testament evidence is found in Jude, which quotes a verse from *First Enoch* and also proclaims that angels left their natural abode and committed the sin of Sodom and Gomorrah. Jude was written in Greek but the verse corresponds to a word for word translation from the Ethiopian version, which, in turn, corresponds to a word for word translation with Aramaic fragments of *First Enoch* found among the Dead

Sea Scrolls. Jude's quote differs significantly from a Greek version that exists, and some evangelical authors have used this to claim that Jude was not actually quoting Enoch. At the same time, these authors are silent about the Ethiopian and Aramaic. Most *Enoch* scholars believe the Greek version is a corruption with the Aramaic being more authentic. If Enoch wrote it, the original was in the Sumerian language.

[62]The story of Simon and Helen and his associating her with Helen of Troy is recounted by Irenaeus.

[63]This helps explain the origins of the two groups at Ephesus contending with Paul in the First Letter of Timothy. Irenaeus claimed that the Simion priests lived in debauchery and from them originated the "knowledge falsely so called" from 1 Timothy 6:20. See Irenaeus, *Against Heresies*, book 1. 23. 5. From the context of 1Timothy, 6, the debauchery included the prosperity doctrine as Paul would write: *They teach that godliness is great gain. . . . But if we have food and clothing, that is enough.*

[64]Irenaeus, *Against Heresies*, 1.23.5.

[65]Menander's doctrine is similar to the one preached by what is known today as the Positive Confession Movement. Menander is given a particularly short treatment by Irenaeus. One wonders if the Gnostics suffered from the same problem as modern proponents of the idea—no amount of faith keeps one from growing old and dying, thus his followers quickly abandoned him.

[66]Irenaeus, 1.24.4 in conjunction with the description of Basilide's ethics by Clement of Alexandria.

[67]Harvard professor Elaine Pagels, in her book,*The Gnostic Gospels*, put forward the thesis that, in the power struggle be tween orthodox leaders and Gnostic leaders, the orthodox used the doctrines of Christ's physical death and resurrection to solidify their church power. One must wonder, however, what that power was worth if they could be murdered at any moment because of those doctrines. A better interpretation of history is that the orthodox used their leadership positions to maintain the orthodox doctrines that were handed down by the Apostles and reflected the true teachings of Jesus. The orthodox were willing to give up their lives, and the power that went with them, for the sake of those doctrines. While some Gnostics were known to die in martyrdom, anti-martyrdom was a doctrine of many Gnostics factions, and members had no problem avoiding martyrdom by sacrificing to idols.

[68]*Against Heresies*, book 25:1 and 3.

[69]For the interpretation of John's Gospel, The Revelation, and John's First Letter in the light of the Nicolaitans and Cerinthus see chapter one above.

[70]Irenaeus, 4, 20:11

[71]Ibid., 5:30.

[72]Irenaeus, 5.28.4. For Irenaeus, the Christians will not avoid the Great Tribulation period by way of the Rapture and the Resurrection as many modern evangelicals believe.

[73]Ibid., 5, 28.2.

[74]Ibid., 5:30:1.

[75]Also see chapter 1, note 43 above concerning the variations in Greek copies

of Revelation 13:10. Irenaeus' statement about the text of Revelation that he approved of is important in helping to determine solutions in the questions surrounding modern textual criticism and, in particular, whether copies known as Sinaiticus or Alexandrinus is the best reading for this verse. Modern commentators who claim the literal interpretation and reading of Revelation inspired violence are either silent on or ignorant of such historical, textual issues. On textual criticism concerning Irenaeus and his accurate quoting from Scripture, see Ben Haupt, "Irenaeus' Citation of Scripture: Intentional or Careless Alterations?" at Academia.edu.

[76]Ibid., 3,12.13.

[77]Ibid., 5, 35:1.

[78]The exact date and authorship of *The Didache* is disputed by scholars. Some believe it was written by the Apostle Matthew in about AD 50, as the document has a linguistic style similar to Matthew's *Gospel*. Others date it as late as Ad 150. The manuscript supports a congregation approach to church government, so this author believes it must have been written sometime before AD 107 and probably while most of the Apostles were still alive and ruling over the churches.

[79]Those who preach a pre-tribulation rapture make a distinction between the church and the Jews who convert to Christ during the Tribulation: the gentile Church is raptured and only Jews are left behind to convert. The church fathers allow no distinctions between the Gentile and Jewish Christians in the Tribulation. Irenaeus believed the time of the Gentiles continues until the end of the Tribulation and that the Millennium is specifically designed to convert Israel. See below in this chapter. Regarding the resurrection, those who hold to a pretribulation rapture believe that the day of resurrection taught in the Gospel of John is meant to be a symbol for a seven year period of resurrection in which many groups are resurrected at different times. This is how they reconcile a number of passages which appear to contradict a pretribulation day of resurrection. Dwight Pentecost is one who preached that there is no such thing as a literal day of resurrection. See his discussion in his book *Things to Come*.

[80]This theology became known as futurist pre-millennialism. Christ returns in the flesh and sets up a thousand year reign on earth. Some scholars today believe that premillennialism was a minority view among the patristic writers of the first three centuries and that most orthodox Christians believed in amillennialism. However, this argument is based on the silence of a number of patristic writings on the subject of a material kingdom rather than on positive evidence in those writings advocating or supporting amillennialism. Justin Martyr wrote that some Christians did not believe in a material kingdom but these were probably a minority and followed Gnostic eschatology while remaining orthodox on the nature of Christ. For details of the arguments and counterarguments see Donald Fairbairn's article, "Who's Side was the Church On?" In Craig L. Blomberg's *A Case for Historic Premillenilism: An Alternative to "Left Behind" Eschatology*, Baker Academic, 2009, Chapter 6. For the emergence of amillennialism and its definition, see chapter 7 below.

[81]It is interesting that in our own time, Gnosticism is resurging in popular-

ity in the mainline Protestant and orthodox churches. The popularity of the writings of Elaine Pagels and Karen King are just some examples.

[82]This is from the document *The Passion of the Scillitan Martyrs*. The version shown here is an abridgement of J.A. Robinson's translation. The dialogue from the original manuscript has been slightly paraphrased for clarity.

[83]The story of Perpetua is recounted in *The Passion of Perpetua and Felicity*. The document is believed by many modern historians to have been based on Perpetua's diary, but also to have been edited. The dialogue here is derived from the narration of the conversations she had with her family members and Saturus in the vision as recorded in the diary.

[84]Some scholars dispute the account of the *Passion* and believe Perpetua and all the other members voluntarily gave themselves up to the authorities-all wishing martyrdom. They cite the fact that Perpetua's family members were not arrested. The probability, however, is that local authorities acted on Emperor Severas' edict forbidding Jews from Proselytizing and applied it to new Christian converts in Carthage. Perpetua was newly baptized and so was targeted by the authorities. Perpetua's relatives were probably Christians for some time. If all had intended to volunteer, it is likely that they would have picked a day and time they could go together, including Saturus.

[85]The date is according to Bishop Epiphanius of the fourth century. Candida Moss uses the date as given by the fourth century bishop Eusebius of Caesarea with some revision by Christine Trevett, who places the origin of the movement in AD 168-171. The later date is one of the pivotal points of Moss's argument that *The Martyrdom of Polycarp* was a fraudulent document of the third century. Moss, however, fails to inform her readers of the earlier date by Epiphanius and the possibility that Eusebius was wrong in his dating. The date by Epiphanius for the emergence of the Montanists correlates well with the AD 155-156 year for Polycarp's death. See note 119 below in this chapter for more on the weaknesses in Moss's argument.

[86]Rex D. Butler, *New Prophecy and New Visions: The Evidence of Montanism in the Passion of Perpetua and Felicitus*, Catholic University of America Press, 2006 p.12.

[87]William Tabbernee archeologically discovered Pepuza and proclaimed the area fit perfectly the dimensions of the New Jerusalem. "Pepouza and Tymion... marked the northern and southern limits of the geographical area where he (Montanus) expected the New Jerusalem....It was flat enough, and large enough to be the landing place of the holy city descending from heaven." See *Pepouza and Tymion: The Discovery and Archaeological Exploration of a Lost Ancient City and Imperial Estate*, Walter de Gruyter, 2008, p.102.

[88]The Prophecy is recorder by Epiphanius, *Panarion, Haer.* 48. 10.3. Compare the prophecy to Revelation 21:23-24: "The city had no need of the sun...for the glory of God illuminated it...and the nations will walk in its light."

[89]Revelation 2:10. See also chapter 2 on Polycarp above.

[90]In my opinion, the fast popularity of the New Prophecy is part of the

evidence that Polycarp and others were murdered in Smyrna in AD 155 or 156. Candida Moss, in her criticism of *The Martyrdom of Polycarp*, chose not to take this into account.

[91]The prophecy was recorded by Epiphanius. Montanism is the word given to the movement by its critics. The new Prophecy is what was used by its supporters.

[92]Judging from the evidence, the group believed it was in the period of the Great Tribulation, and the Antichrist was the Roman emperor.

[93]Revelation 21.4. See the discussion of Maximilla in Butler, p.37.

[94]This prophecy indicates that the New Prophecy maintained the tradition of teaching pacifism in response to persecution as a way of mimicking Jesus' response to His crucifixion. There is no historical evidence that Montanism inspired violence against its enemies as some modern critics, including Jonathan Kirsch, have tried to insinuate.

[95]In his letter to Polycarp, Ignatius of Antioch tells Pastor Polycarp not to allow the congregation to do anything without his permission, while enjoining him not to do anything without permission from God.

[96]The Christian church, as a whole, frowned on voluntary martyrdom. See the document, *The Martyrdom of Polycarp.*

[97]This principle is associated with the Montanists by Tertullian and Epiphanius, 48.9.7. According to Tertullian and Origen of Alexandria, mainstream pastors and elders did not marry again after their wives died, probably following along the lines of the laws of Leviticus where the Priests were forbidden to marry divorced women and the high priests forbidden to marry widows. The Montanists wanted to expand the practice to all Christians.

[98]Revelation 14:4: *These are the ones who were not defiled with women for they are virgins....* Apollonius, as cited in Eusebius,*Hist. Eccl.* 5. 18. 2-3, seems to indicate the Montanists dissolved all marriages. But taking Tertullian and Epiphanius into account, as above, it seems they abolished marriage for only the top prophets. See also the discussion in Butler, p.14 and p.39.

[99]Many modern scholars believe the Montanists set up a rival priesthood, including ordaining women. This is based on Epiphanius's account of a sub-faction of Montanists called the Quintillians. However, Epiphanius does not claim that the entire movement followed this and the Quintillians probably did not emerge until the late second/early third century. William Tabernee points out a funeral inscription found in Phrygia which belonged to a female Montanist named Ammion that proclaims her a "presbytera" (female form of the word priest or elder, although it could also mean elderly woman, as in 1 Tim. 5:2 in context). However, the inscription dates sometime between 180 and 230 AD and might belong to a Quintillian. See Tabbernee, *Montanist Inscriptions and Testimonia*, p.67. The emergence of a rival clergy under the Quintillians probably came as a result of the groups' final excommunication which probably occurred in the late Second Century. There is no evidence that Montanus, or the first generation of Montanists, ordained their own priests. Montanus, however, did appoint financial officers to oversee the support of New Prophecy evangelists and the term koinonoi (those in fellowship with the Spirit) was used by the group to

describe its leaders.

[100]Most Montanists were Trinitarian while some were Modulists: the idea that God is one person but manifests Himself in three modes of being: the Father, Son, and Spirit. However, this was probably nothing more than a representation of the Christian church at large in the later second century with most holding to the Trinity, but some holding to Modulism. Irenaeus's writing is also evidence that the New Prophecy was not ordaining its own priests at this time. Irenaeus is the Patristic who gives us the apostolic succession in Rome, naming each bishop in succession. So it is unlikely he would be tolerant of any rival priesthood as he wrote, "It would be very tedious to recount the succession of all the churches … therefore … as the faith comes down to us through the succession of bishops. It is necessary that every church should agree with this church (Rome) on account of its pre-eminent authority." Irenaeus. Book 3, chapter 3.

[101]Irenaeus, Book 3.11.9. Paraclete is the word John uses for the Holy Spirit in His Gospel and the word favored by the New Prophecy.

[102]Irenaeus, Book 2.32.

[103]Many scholars believe the Montanist movement grew in reaction to the churches de-emphasizing the gifts of the spirit and the new prophets wanted to reinstitute the gifts. This was probably true for some churches. Irenaeus, however, contradicts the claim that all churches were devoid of the gifts, particularly in the west. Origen of Alexandria, writing in the third century, indicated that prophecy was still being practiced in the eastern church at Alexandria. The desire of mainstream church leaders to eliminate the gifts came in reaction to the New Prophecy. In other words, one way to get rid of the New Prophecy was to get rid of prophecy altogether, even though many mainstream churches were practicing it.

[104]The claim was made by the Alogia according to Epiphanius, 51.1.4. He was critical of both the Alogia and the Montanists. He supported the gifts of the Spirit in the churches. It was Epiphanius that refers to the group as the Alogia when he wrote in the fourth century. Apparently, in the beginning, when Irenaeus wrote, the group had no name yet and was simply a group of leaders that bandied together to oppose the New Prophecy.

[105]See chapters 1 and 3 above.

[106]According to Irenaeus.

[107]In reading Irenaeus, it appears that the initial reaction of the Alogia was against the Gospel as he does not indicate they opposed the Revelation at that time. The claim that Cerinthus also wrote the Revelation probably came after A.D.180, the year Irenaeus wrote *Against Heresies*.

[108]There is no mention in Irenaeus that Cerinthus taught this, and there is no hint of a material millennium taught in the Gnostic Nag Hammadi documents. The idea is likely a fabrication of the Alogia as Epiphanius claims, *Haer*, 51.

[109]Some scholars believe that the letter was sent by Victor, his successor, but the argument supporting Eleutherus by Christine Trevett makes the most sense. See Trevett, *Montanism, Gender, Authority, and the New Prophecy*, Cambridge University Press, 2002, p.58. Some of the allegations by Praxeus included Montanus and the two Prophetesses fleecing people of their

money, gambling and sexual intrigues. These seem unlikely, however, with the New Prophecy's emphasis on martyrdom and celibacy. It's hypothetically possible, however, that later members or sub-factions engaged in such activities.

[110]According to Tertullian, *Adversius. Praxeus*, 1.

[111]Alexander Roberts, *The Ante-Nicene Fathers: The Writings of the Fathers Down to A. D. 325 Volume II - Fathers of the Second Century - Hermas, Tatian, Theophilus, Athenago,* Cosimo, Inc.,2007, p.18. Scholars disagree as to the precise dating of Hermas. Part of it may date to AD 90 or before and part to 140. Some modern scholars believe *Hermas* was an anti-Montanist document. However, its dating is too early. Others believe it was written against Marcion, who denied that Christ had a human body, as well as teaching other heterodoxies.

[112]As recorded in the fragments of Gaius by Dionysius Bar Salibi in his commentary on the Apocalypse. Bar Salibi, who wrote in the tenth century, recorded fragments from Hypolitus, who wrote a criticism of Gaius in the early third century. Many scholars believe it is likely that they were part of the debate.

[113]Bar Silibi.

[114]This fragment was recorded as part of the debate by Eusebius of Caesarea in *Eccl History*, 3.31. Eusebius, a critic of the New Prophecy, failed to provide any more quotes from Proculas.

[115]Ibid., 2.25. Peter was buried at the Vatican and Paul was buried on the Ostian Way. The use of tombs in the debate by both opponents demonstrate an importance and veneration of tombs and bones that had to date to somewhere in the second century or bringing up the subject during the debate would not have made sense. The debate demonstrates the weakness in Candid Moss's argument against the document of the *Martyrdom of Polycarp*, she states on page 103 of *The Myth of Martyrdom*, "The practice of collecting and venerating the bodies of martyrs is *completely unparalleled* in the second century (italics are mine for emphasis). Her point is that *The Martyrdom of Polycarp*, which discusses the veneration of Polycarp's bones, could not have been written in the second century, for relics and bones were not venerated until well into the third century. Moss, however, is silent about the debate which took place at AD 202-203, and which indicates that the veneration of the tombs had to be taking place for some time and probably at a point much earlier in the second century by both the Montanists and the mainstream church. Moss is also silent about Eusebius's recording of a letter by the bishop of Ephesus, Polycrates, written to Bishop Victor in Rome to AD 190, which also mentions the location of Phillip's tomb and his prophetess daughters. The letter indicates that Victor would be familiar with the locations and, therefore, veneration was taking place. For Moss to maintain her position, she would need to dispute Eusebius on these points, but she failed to do so. For a discussion on the veneration of these tombs in the second century, see Ulrich Huttner, *Early Christianity in the Lycus Valley*, Brill, 2013, p.195.

[116]Some modern authors still refer to Gaius and advocate that Cerinthus is the author of the Revelation. Unfortunately, these commentators do not

consider the historical background that gave rise to Gaius's accusations, and they discount the report of apostolic authorship by Irenaeus.

[117]According to the criticisms from Epiphanius, Montanists used cheese at their communion celebrations. Candida Moss and some other historians believe that Perpetua was not a Montanist as the Catholic Church canonized her. The incident with cheese is one of the more compelling evidences of Montanism in *The Passion*. In a later Catholic recension, made reference to by Augustine, cheese is replaced by milk in the text, obscuring its association with Montanism. See Butler, p.68.

[118]Kirsch implies in his thesis that the mainstream leaders swung towards the symbolic view of Revelation as a way of keeping the lid down on the boiling pot of violence that the literal interpretation was stirring up: "When they (Church Fathers of the fourth century) cautioned good Christians to engage in a spiritual rather than carnal reading of Revelation, they were struggling to make it safe for human consumption-and thus began the long, ardent, but failed enterprise that one scholar calls the 'taming' of the apocalyptic tradition," *A History of the End of the World*, p.118. In fact, it is the direct opposite of what kirsch maintains. The symbolic (spiritual) view is what led to violence, as will be demonstrated in the next few chapters. The fourth century fathers' opposition to Revelation was born more out of intellectual snobbery and concern for their own power base than any concern about violence. And, in fact, as will be demonstrated, a number of them supported the use of violence.

[119]The story of Origen's confrontation with his mother over his clothes, his desire to volunteer for martyrdom, and his father's execution is recorded by Eusebius. Origen's impulsiveness in his youth is also known from the fact that he castrated himself as he applied Matthew 19:12 to himself. In his later years, he regretted the act.

[120]Whether Origin studied under Clement of Alexandria is a source of debate among historians. On this issue see Henri Crouzel, *Origen*, p.7, and Edward Moore, *Origen of Alexandria and St. Maximus the Confessor: An Analysis and Critical Evaluation of Their Eschatological Doctrines*, p. 17.

[121]Eusebius 6.3,1-8.

[122]According to Eusebius, 1. 6. c 3 4.

[123]From a review of patristic writings, the overall evidence suggests women were not allowed ordination as pastors in the early church, and Origen did not accept the idea of women teaching men. However, it is also clear that women were allowed to hold the office of deacon and prophetess, and, based on this account from Eusebius, could study theology in a formal classroom setting. In keeping with Origen's view, he probably had in mind that his female students would instruct other women. Gnostics allowed women as pastors and a sub-faction of the Montanists ordained women as presbyters.

[124]The term was often used by the church fathers to refer to Christ. The term being applied to Origen showed how highly regarded he became among his students.

[125]The story is related by Epiphanius.

[126]Eventually, Origen hardened his position and taught universal salvation:

all humans and angels, including Satan, will eventually repent and be saved, even if it takes billions of years.

[127]Origen, *De Principiis*, 2.11.1.

[128]See Irenaeus, Book 5, 34.3 and 5, 32.1. Much discussion has been employed on whether Irenaeus and Origen taught a form of Pantheism. That is, human beings will ultimately merge into the Godhead, obliterating any individuality. Some Irenaeus scholars venture to suspect Irenaeus maintained that Christians would retain some individuality while Origen did not.

[129]Origen's view of a future resurrection of the body is not easily discerned. He places the emphasis on the spiritual rather than any physicality of the body, and it does not reside in a material world.

[130]Gnostics referred to the Orthodox Church as "psychic" while the true Gnostic church was "spiritual."

[131]Dan G. McCartney, "Literal and Allegorical Interpretation In Origen's Contra Celsum," *Westminster Theological Journal* 48.2 (Fall 1986) pp. 281-301.

[132]Ibid., p. 287.

[133]These thoughts are related by Origen in his *Commentary on the Gospel of John.*

[134]This dialogue is derived from what Origen wrote about Ambrose in his *Commentary on the Gospel of John.* Here we see the two reasons for Origen's writings. First, he believed the apologies of those like Irenaeus and Justin Martyr were inadequate to counteract Gnosticism. Second, the sheer amount of writings coming forth from the heretics was becoming overwhelming. This last point suggests that most, if not all, the writings found at Nag Hammadi were written at around 215-220 AD. If we also take into account the statements from Irenaeus, it appears that the Gnostic gospels and most other Gnostic documents were written between 150 and 220 AD. There is no papyrology that can place them any earlier. Papyrologists, Carsten Thiede and Sung Yung Kim have demonstrated that fragments from the Gospel of Matthew and the Letters of Paul date earlier than AD 86, including that Pastoral Epistles, of which many scholars place well after AD 90. On this point, see also chapter 2 above.

[135]According to Gregory Nyssen and Eusebius, *Hist.* 6.37.8.

[136]Cyprian, *De lapsis*, 5, 6.

[137]According to Dionysius, as recorded by Eusebius, *De Marta*, 4.8.

[138]One might say that Cyprian was the prelude to the Donatists. On Diocletian's persecution, see chapter five below, and on the Donatists see chapter seven below.

[139]Origen, *In Jesu Nave homiliae*, 26. 9.10.

[140]Origen, Mart. 11. Also see the discussion by Paul L Kolbet in his article: "Torture and Origen's Hermeneutics of Nonviolence," pp.10-11.

[141]Lactantius records the incident in *On the Deaths of the Persecutors*, 10:6. The priest's dialogue is recorded in his narrative.

[142]Romula's and Galerius's attitude and the ensuing meetings are recorded by Lactantius, *Deaths*, chapter 11.

[143]Stephan Williams, *Diocletian and the Roman Recovery,* Psychology Press, 1985, p.62.

[144]Pophyry's lectures are believed by historians to have been based on his written track, *On Philosophy from Oracles*. The dialogue here is based on the tract. Besides Galerius, historian Elizabeth DePalma Digeser has recently put forth the theory that pagan philosophers had an inordinate amount of influence in Diocletian's court and heavily influenced him in his decision to persecute the Christians.

[145]Lactantius recorded his attendance of the lectures and his thoughts while listening to them in *Divine Institutes* 5:2-3.

[146]Dialogue is based on Pophyry's own written words in his tract.

[147]According to Jerome, after Lactantius lost his job with the royal court, he tried to make his living as a writer and fell into poverty.

[148]John H. Smith, *Constantine The Great*, Hamilton, 1971, p. 50.

[149]Lactantius, *Deaths*, 13. 2.

[150]Eusebius records the persecution of Peter and other persecutions.

[151]Eusebius mentions the rebellion but gave no details.

[152]Lactantius claimed the palace was set on fire by lightning strikes. Galerius's thoughts here are based on the description of his actions and attitude by Lactantius.

[153]Some pagan philosophers considered Apollo a manifestation of the sun. It is possible Constantine viewed Apollo in this way.

[154]John Holland Smith, p.53.

[155]Ibid., p.54.

[156]The feelings and thoughts of the crowd are recounted by Lactantius.

[157]Lactantius doesn't name the philosopher he writes against, leaving him anonymous. However, most historians studying the fragments of Pophyry that still exist have no doubt that he lies behind the criticisms in the Institutes.

[158]See the discussion in Elizabeth DePalma Digeser: *The Making of a Christian Empire: Lactantius and Rome*, Cornell University Press, 2000. In particular, the section: "Lactantius's Criticism of the Dominate."

[159]Smith, p.64.

[160]Lactantius, *On the Deaths*, Chapter 33.

[161]The decree is known as the Edict of Toleration and is recorded by Eusebius

[162]The details in the death of Galerius are recorded by Lactantius and Eusebius.

[163]Some historians believe Lactantius did not join Constantine's court until after 313 AD and did not tutor Crispus until 317. This is based on a certain interpretation of the account by Jerome. Digeser, however, argues that this is based on a faulty reading. The syntax of Jerome shows that Crispus was tutored sometime before 317. Digeser also argues that Lactantius was situated in Trier before 313 where Constantine's court was held. In 310, Crispus was anywhere between five and ten years old. Degeser notes that royalty was often professionally tutored beginning at six years of age. She also argues that Constantine's letter to the bishops at Arles in 314 demonstrates certain themes derived from The Divine institutes. For more details of these arguments see her articles: "Lactantius and the Edict of Milan: Does it Determine His Venue?" and "Lactantius and Constantine's Letter

to the Bishops at Arles: Dating the Divine Institutes."

[164]Lactantius' support of religious tolerance is one of the main points in Digeser's book. She also demonstrates that Constantine followed *The Divine Institutes* in emphasizing tolerance toward paganism in his early reign. She makes a point that Constantine did not enforce his early edict against pagan worship and built several temples for the pagans. Eusebius's claim that he tore down the pagan temples hides the fact that he destroyed only four of them. No doubt Eusebius wished Constantine had destroyed them all.

[165]Lactantius: *The Divine Institutes*, translated by Anthony Bowen and Peter Garnsey, p.427.

[166]See Digeser's discussion of Lactantius's golden age in *The Making of a Christian Empire*.

[167]Lactantius, *On the Deaths*, 44. Eusebius also records the dream, but differs in that Constantine had a vision earlier in the day in which Christ tells him he will conquer in the sign of the Chi-rho. Eusebius' account was written many years after the event, while Lactantius's account is contemporary. Thus, Lactantius is probably the more reliable witness.

[168]Symboldictionary.net

[169]After the battle, Constantine announced to the bishops he considered himself one of them, but he also continued to print coins with solar symbols, and the sculpture erected three years later commemorating the battle suggests the divine sun was Constantine's constant companion.

[170]*The Divine Institutes*, Bowen and Garnsey, p.439. Some copies of *The Divine Institutes* exist with the oration and some without it, which has lead scholars to believe Lactantius added the oration sometime after the final battle with Maxentius.

[171]The year of Crispus's birth is debated with some holding to the year 305. See chapter 5 above. It is also unknown whether Crispus's mother was Constantine's wife or concubine. If wife, she would have either died, or Constantine divorced her before he married Fausta, as neither the Greeks nor Romans practiced bigamy or polygamy.

[172]For Lactantius, see Chapter 5 above.

[173]For the civil wars, see Chapter 5 above.

[174]Some historians doubt the story of Crispus and Fausta citing that it too-closely resembles the biblical story of Joseph and Potipher's wife. However, the story is recorded by the pagan historian Zosimus. Modern historians believe that Fausta acted out of jealousy in behalf of her sons while Zosimus recorded she acted out of infatuation for Crispus and engaged in retaliation for being spurned. Eusebius, who championed Constantine to the Christian church, avoids any discussion of how Crispus died, giving evidence that the basics of Zosimus's story were probably correct as the affair probably embarrassed Eusebius.

[175]It is not known by what form of death Crispus was condemned.

[176]This was Helena's desire according to Eusebius, *Life of Constantine*, book 3: 44.

[177]Ibid., 3, 47.

[178]Ibid., 3, 47. Theodoret claims Helena converted Constantine to Christianity as a child, but Eusebius is contemporary with, and knew Constantine

personally and probably knew Helena.

[179]Helena's desire towards charity is ascribed by Eusebius, *Life*, book 3, 45.

[180]Jan Wellam Drijvers, Helen Augusta: Mother of Constantine the Great and the Legend of Her Finding of the True Cross, p. 3. The accompaniment of Eusebius is speculative, but most likely occurred as the Bishop of Caesarea surely would have accompanied her, along with Bishop Macarius of Jerusalem.

[181]The townspeople that directed her may have been comprised of both Christians and Jews. A fifth century account explains that she brought together some 300 Jews and threatened to burn them if they did not cooperate. The account is dubious, but it is probable that Jews aided Helena and that they felt pressure to do so.

[182]The account of the construction of the pagan temple covering the site is given by Eusebius in Life chapter 26.

[183]In his book, *The Quest for the True Cross*, Carsten Thiede made a case that part of the headboard still exists and is housed in the Church of St. Croce in Rome. Upon Thiede's investigation, the Catholic Church allowed the wood to be carbon dated, the results giving a Middle-Ages date. Thiede countered by insisting that the relic cannot be properly carbon dated because it has been handled too much through the ages, thus giving an improper reading. The same criticism has been given for the carbon dating of the Shroud of Turin. A Medieval painting shows the Shroud being handled at the very corner in which the sample was taken for the scientific test.

[184]Several Patristic traditions record the specifics of the discovery of the cross's headboard. The earliest, dated to AD 390, claims the headboard was attached to the cross. A 395 tradition claims the headboard was present alongside the three crosses, but not attached. In this account, Helena distinguished between the three crosses by conducting a healing of a sick woman, laying her on each cross until she was healed by the true cross.

[185]See Chapter 3 above concerning Modulism.

[186]This became known as Sabellianism, named after the theology of Saballium, its most popular teacher.

[187]Tertullian was the first writer to refer to the Son and Father as one substance, but he wrote in Latin. It is likely Tertullian would have translated the Latin "substantia" as "homoousios" if he wrote in Greek.

[188]On Origen, see chapter 4, above.

[189]*Life*, chapter 12. I have abridged and slightly paraphrased the speech recorded by Eusebius.

[190]This is conjecture by J.B. Lightfoot and other historians.

[191]Dionysius does not tell us these people were the Alogia, but this is probable.

[192]Eusebius records Dionysius's words from *On Promises* in Ecclesiastical History, Chapter 25 section 4. Many modern historians, such as Elaine Pagels, leave out this quote in her discussion of Dionysius and other facts when writing on how the book of Revelation became canonized. *In Revelation: Visions, Prophecy, and Politics in the Book of Revelation*, she claimed the book "barely squeezed into the canon" and that Athanasius's inclusion

of the book in his list in AD 360 is "the earliest known record we have of what would become . . . the New Testament canon." (p. 160) While Pagels is technically accurate, her statement is misleading for the book was included in a number of early lists that incorporated all the New Testament books. The difference is that they also included several others that ultimately did not make the canon, while excluding some that did. For example, she is conspicuously silent on the inclusion of Revelation in the Muratorian Canon, which most scholars believe was compiled about AD 170. A few scholars have placed the MC in the fourth century, but Pagels does not even mention this in order to support them in their late date. See the article by C. E. Hill, "The Debate over the Muratorian Fragment and the Development of the Canon." Pagels also failed to discuss Codex Sinaiticus written before AD 360 and which also included the book of Revelation. There is no doubt, however, that the Alogia had an influence in turning some church leaders against the book. But their greater influence was turning the church to allegorize the Revelation.

[193]Italics are mine for emphasis. Some modern historians, such as Jonathon Kirsch, only half-quote Dionysius, leaving out the part of the sentence that indicated these were his opinions. The tactic leaves the reader with the impression that Dionysius was certain and backed by historical fact. The only fact he had on the subject of a different author than the Apostle was from the Alogia who claimed that Cerinthus was the author, something Dionysius rejected. Dionysius claimed he "heard" that there were two monuments in Ephesus. He had not seen them himself and there is no historical verification that two existed.

[194]Eusebius, *Ecclesiastical History*, chapter 25 section 25.

[195]Modern scholars looking at the earliest copies of Revelation, however, have identified these errors. See the article by Stephen Broyles: "The Scribes and the Book of Revelation: How Do You Copy a Book Full of Bad Grammar?" at andreascenter.org

[196]*Eccl. History*, 7.4.

[197]On the Patristic tradition that Bishop Papius helped John write the Gospel, see chapter three, above.

[198] *Eccl. History,* 28.1-2.

[199]See Chapter 4 on the emergence of the Alogia and the debate between Gaius and Proclus. As stated in that chapter, the claim that Cerinthus wrote the book of Revelation is based on this published debate. Eusebius's quote is interesting in that Cerinthus claims he got his own theology from a "great apostle." At the same time, the quote indicates Cerinthus put forward ideas that are not in the Revelation, such as marriage festivals. Therefore, Cerinthus never claimed he wrote the Revelation. If Cerinthus held these views, it's probable that he gleaned off the Revelation after the Apostle John rejected him and then acted as a philosophical chameleon, interjecting some ideas of a physical kingdom on earth with his overall Gnostic view in order to win some converts. Thus Gaius could have used the quote of Cerinthus to try to make the case that Cerinthus wrote the Revelation. The other possibility is that Gaius and the Alogia completely fabricated the quote, as well as Cerinthian authorship, because the idea that Cerinthus held such ideas

on physicality go beyond and contradict anything Irenaeus described about the Gnostic or anything found among the documents of the Gnostic Nag Hammadi Library. See Chapter Three, above, on Irenaeus's description of Cerinthus.

[200]If Eusebius could have eliminated Revelation as Scripture, he probably would have, but as Dionysius indicated, support for the book was too strong to deny and Eusebius grudgingly included it in his own canon. Constantine may have employed Eusebius to make copies of the New Testament which have come down to us as the Codex Sinaiticus. (Modern scholars dispute that Eusebius was the sole copyist. It's probable Eusebius headed up a team of copyists as this would have been too much work for one man, and modern analysis shows the hand of various scribes) The Codex includes the Revelation, but also includes *The Epistle of Barnabas* and *The Shepherd of Hermas*. This shows that the Canon of the New Testament was not yet fixed and yet also shows how strong the church at large supported the Revelation in the middle of the fourth century. As indicated in note 192 above, Elaine Pagels failed to mention Sinaiticus in her discussion on Revelation's canonicity.

[201]One of his contemporaries insinuated that Eusebius bowed to pressure and denied Christ while in prison. However, this critic had no first-hand knowledge and it was probably an unjust slur.

[202]The exact date is unknown, but most scholars believe he wrote it shortly after the Council.

[203]The oration at the Sepulcher dedication is believed to be similar to the one Eusebius gives at the Tricennial, at least when speaking of the Cathedral and Tomb.

[204]*Oration of Eusebius*, chapters 2 and 3. Eusebius quotes Daniel, chapter 7.18.

[205]Ibid., chapter 3:5 and 6.

[206]Ibid., chapter 15.3.

[207]Ibid, chapter 16.6

[208]Eusebius is also silent about Helena's discovery of the Cross in his *Ecclesiastical History* and *Life of Constantine*. Many scholars point to the omission of Helena in order to claim the entire story about Helena and the Cross was a complete fabrication. However, they miss the point of Eusebius's eschatology and agenda in relation to Constantine. No doubt in AD 335, there was already a legend growing about Helena. It is probable Eusebius felt that Constantine's thunder was being stolen by too much emphasis on the Queen. In any case, for Eusebius, it was Constantine and the Tomb, not Helena that were the primary objects of prophecy.

[209]An example is the ritual that developed in the Jerusalem Church: "Then a chair is placed for the bishop in Golgotha behind the [liturgical] Cross... And as all the people pass by one by one, all bowing themselves, they touch the Cross and the title, first with their foreheads and then with their eyes; then they kiss the Cross and pass through, but none lays his hand upon it to touch it."

[210]As already indicated, many scholars claim the Eusebius makes no mention of the Cross at all in his *Life of Constantine* and, again, point to this as

evidence that the story of Helena was a fabrication. Others, such as Thiede, accept Helena's discovery but try to explain the absence in Eusebius by accusing Eusebius of being politically motivated and attempting to put his bishopric higher than Bishop Marcus of Jerusalem, who used the Cross in rituals. However, there is no evidence in Eusebius's writings that he had any dispute with Marcus. All these claims by scholars are overstatements. The Cross is also mentioned in Chapter 9. 18 of the *Oration*: "That Cross which has indeed repaid his (Constantine) pious zeal…and the rewards of virtue bestowed on his noble sons…Thus, clearly have the deeds of God been clearly manifested, and this through the sacred effectiveness of the salutary sign" (the Cross). This is the only mention of the Cross, but, again, while the Cross takes a backseat to the Tomb, these scholars have missed the point of Eusebius's eschatology in relation to the Tomb.

[211]Jonathan Kirsch's main thesis is that the literal interpretation led to violence and that the allegorist fathers did their best to suppress it. Kirsch, however, never mentioned Eusebius. In any discussion of this subject, it's incredulous that Eusebius is completely ignored or omitted from Kirsch's discourse. As indicated in the introduction, one of the main points of this book is to demonstrate how the allegorical interpretation of Revelation chapter twenty led to wars and revolutions—the exact opposite of kirsch's contention.

[212]*Life of Constantine*, book 2:7.

[213]Ibid., book 2: 45. Digeser claimed the laws were not heavily enforced and Eusebius exaggerated their importance.

[214]Ibid., book 3:1.

[215]See Digeser's discussion of Constantine's attitude toward the temples and Eusebius's exaggerations in *The Making of a Christian Empire*.

[216]See chapters 1 through 3 above.

[217]Ambrose, *Ep. 72*.

[218]Craig Alan Satterlee, *Ambrose of Milan's Method of Mystagogical Preaching*, Liturgical press, 202, p.222.

[219]Johannes Roldanus , *The Church in the Age of Constantine: the Theological Challenges*, Taylor & Francis, 2006, p. 151.

[220]The confrontation in the cathedral is recounted by Ambrose in letter 41, written to his sister. The following dialogue was recorded in the letter; I have slightly paraphrased it for the sake of clarity.

[221]Jesse Hoover, "The Contours of Donatism: Theological and Ideological Diversity in Fourth Century North Africa." It is often thought that Donatism refused any forgiveness for lapsed clergy, but this is a hallmark of some later Donatus bishops and not the attitude of Donatus.

[222]The events are based on the descriptions of Bishop Optatus of Milevis, who wrote of the incidents somewhere between the years 366 and 370, in his *third book against the Donatists*.

[223]Optatus records the content of the letter.

[224]Some scholars believe that the origin of the Circumcellions began as a Donatist movement because the brigands encouraged martyrdom. But in reading Optatus, the movement existed before it was associated with martyrdom. The Circumcellions started as a social and economic liberation

movement. Optatus writes somewhat ambiguously, but while he claims the movement was started by two Christians he does not claim they were Donatists. A close reading of Optatus indicates that some Donatists joined only after the movement was already in existence.

[225]As quoted from a fragment of Tyconius known by Beatus of Libana. See Daniel Craner's doctrinal thesis, *Wandering, Begging Monks: Spiritual authority and the promotion of Monasticism in Late Antiquity*, p.230. (2002).

[226]As quoted by Pamela Bright in *The Book of Rules of Tychonius: Its Purpose and Inner Logic*, p.37.

[227]See the rules as discussed by Pamela Bright.

[228]Although modern scholars do not credit Tychonius with establishing a post-millennial theology, this is the logical implications of his eschatology—Christ returns at the end of the millennium. Thus with Tychonius, we see an early form of post-millennialism.

[229]In John 11:24, Mary tells Jesus that she will see her brother again in resurrection on the last day. Modern dispensational premillennialism views the day of resurrection as symbolic for a seven year period of resurrection in which a number of groups and individuals are resurrected throughout the reign of the Antichrist. This is to answer the apparent contradiction of the resurrection occurring at the beginning of the Tribulation, but still including the Revelation's martyrs. Dispensational premillennialism stands in contradiction with Irenaeus who viewed the resurrection of all the righteous occurring at a literal moment within one day, and that day occurring toward the end the Antichrist's reign. See chapter two above.

[230]P. Bright. p.78.

[231]Ibid., p. 87.

[232]The historical interpretation relies heavily on symbolization and clams that the Book of Revelation foretold events that have already occurred over the entire span of church history or the history of western civilization. An example of this interpretation, as it was used in the middle ages, is seen as the seven churches of Revelation were symbolic of seven time periods in the history of the church. Another example is seen in Joachim of Fiore's interpretation of the 12th chapter of Revelation, where he interpreted the seven-headed dragon as indicating seven heads of historical persecutors through the course of church history. He identified the sixth head with the Muslim leader Saladin. See chapter nine below on Joachim. So In Tychonius we have the latent beginnings of the historical interpretation along with postmillennialism.

[233]After the discovery of the Christ's tomb, Constantine, rather than the bishops, played the most instrumental role in Eusebius' thinking. See chapter 6 above.

[234]The reason for the excommunication is recorded by Augustine. Augustine was an anti-premillennialist. If the excommunication was because of Tychonius's overall eschatology and rejection of Premillennial theology, Augustine would have mentioned it.

[235]The symbolic or allegorical interpretation goes beyond the natural symbolism of the Revelation's language. In the literal interpretation, words

mean what they say unless otherwise defined within the context of Scripture. For example, the term millennium according to the literal interpretation means a thousand years. In the symbolic interpretation of Tychonius, it means 350 years.

[236]Augustine,*Confessions*, 5.13.

[237]Ibid.,8.12. The text is from Romans 13:13.

[238]From James Paulgaard's paper written for the University of Saschetchewan, *The Impact of Ambrose of Milan on the Young Augustine*. Besides Augustine's objection to the OT, he had two other impediments to becoming a Christian: he struggled with the question of how it was possible for evil to exist in the presence of an omnipotent God, and he struggled with the thought of embracing celibacy. Augustine reconciled the idea of evil by developing the doctrine of Original Sin, and he embraced celibacy after his experience with Scripture in the garden.

[239]The description of the event is based on a postscript to the description by the Greek historian Zosimus that dates to the Middle Ages. Some historians doubt the Proba part, but accept some of the basics of the story.

[240]The description of the two cities is from the PBS documentary on Augustine's view of the Revelation. Augustine's eschatology has been given the term "amillennialism" because he reinterpreted the millennium to mean the church age. However, the term literally means "no millennium" and does not properly represent Augustine's view. Some followers of Augustine prefer the term "nunc-millennium" or "now-millennium," thus the title of this chapter—The Millennium Now.

[241]Erika T. Hermanowicz, *Possidius of Calama: a study of the North African Episcopate at the time of Augustine*, Oxford University Press, 2008, p.154.

[242]Matthew 26: 51-52.

[243]*Augustine against Petilianus*, chapter 89, 194 and 195.

[244]Epistula 73.

[245]Ibid., 185. In centuries to come, the idea of theologically justifying force against one's enemies out of love for one's neighbor would be advocated by Pope Eugenius III to justify the Second Crusade and the Fifth Monarchy Movement in abolishing all Catholic monarchies. See chapters 8 and 16 below. In the twentieth century, German theologian Dietrich Bonhheoffer, in his book *Ethics*, would use the same philosophy of love to theologically support his involvement in the assassination attempt against Adolph Hitler.

[246]*Letter to Boniface*, chapter 5. The italics are mine for the sake of emphasis.

[247]Ibid., chapter 23. Italics are mine for emphasis.

[248]Some scholars point out that in his *City of God*, Augustine appeared to support a strong separation between church and state which seems to be at odds with his support of heresy laws. But it's his eschatology which explains the apparent contradiction. In Augustine's thinking, some kings would remain at odds with Christianity and remain part of the city of man, but in the church age, or the millennium, Christian kings and civil servants would play a role in helping to bring about the kingdom of God on earth. Here he differs from Eusebius in that he was not so optimistic that the entire world

would become Christian before the day of resurrection, but nonetheless the church would progress throughout the world and Christian kings would aid that progression by way of violence against heretics.

[249]See Kirsch on his portrayal of Augustine in *History of the End of the World*, pp. 118-122. Kirsch attempted to portray Augustine as a valiant but failed hero, "Augustine's stern and austere approach was never wholly successful in extinguishing the fires that the text (Revelation) was meant to ignite in the hearts and minds of its readers," p.122. Throughout his thesis, however, Kirsch ignored many primary sources. In reality, Augustine's view of the millennium helped instigate the fires. Kirsch and other historians neglected to explore the entire body of Augustine's writings and Augustine's eschatological emphasis on heresy laws.

[250]The mentality that led to heresy laws carried over in relation to Jews. Just one example was the publishing of the Corpus Juris Civilis by Emperor Justinian between AD 529 and 534. It included laws restricting citizenship to Christians, established that Jews could not testify against Christians, and the use of the Hebrew language in worship was forbidden. During Justinian's reign, some Jewish communities were converted by force, and their synagogues turned into churches.

[251]The east-west split began with the Council of Chalcedon and the controversy over whether Christ had two natures—one divine and one human, or just one nature—human and divine. The Council sided with the two natures and, at the same time, elevated the Roman Church to the status of supremacy over the church of Constantinople. Various issues continued to deepen the split over the years.

[252]The above recount of the Council of Clermont and Urban's sermon is based on a compilation of the witnesses of Guibert, Abbot of Nogent, who attended the Council and Robert the Monk, who probably attended it. Some historians dismiss the accounts because certain letters written by Urban emphasized his desire to unite Christendom while writing that the desire to march to Jerusalem was the desire of the knights. However, Urban also emphasized the Holy Sepulcher in his preaching before and after the Council. Thus the evidence shows that while he was not a believer in the current prophetic zeal of the people, he used it and played on the peoples' expectations of prophecy in relation to the Holy Sepulcher to gather popular support for the Crusade. Historian Christopher Tyerman holds a different view. While recounting the content of Urban's preaching before and after the Council, Tyerman believes Urban had a sincere desire to liberate the Holy Sepulcher. See Christopher Tyerman, *God's War: A New History of the Crusades*. Cambridge: Belknap Press of Harvard University Press, 2006.

[253]Tyerman.

[254]From an unknown chronicler, but considered reliable by historians

[255]"First Crusade, Siege of Jerusalem," *Military History Magazine*, June 12, 2006.

[256]*Sahih Bukhari, Book 1.*

[257]Efraim Karsh, *Islamic Imperialism, A history*, Yale University Press, New Haven and London, 2006, p. 10. Karsh takes a decidedly critical assessment toward Islam and its conquests, advocating that the conquests were primar-

ily a result of the desire for political power and the attainment of booty. For a pro-Muslim view of the conquests, see M.J. Akbar, *The Shade of Swords: Jihad and the Conflict between Islam and Christianity.* Routlage, 2002. Akbar believes Muhammad's revelations were true and the conquests were primarily religiously motivated. Akbar, however, writes with his own biases and is selective in his recounts of the conquests, leaving out key elements. See note 261 below.

[258]Sura 2: 125-129 and Sura 8: 30-40. A Sura is considered a chapter of the Quran.

[259]*Ibn Isa'd*, a tenth century biography of Muhammad.

[260]The number of the executed is disputed with various historians citing numbers between 300 and 900.

[261]M.J. Akbar recounts the battle of the trenches, but rather than admit and comment on the executions of the Jews, as other Muslim historians have done, he simply ignores the event. This is an example of Akbar's selective history in favor of Muhammad.

[262]As M. J. Akbar put it, "Jesus was given the Holy Spirit, but no weapons for war, his mission was peaceful. Muhammad, as the last messenger, combined the characteristics of all the Prophets, as his mission was greater than any of his predecessors." See *Shade of Swords*, p. 43.

[263]Karsh, p.20.

[264]The story of the night journey is recorded in the seventh chapter of the Quran with details added by the hadith, a series of Muhammad's quotes that Muslims believe supplement the Quran.

[265]The quote is recorded by Romilly James Heald Jenkins in *Byzantium: The Imperial Centuries, AD 610-1071*, University of Toronto Press, 1987, p.34. The statement demonstrates the influence of Eusebius's view of prophecy in relation to the Church of the Holy Sepulcher. By the seventh century, the Holy Sepulcher had replaced a literal Solomon's Temple in both Daniel and the Revelation of John.

[266]This probably explains why no church was built on the site as the Holy Sepulcher took prominence. The site is not without its problems. See chapter 21 below on the possibility that the Temple Mount is not the true site of Solomon's Temple.

[267]*Midzgitha. Pratum spirituale*, 100-102. p. 63.

[268]One version of the prophecy names Constans as the final emperor, giving evidence that it was written about the middle of the fourth century. After Constantine's death in A.D 337, his son, Constans, suppressed pagan sacrifices and supported Nicene theology against Arianism. Thus, early on, it was easy to believe he would be the champion of the prophecy, or the prophecy was written after his death, but the future last king would mimic Constans' oppression of Christianity's enemies.

[269]The date and place of authorship of the prophecy is disputed—views range from 660 to 680 to 691. As indicated above, various areas and revisions may have begun in 660 and finalized in Syria in 691. For one scholar's viewpoint, see Bernard McGinn, *Visions of the End: Apocalyptic Traditions in the Middle Ages*, Columbia University Press, 1998, p. 70.

[270]The full text of *Pseudo-Methodius* is readily available online.

[271] McGinn, p.72.

[272] These prophecies include *Coptic Apocalypse of Pseudo-Shenoute*, *Syriac Apocalypse of Pseudo-Ephraem*, *Coptic Apocalpyse of Pseudo-Athanasius*, and *Greek Interpolation of the Syriac Apocalypse of Pseudo-Methodius*. See chapter 18 below on the possibility that *Pseudo-Ephraem* may be the first document in church history to put forth a pre-tribulation rapture.

[273] Some scholars doubt the legitimacy of the letter to Robert, citing among other criticisms, that Alexius would not have promised to give the treasures of Constantinople to the Latin Church. However, the hostilities between the western and eastern church was beginning to thaw. One also must take into account that Alexius was desperate. He also may have thought he could control the mercenaries once the Muslim insurgents had been taken care of. On Alexius's tendency towards manipulation in diplomacy, see Jason T. Price's master's thesis for Texas Tech University, *An Analysis of the Strategy and Tactics of Alexios I Komnenos*. Another criticism is that the list of relics included the burial cloth of Jesus, which is thought to be impossible since the Shroud of Turin carbon dated to a later period. However, even if the Shroud dating is correct, which is an open question since the carbon sample came from a heavily handled part of the cloth, the burial fabric in Constantinople does not necessarily have to be the same as the Shroud.

[274] Alexius is known to have sent envoys to a council of Urban's at Piacenza in 1095 who urged the liberation of Jerusalem, but what they used as enticements are not recorded. See, *Early Medievalists' Thoughts and Ponderings* by Jonathan Jarrett. Tyerman, however, believes Alexius preached the liberation of the Holy Sepulcher earlier than the year 1095. See *God's War*, p. 69.

[275] Tyerman, p. 62.

[276] Ibid., p. 63.

[277] Raymond was an eyewitness and participant.

[278] Fulk of Charters.

[279] Ambrose, a follower of Origen's system of symbolizing Scripture and one of Augustine's mentors, theologically justified the burning of Jewish synagogues, although there is no evidence he supported the killing of Jews. However, it would be only a small step forward to apply Ambrose's theology of revenge to the murder of Christianity's opponents. See chapter 7 above.

[280] According to Raymond of Aguilers: "With the fall of the city, it was rewarding to see the worship of the pilgrims at the Holy Sepulcher, the clapping of hands, the rejoicing and singing of a new song to the Lord."

[281] For the details and history of the prophecy of the black flags from Khurasan and it current manifestation in modern apocalyptic Islam, see chapter 20 below—On the Threshold of the Nuclear Millennium.

[282] The account is recorded by Roger Cowden, who was an eyewitness to the meeting. Some historians doubt the story. Joachim scholar, Marjorie Holmes, however, accepts the basics of the description. See *The Influence of Prophecy in the Later Middle Ages: A Study in Joachimism*, University of Notre Dame Press, 1993, pp. 7-10.

[283] William of Tyre, *History of Deeds Done Beyond the Sea*, XIV, 4-5.

[284]Ibid.

[285]See Jonathan Riley-Smith's article, "Crusading as an act of Love."

[286]James Reston Jr., *Warriors of God: Richard the Lionheart and Saladin in the Third Crusade*, Doubleday, 2001, p.4.

[287]Ibid., p.5.

[288]Ibid., p.7.

[289]Quote is recorded by Anne-Marie Eddie, *Saladin*, Harvard University Press, 2011, p.218.

[290]Ibid., p.224.

[291]Reston Jr. pp. 262-264.

[292]Ibid., p. 277. Historians debate the reason for Richard's hesitancy. The monk's prophecy is one explanation.

[293]The section on Matthew of Edessa is based on the article by Tara L. Andrews, "THE NEW AGE OF PROPHECY: THE CHRONICLE OF MATTHEW OF EDESSA AND ITS PLACE IN ARMENIAN HISTORIOGRAPHY."

[294]Bret Edward Whalen, *Dominion of God: Christendom and apocalypse in the Middle Ages*, Harvard University Press, 2009. See pp. 102-118.

[295]See chapters 13-15 below on the Protestant reformers use of the historical interpretation and its influence in the support for persecution, war and revolution.

[296]Reeves, p. 39

[297]David Keck, *Angels and Angelology in the Middle Ages*, Oxford University Press, 1998, p.154. Joachim's idea became so widespread throughout the Middle Ages that some even referred to Luther as the angelic pope.

[298]On Joachim's postmillennialism, see Reeves, p. 303.

[299]See Reeves, pp. 306-331 for a rundown of various pseudo-Joachimisms.

[300]For details see chapter 11 below.

[301]Lauro Martines, *Fire in the City: Savonarola and the Struggle for the Soul of Renaissance Florence*, Oxford University Press, 2006, pp. XIV and 21. While not the type of democracy known today, Florence's government was the closest thing to self rule among the city states of Italy.

[302]Paul Strathern, *Death in Florence, Savonarola, the Medici, and the struggle for the Soul of the Renaissance City*, Jonathan Cape, 2011, pp. 11-12. See also Martines, p.292.

[303]Strathern, pp. 14-15.

[304]Richard C. Trexler, Public *Life in Renaissance Florence*, Cornell University Press, 1980, pp. 381-382.

[305]Michael Rocke, *Forbidden Friendships: Homosexuality and Male Culture in Renaissance Florence*, Oxford University Press, 1998, pp. 87-95.

[306]Herbert Millingchamp Vaughan,*The Medici Popes*, G.P. Putnams' Sons, 1908, p.6.

[307]Tim Parks, *Medici Money: banking, Metaphysics, and Art in Fifteenth-Century Florence*, W.W, Norton & Company, London, 2005. pp. 233-234.

[308]Strathern, p.56.

[309]Quoted by Strathern, p.71.

[310]Ibid., p.74.

[311]Pasquale Villari, *The Life and Times of Giralamo Savonarola*, London, 1899, chapter 2.

[312]Quoted by Stathern, p.104.

[313]Ibid., p. 110.

[314]Ibid., p. 114.

[315]Story is recounted by Villari, chapter 9. It's based on a disciple of Savonarola who interviewed him about the incident. Some modern historians dispute some elements of the story. David Weinstein accepts a pro-Medici account and rejects the final part about Savonarola insisting on a return to a republic, believing the monk granted Lorenzo absolution. In contrast, Paul Strathern accepts the Savonarola account but adds his own theory that Savonarola and Lorenzo cut a deal concerning Lorenzo's son, allowing Peiro, to take over the city's government as part of the monk's ultimate goal of reforming and freeing the city's Dominican order from Medici control.

[316]See the treatment of this vision and sermon by Strathern, p.144 and by David Wiensteen,*Savonarola: The Rise and Fall of a Renaissance Prophet*, Yale University Press, Nov 22, 2011, pp. 95-96. The Advent sermons of 1492 have not survived, but historians believe that it was at this time Savonarola gave the prediction of Cyrus based on the monk's later recollections of the prophecy in his *Compendium of Revelations*.

[317]Strathern, p.164. In Strathern's treatment of Cyrus and the renovation of San Marcos, he never mentions any connection to the prophecies of the Last World Emperor and Joachim's's monastic order by Savonarola. However, viewing Savonarola's actions in the light of these Middle Age prophecies appears to give the best understanding of his eschatology.

[318]Marica Tacconi, *Cathedral and Civic Ritual in Late Medieval and Renaissance Florence: The Service Books of Santa Maria Del Fiore*, Cambridge University Press, Dec 8, 2005, p.216.

[319]Martines, p.118. The number of boys, including those less than nine years of age, comes from a letter written by the ambassador of Milan in Florence.

[320]*Selected writings of Girolamo Savonarola: Religion and Politics, 1490-1498*, translated by Anne Borelli and Maria Pastore Passaro, Yale University Press, 2006, p.152.

[321]Strathern, p.216.

[322]The medieval church frowned upon the practice of oral and anal sex as unnatural including by heterosexuals in marriage. While Florence was famous for its homosexual pedophilia, historians such as Martines and Strathern believe Savonarola's law was aimed at all sodomy.

[323]Savonarola made his views known on the value of opposition factions in a later writing made just before he died. On the Puritans and the Fifth Monarchy, see chapters fifteen and sixteen below.

[324]*Selected Writings*, p.171.

[325]On Paine and the American Revolution, see chapter 18 below. Paine's use of I Kings is often not quoted or mentioned in modern secular textbooks.

[326]Patrick Paul Macey, *Bonfire Songs: Savonarola's Musical Legacy*, Oxford University press, 1998, p.74 and 75.

[327]Quoted by Villari, p.167.

[328]Quoted by Starthern, p.265, and Villari, p.170.

[329]Ibid., p.277.

[330]George M'Hardy, *Savonarola*, Charles Scribner's Sons,*1901*, p. 177.

[331]Villari, p.199.

[332]M'Hardy, p. 187.

[333]Quoted by M'Hardy, p 190.

[334]Quoted by Strathern, p. 306.

[335]Landuci as recorded by Weinstein.

[336]Recorded by Strathern, p.365.

[337]Ibid., p. 340.

[338]Herbert Millinchamp Vaughn, p. 90.

[339]Giovanni's homosexuality was alleged by his governor, Francesco Guicciardini and historian and physician to Pope Clement VII, Pailo Giovio.

[340]Ibid., p. 167.

[341]Martin Brecht and James L. schaaf, *Martin Luther, His Road to Reformation, 1483-1521*, Fortress Press, 1993, p.183. See also James hillerbrand, *The Reformation*, Harper and Row, 1964, pp. 41-46.

[342]For Purgatory as a response to Gnosticism, see Joseph Ratzinger's (Pope Benedict XVI) discussion in *Eschatology: Death and Eternal Life*, CUA Press, 2007, p.215. Some trace the beginning of the doctrine to Saint Perpetua who, after praying in tongues, had a vision of her dead brother being released from Hell. Others believe that Perpetua simply reflected a belief that was already widespread in the church. On Perpetua, see chapter 3 above.

[343]Some see point 86 as sarcastic and Luther was aware of the pope's opulent lifestyle.

[344]Luther republished some of Savonarola's works and wrote a favorable introduction to them. No doubt, Luther was also influenced by John Wycliffe and Jon Hus. They were two of the first to question indulgences and the physical presence of Christ in the Eucharist, Wycliffe in the year 1382 and Hus in 1412. Wycliffe also put forth an early form of Justification by faith. Savonarola did not defy the doctrines of the church.

[345]Perhaps a better and more complete formula for salvation has been put forth by Pope Benedict XVI in his book on Paul. Gleaning off Galatians, Benedict indicated that salvation is by faith working through love. See *Saint Paul*, Ignatius Press, 2009, p, 82. See also John Reumann's article on the International Lutheran and Catholic Dialogue Conference that began in 1964 and continued through 1997. In 1985, the Conference published a joint statement on justification and salvation. It included a proclamation that says, "Justifying faith cannot exist without hope and love; it necessarily issues in good works."

[346]Some scholars and writers erroneously claim that Muntzer believed in an imminent return of Christ in the flesh to lead the rebellion. He believed, rather, in an imminent coming of the Spirit to lead the rebellion through himself and his followers.

[347]The above narrative is based on the account by eyewitness conquistador Bernal Diaz, *The Discovery and Conquest of Mexico*, Farrar, Straus and Cudahy, 1956, pp. 26-28.

[348]The Quetzalcoatl myth is recounted by Spanish sources, including a letter written by Cortez, as well as Aztec post-conquest sources. Some historians question the authenticity of the myth because it cannot be verified by pre-conquest Aztec sources.

[349]The story is recounted by Diaz, pp. 102-106.

[350]According to Bernal Diaz.

[351]The story of Columbus and his supporters and detractors at the Spanish Court at Granada is expounded by Felipe Fernandz-Armesto, *Columbus and the Conquest of the Impossible*, Saturday Review Press, 1974, pp. 38-39

[352]Pauline Moffit Watts, 'Prophecy and Discovery: On the Spiritual Origins of Christopher Columbus's "Enterprise to the Indies." *The American Historical Review*, Volume 90, issue 1, Supplement to Vol. 90 (Feb, 1985) p. 95.

[353]Columbus, writing in 1502, described the letter by the Genoese delegates.

[354]Various sides in the debate are exemplified by a number of historians including: Carol Delaney, Felipe Fernandez-Armesto, and Wendy Childs. Delaney advocates that religion and prophecy was Columbus's primary motivation. The opposing side may be found in Fernandez-Armesto, who believes prophecy may have motivated Columbus before his first voyage but only in minor way. He advocates that Columbus later strongly converted to it as result of his failures. The third option is propounded by Childs.

[355]For details of the Florentine Renaissance see chapter 10 above.

[356]Fernando-Amesto considers this meeting legendary and unreliable, believing instead that Columbus first met Perez at Rebido in 1491. The first meeting, however, is attested to by a variety of ancient sources, although the exact date is disputed: 1484-85 or 1486.

[357]There is evidence that the early Observants held millennial beliefs based on Joachim, but their exact eschatology is unknown. See Robert Royal's discussion on the Observants in his article, "Columbus and the Beginning of the World,"

[358]This statement is probably true whether Columbus met with the Franciscans in 1485 or only in 1491.

[359]Fernando-Armesto, *Conquest of the Impossible*, p.23.

[360]Pauline Moffitt Watts, pp. 88-89.

[361]Ibid., p.86.

[362]Fredinand-Amesto, *Conquest of the Impossible*, p.33

[363]Ibid., p.35.

[364]It must be noted, however, that both England and France had their own nationalistic versions of a last world emperor, so it is possible Columbus may have had these prophecies in mind. But the fact that he originally began his quest in Portugal and later returned to Lisbon suggests that prophecy was not his main motivation at this time.

[365]For a more detailed look at the make-up of the Spanish Court, see Conquest of the Impossible, pp. 32-37.

[366]The exact location and identification is not known. The best evidence suggests Watling Island in the Bahamas.

[367]Fernando-Armesto, *Columbus on Himself*, Hackett Publishing Co., 2010, pp. 69-78.

[368]Complicating the reading of the diary is the fact that it was also edited by Bartolome de Las Casas, who also paraphrased some of it. For this reason some scholars, such as Fernandez- Armesto, question large portions of the journal.

[369]Translation is by Fernandez-Armesto, *Columbus on Himself*, p.91. Fernandez-Armesto considers the entry to be reliable, although the author doubts Columbus was wholly devoted to conquering Jerusalem until later voyages. See his article, "Faulty Navigators" written for the *Wall Street Journal*. In the article, he criticizes Carol Delany's work, *Columbus and the Quest for Jerusalem*, which advocated that Columbus was primarily motivated by prophecy. However, Fernandez-Armesto also admits in *on Himself* "... it is at least possible that a chiliastic vision, embracing the recovery of Jerusalem and the end of the world was already in his mind (Columbus) before his departure across the Atlantic." p. 93.

[370]For an example of an argument favoring the letter's authenticity, see Yale professor Margarita Zamora, *Reading Columbus*, University of California Press, 1993, pp. 10-20. Fernando-Armesto, upon completion of *Columbus on Himself*, seems to avoid weighing in on the debate by writing, "After this book was completed, Professor A. Rumeu de Armas drew my attention to a newly discovered MS, purportedly written by Columbus. ... As this collection has no satisfactory history of provenance, I have not added anything from it to the selection for this book," p. 16.

[371]Columbus detailed his thoughts on prophecy after his third voyage.

[372]Buddy Levy, *Conquistador, Hernan Cortes, King Montezuma, and the Last Stand of the Aztecs*, Bantom Books, 2008, pp. 107-109.

[373]Diaz, pp. 218-221.

[374]According to Bernal Diaz. The reason for Montezuma's refusal has become a debate among historians. Some advocate that it was part of Montezuma's tactic to take back full control.

[375]Bernal Diaz, p.290.

[376]Levy, p. 166.

[377]Ibid., p.168.

[378]Bernal Diaz, p.310.

[379]The narrative is based on the descriptions given by Dominican friar Bortolome de Las Casas who was an eyewitness to many of the atrocities. The governor's order was required by the Spanish crown. The original intent of the crown was to allow the natives to respond peacefully to the Spaniards. See *The Devastation of the Indies: A Brief Account*. Trans. Herma Briffault, Baltimore, Johns Hopkins University Press, 1974, pp. 49-50.

[380]*The medieval Heritage of Mexico, Volume 1*, Fordham Univ Press, Jan 1, 1992, p.266.

[381]The story is recorded by La Casas.

[382]John Leddy Phelan, *The millennial kingdom of the Franciscans in the New World: a study of the writings of Gerónimo de Mendieta (1525 - 1604)*, 1980, pp. 24-25.

[383]Ibid., pp. 29-34.

[384]Descriptions of the baptisms are recorded by Motilina, who was one of the twelve. In one example, he claims he presided over fourteen thousand baptisms over a five day span. An indigenous Texacoco record indicates Twenty thousand desired baptism in one day.

[385]This is recorded by missionary Bernardino de Sahagun in the prologue to chapter four in his *A History of Ancient Mexico. Trans.* Fanny R. Bandelier. Glorieta. Rio Grande Press. 1976. See also the article, "On Solid Rock: The Church in New Spain in the Sixteenth Century" by W. Dale Weeks.

[386]Weeks,*On Solid Rock*.

[387]Ibid.

[388]Ibid.

[389]On the discovery of the caves, see Stanislav Chladek, *Exploring Mayan Ritual Caves: Dark Secrets of the Mayan Underworld*. Rowman Altamira, Aug 11, 2011. pp. 91-92.

[390]Matthew Restal and Amari Solari, *2012 and the End of the World: The Western Roots of the Mayan Apocalypse*, Rowan and Littlefield Publishers, Inc., 2011, p. 98

[391]For the description of the mural, see Ibid., p.97.

[392]See David A Timmer's article, "Providence and Perdition; Fray Diego de Landa Justifies His Inquisition against the Yukatan Mayan, " *Church History*Volume 66, no. 3, (Sept 1997) pp. 477-498.

[393]The account of Cabeza de Vaca's exploration is taken from his journal called*The Narracion*and from John Upton Terrel's, *Journey Into Darkness: Cabeza de Vaca's Expedition Across North America 1528-36*, Jarrolds Publishers, London, 1964.

[394]Galveston is now a peninsula and connected to the mainland of Texas.

[395]*Narracion*, chapter 15.

[396]Ibid., chapter 25. Also see Terrell, pp. 167-168.

[397]Ibid., chapter 27.

[398]Terrel, p.216.

[399]The same allegations take place today among some Catholics and Evangelicals regarding the Charismatic Renewal, a movement that supports the receiving and practice of the gifts of the Spirit in Pentecostal, mainline Protestant and orthodox churches. An example among the Catholics was Malachi Martin who believed that the idea of lay people receiving the gifts of the Spirit undermines the authority of the bishops. Some Evangelicals adopt the claims of the ancient Alogia that the gifts have passed from the church and, therefore, healings done today are by the power of the Devil. Pope Benedict XVI, however, claimed that he not only supported the Charismatic Movement, but that he, himself, is a charismatic, and Fr. Raniero Cantalamessa, the Vatican 'chaplain' who preached to the papal household, is a member of the Movement. In addressing the movement in 2008, Benedict claimed, "one of the positive elements and aspects of the Community of the Catholic Charismatic Renewal is precisely their emphasis on the charisms or gifts of the Holy Spirit and their merit lies in having recalled their topicality in the Church." On the bogus claims of the Alogia, see chapter 3 above.

[400]Description and dialogue of these events are taken from *The Life and Illustrious Martyrdom of Thomas More*, by Thomas Stapleton, written in

1558 and translated by Philip Hallet in 1992. Burns and Oats LTD. London.

[401]Robert Bolton's otherwise excellent play and film, *A Man for All Seasons*, ignored this aspect of More's character, but by this time in history, Augustine's theology of justifying state-sponsored persecution of heresy had informed the culture of Europe. If Bolton had included this aspect of More's thinking, he could have titled his play, *A Normal Man of His time.*

[402]Linda Porter, *The First Queen of England: The Myth of Bloody Mary*, St. Martin's press, New York. 2007, p.13.

[403]Ibid., p. 35.

[404]Ibid., p.45.

[405]Exactly when Mary became aware of the conflict is a matter of speculation, but rumors of the King's desire to put away Katherine had circulated for some time, and Margaret Pole knew what was going on. At some time, it is likely Margaret told Mary. See Porter, p.61.

[406]Carolly Erickson, *Mistress Anne: The Exceptional Life of Anne Boleyn*, Summit Books, 1984, p.74 and p. 107.

[407]Porter, p.76. Katherine was, however, allowed to correspond with Mary.

[408]Porter, p.94.

[409]The title for the subheading is derived from the Hollywood film of the same name starring Richard Burton as Henry.

[410]By tradition, kings and queens of England slept in the Tower of London on their wedding nights.

[411]Description and dialogue is from a letter written by Kingston cited by Joann Denny, *Anne Boleyn: A New life of England's Tragic Queen*, De Capo Press, 2004, p.275.

[412]Confessions were attained under torture.

[413]Denny, p.315.

[414]Ibid., p. 315.

[415]Jasper Ridley, *The Life and Times of Mary Tudor*, Weidenfeld and Nicolson, London, 1973 pp. 118-119.

[416]Porter, p. 239.

[417]Description of the wedding and the reaction of the people are recounted by Ridley, pp. 156-157.

[418]Description and dialogue of the event is recorded by John Foxe, *Book of Martyrs*, chapter 16.

[419]Ibid.

[420]Ibid.

[421]Evihu Zakai, *Exile and Kingdom:History and Apocalypse in the Puritan Migration to America*, Cambridge University Press, 2002, pp. 26-28.

[422]Tychonius was the first to propose the day-year theory, and the 1260 day-year theory was also proposed by Joachim.

[423]The description of the seminary and its practices are told by Alice Hogge, *God's Secret Agents: Queen Elizabeth's Forbidden Priests and the Hatching of the Gunpowder Plot*, Harper Perennial, 2006, p.58.

[424]For example, traditional Catholics were offended that the words "take and eat this in remembrance that Christ died for thee" were substituted for "this is the body and blood of Christ" when communion was distributed

to the congregation. Fredrick George Lee, *The Church Under Queen Elizabeth, an historical sketch*, BiblioLife, 2009, p.22.

[425]Ibid., p 62.

[426]Ibid., p. 136.

[427]John Waddington, *Congregational History: 1200-1567.* J. Snow, 1869, p.74. The prayer is cited as typical for such meetings at this time.

[428]Lee, p.277.

[429]Hogge, p. 61.

[430]Ibid., p. 64.

[431]Jesuits, also known as God's Marines, stood at the forefront of the counter-reformation and are credited to reconverting a number of Protestant countries to Catholicism.

[432]Hogge, pp. 66-67.

[433]It's true that the pope instructed the missionaries to avoid politics in order to help make the mission a success. However, he hoped that the missionaries would soften the people to accept a Spanish invasion and the deposing of Elizabeth. Thus he hoped the mission would ultimately end with a political solution. Campion, for his part, always opposed a foreign invasion and disputed Erik Allen on the subject.

[434]Alison Weir, *The Life of Elizabeth*, Ballantine Books, New York, 1988, p. 334.

[435]Quoted from Campion's *Fifth Reason*. Campion's belief in this regard must be an assumption based on Hippolytus's discussion of false prophets. Hippolytus, a third century presbyter, makes no mention of anything that might be interpreted as the Antichrist teaching Luther's justification by faith alone, or anything that may be construed as leading to the debate between Luther and the Catholics.

[436]Richard Simpson, *Edward Campion: A Biography*, Williams and Norgate, London, 1867, p. 276.

[437]Ibid., p. 322.

[438]David Brady, *The contribution of British writers between 1560 and 1830 to the interpretation of Revelation 13.16-18*, J.C.B. Mohr, Tubingen, 1983, p.202.

[439]The rapture is a reference to the "being caught up" referred to in First Thessalonians 4:17, when the "dead in Christ" and "we who are alive and remain" will be caught up in the clouds to meet the Lord. Lacunza makes clear that there are others writing on the same subject but he differs from them in certain respects. Lacunza does not name the others and it's not clear if he had only other Jesuits in mind. Baptist, Morgan Edwards, however, wrote as early as 1742 and published in 1788 and believed that the rapture takes place before the last 3 ½ years before the return of Christ. Lacunza places the rapture at the end of the Tribulation, but before" the day of wrath" which is meant to last 45 days. Taking both Morgan and Lacunza into account, it appears that 1 Thessalonians 4:17 occupied a great deal of discussion in the latter half of the 1700's.

[440]Joseph Mede would also play a part in inspiring premillennial theology as he would combine it with postmillennial concepts. For more on Lacunza's commentary and Irving's role, see chapter 18 below. For Mede, see chapters

15 and 16 below.

[441] A fuller title of Brightman's work is *A Revelation of the Revelation ... and Refutation of Robert Bellarmine Concerning Antichrist in Book Three Concerning the Roman Pontiff*. See Robert Clouse, "The Apocalyptic Interpretations of Thomas Brightman and Joseph Mede" in *The Bulletin of the Evangelical Theological Society*, volume 2, p. 180.

[442] While Augustine appeared to draw a sharp distinction between church and state in *City of God*, he blurs this line with his theology in support of heresy laws in which the state has the obligation in the millennium to protect the church. Thus the line between amillennialism and postmillennialism is also blurred.

[443] Clouse, p.181.

[444] Susan Ronald, *The Pirate Queen: Queen Elizabeth 1, Her Pirate Adventurers, and the Dawn of Empire*, Harper Collins, 2007, p.67.

[445] For details of the plot, see Weir, chapter 23.

[446] Weir, p.389.

[447] For the full details of the Spanish invasion, see Weir, chapter 22.

[448] The narrative here is taken from portions of Gerard's autobiography recorded and edited by John Morris, *The Conditions of Catholics under James the First: Father Gerard's Narrative of the Gunpowder Plot*.

[449] The charter was authored by Edwin Sandys, a Puritan member of Parliament. See the online article, "1607 Virginia and the Gunpowder Plot Aftermath," by Steven C. Smith

[450] Ibid.

[451] Keith L. Sprunger, *Trumpets from the Tower: Puritan printing in the Netherlands, 1600-1640*, p. 91. Brill, 1994.

[452] The content of the chaplains' sermons are recorded by Denis Murphy, *Cromwell in Ireland: A History of Cromwell's Irish Campaigns*, p.72

[453] Cromwell's words are recorded by Antonia Fraser, *Cromwell, our Chief of Men*, Orion, 2011, p. 324

[454] Speech is recorded by Laura Lunger Knoppers, *Monstrous Bodies/political Monstrosities in Early Modern Europe*, Cornell University Press, 2004, p. 96.

[455] The content of the speech is recorded by Murphy, p.78

[456] Speech recorded by Murphy, p.76. On page 78, Murphy explains that Cromwell addressed the troops with the Canaanite speech when he first arrived in port.

[457] Ibid., p.83.

[458] A minority of the troops were made up of English Catholics and Protestants.

[459] Murphy, p. 101.

[460] Ibid., p.109. Some modern historians doubt Cromwell massacred Drogheda. See chapter 16 on this point.

[461] Aviu Zakai, *Exodus and Kingdom: History and Apocalypse in the Puritan Migration to America*, Cambridge University Press, 2002, p.131.

[462] Knollys's 1641 sermon is recorded as part of the Putney Debates held by the military to forge a new constitution in 1649. The inclusion of the sermon demonstrates the importance of eschatology in the debates.

[463]Barry H. Howson, *Erroneous and Schismatic Opinions: The questions of orthodoxy regarding the theology of Hanserd Knollys*, Leiden, Brill, 2001, pp. 248-278.

[464]George Whitby is credited with coining the phrase, postmillennialism. However, the concept is much earlier. As I have argued in this book, the latent form of the theology can be traced back to Lactantius.

[465]Christopher Hill, *Antichrist in Seventeenth Century England*, Oxford University Press, 1971, p.181.

[466]*Clavis Apocalyptica*, section 420.

[467]See*Daniel's Weeks* by Joseph Mede, sections 34-49.

[468]The concept is similar to Lactantius's age of peace, which could be established before Christ's return. See chapter six above.

[469]Tai Liu, *Discord in Zion: The Puritan Divines and the Puritan Revolution, 1640-1660*, Springer, 1973, p.11

[470]Hill, p.46.

[471]Hill. p.79.

[472]Ibid., p.86.

[473]Liu, p.58.

[474]Hill, p.81.

[475]P.G. Rogers, *The Fifth Monarchy men*, Oxford University Press, 1966, p. 15.

[476]Edward Rogers, *The Life and Opinions of a Fifth Monarchy Man: Chiefly Extracted from the Writings of John Rogers.*

[477]Dialogue is recorded by Edward Rogers, Ibid., p. 45.

[478]P.G. Rogers, p. 18.

[479]Liu, p. 63.

[480]Ibid., p.66.

[481]Murphy, p.109.

[482]Some modern historians question Murphy's account, written some one hundred years after the fact and claiming his bias as a Jesuit. Cromwell himself disputed the charge of massacre, claiming that the Irish refused to surrender and give up their arms. In his report to Parliament, however, he reported that only one hundred British soldiers died as opposed to over two thousand Irish troops killed. If the Irish fought to the death, much of which would have taken place house to house and building to building, it seems untenable that they would have killed so few of the British. Cromwell advocated it was a miracle of God. As reported above, he also admitted killing some soldiers after they surrendered. The overall evidence suggests Murphy's account is correct.

[483]The more precise political theology of the Fifth Monarchy advocated that the seventy be elected from the Monarchy congregations, thus the implementation of a democratic theocracy.

[484]Liu, p.90.

[485]P.G.Rogers, p. 34.

[486]Liu, p.95.

[487]According to Edward Rogers. The date of the book is an estimate.

[488]The theology is comparable to Augustine's theology of advocating heresy laws out of love and Mary Tudor's burning heretics out of love.

[489]E. Edwards, p.96.

[490]According to *English Dissenters* website.

[491]A *Door of Hope*, p.1.

[492]Ibid., p.3.

[493]Ibid., p.4. Andrew Stumer was one of the first scholars to draw attention to this passage in relation to postmillennial theology, correctly arguing against earlier scholars that claimed that the Fifth Monarchy was a premillennial movement that expected an imminent coming of Christ. Two of the more recent authors that have made this same mistake are Jonathon Kirsch and Sharan Newman. An example of this mistake may be seen in the statement by Newman in *The Real History of the End of the World*, p 169: "While most who take part in a rebellion think God must be on their side, few expect him to bodily lead an army. The Fifth Monarchist's did." Both Newman and Kirsch based their treatment only on earlier secondary sources and no primary. As I have argued, Fifth Monarchist theology should be most rightly interpreted in the light of Joseph Mede, who mixed a post millennial concept with premillennial by incorporating a time period based on Daniel's seventieth week. English armies were to pave the way for Christ's physical return by eliminating all monarchies. As Edward Rogers wrote, the Fifth Monarchists "were in hot hast to commence this preparatory work." p.56.

[494]A *Door of Hope*, p.8.

[495]This account of Venner's uprising is based on the description by John Donahue, *Radical Republicanism in England, America, and The Imperial Atlantic, 1624-1661.* For a more detailed account of Venner's uprisings, see the compelling descriptions by P.G. Rogers in *The Fifth Monarchy Men.*

[496]Excerpts from the sermon are from *A Discourse, Addressed to the Sons of Liberty, At a Solemn Assembly, near Liberty Tree, in Boston, February 14, 1766.* See the discussion of the sermon by Ruth H. Bloch, *Visionary Republic: Millennial Themes in American thought, 1756-1800,* Cambridge University Press, Cambridge, 1985, p. 53.

[497]Bloch, pp. 53-55.

[498]Samuel Adams' Proclamation of a Day of Fasting as Governor of Massachusetts, March 20, 1797.

[499]John Donoghue, *Radical Republicanism in England, America and the Imperial Atlantic,* PHD thesis, p.3. See also Thomas Jones Howell,*A Complete Collection of State trials and Proceedings for High Treason and Other Crimes from the Earliest Period to the year 1783,* vol. 6, p.107.

[500]Quoted by Avihu Zakai,*Theocracy in Massechusettes: Reformation and Seperation in early Puritan New England,* The Edwin Mellon Press, 1994, introduction.

[501]J.F. Maclear, "New England and the Fifth Monarchy: The Quest for the Millennium in Early American Puritanism," *The William and Mary Quarterly,* Third Series, Vol. 32, No. 2 (Apr., 1975), pp. 223-260, p.237.

[502]Ibid., 251.

[503]John Winthrop, *A History of New England from 1630-1649,* Vol. 1, little, brown and company, Boston, 1853, Note 1, p.38.

[504]George Brinley, James Hammond Trumbull, *Catalogue of the American*

Library of the Late Mr. George Brinley, Volume 1, Case, Lockwood and Brainard, 1897, p. 64.

[505] Maclear, p. 234.

[506] Ibid., p. 235.

[507] Warren Johnson, *Revelation restored: the Apocalypse in later Seventeenth-Century England*, Woodbridge, Suffolk ; Rochester, Boydell Press, 2011 p. 197.

[508] Ibid., p. 202.

[509] Ibid., pp. 203-209.

[510] Ibid., p. 232.

[511] Leroy Edwin Froom, *Prophetic Faith of Our Fathers: The Historical Development of Prophetic Interpretation*, Review and Herald, Washington D.C. 1954, Vol. 3, pp. 117-120.

[512] Quoted by Bloch. p.12.

[513] Harry S. Stout, *The New England Soul: Preaching and Religious Culture in Colonial New England*, Oxford University Press, 1986, p.129.

[514] Bloch, p. 12.

[515] Stout, p.134. Along with republican millennial beliefs, some Anglican scholars originated Deism which would also have a profound effect on the American democratic movement. Toward the latter part of the eighteenth century secular versions of millennialism would dominate colonial preaching.

[516] Nathan Cole, *The Spiritual Travels of Nathan Cole*, 1761.

[517] Jonathon Edwards, *Letters and Personal Writings*, p.17.

[518] Bloch, p. 14.

[519] Nathan O. Hatch, *The Sacred Cause of Liberty: Republican Thought and the Millennium in Revolutionary New England*, Yale University Press, New Haven and London, 1977, p. 29.

[520] Ibid., p. 29.

[521] Ibid., p. 29.

[522] Jonathan Edwards, *A History of the Work of Redemption*, part eight. See also Hatch's discussion, p. 30.

[523] The story of the townspeople, their desire to stay neutral towards the British conflict, and their exile was told by a woman deportee and recorded by Thomas Miller for the Historical and Genealogical Record of Colchester County.

[524] John Mack Faragher, *A Great And Noble Scheme: The Tragic Story Of The Expulsion Of The French Acadians from their American Homeland*, W. W. Norton & Company, 2005 p. 286.

[525] Bloch records excerpts from Davis's sermon, p.40.

[526] Ibid., p.55.

[527] Ibid., pp. 75-77. See also Nathan O. Hatch's overall thesis in *Sacred Cause of Liberty*.

[528] Bloch, p. 77.

[529] Hatch, pp. 86-87.

[530] Ibid., p. 87.

[531] Bloch, p. 79.

[532] James P. Byrd, *Sacred Scripture, Sacred War, The Bible and the American*

Revolution, Oxford University Press, 2013, chapter 4.

[533]From Stephen Newman, "A Note on Common Sense and Eschatology,"*Political Theory*, Vol. 6, 1978 pp. 101-118.

[534]Bloch records Adams' words, p.94.

[535]Italics are mine for the sake of emphasis.

[536]"The September Massacres," *London Times*, Monday, September 10, 1792.

[537]Froom, Vol. 2, p. 643 and p.724.

[538]David Brion Davis, *Revolutions: Reflections on American Equality and Foreign Relations*, Harvard University Press, 1990, p. 44.

[539]Richard Landes quoting Robespierre, *Heaven on Earth: The Varieties of the Millennial Experience*, pp. 256-257 and 270.

[540]Landes proposes that the people turned violent when the French government was unable to fulfill the millennial dream.

[541]Froom, p. 739.

[542]"The Beast, a Sure Word of Prophecy," recorded by Stuart Semmel ,*Napoleon And The British*, Yale University Press, 2004, p.72.

[543]Ben Weider, *Napoleon and the Jews*, Presidents Forum, The international Napoleonic Society.

[544]Ibid., pp. 85-88.

[545]Lacunza, p.59. Lacunza accepted the notion that Cerinthus was a literalist and materialist. However, it is this author's contention that the Alogia spread false rumors that Cerinthus wrote the Revelation. No other document has ever been cited as having been authored by Cerinthus that puts forward a literal interpretation of the Second Coming. On the Alogia, see chapter 3 above.

[546]Lacunza, *The Coming of the Messiah in Glory and majesty*, L.B Seely and Son, London, p.12.

[547]Leroy Edwin Froom, *The Prophetic faith of Our fathers*, Volume 3, Review and Herald Publishing, 1946, p.309.

[548]David Pio Gullon, Two Hundred Years from Lacunza: The Impact of His Eschatological Thought on Prophetic Studies and Modern Futurism, *Journal of the Adventist Theological Society*, 9/1Ð2 ,1998.

[549]Froom, p. 313.

[550]Revelation 20:4-5.

[551]Lacunza, *The Coming of the Messiah*, Vol. 1, pp. 99-101.

[552]Ibid., p. 99.

[553]Daniel 12: 7 and 11-12. Daniel also mentions a 1290 days in the context of the 1335 days. Revelation claims the Antichrist will be given power to rule for 1260 days. This has caused a plethora of speculation from prophecy analysts in their attempts to harmonize the passages.

[554]On Bellarmine's view that the Antichrist will be slain over a forty-five day period, see Froom, Vol. II, p.496. On Lacunza, see *The Coming of the Messiah*, Vol. II p. 214 and pp. 250-251.

[555]Lacunza, Ibid., pp. 215-216. The modern pre-wrath and seventh trumpet raptures are revisions of the post-tribulation rapture. See chapter 21 below.

[556]Some commentators believe Pseudo-Ephraem put forward a post-tribu-

lation rapture. In my own reading, the document suggests either a rapture before a three-and-a-half-year tribulation, or a post-tribulation, pre-wrath rapture.

[557]Thomas Witherby, *A vindication of the Jews: by way of reply to the letters addressed to perseverans to the English Israelite humbly submitted to the consideration of the Missionary Society, and the London Society for promoting Christianity among the Jews*, Stephen Couchman, London, 1809, pp. 220-245.

[558]See the article by John Oddy, "Bicheno and Tyson on the Prophesies, A Baptist Generation Gap," 1955.

[559]*An Attempt to Remove Prejudices Concerning The Jewish Nation*, BiblioLife, reprinted, 2009, pp. 23-24.

[560]John Oddy speculated that Thomas Witherby and William Witherby were brothers, but upon my investigation in William's family tree, only his father is named Thomas with no connection to the Lawyer Thomas.

[561]A number of secondary sources associate Maitland with Ribera's commentary in 1826. However, this author could not find any direct association with this early date in any primary sources. The closest is Froom's statement in his Volume 2: "In 1826 Maitland revived Ribera's Futurist interpretation in England."

[562]Samual Roffey Maitland, *An Enquiry into the Grounds on which the Prophetic period of Daniel and St. John has SUPPOSED to Consist of 1260 Years.* Hatchard and Son, London, 1826 and *A Second Enquiry...*, 1829.

[563]This appears to be the case based on *Memoir of Reverend Daily* which describes the 1826 meetings and states Lady Powerscourt was present at these meetings. The following is an extract: "I am going to the prophets meeting at Mr. Drummond's." p.49. See also Jonathon Burnham, *A story of Conflict, The Controversial Relationship Between Willis Newton and John Nelson Darby*, Paternos Press, 2004, p. 115.

[564]Irving describes the conference in the postscript at the end of his prologue in his translation of Lacunza's book.

[565]Joseph Wolf, *Travels and Adventures of the Reverend Wolf*, Oxford university press, 1861, digital version 2012, p.237. Lacunza symbolized the Antichrist as a principle of heresy that would be espoused by a group of apostate Catholic clergy, but not the pope. It's also possible that Maitland's work influenced the conference on this point about the pope.

[566]Henry Drummond, *Dialogues*, p.377.

[567]Commentators argue whether Irving believed in a pre or post-tribulation rapture.

[568]Letter 23, *Letters and papers of the Late Theodosia A. Viscount Powerscourt*, edited by Robert Daily, Seeley, Burnside, and Seeley, London.

[569]From John Nelson Darby's collected works, quoted by Max S. Weremchuk, research paper 3 on J. N. D. On governing itself, he meant that the church should be free from government interference.

[570]See the article," The Politics of Conversion in Ireland," *Third Way*, February, 1991, Vol., 14, pp.14-15.

[571]The numbers of conversions are given by J.N. Darby, *Considerations Ad-*

dressed to the Archbishop of Dublin and the Clergy Who Signed the Petition to the House of Commons for Protection, 1827.

[572]Ibid.

[573]J.N. Darby, *Considerations on the Nature and Unity of the Church of Christ*, 1828.

[574]Ibid.

[575]See the article by Thomas Ice for the argument that Darby believed in a pre-tribulation rapture as early as 1826/27, *When Did J. N. Darby Discover the Rapture?* On the position that Darby later exaggerated his convalescence experience, see Max S. Weremchuk, research paper #7: "Of course many seek to read back into his early statements insights gained later (Darby does that himself as to the 1827/28 experience)."

[576]While he was a historicist, it was impossible for Darby to believe in a pre-tribulation rapture. In 1829, then, Darby believed in an imminent return of Christ and a post-tribulation, pre-wrath rapture. He does not, however, give any indication that he agreed with Lacunza on the length of the wrath. His tract seems to indicate a literal twenty-four-hour "Day of the Lord's Wrath," while Lacunza believed it covered a forty-five day period. In reading his later recollections, one has to understand that Darby referred to events and concepts that he believed eventually led him to a conviction in a pre-tribulation rapture.

[577]Burnham, pp.116-117. No detailed minutes remain of the meetings, only the outlines of topics recorded by the *Christian Herald*.

[578]Ibid., 119.

[579]W. Kelly's article, *The Rapture of the Saints: who suggested it, or rather on what Scripture?* T. Weston, 1903. Speculation that tweedy borrowed from Lacunza is my own.

[580]From Darby's collected writings. That the missionary was tweedy is speculation by Max S. Weremchuk in research paper 7. The recollection of the missionary by Darby correlates well with the on article on Tweedy by Kelly cited in note 579.

[581]The meeting is recollected in a letter by eye-witness J.G. Bellett to J. McAllister. Burnham differs from Bellett, citing a memoir by Mrs. Maddon that the Lady Powerscourt's break from the church occurred at the 1832 conference.

[582]Revelation 17:3-5.

[583]J.N. Darby, *An Examination of the statements made in the "Thoughts on the Apocalypse," by B. W. Newton; and an enquiry how far they accord with Scripture*. Section 8 in Collected Works.

[584]Burnham, p.129.

[585]According to Burnham, Darby proposed a three-and-a-half year tribulation until at least 1845, note 126, p.122.

[586]A seven-year Tribulation caused new problems for Darby to reconcile. For a thorough run-down on difficult biblical passages for a seven year pre-tribulation rapture and imminent return of Christ, see chapter 20 below. See also chapters 1 and 2 above.

[587]This was related to me by a former member of the Brethren that I met while attending Seminary in 1993.

[588]Jonathon Moorehead, "The Father of Zionism: William E. Blackstone?" *Journal of the Evangelical Theological Society*, December 2010. pp. 787-800.

[589]Revelation 12:5: "Her male child (Jesus) was *caught up* to God and his throne." Some Bible versions translate the word as "snatched" which suggests disappearing, but this is not the sense of the Gospels' and Acts' accounts of the Ascension of Jesus. The Gospel of John, chapter 6 is particularly compelling in suggesting that Jesus did not vanish: "What if then you shall see the Son of Man ascend up where He was before?"

[590]For the background of Edmund Ruffin and details of his writings, see Jason Phillips, "The Prophecy of Edmund Ruffin" in *Apocalypse and the Millennium in the American Civil War Era*, Edited by Ben Wright and Zachary W. Dresser, LSU Press, 2013, pp.13-23. For the excerpts from Ruffin's stories, see Edmund Ruffin, *Anticipations of the Future to Serve as Lessons for the Present Time*, J.W Randolph, Richmond, Virginia, 1860, pp. 279-326. The date of June for the newspaper stories is approximate based on certain statements Ruffin made in his diary.

[591]Levi Purviance, *The Biography of Elder David Purviance, Written by Himself, with a Sketch of the Kentucky Revivals By Levi Purviance*, G.W. Ells, 1848. p.58

[592]Ibid., pp. 298 and 301.

[593]Pamela Elwyn Thomas Colbenson, *Millennial Thought Among Southern Evangelicals: 1830-1885*, Georgia State University, 1980, p. 32.

[594]Bruce T. Gorely notes that the Republican Party had its roots in postmillennialism. See his article *Recent Historiography on religion and the American civil war.*See also *Apocalypse and the Millennium in the American Civil War Era*, edited by Ben Wright, Zachary W. Dresser, LSU Press, Nov. 4, 2013.

[595]David B. Chesebrough, *Clergy Dissent in the Old South, 1830-1865*, Southern Illinois University Press, 1996, pp. 72-79, 114-115.

[596]Colbenson, p. 50.

[597]Samuel Davies Baldwin, *Armageddon: or the Overthrow of Romanism and Monarchy; the Existence of the United States Foretold in the Bible*, Cincinnati Applegate, 1854. p.33.

[598]Ibid., p.34.

[599]Baldwin , *Dominion; The Divine Rights of Shem, Ham, and Japheth*, Stevenson and Owen, Nashville, Tennessee, 1857, p.51.

[600]Colbenson , p.158.

[601]The Sons of Confederate Veterans on the history of South Carolina's Secession Convention.

[602]Colbenson, p. 138.

[603]*Exploded Graces: Providence and the Confederate Israel in Evangelical Southern Sermons, 1861 -1865*, Master's Thesis, Rice university, 1990, p.36

[604]Ibid., p.94.

[605]John Thorton, "The African Experience of the '20 and Odd Negroes' Arriving in Virginia in 1619," *The William and Mary Quarterly*, 3rd Ser., Vol. 55, No. 3, Jul., 1998, pp. 421-434. p. 425.

[606]Ibid., p. 426.

[607]Ibid., p. 430.

[608]Ibid., p. 431.

[609]Ibid., p. 434.

[610]Stephen Elliot, *Our Cause in Harmony with the Purposes of God in Christ Jesus*, Power Press of John Cooper, 1862, p. 5.

[611]Ibid., p.7.

[612]Ibid., p.9.

[613]Stephen Elliot, *Address to the Thirty-Ninth Annual Convention of the Protestant Episcopal Church in the Diocese of Georgia*, 1861. p. 9.

[614]"The issue of 'slavery' in the NT/Apostolic world," The website quotes from *A History of Ancient Near Eastern Law*: "Many of the documents (concerning slavery) emphasize that the transaction is voluntary. This applies not only to self-sale but also to those who are the object of sale, although their consent must sometimes have been fictional, as in the case of a nursing infant." Raymond Westbrook (ed.), (2 vols.). Brill: 2003 1:665.

[615]Colleen A. Vasconcellos, "Children in the Slave Trade," in Children and Youth in History, Item #141,(accessed October 5, 2013). Based on a baptismal record from South Carolina, Some historians have questioned the truthfulness of Olaudah's account that he was born in Africa. Other historians argue for the story's authenticity. In any case, the story represents accurate accounts of kidnapping for the slave trade For a rundown of the debate, pro and con, see the article: "Where was Oldoula Equiano Born?"

[616]Excerpts are from Gilbert Haven's sermon, "The war and the Millennium," *National sermons.: Sermons, speeches and letters on slavery and its war: from the passage of the Fugitive slave bill to the election of President Grant*, By Gilbert Haven, pp. 373-392.

[617]James H. Moody, "The Erosion of Postmillennialism in American Religious Thought, 1865-1925," *JSTOR*, Vol. 53, March 1984, pp. 61-77.

[618]Emiko Ohnuki-tierney, *Kamikaze Diaries: Reflections of Japanese Student Soldiers*, University of Chicago Press, 2006, pp. 9-10 and 163-185.

[619]In the earliest days of Attack Force, some pilots did volunteer out of patriotism and emperor worship, but after these few initial pilots died, the navy ran out of volunteers and so had to draft a number college students into the Force.

[620]Ibid., xiii.

[621]On Tanaka's timeline, see Jacqueline Stone, "Japanese Lotus Millennialism: From Militant Nationalism to Contemporary Peace Movements", in Millennialism, Persecution and Violence, edited by Catherine Wessinger, Syracuse University Press, 2000, p.267.

[622]Stone, pp.262-264.

[623]Ibid., p. 265.

[624]Ibid., pp.267 and 269.

[625]Ibid., p.270.

[626]Ibid.,pp. 269 and 270.

[627]Louis G. Perez, *Japan at War: An Encyclopedia*, ABC-CLIO, 2002, P.180.

[628]Stone, pp.272 and 273.

[629]See Walter A. Skya's discussion on Ishiwara in *Japan's Holy War: The ideology of Radical Shinto Ultranationalism*, Duke University Press, 2009, p.247and p. 248.

[630]Francis X. Winters *Remembering Hiroshima: Was it Just?*, Ashgate Publishing, Ltd, 2009, p.102

[631]Ikuhiko Hata, *Hirohito: the Showa Emperor in War and Peace*, Global Oriental Ltd, 2007, p. 161

[632]Matthew, chapter 24.

[633]Revelation 16:16.

[634]Ibid., pp. 92-94. See also the Wikipedia article on *The Protocols*.

[635]Filiu, p. 32 and p. 87.

[636]Ibid., p.146.

[637]Some commentators have written that Khamenei does not share the eschatological views of Ahmadinejad. However, according to a blog from the Institute of Religion and Democracy it was stated "There are indications that Khamenei is not at odds with Ahmadinejad when it comes to their role in prophecy. In July 2010, a senior cleric claimed that Khamenei told his inner circle that he had met the Mahdi, who promised to return while Khamenei remained alive. When mostly-Shiite protesters challenged the pro-American monarchy of Bahrain, a representative of Khamenei said it is 'the best opportunity to begin setting the stage for the emergence of the 12th imam, our Mahdi.'" See "Iran reports Saudi king's Death: A Green Light for War?" September 5, 2013.

[638]The video can be seen in an abridged version on YouTube and on Reza Kahlili's website, *A Time To Betray*, based on his book of the same name. In a review of Kahlili's book, his identity as a former CIA agent working in Iran was verified by *Washington Post* associate editor David Ignatius in *The Washington Post Book World Review*, Sunday, April 11, 2010. In his investigation into Kahili, Ignatius reported a current government official's words about the author: "I can't confirm every jot and title in the book, but he did have a relationship with U.S. intelligence." Ignatius goes on to write: "I spoke with Kahlili's lawyer, too, who told me that the book was 'submitted for prepublication review' at a certain unnamed U.S. government agency and that this agency confirmed that Kahlili did have an operational relationship. Eventually, I found one of Kahlili's former case officers, who described him as 'legit' and 'a very brave guy.'

[639]Ali H. Soufan, *The Black Banners: The Inside Story of 9/11 And the War against Al-Qaida*, W.W Norton & Company, Sept. 20011, prologue. The dialogue is derived from Soufan's account of the interrogation.

[640]This statement has been quoted on sympathetic Muslim websites. I assume the quote is correct.

[641]Anonymous Author, *Black flags from the East: The Movements, Past Present and Future—1979-2012*, pp. 48-49.

[642]Ibid., p.63.

[643]The video and connection to Tamerlan Tsarnaev was first reported by Adam Serwer on the website for *Mother Jones* magazine on April 19, 2013.

[644]It is unclear at this time whether ISIS, a Sunni organization, considers

Jesus to be the Mahdi or if the leader of ISIS considers himself to be the Mahdi. It is possible that the ISIS' head, Abu Bakr al-Baghdadi, believes he will lead the way for the Mahdi. Perhaps future issues of *Dabiq* will clarify this. See the articles discussing ISIS atMahdiWatch website.

[645]See the article, "Dabiq: What Islamic State's New Magazine Tells Us about Their Strategic Direction, Recruitment Patterns and Guerrilla Doctrine," The Jamestown Foundation, August 1, 2014.

[646]Tabari, *The History of al-Tabari Volume 27, The Abbasid Revolution*, SUNY Press, 1985 p.30. See also the discussion in Hayrettin Yücesoy, *Messianic Beliefs and Imperial Politics in Medieval Islam: The 'Abbasid Caliphate in the Early Ninth Century*, University of South Carolina Press, 2009 p.41.

[647]Moshe Sharon, *Revolt: The Social and Military Aspects of the 'Abbasid Revolution*, JSAI, 1990 p.27.

[648]Yucesoy, *Messianic Beliefs*, p.21. See also Salih Sa id Agha, *The Revolution which Toppled the Umayyads: Neither Arab Nor 'Abbasid*, Brill, 2003, p.4.

[649]Yucesoy, pp.108-110.

[650]See chapter 8 above for details of the prophecy of the Last World Emperor and its relationship to the Crusades.

[651]Soufan, *Black Banners*, Prologue. Soufan quotes Sheik Salmon al-Qadah: "If a Muslim believes in this hadith, he believes in something false."

[652]Timothy R. Furnish quotes Tabor in his article,"The Importance of Being Mahdist." SEP 8, 2008.

[653]Ibid.

[654]Nour Samaha, "The Brothers Larijani: A sphere of power," *Aljazeera*, June 9, 2013.

[655]Elad benari, *Israel National News.*

[656]*The Times of Israel*, January 21, 2013.

[657]On Russia's development of binary systems, see Eric A. Coddy and James J. Wirtz, *Weapons of Mass destruction*, ABC CLIO, pp. 41-42

[658]Most modern scholars shed doubt upon the authenticity of Aristeas' letter, preferring to accept only a shred of truth to the story of the origins of the Greek Septuagint. However, Nina Collins, from the University of Leeds, argues for the letter's overall reliability. See *The Library in Alexandria and the Bible in Greek*, Brill, August, 2000. The Dead Sea Scrolls, while shedding no light on the letter, have bolstered the Septuagint as a more reliable text of the Old Testament than that of the Hebrew Masorite text, which has now been shown to have a variety of errors. See Carsten Thiede, *The Dead Sea Scrolls and the Jewish Origins of Christianity.*

[659]Tacitus, *The Histories*, Book 5, part 12. According to the Jewish historian Josephus, in the midst of Jerusalem's destruction, Vespasian's son Titus cut a deal with Temple authorities to leave the Temple untouched. Renegade Roman soldiers, however, defied Titus' order and set fire to the building, burning it to the ground.

[660]Ralph Martin, *The Temples that Jerusalem Forgot*, Associates for Scriptural knowledge, 1994.

[661]There is another spring attested to in scripture—the En Rogel. Its loca-

tion is disputed, but scholars place it outside Jerusalem. However, it was evidently close enough to the Gihon so that loud noises could be heard from one to the other.

[662]See the articles, *"A Response to Dr. Ernest Martin" – By: Leen Ritmeyer* and *A Critique by Dr. Leen Ritmeyer and a Rebuttal to Ritmeyer by Dr. Ernest L. Martin Concerning the New Research of Ernest L. Martin regarding the true site of the Temple in Jerusalem.*

[663]*Against Heresies*, book 5:30.

[664]Eusebius, book. 3:18.

[665]See 1 John chapters 1, 4, and 5.

[666]Joel Robinson, *The Islamic Antichrist: The Shocking Truth About The Real nature of the Beast*, WND Books, July, 2009.

[667]Having said the above, it is interesting that Francis has recently elevated Bishop Rainer Woelki to head the largest diocese in Germany. The bishp is noted for his liberal view of Homosexuality. In 2012, he stated, "If two homosexuals take responsibility for each other, if they are loyal to each other over the long term, then one should see this in the same way as heterosexual relations." Could this be the beginning of a sea-change in the Catholic stance on human sexuality toward the viewpoint of the Nicolaitans?

[668]2 Maccabees, 2:4-8. The mountain is probably Mount Nebo in Jordan. There are five traditions about what happened to the Ark just prior to the Babylonian invasion: One, the Maccabean account, two, the Ark was smuggled into Egypt, three, it was captured by the Babylonians and destroyed, four, it was smuggled into Ethiopia, and five, it was hidden in a cave under the Temple. This book assumes the Maccabean version to be correct.

[669]See R. Grant Jones website, Notes on the Septuagint. In particular, see Appendix: A Collection of References to the 'Septuagint Plus' in the New Testament."

[670]On this point, see William W. Combs, Detroit Baptist Seminary Journal, "Is *Apostasia* in 2 Thessalonians 2:3 a Reference to the Rapture?" Vol. 3 (Fall 1998): 63–87.

[671]Irenaeus, book 5, chapter 35, section 2, and chapter 36, section 2.

About the Author

Kevin Timothy O'Kane has earned a Bachelor in Pre-Seminary from Bethany College and a Master of Divinity from Austin Presbyterian Theological Seminary. In his studies, he has traveled to Syria, Jordan, and Israel. He has researched the history of Christian prophecy and its influence on western civilization for over twenty years.

Kevintimothyokane.com

www.ingramcontent.com/pod-product-compliance
Lightning Source LLC
LaVergne TN
LVHW011217080426
835509LV00005B/176